MINNESOTA SPORTS ALMANAC

Best wishes
Joel Rippel

MINNESOTA SPORTS ALMANAC

Joel A. Rippel

Foreword by Patrick Reusse

 Minnesota Historical Society Press

125 GLORIOUS YEARS

www.mhspress.org

The Minnesota Historical Society Press is a member of
the Association of American University Presses.

Book and cover design: Dennis Anderson, Duluth, Minnesota

Cover photo credits—FRONT (*clockwise from top*): Gopher hockey's 2002 NCAA championship
team and Coach Don Lucia, Gopher basketball's Lindsay Whalen, and Gopher golf's
Tom Lehman (all University of Minnesota Athletics); Minnesota Twins batter Torii Hunter
(Minnesota Twins); Minnesota Vikings running back Robert Smith (Minnesota Historical
Society); SPINE: Minnesota Wild goalie Manny Fernandez (Bruce Kluckhohn); BACK (*left to right*):
Gopher diving's P. J. Bogart (University of Minnesota Athletics); Bemidji curler Cassie Johnson
(Monte Draper, *Bemidji Pioneer*)

Overleaf: Harmon Killebrew of the Minnesota Twins bats a home run, 1971.

Manufactured in the United States of America

10 9 8 7 6 5 4 3 2 1

♾ The paper used in this publication meets the minimum requirements of the American
National Standard for Information Sciences—Permanence for Printed Library Materials,
ANSI Z39.48-1984.

International Standard Book Numbers:
10-digit: 0-87351-558-7 (paper)
13-digit: 978-0-87351-558-0 (paper)

Library of Congress Cataloging-in-Publication Data

Rippel, Joel A., 1956–
Minnesota sports almanac / Joel A. Rippel ; foreword by Patrick Reusse.
    p. cm.
Includes bibliographical references.
ISBN-13: 978-0-87351-558-0 (pbk. : alk. paper)
ISBN-10: 0-87351-558-7 (pbk. : alk. paper)
1. Sports—Minnesota—History. I. Title.
GV584.M65R57 2006
796.09776—dc22   006012642

Acknowledgments

Several years ago, I presented an idea to Minnesota Historical Society Press publisher Greg Britton. Fortunately, he had a better idea, which became *75 Memorable Moments in Minnesota Sports.*

Then, I had another idea for Britton. And, again, he had a better plan. The result is the *Minnesota Sports Almanac.* This book is a combination of almanac, trivia book and record book for Minnesota sports.

I had a tremendous amount of fun working on this project. While putting this together, I got a lot of help.

The book would not and could not have been completed without former Minnesota Historical Society Press editor Sally Rubinstein. From the initial discussion about the project, Sally was a strong supporter and staunch advocate. Along the way, she provided direction and kept the project in focus. Sally, along with her daughter Rebecca, routinely brought to my attention ideas and items to be included in the book.

There are many others I would like to thank, especially Marilyn Ziebarth and Shannon Pennefeather of Minnesota Historical Society Press. Volunteer Helen Newlin assisted the work.

It would be difficult to find someone who knows more about Minnesota sports history than Dave Mona. Dave provided background on the Minnesota Sports Hall of Fame and offered numerous helpful suggestions.

I would also like to think Lisa Mushett and David Shama of the United States Tennis Association/Northern Section; Lois Hendrickson and Karen Klinkenberg of the University of Minnesota archives; Augsburg College Sports Information Director Don Stoner; the staff of the news library of the *Minneapolis Star Tribune;* Rob Daves, who oversees the Minnesota Poll for the *Star Tribune;* Stew Thornley and John Mueller.

* * *

For the record—

All almanacs need to have cut-off dates. *Minnesota Sports Almanac* uses the date July 2005—with a few major additions through the spring of 2006.

Contents

Foreword by Patrick Reusse   xiii

1   **Minnesota Immortals and Olympians**   1

     Minnesota Sports Hall of Fame

     Minnesota Olympians

2   **Baseball and Softball**   25

     Minnesota Twins

     Twins Players

     Other Professional Players

     Minor League Baseball

     Other Professional Leagues

     All-American Girls Professional Baseball League

     College Baseball

     Amateur Baseball

     Softball

3   **Football**   79

     Minnesota Vikings

     Other Professional Football

     College Football—University of Minnesota

     College Football—Other Conferences

4   **Basketball**   123

     Minnesota Timberwolves

     Minneapolis Lakers

     Other Professional Basketball

     Women's Professional Basketball—Lynx

College Basketball

University of Minnesota Basketball Gophers—Men

University of Minnesota Basketball Gophers—Women

College Basketball—Other Conferences

5 **Hockey**   175

Minnesota Wild

Fighting Saints

Minor League Hockey Teams

Olympic Hockey

Amateur Hockey

College Hockey

6 **High School Sports**   203

Basketball

Curling

Football

Hockey

Girls' Swimming

Track and Field

Wrestling

Boys' State Champions

Girls' State Champions

7 **Bowling, Golf, Lacrosse, Soccer, Tennis,
and Volleyball**   273

Bowling

Golf

University of Minnesota Golf

Amateur Golf

Lacrosse

Soccer—Minnesota Thunder

Minnesota Strikers

Minnesota Kicks

Women's Soccer

Tennis

College Tennis

Volleyball

8   Wrestling and Boxing   305

Wrestling

Boxing

9   University of Minnesota Athletics   321

Gymnastics

Swimming and Diving

Track and Field

Volleyball

10   Racing: Marathons, Skating, Horses, and Autos   331

Marathons

Inline Roller Skating

Horse Racing

Auto Racing

11   Fishing, Hunting, and Other Outdoor Sports   339

Fishing

Hunting

Curling

Figure Skating

Outdoor Adventurers

Skiing

Snowmobiling

Water Skiing

12 Venues, Commentators, Officials, and the Poll   357

Major Sports Venues

University of Minnesota Sports Venues

Amateur Sports Venues

Sports Commentators

Sports Officials

Minnesota Poll on Sports

Bibliography   379

Foreword

Patrick Reusse

There is a feeling in this age where 24 daily hours of sports babble is available on the radio, where ESPN can take Sammy Sosa having cork in his bat and turn it into a five-day, round-the-clock, shout-a-thon, and where Internet bloggers can offer their hallucinations as fact—there's a feeling that we're in the generation that has turned rumor mongering in the world of sports into a science.

Guess what?

The generations before us, before World War II, might have been lowly, underpaid newspaper reporters, but they set a standard for rumor mongering that the bloggers are still trying to equal.

Among the many fascinating items in Joel Rippel's history of Minnesota sports, this ranked near the top for me:

"On September 22, 1940, a headline in the *Minneapolis Star-Journal* read, 'Ruth as St. Paul manager?' The newspaper reported, 'Possibilities that Babe Ruth may become manager of the St. Paul (Saints) baseball club developed Saturday night. Lou McKenna, business manager, said he may contact Ruth, following the receipt of a letter from Ray Doan, close friend of Babe, in which Ray said that he thinks the great home run hitter of another day is in a receptive mood.'"

Babe Ruth, the greatest name in the history of American sports, might be coming to the Twin Cities to manage St. Paul's American Association team?

Take that, bloggers!

Can you imagine what a talker that was among Minnesota's sports fans, after they saw the headline and read McKenna's scenario (vague though it was) for hiring Ruth?

Sadly, but in true rumor-mongering fashion, the Saints never did get the Babe signed as manager for 1941. They wound up with Ralph Kress, who presumably created less of a stir among McKenna's potential ticket buyers.

I consider myself something of a Minnesota sports historian. I started working as a copy boy in the sports department of the *Minneapolis Morning Tribune* out of high school in August 1963. I was hired by the late, great Ted Peterson, the *Tribune*'s link to outstate high schools and towns.

In January 1966, I gave up a long-shot attempt at a University of Minnesota degree and was hired as a sportswriter at the *Duluth News-Tribune*. I just couldn't turn down that $76.08 a week the Ridders were paying a novice reporter back then.

Here's the point: As I went through the pages of this Minnesota sports history, there were a couple of hundred times when I said: "I didn't know that."

My guess is, if you're among the Minnesotans who have not been in the sports business for more than two decades, you figure to multiply the I-didn't-know-that's several times.

Back in 1999, we took on a year-long project in the *Star Tribune*'s sports department to celebrate a century of sports in Minnesota. There were monthly spreads on specific topics (hoops, hockey, high schools, and the like), wrapped up by an attempt to name the state's 100 most important sports people for the 20th century.

We gave it a good shot, but a list such as that is destined to be imperfect. There's no doubt that if the resource Mr. Rippel and the Minnesota Historical Society are making available to us now had been available then, there would have been fewer flaws in our list.

For instance: Solomon Hughes would have made it. He was one of the nation's first prominent black golfers in the 1930s and into the '40s. He slipped past us, but you can read about him here.

You also will find out that

- In 1947 Max Winter wanted to name Minneapolis' newly acquired pro basketball team the "Vikings." He was persuaded to go with "Lakers," the winning entry in a newspaper-sponsored contest. Max kept that Vikings name in his hip pocket and broke it out 13 years later, after landing an NFL expansion franchise for Minnesota.
- You know what I said to myself when coming across that item here? "I didn't know that."
- Minnesota's first-ever baseball game was played in 1857 in Nininger. I didn't even know we had a Nininger.
- The state high school basketball tournament—Minnesota's greatest annual event until it started being played in classes after 1970—started in 1913.

I knew that. What I didn't know was that there was a second public school tournament, for schools that had not yet been given the blessing of the State High School League, played from 1923 through 1927.

You can't find those state championships for East Chain, Stewart, Chisago City, Brewster, and Henning in any of the state league's literature, but they get a mention in this history of Minnesota sports.

- "Unser Joe" Hauser took advantage of Nicollet Park's extra-short fence in right field to shatter minor league home run records for the Minneapolis Millers in the 1930s.

Knew that. The Millers' slugger I didn't know a thing about was Perry Werden, who was smashing home runs for the team in the 1890s, back when the baseballs were wrapped as tight as what . . . Randy Moss's thoughts?

Werden's advantage was Athletic Field, a bandbox that sat on the space now occupied by Butler Square in downtown Minneapolis.

Really. There's too much good stuff here.

We knew the North Stars were a chaotic operation during their time in Bloomington, but 15 different men as coaches in 26 years . . . and several more than once?

Amazing.

We knew Gustavus Adolphus, the Golden Gusties, had some football greatness in its history, but not that 13 players from the MIAC have been selected in the NFL Draft.

You'll find out that St. Paul voters passed—that's right, passed—by a huge margin a bonding bill that included money for a new ballpark—in 1953.

You'll find out Bobby Riggs was hustling Minnesota for bucks long before he was hustling the nation for bucks with his notorious match with Billie Jean King.

You will find out the Iron Range was more than the birthplace of hockey in Minnesota. It was also the early source of great swimmers and prep powerhouses.

Big stuff. Little stuff. It's all here. Learn and enjoy.

Minnesota Immortals and Olympians

DID YOU KNOW ?

At the 2002 Winter Olympics in Salt Lake City, 21 Minnesota-born athletes—more than any other state—represented the United States. At the 2006 Winter Olympics in Turin, Italy, 34 Minnesotans represented the United States.

Hennepin and Ramsey Counties have produced 108 Winter Olympians. Hennepin County is tied with Middlesex County, Massachusetts, for producing 60, the most Olympians from one county.

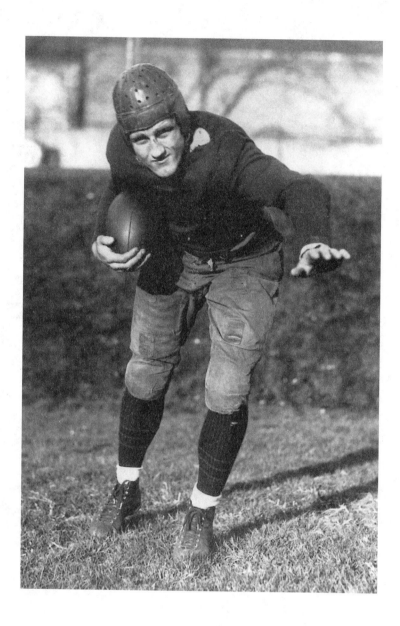

Minnesota Sports Hall of Fame

O N MAY 5, 1958, more than 1,400 Minnesotans gathered at the Leamington Hotel in downtown Minneapolis for what longtime Minneapolis journalist Charles Johnson called "the most enthusiastic, most impressive, biggest and most successful sports dinner these parts have ever known."

The occasion was the Minnesota Sports Champions Award Dinner, sponsored by the Minnesota Centennial Commission to honor a "sports champion" from each of the state's 87 counties. The keynote speakers at the event were University of Oklahoma football coach Bud Wilkinson, former heavyweight boxing champion Jack Dempsey, and Olympic champion Bob Richards. The highlight of the two-hour banquet was the announcement of the inaugural class of the Minnesota Sports Hall of Fame. The initial class numbered 17, with 10 honorees in attendance.

In the next day's *Minneapolis Star,* Johnson wrote that the presentation of the members of the Hall of Fame "was a dramatic and exciting finish to a gathering of champions such as this state has never known before and may never see again in one dining room."

Indeed. The Minnesota Sports Hall of Fame, originally housed in the Minneapolis Star and Tribune building, added members to the Hall of Fame irregularly: five in 1959, nine in 1963 and six in 1972. Then the Hall of Fame fell dormant until being reactivated in 1986. That year, five new members were inducted, and the Hall of Fame relocated to the concourse of the Metrodome. Four more classes were inducted for 1987, 1988, 1989, and 1990. Then the Hall of Fame went inactive again.

According to the *Minneapolis Tribune,* "Members of the Minnesota Sports Hall of Fame are selected because of their greatness in their chosen sport without regard to the popularity of their sport. To be a member, one must be primarily identified with Minnesota more than with any other state and must have performed feats on the championship level which reflected honor and glory on the state."

Hall of Fame Members

1958 Bernie Bierman, Tommy Gibbons, Frank Goheen, Fortune Gordien, Walter Hoover, Harrison "Jimmy" Johnston, George Mikan, Tommy

Herb Brooks led the Gophers to three NCAA titles and the U.S. team to the 1980 Olympics gold medal.

Milton, John McGovern, Bronko Nagurski, Patty Berg, Mike Gibbons, Bob Dunbar, William W. "Pudge" Heffelfinger, Dr. Henry L. Williams, Mike O'Dowd, Charles Albert "Chief" Bender

1959 John Johnson, Ken Bartholomew, Garfield "Gar" Wood, Mike Kelley, Emmett Swanson

1963 George Loomis, Edwin Widseth, Clarence "Biggie" Munn, Robin Lee, Dorothy Langkop, Nick Kahler, George Quam, Gil Dobie, Dr. L. J. Cooke

1972 Jimmy Robinson, Charles "Bud" Wilkinson, Joe Hutton Sr., Earl Martineau, Les Bolstad, Harmon Killebrew

1986 Jim Marshall, Jeanne Arth, Bruce Smith, John Mariucci, Calvin Griffith

1987 John Mayasich, Max Winter, Fran Tarkenton, Bud Grant, Dick Siebert

1988 Frank Brimsek, Tony Oliva, Jean Havlish, Bobby Marshall, Vern Mikkelsen

1989 Carl Eller, Walter Bush, Alan Page, Halsey Hall, Janet Karvonen

1990 Herb Brooks, Paul Giel, John Kundla, Pug Lund, Cindy Nelson

DID YOU KNOW ?

LeRoy Neiman, born in St. Paul in 1921, became one of the most widely known artists of the twentieth century. He was the official artist for five Olympic games: 1972 (summer), 1976 (winter), 1980 (winter), 1984 (winter and summer).

Hall of Fame Biographies

Jeanne Arth teamed with Californian Darlene Head to win the doubles title at Wimbledon in 1959. Arth and Head won the U.S. doubles title in 1958 and 1959.

Ken Bartholomew won four North American speed-skating titles (three outdoors and one indoors). He tied for the silver medal in the 500 meters at the 1948 Olympics.

Charles Albert "Chief" Bender, who was raised on Minnesota's White Earth Ojibwe Indian Reservation, was the first Minnesotan to be named to the National Baseball Hall of Fame. He won 212 games in a major league career from 1903 to 1917.

Patty Berg, a Minneapolis native who helped found the Ladies Professional Golf Association, is considered one of the top female golfers of all time. Named the Associated Press female athlete of the year in 1938 and 1943, Berg won 44 tournaments between 1944 and 1962.

Bernie Bierman, the second "winningest" coach in University of Minnesota football history, directed the Gophers to five national titles.

Les Bolstad is considered the godfather of Minnesota golf. After winning the U.S. Public Links title in 1926 at the age of 18, he coached the University

Charles Albert "Chief" Bender, an Ojibwe Indian, was the first Minnesotan named to the National Baseball Hall of Fame.

of Minnesota golf team for 30 years. He was also a mentor to many of the state's most successful golfers, including Patty Berg.

Frank Brimsek, a native of Eveleth, won the National Hockey League's Calder Trophy as the top hockey rookie in 1938. A six-time NHL all-star, he is a member of the Hockey Hall of Fame in Toronto and the U.S. Hockey Hall of Fame.

Herb Brooks, who played hockey for the Gophers, is best known for coaching the Gophers to three national titles and the U.S. Olympic team to the Gold Medal at the 1980 Olympics.

Patty Berg, top female golfer and two-time female Athlete of the Year

Walter Bush grew up in Hopkins before playing college hockey at Dartmouth. Instrumental in bringing the NHL to Minnesota in 1966, Bush is a member of the Hockey Hall of Fame and the U.S. Hockey Hall of Fame.

L. J. Cooke coached the University of Minnesota basketball team to two national and five conference titles during his 28-season tenure. Cooke, who is the "winningest" coach in school history, also served as the school's athletic director.

Gil Dobie, a native of Hastings, played for the University of Minnesota football team before embarking on a Hall of Fame coaching career. In 31 years as a college football coach, his teams had a 180–45–15 record and won two national titles. He coached 14 unbeaten teams, and his teams had a 58-game unbeaten streak. He was elected to the College Football Hall of Fame in 1951.

Bob Dunbar won every major bonspiel in North America and became one of the greatest curlers in American history.

Carl Eller, a native of North Carolina, played football for the Gophers before becoming a first-round draft choice of the Minnesota Vikings. During his 14-year career with the Vikings, he was a six-time Pro Bowl selection. Eller was inducted into the Pro Football Hall of Fame in 2004.

Tommy Gibbons, a St. Paul native, held the American light-heavyweight boxing title during a professional career that spanned the years 1908 to 1925. His 15-round bout against Jack Dempsey in 1923 is still one of the most talked-about fights. In his 106 professional bouts, he lost only three times—to Dempsey in 1923, Harry Grebe in 1924, and Gene Tunney in 1927. After his fighting career, he became Ramsey County sheriff.

Mike Gibbons, brother of Tommy Gibbons, was known as the St. Paul Phantom. He is regarded as one of the best middleweight boxers of all time.

Paul Giel, a Winona native, was a two-sport star for the Gophers—an All-American in football and in baseball. He played major league baseball before serving as the university's athletic director for 17 years.

Francis "Moose" Goheen, one of the greatest American-born hockey players, played for the St. Paul Athletic Club and is a member of the Hockey Hall of Fame and the U.S. Hockey Hall of Fame.

Fortune Gordien, a former Minneapolis Roosevelt High School and University of Minnesota track and field star, was a member of three U.S. Olympic teams and held the world record in the discus for nine years.

Bud Grant, a three-sport standout at the University of Minnesota, went on to play professional football and basketball. He gained fame as the coach of the Minnesota Vikings, leading them to four Super Bowls. He is a member of the Pro Football Hall of Fame.

William W. "Pudge" Heffelfinger, named to the first All-American football team in 1889

Calvin Griffith brought major league baseball to Minnesota when he relocated the Washington Senators franchise to the Twin Cities in October 1960. In 1984, Griffith sold the franchise, which his family had owned for more than 70 years, to Carl Pohlad.

Halsey Hall's career in newspapers and broadcasting spanned the years 1919 until his death in 1977. He was the first to call the Gophers "Golden" and his trademark saying was "Holy cow."

Jean Havlish, a St. Paul native, won the Women's International Bowling Congress Championship Tournament singles-events title in 1964 and the all-events title in 1980. She is a member of the National Bowling Hall of Fame.

William W. "Pudge" Heffelfinger, who graduated from Minneapolis Central High School in 1888, is considered one of the greatest college football players of all time. After playing for the University of Minnesota while still in high school, Heffelfinger went on to Yale, where he earned All-American honors for three consecutive seasons. After a brief coaching career, he became a Hennepin County commissioner.

Walter Hoover, considered one of the greatest scullers in American history, was the first American to win the Diamond Sculls at Henley, England. He won many national and international championships for the Duluth Boat Club.

Joe Hutton Sr. coached the Hamline University basketball team to 591 victories, three small-college national titles, and 17 MIAC conference titles in 34 seasons.

John Johnson, a Minneapolis native, was a champion bicyclist and speed skater. In 1892, at the age of 19, he became the first to bicycle one mile in less than two minutes when he went one mile in 1:56.6. A member of the U.S. Bicycling and Speed Skating halls of fame, he also set several world records in speed skating.

Harrison R. "Jimmy" Johnston was the first Minnesotan to win the U.S. Amateur golf championship (1929, at Pebble Beach, California). He won seven state titles and was a member of five U.S. Walker Cup teams.

Nick Kahler, a member of the U.S. Hockey Hall of Fame, was one of the first great players in Minnesota. He was a member of the St. Paul Athletic Club team that won the MacNaughton Cup in 1916. He founded the Minneapolis Millers hockey team.

Janet Karvonen, a legend before finishing high school, led New York Mills to three consecutive girls state basketball titles. Karvonen was the first player in state history to score more than 3,000 points in a career and was the U.S. High School Player of the Year as a senior. Karvonen is a member of the National High School Hall of Fame.

Mike Kelley was associated with professional baseball in Minneapolis and St. Paul for nearly 50 years. He owned the Minneapolis Millers from 1923 to 1946.

Harmon Killebrew, one of the greatest home run hitters in major league history, played for the Minnesota Twins from 1961 to 1974. From 1961 to 1970 he hit 403 home runs for the Twins. He finished his career with 573 home runs.

John Kundla, who played baseball and basketball for the Gophers, coached the Minneapolis Lakers to six titles and coached the Gophers for nine seasons. He is a member of the Basketball Hall of Fame.

Dorothy Franey Langkop, a speed skater from St. Paul, won three U.S. and North American championships. She won a bronze medal in the 1,000 meters at the 1932 Olympics. During her career, she broke 25 American and Canadian records. At one time, she held five U.S. records.

Dorothy Franey Langkop, Olympic medalist speed skater who broke 25 American and Canadian records, 1931

R. W. "Bobby" Marshall, first African American to earn All-American status in the Big Ten and be named to the Football Foundation Hall of Fame

Robin Lee, at the age of 13, won the Midwestern Championship as a member of the St. Paul Figure Skating Club. He won five consecutive senior men's figure skating titles. He was the top skater on two U.S. Olympic teams (1936 and 1940). After retiring from competition, he continued to train skaters at the Figure Skating Club of Minneapolis until retiring in 1990. He is a member of the U.S. Figure Skating Association Hall of Fame.

George Loomis is one of the foremost trainers and drivers of harness horses in state history. He trained and drove horses for nearly 50 years.

Francis "Pug" Lund, the captain of the Gophers 1934 national championship football team, is a member of the College Football Hall of Fame.

John Mariucci, an Eveleth native, is called the "godfather of Minnesota hockey." After playing for the Gophers, he went on to be one of the few Americans playing in the NHL. He coached the Gophers for 14 seasons and coached the 1956 U.S. Olympic team. He is a member of the U.S. Hockey Hall of Fame and the Hockey Hall of Fame.

Bobby Marshall played football and baseball for the Gophers in the early 1900s. He was the first African American to earn All-American status in the conference that became known as the Big Ten. He is a member of the National Football Foundation's Hall of Fame.

Jim Marshall, who was an All-American at Ohio State, played one year in the CFL and one year for the Cleveland Browns before joining the Minnesota Vikings in 1961. He would play in 302 consecutive games and became the first African American to be named to the Minnesota Sports Hall of Fame.

Earl Martineau, a graduate of Minneapolis West High School, played for the Gophers football team from 1921 to 1923. He was All-American in 1923. He served in the marines during World War I, earning several medals for bravery before returning home to play for the Gophers.

John Mayasich paced Eveleth High School to four state hockey titles and was a three-time All-American at the University of Minnesota. Mayasich was a member of the 1956 and 1960 U.S. Olympic teams and is a member of the U.S. Hockey Hall of Fame.

John McGovern, a native of Arlington, Minnesota, was the second University of Minnesota football player to earn All-American honors, when he was named in 1909. McGovern missed just one game in his three-year career—playing every minute in every other game.

George Mikan, who was named the greatest basketball player for the first 50 years of the 20th century, led the Minneapolis Lakers to six championships in seven years.

Vern Mikkelsen, an Askov native, led Hamline to the 1949 small-college

George Mikan, voted greatest basketball player for the first 50 years of the 20th century

Tommy Milton, 1923, first driver to win the Indianapolis 500 twice

basketball title. He was a member of four Minneapolis Lakers championship teams.

Tommy Milton, a St. Paul native regarded as one of the greatest auto racers in American history, was the first to win two Indianapolis 500 races (he won in1921 and 1923). He finished in the top three in 82 of his 104 career starts. He won 23 races and at one time held 50 records.

Clarence "Biggie" Munn, a Minneapolis native and graduate of Minneapolis North High School, was an All-American for the Gophers in 1931. He earned six letters at the university—three in football and three in track. He went on to a successful coaching career at Michigan State, where he also served as athletic director.

Bronko Nagurski, a member of the College Football Hall of Fame and the Pro Football Hall of Fame, was the first player to be named an All-American at two positions in the same year (tackle and fullback in 1929). After his career at the University of Minnesota, Nagurski played eight seasons of professional football for the Chicago Bears. He also won three professional wrestling world titles. In 1999, *Sports Illustrated* named Nagurski Minnesota's top athlete for the 20th century.

Cindy Nelson, a native of Lutsen, Minnesota, is the only woman to ski on four U.S. Olympic teams. She won a bronze medal in downhill at the 1976 Olympic Games in Austria.

Mike O'Dowd, known as the "St. Paul Harp" and as one of the toughest fighters of his time, won the world middleweight boxing title in 1917. He held the title for three years.

Tony Oliva, a native of Cuba, was named to the American League All-Star team eight times during his career with the Minnesota Twins. He won the American League Rookie of the Year award and won three American League batting titles.

Alan Page was a first-round draft choice of the Minnesota Vikings in 1971, following an impressive college football career at Notre Dame. He played in nine consecutive Pro Bowls and, in 1971, was the first defensive player to be named MVP of the NFL. Page is now a member of the Minnesota Supreme Court.

George Quam won the Minneapolis Athletic Club handball championship 25 consecutive times, despite having just one arm. (He lost his left arm in an accident at the age of seven.) Quam, who won 140 of 154 matches on a national tour, is a member of the Helms Foundation Hall of Fame.

Jimmy Robinson, the most notable Minnesota sportsman of the 20th century, is a member of five halls of fame. He was the first outdoors writer for the *Minneapolis Star,* and he wrote for *Sports Afield* magazine from 1926 to 1986. He also ran the Sports Afield duck camp in Manitoba.

Dick Siebert coached the University of Minnesota baseball team for 31 seasons. He led the Gophers to three NCAA titles (1956, 1960, and 1964) in an eight-year span. He coached future Hall of Famers Dave Winfield and Paul Molitor.

Bruce Smith, a Faribault native, is the only Gopher football player to win the Heisman Award. Smith won the award in 1941 after helping the Gophers gain the national title. After World War II, he played in the NFL.

Emmett Swanson, one of the top rifle-pistol marksmen in American history, appeared in two Olympics (1948 and 1952) as a competitor. The winner of numerous national championships, he also won at least three world titles. As captain of the University of Minnesota's rifle team in 1925, he earned All-American honors.

Fran Tarkenton, a member of the Pro Football Hall of Fame, played for the Minnesota Vikings for 13 seasons. He was the quarterback of three Vikings Super Bowl teams.

Edwin Widseth, a native of Gonvick, played football for the University of Minnesota from 1934 to 1936 and was an All-American in 1935 and 1936. The Gophers were 23–1 during that span. Widseth, who is a member of the College Football Hall of Fame, played four seasons of pro football.

Charles "Bud" Wilkinson, a Minneapolis native and a graduate of Shattuck Academy in Faribault, played football for the Gophers from 1934 to 1936. Wilkinson, who also earned three letters in hockey for the Gophers, was an All-American in football in 1935. He went on to a successful coaching career at the University of Oklahoma for 17 seasons. During that time, the

Bruce Smith, the only Gopher to earn the Heisman Trophy

Sooners compiled a 145–29–4 record and put together a 47-game winning streak.

Henry L. Williams, a graduate of Yale, became the first full-time, salaried football coach at the University of Minnesota in 1900. In 22 seasons, he coached the Gophers to a 136–33–11 record.

Max Winter introduced major league sports to the area when he helped bring the Minneapolis Lakers to Minnesota in 1947. He was part of the group that was awarded the expansion team Minnesota Vikings by the NFL in 1960.

Garfield "Gar" Wood, who grew up on a farm near Lake Osakis, dominated speedboat racing from 1920 to 1933. Thousands lined the banks of the Mississippi River to watch him race.

Minnesota Olympians

Minnesota athletes who have competed in either the summer or winter Olympics number 258 (after the 2006 Winter Games in Turin, Italy), according to the United States Olympic Committee. But that figure doesn't tell the complete story.

Tracy Caulkins was born in Winona but did not live in Minnesota. Her parents were teachers in Cochrane, Wisconsin, and Winona had the nearest hospital. Caulkins grew up in Nashville and swam at the University of Florida. In addition to the three gold medals she won at the 1984 Olympics in Los Angeles, she won 48 national titles, the most ever won by an American swimmer.

J. Ira Courtney, a Minnesota-born student attending the University of Washington, competed in three events in track and field at the 1912 games in Stockholm, Sweden. He is the first Minnesota-born athlete to compete in the Olympics. Courtney is also credited with being the first Olympian from the Pacific Northwest.

Fortune Gordien, who was born in Spokane, Washington, is an Olympian and a member of the Minnesota Sports Hall of Fame. He competed in three Olympics after leading the University of Minnesota to the NCAA track and field title in 1948. Gordien, who was the top-ranked American in the discus for seven years, held the world record for six consecutive years. He won a bronze medal at the 1948 games and a silver in 1956.

Tom Malchow is the only Minnesota-born and Minnesota-raised athlete who has won a gold medal at the Summer Olympics. The St. Paul native

Amy Peterson, speed skater and winner of three Olympic gold medals

claimed the gold medal in the 200-meter butterfly at the 2000 Olympics
in Sydney, Australia.

Amy Peterson is the only other Minnesota-born athlete (other than Caulkins)
to have won three individual Olympic medals. The speed skater, a Maplewood native who has competed in five Olympics, won a silver medal in
1992 and two bronzes in 1994.

Robert Seguso, born in Minneapolis in 1963, grew up in Sunrise, Florida.
He teamed with Ken Flach to win the gold medal in tennis doubles at the
1988 Olympics. After his collegiate career at Southern Illinois University–
Edwardsville, Seguso eventually reached No. 22 in the singles rankings but
earned his fame in doubles. He and teammate Ken Flach reached No. 1 in
the rankings and won 29 titles.

Of the eight Minnesota athletes who have won two or more Olympic medals, only two—Austin's **Burdette Haldorson** and Dayton's **Briana Scurry**—have earned two gold medals. Haldorson, who played on Austin's team in the 1951 state basketball tournament and played collegiately at Colorado, was a member of the 1956 and 1960 U.S. basketball teams. Scurry was the goalkeeper on the 1996, 2000, and 2004 U.S. women's soccer teams. The U.S. won gold medals in 1996 and 2004 and a silver in 2000.

At least 20 Minnesota-born athletes have won gold medals in hockey. Minnesota natives on the 1980 Olympic hockey team were **William Baker, Neal Broten, David Christian, Steve Janaszak, Mark Johnson, Robert McClanahan, Mark Pavelich, Mike Ramsey, Buzz Schneider, Eric Strobel, Kent Thometz,** and **Philip Verchota.**

Summer Olympians

1912 J. Ira Courtney (track and field)

1920 Frank Loomis (track and field, 400-meter hurdles, gold medal)

1924 Karl Anderson (track and field), Leonard Carpenter (rowing, eight oars with coxswain, gold medal); John Faricy (swimming); Raymond Fee (boxing, 112.5 pounds, bronze medal); Thomas Lieb (track and field, discus, bronze medal)

1928 Walter Hoover (rowing)

1932 Evelyne Hall (track and field, 80-meter hurdles, silver medal); Edwin Moles Jr. (swimming); Ann Govednik Van Steinburg (swimming)

1936 Charles Leonard (modern pentathlon, silver medal); Milo Matteson (equestrian); Ann Govednik Van Steinburg (swimming); Gene Venzke (track and field)

1948 Verne Gagne (wrestling); Emmett Swanson (shooting)

1952 Frank McCabe (basketball, gold medal); Emmett Swanson (shooting)

1956 John Beaumont Jr. (shooting); Burdette Haldorson (basketball, gold medal); Robert Horn (water polo); Charles Jones (track and field); Alan Rice (Greco-Roman wrestling)

1960 Burdette Haldorson (basketball, gold medal); Robert Horn (water polo); Charles Jones (track and field)

1964 Robert Christopherson (boxing); Virgil Luken (swimming)

1968 David Brink (cycling); John Clawson (basketball, gold medal); Ronald Daws (marathon); John Hartigan (rowing); Larry Lyden (Greco-Roman wrestling); James McNally (shooting); Van Nelson (track and field); Trina Radke (swimming)

1972 William Allen (sailing, soling class, gold medal); Duane Bobick (boxing);

Craig Lincoln (diving, 3-meter springboard, bronze medal); James McNally (shooting); Angus Morrison (canoe and kayak); Gary Neist (Greco-Roman wrestling); Philip Rogosheske (canoe and kayak)

1976 Gary Alexander (wrestling); Garry Bjorklund (track and field); Kolleen Casey (gymnastics); Dan Chandler (Greco-Roman wrestling); John Hartigan (rowing); Evan Johnson (Greco-Roman wrestling); Lawrence Klecatsky (rowing); Mark Lutz (track and field); Patrick Marcy (Greco-Roman wrestling); Angus Morrison (canoe and kayak); Brad Rheingans (Greco-Roman wrestling); Bruce Thompson (Greco-Roman wrestling)

1980 The United States boycotted the 1980 Summer Olympic Games in Moscow because of the Soviet Union's war in Afghanistan. The following native Minnesotans had qualified for the U.S. Olympic team: Colin Anderson (track and field); Tracy Caulkins (swimming); Dan Chandler (Greco-Roman wrestling); Brian Gust (Greco-Roman wrestling); Angus Morrison (canoe and kayak); Brad Rheingans (Greco-Roman wrestling); Peter Schnugg (water polo); Steven Seck (judo); John Simons Jr. (swimming); Bruce Thompson (Greco-Roman wrestling)

1984 Tracy Caulkins (swimming, 200-meter individual medley, gold medal; 400-meter individual medley, gold medal; 400-meter medley relay, gold medal); Dan Chandler (Greco-Roman wrestling); Stephen Erickson (sailing, star class, gold medal); James Martinez (Greco-Roman wrestling, 68 kilograms, bronze medal); Steven Roller (track and field)

1988 John Morgan (Greco-Roman wrestling); Lynn Nelson (track and field); Carol Ann Peterka (team handball); Robert Seguso (tennis, doubles, gold medal)

1992 Peter Durben (shooting); Yasmin Farooq (rowing); Tami Jameson (team handball); Robert Kempainen (marathon); Janis Klecker (marathon); Manuel Lagos (soccer); Lori Ogren (team handball); Carol Ann Peterka (team handball)

1996 William Carlucci (rowing, lightweight four without, bronze medal); Yasmin Farooq (rowing); Tami Jameson (team handball); Toni Jameson (team handball); Robert Kempainen (marathon); Thomas Malchow (swimming, 200-meter butterfly, silver medal); Gordon Morgan (Greco-Roman wrestling); Brandon Paulson (Greco-Roman wrestling, 52 kilograms, silver medal); Carol Ann Peterka (team handball); Debra Richardson (volleyball); Briana Scurry (soccer, gold medal)

2000 Kristin Kuehl (track and field); Thomas Malchow (swimming, 200-meter butterfly, gold medal); Sarah Noriega (volleyball); Sara Reiling (diving); Briana Scurry (soccer, silver medal); Michael Wherley (rowing)

2004 Wiz Bachman (volleyball); Sara Hildebrand (diving); Thomas Malchow (swimming); Victor Plata (triathlon); Briana Scurry (soccer, gold medal); Carrie Tollefson (track and field); Michael Wherley (rowing)

DID YOU KNOW ?

On June 1, 1979, Gerry Spiess, a 39-year-old electronics engineer from White Bear Lake, left Virginia Beach, Virginia, in his homemade 10-foot sailboat *Yankee Girl*. When he docked the boat in Falmouth, England, 54 days later, his craft became the smallest ever to cross the North Atlantic. Two years later Spiess sailed alone from California to Australia.

Winter Olympians

1920 Francis Goheen (ice hockey)

1932 Margaret Bennett (figure skating); Dorothy Franey Langkop (speed skating, 1,000 meters, bronze medal)

1936 Philip La Batte (ice hockey, bronze medal); Robin Lee (figure skating); Alfred Lindley (skiing); Erle Reiter (figure skating)

1940 Robin Lee (figure skating)

1948 Robert Fitzgerald (speed skating); Roy Ikola (ice hockey); Allen Van (ice hockey); John Werket (speed skating)

1952 Reuben Bjorkman (ice hockey, silver medal); John Burton (skiing); Robert Fitzgerald (speed skaing); Andre Gambucci (ice hockey, silver medal); Janet Griffiths-Allen (figure skating); George Hovland (skiing); Willard Ikola (ice hockey, silver medal); Matt McNamara (speed skating); John Nightingale (figure skating); John Noah (ice hockey, silver medal); Arnold Oss Jr. (ice hockey, silver medal); Robert Rompre (ice hockey, silver medal); James Sedin (ice hockey, silver medal); Allen Van (ice hockey); John Werket (speed skating); Kenneth Yackel (ice hockey, silver medal)

1956 Wendell Anderson (ice hockey, silver medal); Eugene Campbell (ice hockey); William Carow (speed skating); Gordon Christian (ice hockey, silver medal); Willard Ikola (ice hockey, silver medal); John Matchefts (ice hockey, silver medal); John Mayasich (ice hockey, silver medal); Daniel McKinnon (ice hockey, silver medal); Matt McNamara (speed skating); Eugene Sandvig (speed skating); John Werket (speed skating)

1960 Floyd Bedbury (speed skating); William Carow (speed skating); Roger Christian (ice hockey, gold medal); William Christian (ice hockey, gold medal); Paul Johnson (ice hockey, gold medal); Gene Kotlarek (ski jumping); John Mayasich (ice hockey, gold medal); Jack McCartan (ice hockey, gold medal); Edwyn Owen (ice hockey, gold medal); Thomas Williams (ice hockey, gold medal)

1964 John Balfanz (ski jumping); Floyd Bedbury (speed skating); David Brooks (ice hockey); Herb Brooks (ice hockey); Roger Christian (ice hockey), William Christian (ice hockey); Daniel Dilworth (ice hockey); Dates Fryberger (ice hockey); Thomas Gray (speed skating); David Hicks (ski jumping); Paul Johnson (ice hockey); Gene Kotlarek (ski jumping); Janice Lawler (speed skating); Jay Martin (ski jumping); Thomas McCoy (ice hockey); Donald Ross (ice hockey); Gary Schmalzbauer (ice hockey); James Westby (ice hockey); Thomas Yurkovich (ice hockey)

1968 Herb Brooks (ice hockey); William Cox (speed skating); John Dale (ice hockey); Craig Falkman (ice hockey); Thomas Gray (speed skating); Leonard Lilyholm (ice hockey); Jay Martin (ski jumping); Mary Meyers (speed skating, 500 meters, silver medal); James Moriarty (luge); John Morrison (ice hockey); Robert Paradise (ice hockey); Misha Petkevich (figure skating); Donald Ross (ice hockey); Larry Stordahl (ice hockey)

1972 Larry Bader (ice hockey, silver medal); Henry Boucha (ice hockey, silver medal); Charles Brown (ice hockey, silver medal); Mike Curran (ice hockey, silver medal); Jerry Martin (ski jumping); James McElmury (ice hockey, silver medal); Bruce McIntosh (ice hockey, silver medal); Ronald Naslund (ice hockey, silver medal); Misha Petkevich (figure skating); Franklin Sanders Jr. (ice hockey, silver medal); Craig Sarner (ice hockey, silver medal); Timothy Sheehy (ice hockey, silver medal)

1976 Steven Alley (ice hockey); Blane Comstock (ice hockey); James Denney (ski jumping); Peter Hoag Jr. (biathlon); Jeffrey Hymanson (ice hockey); Paul Jensen (ice hockey); Steve Jensen (ice hockey); Terry Kern (ski jumping); Kim Kostron (speed skating); Robert Lundeen (ice hockey); James Maki (ski jumping); Jerry Martin (ski jumping); James Moriarty (luge); Cindy Nelson (skiing, downhill, bronze medal); Doug Peterson (skiing); Michael Randolph (ice hockey); Gary Ross (ice hockey); Buzz Schneider (ice hockey); Mary Seaton (skiing); Cindy Seikkula (speed skating); Stephen Sertich (ice hockey); Kip Sundgaard (ski jumping); John Taft (ice hockey); Greg Windsperger (ski jumping)

1980 William Baker (ice hockey, gold medal); John Broman (ski jumping); Neal Broten (ice hockey, gold medal); David Christian (ice hockey, gold medal); James Denney (ski jumping); James Grahek (ski jumping); Peter Hoag Jr. (biathlon); Steve Janaszak (ice hockey, gold medal); Mark Johnson (ice hockey, gold medal); Todd Kempainen (skiing); Kim Kostron (speed skating); James Maki (ski jumping); Robert McClanahan (ice hockey, gold medal); Cindy Nelson (skiing); Mark Pavelich (ice hockey, gold medal); Mike Ramsey (ice hockey, gold medal); Buzz Schneider (ice hockey, gold medal); Eric Strobel (ice hockey, gold medal); Kent Thometz (speed skating); Philip Verchota (ice hockey, gold medal)

1984 Scott Bjugstad (ice hockey); Kevin Brochman (skiing); Katie Class (speed skating); Steven Griffith (ice hockey); John Harrington (ice hockey); Thomas Hirsch (ice hockey); David Jensen (ice hockey); Bob Mason (ice hockey); Mark Mitchell (speed skating); Cindy Nelson (skiing); Michael Randall (skiing); Tim Thomas (ice hockey); Kent Thometz (speed skating); Nick Thometz (speed skating); Philip Verchota (ice hockey)

1988 John Baskfield (speed skating); Kevin Brochman (skiing); Peggy Clasen (speed skating); Katie Class (speed skating); James Johannson (ice hockey); Thomas Locken (curling); Todd Okerlund (ice hockey); Amy Peterson (speed skating); Dave Snuggerud (ice hockey); Tricia Stennes (speed skating); Nick Thometz (speed skating); Jill Trenary (figure skating)

1992 Patrice Anderson (biathlon); John Bauer (skiing); Peggy Clasen (speed skating); James Johannson (ice hockey); Carrie Johnson (speed skating); Rachel Mayer (ice dancing); Amy Peterson (speed skating, 3,000 meter relay, silver medal); Tricia Stennes (speed skating); William Strum (curling, bronze medal); Nick Thometz (speed skating)

1994 Randy Bartz (short track, 5,000 meter relay, silver medal); Troy Benson (skiing); Peggy Clasen (speed skating); Brett Hauer (ice hockey); Darby Hendrickson (ice hockey); Amy Peterson (speed skating, 3,000 meter relay, silver medal; 500 meter, bronze medal)

1998 John Bauer (skiing); Alana Blahoski (ice hockey, gold medal); Andrew Erickson (biathlon); Mike Keuler (ski jumping); Kristina Koznick (skiing); Jamie Langenbrunner (ice hockey); Stacy Liapis (curling); Joel Otto (ice hockey); Amy Peterson (speed skating); Kara Salmela (biathlon); Amy Sannes (speed skating); Jennifer Schmidgall (ice hockey, gold medal)

2002 John Bauer (cross-country skiing); Natalie Darwitz (ice hockey, silver medal); Kristina Koznick (skiing); Stacy Liapis (curling); Amy Peterson (speed skating); Amy Sannes (speed skating); Jennifer Schmidgall (ice hockey, silver medal); Krissy Wendell (ice hockey, silver medal)

2006 Mason Aguirre (snowboarding); Scott Baird (curling, bronze medal); Tony Benshoof (luge); Jason Blake (ice hockey); Maureen Brunt (curling); Natalie Darwitz (ice hockey, bronze medal); Jim Denney (ski jumping); Tricia Dunn-Luoma (ice hockey, bronze medal); Pete Fenson (curling, bronze medal); Courtney George (curling); Bret Hedican (ice hockey); Cassie Johnson (curling); Jamie Johnson (curling); Lindsey Kildow (alpine skiing); Kristina Koznick (alpine skiing); Abby Larson (cross-country skiing); Jordan Leopold (ice hockey); Mark Parrish (ice hockey); Joe Polo (curling, bronze medal); Jennifer Schmidgall Potter (ice hockey, bronze medal); Kaylin Richardson (alpine skiing); Shawn Rojeski (curling, bronze medal); Amy Sannes (speedskating); Jessica Schultz (curling); John Shuster (curling, bronze medal); Carolyn Treacy (biathlon); Lindsey Weier (cross-country skiing); Krissy Wendell (ice hockey, bronze medal); Lindsay Williams (cross-country skiing).

Baseball
and Softball

2

Minnesota Twins

I N 1948, one year after obtaining a professional basketball team, the Minneapolis Lakers, civic leaders in the Twin Cities set out to lure a professional football franchise or major league baseball team to the area. Over the next dozen years, the quest for a major league baseball team left the Twin Cities disappointed. In the 1950s, at least five teams—the New York Giants, Philadelphia Athletics, St. Louis Browns, Cleveland Indians, and Washington Senators—flirted with the idea of moving to the Twin Cities. The financially troubled Washington Senators became the focus of the civic leaders in the late 1950s.

In July 1958 Washington Senators' owner Calvin Griffith reportedly was ready to ask the other American League owners for permission to relocate his team to Minnesota. Two days later, at a Congressional hearing about antitrust legislation, Griffith testified he would never move the team. In September 1958, Griffith again appeared ready to request permission to move, but he apparently changed his mind, announcing the team would remain in Washington.

Things heated up in July 1959, when a group of New York businessmen, frustrated with major league baseball's reluctance to expand, announced they would form a third major league. The eight-team league, dubbed the Continental League and scheduled to begin play in 1961, awarded a franchise to the Twin Cities. During the 1959 World Series, a national publication prematurely reported that the transfer of the Senators to the Twin Cities for the next season was a certainty.

In October 1960 the National League owners voted to expand to 10 teams by granting franchises to New York and Houston. American League owners convened in New York a week later for an "expansion and re-alignment session." The meeting produced dramatic changes when the owners allowed the Senators to move to Minnesota and added two expansion teams—one in Washington to replace the departing Senators and another in Los Angeles.

Minnesota Governor Orville Freeman and Senator Hubert Humphrey lauded the announcement in the October 27 edition of the *Minneapolis Tribune*. "Major league baseball will be a real stimulus to a bigger and better Minnesota," said Freeman. Humphrey called the announcement "a great day for the Twin Cities and a great day for Minnesota. A long struggle to bring major league baseball here has culminated in success."

Harmon Killebrew of the Minnesota Twins crossing home plate after hitting a game-winning home run, 1965

Twins owner Cal Griffith, with Karl Rolvaag and Hubert Humphrey, 1965 World Series, Met Stadium

Minnesota had acquired a franchise that had inspired the quip, "Washington—first in war, first in peace and last in the American League." But the franchise, renamed the Minnesota Twins, initially flourished in its new home. The Twins team won the American League pennant in 1965 and the American League West Division titles in 1969 and 1970. From 1961 to 1970, the Twins led the American League in attendance.

At the end of the 1981 season, after 21 seasons at Metropolitan Stadium, the Twins moved to downtown Minneapolis to play in the Hubert Humphrey Metrodome. Some 2½ years later, after entertaining the thought of moving his team, Griffith sold the franchise to banker Carl Pohlad.

In 1987 the Twins won their first division title in 17 years and then went on to stun most baseball observers by winning the World Series. The championship was the first won by a Minnesota major league sports franchise since the Lakers won the NBA title in 1954.

Just four years later in 1991, the Twins won another World Series. After a second-place finish in 1992, the Twins' fortune took a nosedive, and the team suffered through eight consecutive losing seasons—including 90-loss seasons in 1997, 1998, and 1999. The low point for the franchise came in November 2001, when Commissioner Bud Selig announced that major league baseball intended to "contract" two teams, targeting the Twins and Montreal Expos.

Owner Pohlad, who had been praised for keeping the team in Minnesota after buying it in 1984, reportedly offered the franchise for contraction—believing that a check to fold the franchise was better than the annual budget losses and the ongoing fight for a new stadium. But before the plan could be put in motion, a Hennepin County District Court judge issued an injunction that forced the team to honor its lease for the 2002 season. Major League Baseball challenged that decision, but Minnesota's Court of Appeals upheld it on January 22, 2002. The contraction plans were put on hold on February 5, 2002, after the state supreme court refused to hear the case.

Given a reprieve, the Twins have again flourished. After a respectable 85-victory season in 2001, the Twins have won three consecutive Division titles. From 2002 to 2004, the team won at least 90 games in each season—the first time in Twins history that has happened.

The Twins failed to reach the playoffs in 2005—finishing third in the American League Central, with an 83–79 record. On a positive note, it was the fifth consecutive winning season for the Twins, the first time the team has accomplished that. Pitcher Johan Santana led the major leagues with 238 strikeouts—a first for a Twins pitcher.

DID YOU KNOW ?

Game 1 of the 1987 World Series (October 17, 1987) was the first World Series game played indoors. The Twins defeated the St. Louis Cardinals, 10–1, before a crowd of 55,171 at the Metrodome.

League Organization

From 1961 until 1968, the American League was a 10-team league. In 1969 the American League split into divisions. From 1969 to 1993, the Twins played in the American League West Division. In 1994 major league baseball reorganized and the Twins were placed in the American League Central.

Work Stoppages

Since the Major League Baseball Players Association was formed in 1966, there have been eight work stoppages (a ninth was averted at the last minute). Of the eight stoppages, five have been strikes by the players, and the other three have been lockouts by the owners.

Date	Reason	Effect
Apr. 1–13, 1972	Strike	13 days and 86 games missed
Feb. 8–25, 1973	Lockout	17 days, 0 games missed
Mar. 1–17, 1976	Lockout	17 days, 0 games missed
Apr. 1–8, 1980	Strike	8 days, 0 games missed
Jun. 12–Jul. 31, 1981	Strike	50 days, 712 games missed
Aug. 6–7, 1985	Strike	2 days, 0 games missed
Feb. 15–Mar. 18, 1990	Lockout	32 days, 0 games missed
Aug. 12, 1994–Mar. 31, 1995	Strike	232 days, 920 games missed, inc. 1994 World Series

NOTE: A strike was narrowly averted in 2002. The Players Association had set a deadline of August 30 to reach a new agreement. The agreement was reached on August 31, just 3½ hours before the first game that would have been affected by a strike. The agreement was the first achieved without a work stoppage since 1970.

Twins Year-by-Year

Season	Record	Manager
1961	70–90–1	Cookie Lavagetto (25–41), Sam Mele (45–49–1)
1962	91–71–1	Mele
1963	91–70	Mele
1964	79–83–1	Mele
1965	102–60	Mele
1966	89–73	Mele
1967	91–71–2	Mele (25–25), Cal Ermer (66–46–2)
1968	79–83	Ermer
1969	97–65	Billy Martin
1970	98–64	Bill Rigney
1971	74–86	Rigney
1972	77–77	Rigney (36–34), Frank Quilici (41–43)
1973	81–81	Quilici
1974	82–80–1	Quilici
1975	76–83	Quilici
1976	85–77	Gene Mauch

1977	84–77	Mauch
1978	73–89	Mauch
1979	82–80	Mauch
1980	77–84	Mauch (54–71), John Goryl (23–13)
1981	41–68–1	Goryl (11–25–1), Billy Gardner (30–43)
1982	60–102	Gardner
1983	70–92	Gardner
1984	81–81	Gardner
1985	77–85	Gardner (27–35), Ray Miller (50–50)
1986	71–91	Miller (59–80), Tom Kelly (12–11)
1987	85–77	Kelly
1988	91–71	Kelly
1989	80–82	Kelly
1990	74–88	Kelly
1991	95–67	Kelly
1992	90–72	Kelly
1993	71–91	Kelly
1994	53–60	Kelly
1995	56–88	Kelly
1996	78–84	Kelly
1997	68–94	Kelly
1998	70–92	Kelly
1999	63–97	Kelly
2000	69–93	Kelly
2001	85–77	Kelly
2002	94–67	Ron Gardenhire
2003	90–72	Gardenhire
2004	92–70	Gardenhire
2005	83–79	Gardenhire

Twins Titles

American League	1965, 1987, 1991
American League West	1969, 1970, 1987, 1991
American League Central	2002, 2003, 2004

Twins in the Postseason

1965 World Series — Los Angeles Dodgers 4, Twins 3
1969 American League Championship Series — Baltimore Orioles 3, Twins 0
1970 American League Championship Series — Baltimore Orioles 3, Twins 0
1987 American League Championship Series — Twins 4, Detroit Tigers 1

1987	World Series	Twins 4, St. Louis Cardinals 3
1991	American League Championship Series	Twins 4, Toronto Blue Jays 3
1991	World Series	Twins 4, Atlanta Braves 3
2002	American League Division Series	Twins 3, Oakland Athletics 2
2002	American League Championship Series	Anaheim Angels 4, Twins 1
2003	American League Division Series	New York Yankees 3, Twins 1
2004	American League Division Series	New York Yankees 3, Twins 1

Twins Managers' Records

Tom Kelly	1,140–1,244
Sam Mele	522–431
Gene Mauch	376–394
Ron Gardenhire	359–288
Frank Quilici	280–287
Billy Gardner	268–353
Bill Rigney	208–184
Cal Ermer	145–129
Ray Miller	109–130
Billy Martin	97–65
John Goryl	34–38
Cookie Lavagetto	25–41

Twins Players' Records

Game (batting)

Hits	6, by Kirby Puckett (Aug. 30, 1987, and May 23, 1991)
Home runs	3, by Bob Allison (May 17, 1963); by Harmon Killebrew (Sept. 21, 1963); by Tony Oliva (Jul. 3, 1973)
Runs batted in	8, by Glenn Adams (Jun. 26, 1977); by Randy Bush (May 20, 1989)
Stolen bases	4, by Larry Hisle (Jun. 30, 1976)

Game (pitching)

Innings pitched	13, by Jim Merritt (Jul. 26, 1967)
Strikeouts	15, by Camilo Pascual (Jul. 19, 1961); by Joe Decker (Jun. 26, 1973); by Jerry Koosman (Jun. 23, 1980); by Bert Blyleven (Aug. 1, 1986)

Season (batting)

Games played	164, by Cesar Tovar (1967)
Longest hitting streak	31 games, by Ken Landreaux (Apr. 23 to May 30, 1980)
Batting average	.388, by Rod Carew (1977)
Hits	239, by Rod Carew (1977)

Home runs	49, by Harmon Killebrew (1964, 1969)
RBI	140, by Harmon Killebrew (1969)
Stolen bases	62, by Chuck Knoblauch (1997)

Season (pitching)

Wins	25, by Jim Kaat (1966)
Saves	45, by Eddie Guardado (2002)
Innings pitched	325, by Bert Blyleven (1973)
Strikeouts	265, by Johan Santana (2004)

Career (batting)

Games	1,939, by Harmon Killebrew
Batting average	.334, by Rod Carew
Hits	2,304, by Kirby Puckett
Home runs	475, by Harmon Killebrew
RBI	1,325, by Harmon Killebrew
Stolen bases	276, by Chuck Knoblauch

Career (pitching)

Wins	189, by Jim Kaat
Saves	254, by Rick Aguilera
Strikeouts	2,035, by Bert Blyleven
ERA	2.67, by Dean Chance

Team records

Longest winning streak	15, Jun. 1–16, 1991
Longest losing streak	14, May 19–Jun. 2, 1982

Longest games

22 innings (6:17)	Twins 5, Cleveland 4 (Aug. 31, 1993)
22 innings (5:47)	Milwaukee 4, Twins 3 (May 12–13, 1972)
20 innings (5:40)	Washington 9, Twins 7 (Aug. 9, 1967)
19 innings (5:27)	New York 5, Twins 4 (at New York, Aug. 25, 1976)

No-hitters

Name	Date	Opponent	Score
Jack Kralick	Aug. 26, 1962	Kansas City	1–0
Dean Chance	Aug. 6, 1967	Boston	2–0*
Dean Chance	Aug. 25, 1967	at Cleveland	2–1
Scott Erickson	Apr. 27, 1994	Milwaukee	6–0
Eric Milton	Sept. 11, 1999	Anaheim	7–0

*5 innings

Twins 20-Game Winners

Pitcher	Year	Record
Camilo Pascual	1962	20–11
Pascual	1963	21–9
Jim Grant	1965	21–7
Jim Kaat	1966	25–13
Dean Chance	1967	20–14
Dave Boswell	1969	20–12
Jim Perry	1969	20–6
Perry	1970	24–12*
Bert Blyleven	1973	20–17
Dave Goltz	1977	20–11
Jerry Koosman	1979	20–13
Frank Viola	1988	24–7*
Scott Erickson	1991	20–8
Brad Radke	1997	20–10
Johan Santana	2004	20–6*

*won Cy Young award.

Twins League Batting Titles

Tony Oliva	1964 (.323), 1965 (.321), 1971 (.337)
Rod Carew	1969 (.332), 1972 (.318), 1973 (.350*), 1974 (.364*), 1975 (.359*), 1977 (.388*), 1978 (.333)
Kirby Puckett	1989 (.339)

*led major leagues

Twins Hitting Streaks

31	Ken Landreaux (Apr. 23–May 30, 1980)
25	Brian Harper (Jul. 6–Aug. 4, 1990)
24	Lenny Green (May 1–28, 1961)
23	Kent Hrbek (Apr. 17–May 13, 1982)
23	Kirby Puckett (Sept. 26, 1993–Apr. 20, 1994)
23	Marty Cordova (Jun. 5–29, 1996)
23	Cristian Guzman (Aug. 1–25, 2002)
22	Shane Mack (Jul. 26–Aug. 18, 1992)
20	Ted Uhlaender (Aug. 16–Sept. 7, 1969)
20	Chuck Knoblauch (Sept. 2–25, 1991)

Twins Award Winners

American League MVP
1965 Zoilo Versalles; **1969** Harmon Killebrew; **1977** Rod Carew

American League Rookie of the year
1964 Tony Oliva; **1967** Rod Carew; **1979** John Castino (co-rookie of the year with Toronto's Alfredo Griffin); **1991** Chuck Knoblauch; **1995** Marty Cordova

---

DID YOU KNOW ?

In their first 44 seasons in Minnesota, the Twins had just one public address announcer—Bob Casey. Between 1961 and 2004, Casey worked more than 3,400 Twins home games. Casey, who had also worked for the Minneapolis Lakers and Minneapolis Millers in a career that began in 1947, is probably best remembered for several announcements, including "no smoking in the Metrodome," his introduction of Kirby Puckett—and an announcement on August 25, 1970.

That night, during a Twins game against the Boston Red Sox, a bomb threat was called into Metropolitan Stadium and passed along to Casey. Joe Soucheray's history of Metropolitan Stadium reports that Casey told the crowd of nearly 18,000, "Your attention please. There will be an explosion in the stadium at 9:30 p.m. I repeat, there will be an explosion!" During a 40-minute delay, many fans gathered in the infield, but there was no explosion.

American League Manager of the year
1991 Tom Kelly

Gold Gloves (with the Twins)

Earl Battey	1961, 1962
Jim Kaat	1962, 1963, 1964, 1965, 1966, 1967, 1968, 1969, 1970, 1971, 1972
Vic Power	1962, 1963

Zoilo Versalles	1963, 1965
Tony Oliva	1966
Gary Gaetti	1986, 1987, 1988, 1989
Kirby Puckett	1986, 1987, 1988, 1989, 1991, 1992
Chuck Knoblauch	1997
Torii Hunter	2001, 2002, 2003, 2004
Doug Mientkiewicz	2001

Twins All-Stars

1961 Harmon Killebrew, Camilo Pascual

1962 Earl Battey, Jim Kaat, Camilo Pascual, Rich Rollins

1963 Bob Allison, Earl Battey, Harmon Killebrew, Zoilo Versalles

1964 Bob Allison, Jimmie Hall, Harmon Killebrew, Tony Oliva, Camilo Pascual

1965 Earl Battey, Jim Grant, Jimmie Hall, Harmon Killebrew, Tony Oliva, Zoilo Versalles

1966 Earl Battey, Jim Kaat, Harmon Killebrew, Tony Oliva

1967 Rod Carew, Dean Chance, Harmon Killebrew, Tony Oliva

1968 Rod Carew, Harmon Killebrew, Tony Oliva

1969 Rod Carew, Harmon Killebrew, Tony Oliva, John Roseboro

1970 Rod Carew, Harmon Killebrew, Tony Oliva, Jim Perry

1971 Leo Cardenas, Rod Carew, Harmon Killebrew, Tony Oliva, Jim Perry

1972 Rod Carew

1973 Bert Blyleven, Rod Carew

1974 Rod Carew

1975 Rod Carew

1976 Rod Carew, Butch Wynegar

1977 Rod Carew, Larry Hisle, Butch Wynegar

1978 Rod Carew

1979 Roy Smalley

1980 Ken Landreaux

1981 Doug Corbett

1982 Kent Hrbek

1983 Gary Ward

1984 Dave Engle

1985 Tom Brunansky

1986 Kirby Puckett

1987 Kirby Puckett

1988 Gary Gaetti, Tim Laudner, Kirby Puckett, Jeff Reardon, Frank Viola

1989 Gary Gaetti, Kirby Puckett

1990 Kirby Puckett

1991 Rick Aguilera, Jack Morris, Kirby Puckett
1992 Rick Aguilera, Chuck Knoblauch, Kirby Puckett
1993 Rick Aguilera, Kirby Puckett
1994 Chuck Knoblauch, Kirby Puckett
1995 Kirby Puckett
1996 Chuck Knoblauch
1997 Chuck Knoblauch
1998 Brad Radke
1999 Ron Coomer
2000 Matt Lawton
2001 Cristian Guzman, Joe Mays, Eric Milton
2002 Eddie Guardado, Torii Hunter, A.J. Pierzynski
2003 Eddie Guardado
2004 Joe Nathan
2005 Joe Nathan, Johan Santana

Retired Twins numbers

3   Harmon Killebrew, on May 4, 1975
6   Tony Oliva, on July 14, 1991
14   Kent Hrbek, on Aug. 13, 1995
29   Rod Carew, on July 19, 1987
34   Kirby Puckett, on May 25, 1997
42   honoring Jackie Robinson, on May 23, 1997

Memorable Trades by the Twins

December 2, 1966 Acquired Dean Chance and Jackie Hernandez from California in exchange for Pete Cimino, Jimmie Hall and Don Mincher.

November 28, 1967 Acquired Bob Miller, Ron Perranoski and John Roseboro from Los Angeles in exchange for Jim Grant and Zoilo Versalles.

December 12, 1969 Acquired Luis Tiant and Stan Williams from Cleveland in exchange for Dean Chance, Bob Miller, Graig Nettles and Ted Uhlaender.

June 1, 1976 Acquired Mike Cubbage, Jim Gideon, Bill Singer and Roy Smalley from Texas in exchange for Bert Blyleven and Danny Thompson.

February 3, 1979 Acquired Dave Engle, Paul Hartzell, Brad Havens and Ken Landreaux from California in exchange for Rod Carew.

February 3, 1987 Acquired Tom Nieto and Jeff Reardon from Montreal in exchange for Al Cardwood, Neal Heaton, Yorkis Perez and Jeff Reed.

July 31, 1989 Acquired Rick Aguilera, Tim Drummond, Jack Savage, Kevin Tapani and David West from the New York Mets in exchange for Frank Viola.

February 6, 1998 Acquired Brian Buchanan, Cristian Guzman, Eric Milton and Danny Mota from the New York Yankees in exchange for Chuck Knoblauch.

November 14, 2003 Acquired Joe Nathan, Boof Bonser and Francisco Liriano from San Francisco in exchange for A.J. Pierzynski and cash.

December 3, 2003 Acquired Carlos Silva, Nick Punto and Bobby Korecky from Philadelphia in exchange for Eric Milton.

Twins First-Round Draft Choices

1965 Eddie Leon; **1966** Bob Jones; **1967** Steve Brye; **1968** Alex Rowell; **1969** Paul Powell; **1970** Bob Gorinski; **1971** Dale Soderholm; **1972** Dick Ruthven; **1973** Eddie Bane; **1974** Ted Shipley; **1975** Rick Sofield; **1976** Jamie Allen; **1977** Paul Croft; **1978** Lenny Faedo; **1979** Kevin Brandt; **1980:** Jeff Reed; **1981** Mike Sodders; **1982** Bryan Oelkers; **1983** Tim Belcher; **1984** Jay Bell; **1985** Jeff Bumgarner; **1986** Derek Parks; **1987** Willie Banks; **1988** Johnny Ard; **1989** Chuck Knoblauch; **1990:** Todd Ritchie; **1991** David McCarty; **1992** Dan Serafini; **1993** Torii Hunter, Jason Varitek; **1994:** Todd Walker; **1995** Mark Redman; **1996** Travis Lee; **1997** Michael Cuddyer, Matthew LeCroy; **1998** Ryan Mills; **1999** B.J. Garbe; **2000:** Adam Johnson; **2001** Joe Mauer; **2002** Denard Span; **2003** Matt Moses; **2004** Trevor Plouffe, Glen Perkins, Kyle Waldrop; **2005** Matt Garza.

NOTE: Between 1965 and 2004, the Twins had 44 first-round picks. Six of them—Leon, Allen, Ruthven, Belcher, Varitek, and Lee—did not sign with the Twins. Through the 2004 season, 21 of them—Brye, Powell, Gorinski, Bane, Sofield, Faedo, Reed, Oelkers, Parks, Banks, Knoblauch, Ritchie, McCarty, Serafini, Hunter, Walker, Redman, Cuddyer, LeCroy, Johnson, and Mauer—have played for the Twins.

Twins Players

Minnesota-Born Twins

Through the 2004 season, 145 native Minnesotans had appeared in a major league baseball game, including these 26 Minnesotans who played for the Twins:

Fred Bruckbauer (New Ulm), Tom Burgmeier (St. Paul), Jim Eisenreich (St. Cloud), Bob Gebhard (Lamberton), Paul Giel (Winona), Dave Goltz (Pelican Rapids), Kent Hrbek (Minneapolis), Tom Johnson (St. Paul), Tom Kelly (Graceville), Jerry Kindall (St. Paul), Jerry Koosman (Appleton), Mike Mason (Faribault), Joe Mauer (St. Paul), Paul Molitor (St. Paul), Jack Morris (St. Paul), Greg Olson (Marshall), Mike Poepping (Little Falls), Tom Quinlan (St. Paul), Brian Raabe (New Ulm), Michael Restovich (Rochester), Terry Steinbach

(New Ulm), Dick Stigman (Nimrod), Jerry Terrell (Waseca), George Thomas (Minneapolis), Charley Walters (Minneapolis) and Dave Winfield (St. Paul).

Jim "Mudcat" Grant

In 1965 Jim "Mudcat" Grant became the first African American to win 20 games in the American League, when he went 21–7 for the Twins. Grant also became the first African American pitcher on an American League team to win a World Series game; he won Game 1 of the 1965 series.

In 1954, while pitching for Fargo-Moorhead of the Class C Northern League, Grant became the first African American to win 20 games in minor league baseball. Grant won 21 games for Fargo-Moorhead, which went 85–55 in the regular season and won the league's playoffs.

Grant, who made his major league debut in 1958, spent 14 seasons in the major leagues. Playing for the Twins from 1964 to 1967, he went 50–35 for the team.

Kirby Puckett

In March 1996, Kirby Puckett was preparing for his 13th major league season. Puckett, 35, batted .344 in 20 spring-training games to show there were no ill effects from being hit in the face by a pitch the previous September. But on the morning of March 28, 1996, Puckett woke up with blurred vision. Puckett, who had never been on the disabled list, was eventually diagnosed with glaucoma and retired. He died on March 6, 2006, after suffering a stroke.

Winning Streak

Between July 12, 2004, and May 1, 2005, Johan Santana of the Minnesota Twins put together the fourth-longest winning streak by a pitcher in modern (since 1900) major league baseball history.

Starting with a 4–1 victory over the Kansas City Royals on July 17, 2004, Santana won 17 consecutive games (in a span of 20 starts) before losing to the Los Angeles Angels, 2–1, on May 1, 2005. In that span, Santana was 17–0 with a 1.77 ERA.

Santana's streak was the longest in the majors in five years (Roger Clemens won 20 consecutive games from June 3, 1998, to June 1, 1999). The two other streaks longer than Santana's are: 24 by the New York Giants' Carl Hubbell (June 17, 1936, to May 27, 1937) and 19 by the New York Giants' Rube Marquard (April 11 to July 3, 1912).

Baseball Hall of Famer Kirby Puckett making "the Catch" in game six of the 1991 World Series

Mr. Versatile

One Minnesota Twin—Cesar Tovar—has played all nine positions in one game. On September 22, 1968, Tovar accomplished the feat against the Oakland Athletics at Metropolitan Stadium.

Tovar started at pitcher—the only position player in Twins history to be the team's starting pitcher—and pitched a scoreless first inning. He struck out future Hall of Famer Reggie Jackson. In the second inning, he moved to catcher. From there, in order, he went to first base, second base, shortstop, third base, left field, center field and right field. Tovar was the second major leaguer to play all nine positions in the same game. The Athletics' Bert Campaneris was the first.

Minnesotans in the Hall of Fame

Three native Minnesotans have been inducted into the National Baseball Hall of Fame in Cooperstown, New York: Chief Bender (1953), Dave Winfield (2001), and Paul Molitor (2004).

Six Minnesota Twins players have been inducted into the Hall of Fame: Rod Carew (1991), Steve Carlton (1994), Harmon Killebrew (1984), Kirby Puckett (2001), Winfield, and Molitor.

More Player Records

The Twins' Tony Oliva is the only major league baseball player to win batting titles his first two years in the big leagues. Oliva won the American League batting title in 1964 with a .323 batting average. In 1965 he won the title with a .321 average.

In December 1972, the American League adopted the designated hitter rule. On April 6, 1973, Oliva became the first designated hitter to hit a home run when he connected off Oakland's Catfish Hunter.

In 1997 the Twins' Brad Radke tied a team record with 12 consecutive victories. Radke, who equaled the mark set by Scott Erickson in 1991, accomplished the feat in 12 consecutive starts. Radke became just the third pitcher in 50 years to win 12 consecutive starts—joining Pat Dobson (1971) and Bob Gibson (1968).

In July 2004 Radke, Johan Santana and Kyle Lohse pitched consecutive shutouts. Radke started the streak with a 9–0 victory over Kansas City on July 6. The next night, Santana beat the Royals, 4–0. Lohse followed with a 12–0 victory over the Royals to run the Twins' consecutive shutout innings streak to a

team record 27 innings. On July 9, the Twins got five more shutout innings—
to stretch the streak to 32 innings—in an eventual 7–1 victory over Detroit.

On July 19, 2004, Twins pitcher Terry Mulholland defeated the Detroit
Tigers, 3–1, for his second victory of the season. The victory meant that
Mulholland has defeated all 30 major league teams in an 18-year major
league career. Mulholland, a 41-year-old left-hander, became just the third
pitcher in major league history to achieve the feat, joining Kevin Brown and
Al Leiter. The Twins were Mulholland's 10th major league team.

In his first five major league seasons, Twins' third baseman Corey Koskie
was hit by pitch, 37 times. On July 27, 2004, Koskie tied a major league record
when he was hit three times during the Twins' 7–3 victory over the Chicago White Sox. Koskie equaled the mark held by 20 others. For the season,
Koskie was hit 12 times.

DID YOU KNOW ?

Eight native Minnesotans have won at least 100 games in major league
baseball:

Jack Morris (254), Jerry Koosman (222), Chief Bender (212), Joe Bush
(195), Bill Gullickson (162), Rube Walberg (155), Aaron Sele (131), and
Dave Goltz (113).

3,000 Hits

St. Paul natives Dave Winfield and Paul Molitor each played baseball for the
University of Minnesota before embarking on long major league baseball
careers, which included brief stops with the Minnesota Twins. Each has been
elected to the Baseball Hall of Fame.

They have another thing in common—3,000 hits. Both reached the milestone while playing for the Twins, and they both recorded the milestone on
the same date. Winfield got his 3,000th hit off Oakland's Dennis Eckersley at
the Metrodome on September 16, 1993. Three years later, to the day, Paul
Molitor got his 3,000th hit against the Royals in Kansas City. Molitor hit a
triple off the Royals' Jose Rosado.

Coincidentally, the Metrodome was also the site when Eddie Murray (on
June 30, 1995, while playing for Cleveland) and Cal Ripken (on April 15, 2000,
while playing for Balitmore) reached 3,000 hits.

Ground-Rule Double

The old adage that what goes up must come down is usually true. Probably the strangest moment in Metrodome history occurred on May 4, 1984, when Dave Kingman of Oakland lifted a pop-up that disappeared. The ball apparently went into a hole in the lining at roof level (195 feet above the playing surface) and never came down. Kingman was awarded a ground-rule double. Kingman was the only batter ever to hit a ball that stayed in the Metrodome roof.

Triple Plays

The Twins, who have recorded 10 triple plays in their history, are the only major league team to record two in the same game. Against the Red Sox in Boston on July 17, 1990, the Twins' Gary Gaetti, Al Newman and Kent Hrbek combined to complete triple plays in the fourth and eighth innings. The Red Sox won the game, 1–0.

The next night, the Twins set a team record—tying an American League record—by turning six double plays in a 5–4 loss to the Red Sox.

Long Home Runs

Metropolitan Stadium

The longest home run in Twins' history was a 520-foot home run by Harmon Killebrew. On June 3, 1967, Killebrew slugged the home run—the first to reach Metropolitan Stadium's second deck in left. On May 26, 1974, Bobby Darwin became the second player to reach the second deck when he slugged a 515-foot home run off Ferguson Jenkins in the Twins' 6–1 victory over Texas.

Metrodome

The longest home run in Metrodome history was a 481-foot shot to right field by Milwaukee's Ben Oglivie on June 27, 1983, off the Twins' Brad Haven. The longest home run by a Twin in the Metrodome was a 480-foot blast to right by Kent Hrbek on September 9, 1984.

The longest home run to center field was a 473-footer by the Twins' Pedro Munoz on April 5, 1994; the longest to left field was a 475-foot home run by Oakland's Mark McGwire on June 1, 1996.

Twins and Outdoor Baseball

Even after he agreed to move his Twins team to the Metrodome, owner Calvin Griffith said, "I don't think you'll find anybody around here who will argue with you baseball wasn't meant to be played outdoors in the sunshine." He told the *Minnesota Daily*, "I still believe that. But with the economics of the game of baseball today [1981], I think the majority of owners would prefer to have a stadium that would guarantee that they can get their 80 games in each year. Now we can stop worrying about the weather because when there is a game scheduled, we know we'll get it in."

In the 1,671 games played over 21 seasons (1961–81) at Metropolitan Stadium, 82 were rainouts, an average of four per year. Griffith told the *Minnesota Daily* that this figure was misleading. "In Minnesota, we play so many games, especially in April, May and September, that we shouldn't play, but we do because we have to get them in," said Griffith. "I don't like seeing fans at a game freezing and wet."

Met Stadium Weather for Twins Games

First home game	63° on Apr. 21, 1961
Average date for home opener	Apr. 15
Earliest date for home opener	Apr. 6
Latest date for home opener	Apr. 23
Average temp. for home opener	56.4°
Warmest temp. for home opener	89° on Apr. 10, 1980
Coldest temp. for home opener	33° on Apr. 14, 1962. (On Apr. 12, the game was snowed out by 6 inches of snow, and on Apr. 13 it was -2°.)
Average attendance for opener	20,803
Latest date of a snowed-out game	May 2, 1976. (Snow forced postponement of game against the Milwaukee Brewers; at 1:15 P.M. game time, it was 43°.)

Weather and the Metrodome

November 19, 1981 Less than two months after the Metrodome roof was first inflated, a major storm dumped 10 inches of heavy, wet snow on Minneapolis. The weight caused the roof to partially deflate. A tear in the roof was fixed within four days.

April 6, 1982 It was 28° outside as the Minnesota Twins played their first regular-season game in the Metrodome.

April 14, 1983 A snowstorm caused the Twins' game against the California Angels to be postponed. It is the only postponement in Metrodome history.

Homer Hanky

Terrie Blair, a promotions manager for the *Minneapolis Star Tribune*, invented the Homer Hanky in 1987. The hanky, manufactured in China, sold for $1 and immediately became a sought-after piece of sports memorabilia. During the American League playoffs, the Homer Hanky was so popular that the *Star Tribune* sold out its initial supply of 430,000 and had to order another 600,000. That year the Twins won the American League West title, earning their first postseason berth since 1970.

Since 1987, the Homer Hankies have returned each time the Twins reached the playoffs—1991, 2002, 2003 and 2004.

Spring Training

The Minnesota Twins have had just two spring training homes. From 1961 to 1990, the Twins trained in Orlando, Florida, and played their home exhibition games at Tinker Field.

Since 1991, the Twins have trained in Fort Myers, Florida, and played their home exhibition games at the Lee County Sports Complex.

All-Star Game

The Twins have played host to major league baseball's All-Star game twice—in 1965 and 1985. On July 13, 1965, the National League All-Stars defeated the American League All-Stars, 6–5, before 46,706 at Metropolitan Stadium. On July 16, 1985, the National League defeated the American League, 6–1, before 54,960 at the Metrodome.

Other Professional Players

Moonlight Graham's Field of Dreams

About 14,000 players have appeared in a major league baseball game. Archibald "Moonlight" Graham's brief stint with the New York Giants might be one of the shortest.

On June 29, 1905, Graham made his major league debut by playing the final

1½ innings of the Giants' 11–1 victory over the Brooklyn Dodgers. Graham, who was 28, played in right field and had no chances and did not bat. It was his only major league appearance.

The next day he was sent back to the minor leagues. He soon decided to pursue a medical career, and after receiving his medical degree, the North Carolina native began practice in the northern Minnesota town of Chisholm in 1909. For the next 50 years, Graham practiced medicine in Chisholm. He gained national recognition for an extensive study of children's blood pressure. Graham died on October 25, 1965, three months shy of his 89th birthday.

A quarter-century after his death, Graham again received national attention. In 1989 Graham's brief major league career and medical career were highlighted in a movie called *Field of Dreams*. The movie, which starred Kevin Costner, was based on a novel titled *Shoeless Joe*, which was written by W. P. Kinsella.

Babe Ruth in Minneapolis

Baseball Hall of Famer Babe Ruth made two appearances in the Minneapolis. On October 14, 1924, Ruth, who had just completed his fifth season with the New York Yankees, and teammate Bob Meusel made an appearance in an exhibition game at Nicollet Park. Ruth played for the Odd Fellows, who were the Minneapolis amateur champions, while Meusel played for Al Dretchko's All-Stars. Ruth played first base and went 4-for-5 with two home runs and six RBIs in the Odd Fellows' 8–5 victory.

Ruth returned to Minneapolis eleven years later. On September 1, 1935, Ruth, who had been released earlier in the season by the Boston Braves, appeared at Nicollet Park. About 13,000 fans turned out to see Ruth play in the annual Minneapolis/St. Paul police benefit game. Ruth, who played half of the game for each team, went 1-for-3 with a double and two walks. Minneapolis pitcher Pete Guzy struck out 18 in the game.

On September 22, 1940, a headline in the *Minneapolis Star-Journal* read, "Ruth as St. Paul manager?" The newspaper reported, "Possibilities that Babe Ruth may become manager of the St. Paul (Saints) baseball club developed Saturday night. Lou McKenna, business manager, said he may contact Ruth, following the receipt of a letter from Ray Doan, close friend of Babe, in which Ray said that he thinks the great home run hitter of another day is in a receptive mood. Once Babe refused to consider minor league jobs, but inactivity of recent years has prompted him to change his mind. Babe Ganzel recently resigned as the St. Paul manager."

Babe Ruth playing an exhibition game at Nicollet Park, 1924

Ruth, who had retired from major league baseball in 1935, did not become the manager of the Saints. Ralph Kress managed the Saints in 1941. Ruth, who died in 1948 at age 53, never became a manager.

DID YOU KNOW ?

In 1933 Joe Hauser, who played for the Millers (1932–36), hit 69 home runs, becoming the first player to hit at least 60 home runs twice. Hauser hit 202 home runs in his five seasons with the Millers.

Minor League Baseball

Semi-professional baseball came to the Twin Cities as early as 1877, when Minneapolis and St. Paul fielded teams in the League Alliance. Not until 1884 did professional baseball "officially" arrive in Minnesota. That year, Minneapolis, St. Paul, Stillwater, and Winona fielded teams in the Northwestern League. After the league disbanded on September 3, St. Paul also played in the Union Association. St. Paul played nine games in the league after replacing Wilmington, which had disbanded.

There was no professional baseball in the Twin Cities in 1885, but Minneapolis and St. Paul returned to the Northwestern League in 1886 and 1887. In 1888, both Minneapolis and St. Paul joined the Western Association. They would remain in the league until 1899 (except for two interruptions—neither team competed in 1893, and St. Paul also missed 1894).

Following the 1899 season, two big changes occurred—the Western League was renamed the American League and St. Paul owner Charles Comiskey moved his team to Chicago where they became the White Sox. In 1900 Minneapolis fielded a team in the American League, and in 1901 both Minneapolis and St. Paul fielded teams in the Western League.

American Association

In 1901 Thomas J. Hickey wrote to postmasters in eight cities requesting their opinion on the prospects of organizing a new professional baseball league incorporating their cities.

Hickey received favorable responses from all eight postmasters—Columbus, Indianapolis, Kansas City, Louisville, Milwaukee, Minneapolis, St. Paul and Toledo. How well Hickey chose cities for the circuit is shown by the fact that the league's original lineup remained constant for the next 50 years.

From the league's first season in 1902 until 1952, the league's membership was unchanged (except for two years, 1914 and 1915, when the Toledo club operated in Cleveland).

The Minneapolis Millers and St. Paul Saints remained in the league until 1960.

Millers vs. Saints Rivalry

Professional baseball teams from Minneapolis and St. Paul have been natural rivals since the late 1800s when the teams played in the Northwestern League and the Western League, but the rivalry really took off in 1902 when both cities joined the eight-team American Association.

From the very start, the rivalry was strong. The teams were scheduled to meet as members of the American Association for the first time on May 26, 1902, but the game was called off by the St. Paul team because of wet grounds.

Fans at Nicollet Park clamor for a Miller hit, 1904

St. Paul Saints team, 1911

According to the *Minneapolis Tribune,* the "afternoon cleared up so a game could have been played without submitting the players to too much discomfort." The headline above the story said, "Saints wanted to take a rest."

The *Tribune* went on to report that several members of the St. Paul team "were not in the best of shape" and the team was "leery" of facing the Millers. Going into the game the Millers had an 8–18 record while the Saints were 15–11. The teams finally played the next day, and the Millers won 8–4 at Lexington Park. The Saints went on to win the season series, 12–8.

For the next 59 seasons, the two teams were the cornerstones of the league. The Millers and the Saints were the two winningest teams in the league from 1902 and 1960. Each team won nine regular-season titles, and each team had seven second-place finishes.

The rivalry featured as many as 24 games per season—highlighted by doubleheaders on Memorial Day, the Fourth of July and Labor Day where one game was played at each team's park (Nicollet Park in Minneapolis and Lexington Park in St. Paul). (One memorable holiday doubleheader occurred on July 4, 1929, when a bench-clearing brawl erupted between the two teams at Nicollet Park during the morning game. It took 12 police officers to restore order on the field.)

In all, the teams met more than 1,300 times as members of the American Association. The Saints claimed bragging rights by winning the overall series 680–623. Ten games were played to a tie. The Saints also won the season series 32 times. The Millers won the series 20 times. In seven years, the series ended in a tie. The Millers won the season series eight times in the first 13 seasons. After that the Saints dominated the series in two long stretches. Between 1915 and 1932, the Saints won the series 16 times—including 12 consecutive years—with one tie. The team dominated the final 18 seasons of the rivalry. From 1943 to 1960, the Millers won the season series just three times (1950, 1950 and 1957). In 1960, the Saints won the final season series, 13–9.

The Minneapolis–St. Paul rivalry came to end when Calvin Griffith announced in October 1960 that he was moving his Washington Senators franchise to the Twin Cities. In January 1961, Griffith paid the American Association a reported $550,000 for moving into the American Association's "territory." Bill O'Neal, a minor league baseball historian and author, wrote in his history of the American Association, "No sports rivalry was more bitterly contested over a longer period than the baseball competition between Minneapolis and St. Paul."

Affiliations

The first year that the Minneapolis Millers and St. Paul Saints were affiliated with a major league team was in 1936. The Saints spent seven seasons as a farm team of the Chicago White Sox and 17 seasons as an affiliate of the Brooklyn/Los Angeles Dodgers. The Millers spent six seasons as a farm team of the Boston Red Sox and 12 seasons as a farm team of the New York Giants.

St. Paul Saints—Chicago White Sox (1936–42); (1943: none); Brooklyn/Los Angeles Dodgers (1944–60).

Minneapolis Millers—Boston Red Sox (1936–38, 1958–60), New York Giants (1946–57).

Millers and the Weather

On May 1, 1908, the Minneapolis Millers' home opener (against Indianapolis) was postponed because of snow and cold. At mid-day there were snow showers in Minneapolis.

The Millers' 1947 season got off to a slow start when six of the first seven games were postponed because of weather. The Millers were scheduled to open the season on April 16 in Milwaukee, but the game was called because of snow. The teams managed to play on April 17, but the April 18 game was postponed because of cold. The Millers were rained out in Kansas City on April 19 and 20 before an off day on April 21. The Millers' home opener was scheduled for April 22, but that game and the April 23 game were postponed because of rain. The Millers finally played their home opener on April 24—beating Milwaukee, 4–0.

On May 1, 1951, future Hall of Famer Willie Mays went 3-for-5 in the Minneapolis Millers' 11–0 victory in their home opener before 6,477 at Nicollet Park. It was a rainy, windy day, and later that afternoon, 75 mph winds hit the Twin Cities.

On September 29, 1959: Because of cold temperatures (50 degrees) and windy conditions in Bloomington, Game 3 of the Junior World Series between the Minneapolis Millers and Havana Sugar Kings was called off. The remainder of the series was moved to Havana, Cuba.

DID YOU KNOW ?

On May 22, 1948, Roy Campanella became the first African American to play in the American Association when he made his debut with the St. Paul Saints. Campanella batted .325 in 35 games with the Saints before being recalled by the Brooklyn Dodgers on June 30.

American Association Pennants Won by the Millers and Saints

Millers 9—1910, 1911, 1912, 1915, 1932, 1934, 1935, 1950, 1955. Also won playoff titles in 1955, 1958, and 1959.

Saints 9—1903, 1904, 1919, 1920, 1922, 1924, 1931, 1938, and 1949. Also won a playoff title in 1948.

Hall of Fame members

Millers 16—Roger Bresnahan (1898–99), Jimmy Collins (player/manager 1909), Rube Waddell (1911–13), Urban Faber (1911), Bill McKechnie (1921), Zack Wheat (1921), George Kelly (1930–31), Ted Williams (1938), Billy Herman (player/manager 1948), Ray Dandridge (1949–52), Hoyt Wilhelm (1950–51), Willie Mays (1951), Monte Irvin (1955), Orlando Cepeda (1957), Carl Yastrzemski (1959–60), and Dave Bancroft (manager, 1933).

Roy Campanella of the St. Paul Saints hits a home run at Nicollet Park, 1948

Saints 6—Miller Huggins (1901–03), Bill McKechnie (1913), Lefty Gomez (1930), Duke Snider (1947), Roy Campanella (1948), and Walter Alston (manager, 1948–49)

Millers or Saints in the Junior/Little World Series

1904 Buffalo (Eastern) defeat Saints, 2–1

1920 Baltimore (IL) defeat Saints, 5–1

1922 Baltimore (IL) defeat Saints, 5–2

1924 Saints defeat Baltimore (IL), 5–4 (with one tie game)

1931 Rochester (IL) defeat Saints, 5–3

1932 Newark (IL) defeat Millers, 4–2

1948 Montreal (IL) defeat Saints, 4–1

1955 Millers defeat Rochester (IL), 4–3

1958 Millers defeat Montreal (IL), 4–0

1959 Havana (IL) defeat Millers, 4–3

Saints in the Big Leagues

Since 1993, the St. Paul Saints of the independent Northern League have sold the contracts of 78 players to major league organizations, and 14 have gone on to play in the major leagues. Former Saint Kevin Millar played for the 2004 World Series champion Boston Red Sox.

Name	(Years with Saints)
Frank Charles	1993
Doug Dascenzo	1995
J.D. Drew	1997–98
Matt Duff	2001
Luis Lopez	1995
Julio Manon	1999
Kevin Millar	1993
Mike Mimbs	1993
Rey Ordonez	1993
Eddie Oropesa	1993
Dan Peltier	1995
Roy Smith	1997–98, 2004
Scott Stewart	1996
Darryl Strawberry	1996

NOTE: In addition, former major leaguers J.T. Bruett, Jim Eppard, Jack Morris, and Matt Nokes have played for the Saints. Saints manager George Tsamis pitched in 41 games with the Minnesota Twins in 1993.

Ila Borders

In 1997 Borders, the first woman to receive a college baseball scholarship (at Southern California College), was invited to try out for the Saints. The Saints signed her to a contract, and on May 31, 1997, the 5-foot-10 left hander became the first woman to appear in a regular-season minor league game in the 20th century. She pitched for the Saints against the Sioux Falls Canaries in Sioux Falls, South Dakota.

After just six innings with the Saints, she was traded to Duluth-Superior in June 1997. On July 9, 1998, she became the first woman to start a men's professional baseball game. Two weeks later, she became the first woman to win a game.

In 1999 Borders was waived by Duluth-Superior and signed with Madison of the

Ila Borders, one of the first women to pitch for a pro baseball team, started with the St. Paul Saints in 1987.

Northern League. In 2000 Borders signed with the Zion (Utah) Pioneerzz of the Western Baseball League and was guaranteed a spot on the roster for the rest of the season, regardless of her record. But on June 30, one day after allowing three runs, she retired at the age of 26.

"I'll look back and say I did something nobody ever did," Borders told the *Salt Lake Tribune*. "I'm proud of that. I wasn't out to prove women's rights—or anything. I love baseball. Ask a guy if he's doing it to prove men's rights. He'll say he's doing because he loves the game."

DID YOU KNOW ❓

In 1951 Willie Mays batted .477 in 35 games with the Millers before being recalled by the New York Giants. The 1951 Millers' roster had three future Hall of Famers—Mays, Ray Dandridge, and Hoyt Wilhelm.

Ray Dandridge and Dave Barnhill

In June 1949, Ray Dandridge became the first African American to play for the Minneapolis Millers. Dandridge and Dave Barnhill were purchased from the New York Cubans by the New York Giants of the National League and assigned to the Millers.

Dandridge, age 36, batted .362 for the Millers that season. In 1950 he batted .311 and was named the American Association's MVP. In 1951 he batted .324 for the Millers, and he batted .291 in 1952.

Dandridge never made it to the major leagues. He played for nine teams in a 20-year professional career. He was elected to the National Baseball Hall of Fame in 1987.

Barnhill spent three seasons with the Millers, going 7–10 in 1949, 11–3 in 1950 and 7–2 in 1951.

Hits Leader Spence Harris

The all-time leading hits leader in the minor leagues is Duluth native Anthony "Spence" Harris. Harris, who spent parts of four seasons in the major leagues, played professional baseball for 28 seasons (1921–48). In 1948, at the age of 48, he appeared in 45 games in the minor leagues. He spent 10 seasons

Minneapolis Millers celebrating victory in the Little World Series, 1955

(1928–37) with the Minneapolis Millers. In 3,258 career minor league games, he had 3,617 hits and a career batting average of .318.

Monte Irvin

Future Hall of Famer Monte Irvin spent part of the 1955 season with the Minneapolis Millers. He batted .352 in 75 games. Irvin was elected to the National Baseball Hall of Fame in 1973.

Mike Kelley

Mike Kelley is synonymous with professional baseball in the Twin Cities for the first 50 years of the 20th century. Except for a little over two years, Kelley was associated with either the St. Paul Saints or the Minneapolis Millers from 1902 to 1946.

Kelley, who played in the National League in 1899, joined the Saints in 1902. He managed the Saints from 1902 to 1905 and then joined the Millers in 1906. In 1908 he rejoined the Saints and managed them from 1908 to 1912 and 1915 to 1923. In late 1923, he purchased the Minneapolis Millers and was with them until he sold the team to the New York Giants in 1946. He managed the Millers from 1924 to 1931 before concentrating on his duties as president and owner of the team.

Kelley, who also managed parts of four other seasons in the minor leagues, is the third-winningest manager in minor league baseball history. In 30 seasons, his teams compiled a 2,390–2,102 record. In 17+ seasons with the Saints, his teams compiled a 1,480–1,161 record. In nine seasons with the Millers, his teams were 745–722. (The winningest manager in minor league history is Stan Wasiak, whose teams won 2,530 games.)

In 2001 a Web site named the top 100 minor league baseball teams of the previous 100 years. Two of the St. Paul Saints teams managed by Kelley made the list. The Saints' 1920 team, which won an American Association–record 115 games, was named the No. 6 team of the top 100. The Saints' 1922 team, which won 107 games, was named No. 88.

Minnie Minoso

Minnie Minoso is the only player to appear in a professional baseball game in seven different decades. After playing in the Negro League in the 1940s, Minoso made his major league debut with the Cleveland Indians in 1949. His last full major league season was 1964. Minoso became a five-decade man when he made two pinch-hitting appearances for the Chicago White Sox in 1976 and 1980.

In 1993 Minoso became a six-decade man when he had one at-bat with the St. Paul Saints. The Saints are co-owned by Mike Veeck, who is the son of Bill Veeck, who owned the Cleveland Indians when Minoso made his major league debut.

On July 16, 2003, at age 77, Minoso made another cameo appearance for the Saints to qualify as a seven-decade man. Minoso drew a first-inning walk against the Gary Railcats at Midway Stadium. To make the at-bat official, Minoso signed a standard Northern League player contract (for $1,000 per month). For his one game, Minoso was paid a pro-rated $32.26.

Bill Sharman

Bill Sharman was one of only three sportsmen (along with John Wooden and Lenny Wilkens) to be elected to the Naismith Memorial Basketball Hall of Fame as both a player and a coach. He also played minor league baseball from 1950 to 1955. In 1952 Sharman batted .294 with 16 home runs and 77 RBIs for the St. Paul Saints. In 1955 with the Saints, he batted .292 with 11 home runs and 58 RBIs.

Sharman, who played for the Boston Celtics from 1951 to 1961, went on to a successful career as a coach. He coached the Los Angeles Lakers to an NBA record 33 consecutive victories during the 1971–72 season. Sharman was elected to the Hall of Fame as a player in 1976 and as a coach in 2004.

Monty Stratton

In 1935 Monty Stratton went 17–9 for the St. Paul Saints and appeared headed to a successful major league career. In 1937 and 1938 with the Chicago White Sox, Stratton went 30–14. Following the 1938 season, he suffered a leg injury in a hunting accident, and the leg was amputated.

For the next three seasons, he served as a coach with the White Sox, but he decided to return to pitching, winning 18 games with Sherman in the East Texas League in 1946. In 1949 Stratton's life was the subject of a movie. *The Stratton Story* starred James Stewart as Stratton.

Home Run King

Before Babe Ruth hit a professional-baseball record 54 home runs for the New York Yankees in 1920, the record-holder resided in Minneapolis.

In 1894, Perry Werden hit a record 43 home runs (in just 114 games) for the Minneapolis Millers. The next season, he hit 45 home runs (in 123 games) for the Millers. In 1896, he hit 18 home runs for a three-season total of 104.

In a professional career, which lasted from 1884 to 1908, those were the only times he hit more than 10 home runs in a season. The 6-foot-2, 220-pound first baseman, known as "Moose," benefited from the Millers playing their home games in tiny Athletic Park (located in downtown Minneapolis where the Butler Square building is today). Werden, who spent parts of six seasons in the major leagues, hit 195 home runs in his 25-season career.

After retiring, he umpired in the American Association and Northern League and coached the Gophers baseball team briefly. He died on January 9, 1934.

Northern League

The Northern League began in 1902 as a six-team league, with Crookston being the only Minnesota team. In 1906 the league combined with the Copper Country–Soo League to form the Northern–Copper Country League.

The league folded in August 1908, reformed itself in 1913, and disbanded on July 4, 1917. It then reformed as a seven-team league in 1933 and remained in existence until 1971. (It did not operate from 1943 to 1945 because of World War II.) In 1993 the league reappeared as a six-team independent league.

The Northern League has sent at least 335 players to the major leagues, including Hall of Famers Hank Aaron (Eau Claire, 1952), Lou Brock (St. Cloud, 1961), Steve Carlton (Winnipeg, 1964), Orlando Cepeda (St. Cloud, 1956), Jim Palmer (Aberdeen, 1964), Gaylord Perry (St. Cloud, 1958), and Willie Stargell (Grand Forks, 1960). Another member of the Hall of Fame—Earl Weaver—managed Aberdeen in 1959.

Aaron won the Northern League batting title in 1952, hitting .336 with nine home runs in 87 games as an 18-year-old shortstop. Two years later, Aaron was playing in the major leagues with the Milwaukee Braves.

Cepeda won the Northern League triple crown in 1956, leading the league in batting average (.355), home runs (26) and RBIs (112). In 1961 Brock batted .361 to win the league batting title.

Other future major leaguers to play in the Northern League include Matty Alou (St. Cloud, 1958), Bo Belinsky (Aberdeen, 1958), Willie Horton (Duluth-Superior, 1962), Denny McLain (Duluth-Superior, 1963), Don Mincher (Duluth-Superior, 1956), Vada Pinson (Wausau, 1956) and Joe Torre (Eau Claire, 1960).

DID YOU KNOW ?

On July 24, 1948, five members of the Duluth Northern League baseball team riding the team's bus to a game in St. Cloud died in a head-on collision near St. Paul. Killed were manager George Treadwell and players Steve Lazar, Gerald Peterson, Gilbert Trible and Donald Schuchman, along with the driver of the other vehicle. Thirteen others were injured.

Northern League Champions

1902 Winnipeg; **1903** Winnipeg; **1904** Duluth; **1905** Duluth; **1906** Calumet; **1907** Winnipeg; **1908** Brandon; **1913** Winona; **1914** Duluth; **1915** Fargo-Moorhead; **1916** Winnipeg; **1917** Fargo-Moorhead; **1933** Winnipeg, Superior; **1934** Fargo-Moorhead; **1935** Winnipeg; **1936** Jamestown, Eau Claire; **1937** Duluth; **1938** Superior, Duluth; **1939** Winnipeg; **1940** Grand Forks; **1941** Wausau, Eau Claire; **1942** Eau Claire, Winnipeg; **1946** St. Cloud; **1947**

Aberdeen, Sioux Falls; **1948** Grand Forks; **1949** Eau Claire, Aberdeen; **1950** St. Cloud, Sioux Falls; **1951** Eau Claire, Grand Forks; **1952** Superior; **1953** Fargo-Moorhead; **1954** Fargo-Moorhead; **1955** Eau Claire, St. Cloud; **1956** Eau Claire, Duluth-Superior; **1957** Duluth-Superior, Winnipeg; **1958** St. Cloud, Fargo-Moorhead; **1959** Winnipeg; **1960** Winnipeg; **1961** Duluth-Superior, Aberdeen; **1962** Grand Forks, Eau Claire; **1963** Duluth-Superior, Grand Forks; **1964** Aberdeen; **1965** St. Cloud; **1966** St. Cloud; **1967** St. Cloud; **1968** St. Cloud; **1969** Duluth-Superior; **1970** Duluth-Superior; **1971** St. Cloud

NOTE: From 1933 to 1964, the league had regular-season and playoff champions. When two teams are listed for the same year, the first one is the regular-season champion, while the second is the playoff champion.

Independent Northern League Playoff Champions

1993 St. Paul; **1994** Winnipeg; **1995** St. Paul; **1996** St. Paul; **1997** Duluth-Superior; **1998** Fargo-Moorhead; **1999** Winnipeg; **2000** Duluth-Superior; **2001** Winnipeg; **2002** Winnipeg; **2003** Fargo-Moorhead; **2004** St. Paul; **2005** Gary

NOTE: From 1999 to 2002, the league merged with the Northeast League to form a 16-team league. The playoffs winner listed above (the Central Division winner) played the Eastern Division champion for the league title. In 1999 Winnipeg lost to Albany-Colonie; in 2000 Duluth-Superior lost to Adirondack; in 2001 and 2002 Winnipeg lost to New Jersey. In September 2005, the St. Paul Saints announced that it and two other Northern League teams (the Sioux Falls Canaries and Lincoln Saltdogs) were leaving the 12-team Northern League to form a new league—the American Association—in 2006.

Other Professional Leagues

Several other professional leagues have fielded Minnesota teams. The Minnesota-Wisconsin League operated from 1909 to 1912. Duluth, Red Wing, Rochester, and Winona fielded teams in this league.

In 1912 Duluth fielded a team in the Central International League.

In 1943 the four-team Twin Ports League (the only professional league to be classified Class E), operated in Duluth and Superior before disbanding on July 13.

In 1958 Rochester and Winona fielded teams in the Three-I league, while Worthington had a team in the Class D Western League in 1939 and 1940.

In 1993 the Northern League returned after a 22-year absence as an independent league (no affiliation with organized baseball). While the league has flourished, several other start-up independent leagues appeared briefly on the scene.

St. Paul's Uptown Sanitary Shop baseball team, 1930s

In 1994 the Great Central and North Central Leagues started up. Minneapolis had a team in the four-team Great Central League, which lasted just one season. The six-team North Central League had three Minnesota teams—Brainerd, Marshall and Minneapolis). In 1995 the North Central League started its second season, but it disbanded in mid-July.

In 1995 the eight-team Prairie League started with one Minnesota team—the Minneapolis Loons, managed by former major leaguer Greg Olson. The Loons relocated to Austin in 1996, but the team and Brainerd were unable to complete the league's second season. The league disbanded after the season.

Segregated Baseball

A handful of African Americans played professional baseball in the late 19th century, including Bud Fowler with Stillwater of the Northwestern League in 1884. By 1898, however, "organized" baseball had become segregated. For the next 50 years, African Americans were kept out of organized baseball.

In the early 20th century, African Americans formed independent teams that barnstormed. Eventually, a Chicago businessman named Rube Foster formed the Negro National League, which had eight teams primarily in the Midwest. Baseball historian Stew Thornley writes that the Negro National League never included a team from Minnesota, but several independent teams rose to prominence in the first 20 years of the 20th century.

Bud Fowler

Fowler was one of the first African Americans to play professional baseball. Fowler's professional career began with Lynn (Massachusetts) Live Oaks of the International Association (the first minor league) in 1878. In 1884, Fowler was signed by Stillwater of the Northwestern League. Minneapolis and St. Paul also fielded teams in the eight-team league. The Stillwater team lost its first 16 games before Foster pitched complete-game victories on May 26, 28, 29 and 31. On June 15, he pitched another victory, but the team folded in August. The team had compiled a 21–46 record.

Fowler went on to play for 10 teams in four professional leagues. In 1895, he helped form a touring team called the Page Fence Giants.

Bobby Marshall

Bobby Marshall graduated from Minneapolis Central High School and lettered in three sports—football, baseball and track—at the University of Minnesota.

After earning a law degree from the University of Minnesota, he coached football at Minneapolis Central and at Parker College (in Winnebago, Minnesota), but his coaching career was brief. In 1908 Marshall began playing for the Minneapolis Keystones. The next season, he joined the Twin Cities Gophers. He also played for the Chicago Leland Giants and the Chicago Giants. In 1911 Marshall formed the St. Paul Gophers, a team that lasted just one season. In 1912 he played for a team called the Minneapolis Hennepins.

Marshall also played semi-professional and professional football. From 1910 to 1917, he played for the semi-pro Minneapolis Marines. In the early 1920s, he returned to the Marines, who were by then a member of the American Professional Football Association (eventually the National Football League). In 1925 he played for the Duluth Kelleys of the NFL.

Marshall continued to play semi-professional baseball until he was in his early 50s. He died in 1958 at age 78 and was elected posthumously to the National Football Foundation Hall of Fame in 1971.

Satchel Paige

For much of his time with the Kansas City Monarchs, Hilton Smith was a teammate of the legendary Satchel Paige. During the 1930s Paige played on teams that barnstormed the United States, and he made several appearances in Minnesota. Paige made his major league debut in 1948 at age 42 and was elected to the National Baseball Hall of Fame in 1971.

Hilton Smith

In 1949 Hilton Smith spent the summer playing for the amateur Fulda (Minnesota) Giants. Smith, who was 42, had been recruited from the Kansas City Monarchs.

Smith was elected to the National Baseball Hall of Fame in 2001, the same year as former Twins Kirby Puckett and Dave Winfield. He died in 1983 at age 76.

DID YOU KNOW ?

University of Minnesota women's hockey player Krissy Wendell, a member of the U.S. women's Olympic team in 2002 and 2006, was the fifth girl to play in the Little League World Series. She played for Brooklyn Center in 1994.

All-American Girls Professional Baseball League

World War II had caused many minor league teams to disband because young men 18 years of age and older were being drafted into the armed services. By the fall of 1942, Philip Wrigley, the owner of the Chicago Cubs, was worried that attendance at baseball games would fall if franchises continued to lose quality players to the armed services. Wrigley asked Ken Sells, the general manager of the Chicago Cubs, to head a committee to come up with ideas to bolster attendance. The committee recommended the All-American Girls Professional Baseball League.

In 1943 the league fielded four teams—Racine (Wis.), Rockford (Ill.), Kenosha (Wis.) and South Bend (Ind.). The first season was a success as the Racine Belles won the inaugural championship.

For the 1944 season, the league decided to expand by two teams—adding franchises in Milwaukee and Minneapolis. The Minneapolis team, called the Millerettes, would play at Nicollet Park.

The Millerettes held their first training camp in Peru, Ill. Two women from the Twin Cities—Lorraine Borg and Peggy Torrison—survived the tryouts to make the team. On May 27, 1944, the Millerettes played their first game against the Rockford Peaches at Nicollet Park. The Peaches rallied for a 5–4 victory over the Millerettes, in front of a crowd of "several hundred" according to the *Minneapolis Tribune.*

The Millerettes compiled a 23–36 record in the first half of the season and attendance dropped off, so in late July it was decided the Millerettes would play the remainder of their games on the road. The Millerettes finished the season with a 45–72 record. After the season, the team was relocated to Fort Wayne, Ind.

The star of the Millerettes was Helen Callaghan, who batted .287. Callaghan would have a son, Casey Candaele, who would go on to play in the major leagues. Annabelle Lee, a pitcher for the Millerettes, was the aunt of the future major league pitcher Bill Lee. Jean Havlish, who would gain fame as a bowler, played for the Fort Wayne Daisies in the 1950s.

Toni Stone

Toni Stone lived in the Rondo neighborhood of St. Paul in the 1930s. During the 1950s, she became the first woman to play regularly for a men's professional team, handling second base for the Indianapolis Clowns of the Negro Leagues in 1953. She also played for the Kansas City Monarchs. She was inducted into the Women's Sports Hall of Fame and is honored in a display at the National Baseball Hall of Fame in Cooperstown.

College Baseball

Baseball was first played in Minnesota in 1857, the year before Minnesota achieved statehood. Nineteen years later, baseball became the first sport played at the University of Minnesota.

In May 1876 the university baseball team played an amateur team called the Crescents. According to the *Minneapolis Tribune,* the university team was "badly beaten" by the Crescents, and no team was fielded for the next six years. Baseball returned to the Minnesota campus in 1883 when the university won two of three games against Hamline and Carleton.

Since then, the university has fielded one of the most successful programs in college baseball history. In May 2000 the Gophers earned the 2,000th victory in program history. The Gophers have won three NCAA titles (1956, 1960 and 1964) and 20 Big Ten conference titles and have been to the NCAA playoffs 26 times since 1956.

In the first 50 years of the 20th century, the Gophers won just two conference titles. That drought changed with the arrival of Dick Siebert as coach in

Toni Stone, the first woman to play regularly for a men's professional baseball league, meets boxer Joe Louis.

1948. Siebert, who played college baseball at Concordia (St. Paul), spent 11 seasons in the major leagues before retiring following the 1945 season.

Siebert won his first conference title in 1956, his ninth season at the university. Between 1956 and 1977, the Gophers won 11 conference titles under Siebert. Siebert passed away in December 1978. Former Gopher and major leaguer George Thomas took over the program and coached the Gophers for three seasons.

In 1982 former Gophers student manager and graduate assistant John Anderson took over. At the time the 26-year-old was the youngest head coach in the history of the Big Ten Conference baseball history. The Gophers won the conference title in Anderson's first season.

In 1998 Anderson became one of the youngest coaches in college baseball history to reach 600 victories. In 2002 Anderson surpassed Siebert as the winningest coach in school history. He also became the winningest coach in Big Ten baseball history. Through the 2005 season, Anderson had an 871–544 record.

The 2005 season was the Gophers' 43rd consecutive winning season. The Gophers have had just one losing season since 1950.

Since former Gopher Ralph Capron played for the Pittsburgh Pirates in 1912, 27 former Gophers have gone on to play in the major leagues. Former Gophers Dave Winfield and Paul Molitor have been elected to the National Baseball Hall of Fame.

Retired Gophers Baseball Numbers

5	Herb Isakson
11	Paul Molitor
25	Dick Siebert
26	David Chelesnik
31	Dave Winfield
34	Paul Giel

DID YOU KNOW ?

The winningest coach in Minnesota college history is former Winona State baseball coach Gary Grob. Grob coached Winona from 1965 to 2000 and became just the sixth coach in NCAA Division II baseball history to reach 1,000 victories. Grob's record was 1,020–563–10.

Amateur Baseball

A year before Minnesota's statehood, citizens of the territory were already enjoying baseball. On August 15, 1857, the first known baseball game in state history was played in Nininger, a small (now vanished) community on the banks of the Mississippi River near Hastings.

Baseball quickly moved upstream to St. Paul, and following the Civil War, the number of teams in the state dramatically increased. Just 10 years after the game was introduced to the territory, the first state tournament was held. On September 24, 1867, the St. Paul North Stars won the tournament.

The sport continued to grow steadily. The first "official" state amateur tournament was held at Lexington Park in St. Paul in 1924, when the champions of eight leagues competed for the state title. Six years later, the tournament became a two-class tournament, and by 1940 there were 423 amateur teams in the state.

After World War II, many of the teams were no longer really "amateur," since they recruited and paid players. In 1948 a third class was added to the state tournament. Teams in this class were prohibited from paying players, and all the players on the team had to be local.

In the late 1940s and 1950s former professional players playing in state amateur leagues included Dick Siebert, Howie Schultz and Hy Vandenberg. At the midway point of the 20th century, there were 799 teams in the state. The 1950 state tournament, held in St. Cloud, drew a record 35,318. In the 1950s the number of teams began declining. In 2004 only 303 teams competed in three classes.

State Amateur Baseball Champions

2005 Wesley Homes (Class A), Mankato (Class B), Holdingford (Class C)
2004 Minnetonka (Class A), Jordan (Class B), Blue Earth (Class C)
2003 Minnetonka (A), Austin (B), Green Isle (C)
2002 St. Louis Park (A), Austin (B), Granite Falls (C)
2001 Minnetonka (A), Cold Spring (B), Watkins (C)
2000 Glynn Building (A), Cold Spring (B), Brainerd (C)
1999 Minnetonka (A), Dundas (B), Buckman (C)
1998 Minnetonka (A), Dundas (B), Glencoe (C)
1997 Minnetonka (A), Hamel (B), St. Michael (C)
1996 St. Paul Highland Park (A), Cold Spring (B), Plato (C)
1995 St. Paul Rosetown (A), Miesville (B), Sauk Rapids (C)
1994 Minneapolis Angels (A), Jordan (B), Belle Plaine (C)
1993 St. Paul Highland Park (A), Red Wing (B), Granite Falls (C)
1992 Minneapolis Angels (A), Miesville (B), Sartell (C)
1991 Minneapolis Angels (A), Rochester (B), Regal (C)
1990 St. Paul Conquest Rooster (A), Red Wing (B), Bovey (C)
1989 Columbia Heights (A), Miesville (B), Morris (C)
1988 Minneapolis J. Botten (A), Dundas (B), Delano (C)
1987 Bloomington (A), Hamel (B), Chaska (C)

1986 Columbia Heights (A), Cold Spring (B)
1985 Minneapolis Halek's (A), Arlington (B)
1984 St. Paul Frontier Bar (A), Arlington (B)
1983 St. Paul Steichens (A), St. Cloud (B)
1982 Brooklyn Center (A), Dundas (B)
1981 Winona (A), Cold Spring (B)
1980 Richfield (A), New Ulm (B)
1979 West St. Paul (A), Arlington (B)
1978 Columbia Heights (A), Miesville (B)
1977 Minneapolis Mr. Roberts (A), Bemidji (B)
1976 Prior Lake (B)
1975 Prior Lake (B)
1974 Red Wing (B)
1973 Cold Spring (B)
1972 Columbia Heights (B)
1971 Chaska (B)
1970 Columbia Heights (A), Deer Creek (B)
1969 St. Paul Sport Spec. (A), Arlington (B)
1968 Columbia Heights (A), Dassel-Cokato (B)
1967 Columbia Heights (A), Arlington (B)
1966 Winona (A), Perham (B)
1965 Bloomington (A), St. Bonifacius (B)
1964 St. Paul Como Red (A), St. Bonifacius (B)
1963 Minneapolis A&B Sports (A), Braham (B)
1962 St. Paul Ganzers (A), Little Falls (B)
1961 Minneapolis T.C. Federal (A), St. Bonifacius (B)
1960 Bloomington (A), Pipestone (B)
1959 Fairmont (A), Shakopee (B)
1958 Austin (A), Pipestone (B)
1957 Waseca (A), Braham (B)
1956 Minneapolis Teamsters (A), Bemidji (B)
1955 St. Peter (A), Cold Spring (B)
1954 Benson (A), Milroy (B)
1953 Austin (AA), Delavan (A), Rollingstone (B)
1952 Willmar (AA), Cannon Falls (A), Soderville (B)
1951 Litchfield (AA), Watertown (A), Soderville (B)
1950 Fergus Falls (AA), Le Center (A), Lester Prairie (B)
1949 Austin (AA), Excelsior (A), Little Falls (B)
1948 Albert Lea (AA), Winsted (A)
1947 Albert Lea (AA), Chaska (A)

1946 Albert Lea (AA), Springfield (A)
1945 Albert Lea (AA), Excelsior (A)
1944 Albert Lea (AA), Springfield (A)
1943 Minneapolis Mitby Sathers (AA), New Ulm (A)
1942 Austin (AA), Fairfax (A)
1941 Owatonna (AA), New Ulm (A)
1940 Albert Lea (AA), Shakopee (A)
1939 St. Paul T. H. Shoe (AA), Maple Lake (A)
1938 St. Paul N. St. Env. (AA), Owatonna (A)
1937 Minneapolis Heinies (AA), Austin (A)
1936 St. Paul Comm. Row (AA), Windom (A)
1935 St. Paul J.J. Kohn (AA), Red Wing (A)
1934 Minneapolis Jerseys (AA), Willmar (A)
1933 St. Paul E.M.B.A. (AA), St. Peter (A), Harmony (B)
1932 St. Paul Milk Drivers (A), Chaska (B), Brooten (C)
1931 St. Paul Bohn Ref. (A), Maple Lake (B), Madelia (C)
1930 Fairmont (A), South St. Paul (B)
1929 Albert Lea
1928 Mankato
1927 Mora
1926 St. Paul Armour's
1925 White Bear Lake
1924 St. Paul Armour's

Amateur Baseball Hall of Fame

Since the Minnesota Amateur Baseball Hall of Fame was founded in 1963 in St. Cloud, 230 men have been inducted (about four to six each year):

A George Alshire, Waite Park; Clarence Anderson, Brandon; Eldred Anderson, Hutchinson; H. F. Anderson, Lafayette; Vernie Anderson, Sebeka; Vic Arlt, Hutchinson; Gene Athmann, Greenwald; Bernard Atkinson, New York Mills; Fred Atkinson, New York Mills; Mike Augustin, St. Paul

B Robert Baab, Crookston; Herman Backus, Browns Valley; Mike Barry, Red Wing; Harry Bealke, St. Paul; Elmer Becker, Deer Creek; Buddy Beier, Regal; Donald Bigalke, Randall; Clarence Bloomer, Waite Park; Kenneth Borg, Ashby; Leo Braind, Faribault; John Breimhorst, Jordan; William J. Breimhorst, Jordan; Dennis Brennan, Hinckley; James Brennan, Hinckley; J. M. Brennan, Hinckley; Wayne Bright, Cyrus; Leon Brinkman, Glencoe; Earl Broadbent, Elysian; William Burkhard, St. Cloud

Members of the Stillwater amateur baseball team, including Bud Grant (4th from left), 1954

C Denis Campbell, Winsted; Glenn Carlson, St. Cloud; Nick Chanaka, St. Cloud; Bill Cline, Aitkin; Harlan Conley, Verndale; Judge F. J. Connelly, Shakopee; Donald Cook, Comfrey; Mel Cook, Comfrey; Joseph J. Cory, St. Paul; Stan Cyson, Minneapolis

D Harlan Dammann, Hamburg; M. E. Dekko, Gary; Lee Denny, Verndale; Earl Dibb, Lester Prairie; Perry Ditty, Delano; Richard Ditty, Delano; John Dolan, Milroy; Mark Dolan, Albert Lea; Pat Dolan, Milroy; Casey Dowling, Sleepy Eye; Loren Downes, Nashwauk; George Droege, Hamburg; Roy Dunlap Sr., St. Paul

E Ambrose Ebnet, Holdingford; Bruce Edgar, St. James; Harold Eng, Braham

F George Fabel, Worthington; Bill Fairbanks, Buffalo; Russ Fechter, Red Wing; Marvin Fiemeyer, Courtland; James Fischer, Pierz; Jerry Flathman, St. Paul; Paul Fortin, Hamel; Lyle Freer, Wadena; A. H. Frick, Grand Rapids; Charles Fuller, Owatonna; Joseph Furnstahl, Randall

G Roy Gebhard, New Ulm; Alvin Gisvold, Springfield; Angelo Giuliani, St. Paul; Obert Gjerde, Sunberg; Sam Gnifkowski, St. Cloud; Maurice Gorham, Fairmont; Alan Gothmann, Waconia; Art Grangaard, Willmar; Loran Graupmann, Hamburg; Dick Grewe, Wadena; Calvin Griffith, Minneapolis; William J. Grose, Waterville; Richard Grunhoffer, Montgomery; Clarence Guetzkow, Mayer

H Jerome Hahn, St. Louis Park; Joseph P. Hahn, Belle Plaine; Jack Hall, St. Cloud; Oscar Halvorson, Milan; Andy Hamm, St. Cloud; Joe Harmala, Cokato; Steve Hecomovich, Marble; Robert Heidmann, Gaylord; Don Heinen, Roscoe; Victor Helget Sr., Stark; Donald Herd, Green Isle; Elmer Hierlinger, Anoka; Gerald Hochsprung, Brownton; Raymond Hoffmann, St. Peter; Lester Hoien, Twin Valley; Louis Holm, Essig; Cletus Huiras, Sleepy Eye; Bill Huls, Cold Spring

J Russell Jacobson, New York Mills; Tom Jameson, Le Center; Ernest Johnson, St. Paul; Iver Johnson, Faribault; Rick Johnson, Wadena

K Norbert Kalthoff, Cold Spring; Hal Kamsen, Sauk Centre; Herman Kampsen, Elrosa; Francis Kappel, Winsted; Jim Karn, Crookston; Harley Karvonen, Perham; Jay Katzenmeyer, Madison; Lyle G. Katzenmeyer, Brownton; Walt Katzenmeyer, Brownton; Fred J. Keup Sr., Belle Plaine; Arnold J. Klaers, Loretto; Larry Knigge, Marshall; Robert K. Knowlton, Monticello; John Koch, Trimont; Wendelin Koep Sr., Urbank; Alan Krueger, Perham; LaVerne Kuck, Searles; Al Kuebelbeck, Cold Spring

L Tink Larson, Waseca; Leo Litke, Pierz; Conrad Lueck, Aitkin; Al Luetmer, Meire Grove

M Tom Mallery, Hastings; Michael Mandich, Coleraine; Vint McDonald, Hawley; William H. McGowan, Gibbon; Lou McKenna, St. Paul; Louis Melius, Winthrop; Gerald J. Meyer, Belle Plaine; Edward Mohs, Belgrade; Dave Mooney, Hutchinson; Edmund G. Mueller, Arlington; Bill Murray, Delavan

N Rueben Nathe, Litchfield; Henry Nicklasson, New Ulm; Ted Nikolai, Chaska; Virgil Nordby, Wolf Lake; Ken Norman, Winsted

O Gene F. O'Brien, Faribault; James O'Brien, Arlington; Marty O'Neill, St. Paul; Dave Odman, Red Wing; John Oistad, Karlstad

P Howard Pennertz, Litchfield; Howard C. Pennertz, Litchfield; Ted Peterson,

A Glencoe player sliding into home, about 1950

Alexandria; Maurice Potter, Windom; Walt Prust, Ceylon; Dick Putz, St. Cloud

Q Wally Quaas, Chaska

R Frank Rabbit, Inger; Tom Rademacher, Rosen; Lawrence Rassier, St. Cloud; Willard Reigstad, Pennock; William Richter, Granite Falls; Gerald Riewer, Staples; L. R. Ringhofer, Owatonna; Bernie Roberts, Battle Lake; Gerald Roepke, New Germany; Dennis Roisum, Glencoe; Art Rolfzen, New Munich; Jack Ruhr, Hastings; Oscar Running, Ashby

S Archie Sailer, Frazee; Andrew Saloka, Rush City; Lee Sand, Greenwald; Bob Schabert, St. Paul; Marvin Scheele, Hamburg; Emil Scheid, Austin; Mel Schiller, Courtland; Milton Schilling Sr., Litchfield; Arthur Schlangen, Roscoe; Elmer Schleper, Farming; Joseph B. Schleper, Shakopee; Howard Schmidtke, St. James; Leo Schultz, St. Paul; Myron Seidl, Stark; Norbert Seidl, Stark; Martin Siewert, Hamburg; Otto Siewert, Redwood Falls; Tony Sipe, Ada; Lyle Smith, Big Lake; Al Solum, Erhard; Victor J. Sondag, New Ulm; Jake Spanier, St. Martin; Nic Spanier, Luxemburg;

Urban Spanier, Spring Hill; John Spier, Bethel; Bernie Steidl, Miltona; James Stoll, Arlington; Kenneth Strandemo, Kenyon; Mathew Stuckel, Ely; Valentine Styrbicky, Delano; Joseph Svoboda, Lonsdale; Woodrow Swanson, Carver

T Dewey Tauer, Red Wing; Frank Tauscheck, New Ulm; George Thompson, Big Lake; Joseph Trobec, St. Stephen

V Phil von Fischer, Springfield

W Bassie Wagner, Springfield; Bill Walsh, Gaylord; Charles Warner, Brownton; Erwin Warner, Halstad; Herb Weber, Springfield; Jerome G. Wegscheid, Wadena; Rich Weigel, Little Falls; Elmer Wellman, Hanska; Dale Welter, Chaska; Dave Wendlandt, Brownton; Warren West, Brownton; Wes Westrum, Clearbrook; Dana Wheeler, Henning; Norman Wilson, Springfield; Cletus Winter, St. Cloud; Leo J. Wirth, Kimball; Herman Woock, Aitkin; Milton Woodall, Blue Earth

Y Ray Yaeger, St. Cloud; Sheridan H. Young, Redwood Falls

Z Gaylord Zelinski, Brainerd; Robert J. Zellmann, Norwood; Virgil Zellmann, Young America; Al Zieper, Norwood; Robert Zwach, Milroy

DID YOU KNOW ?

Going into the 2006 season, Minnesota State University–Mankato coach Dean Bowyer is one of six active NCAA Division II baseball coaches with at least 900 victories. In 33 seasons as a college baseball coach (four at Minot State), Bowyer has a 948–490–7 record.

Eugene McCarthy

In the 1920s and 1930s future U.S. Senator Eugene McCarthy played amateur baseball in the Great Soo League. (The league was named after the Great Northern and the Soo Line, railroads that cut through the region.) McCarthy's hometown was Watkins, and other towns that fielded teams during the league's 40 years included Albany, Avon, Cold Spring, Holdingford, Melrose, New Munich, Paynesville, Richmond, Rockville, St. Anthony, St. Cloud, St. Joseph and St. Martin. McCarthy played in the league from age 16 to 20 and then played another season at age 29.

American Legion Baseball

Minnesota has participated in the national American Legion baseball program since its inception in 1925. All 50 states (and Puerto Rico) sponsor teams. In 2000 Minnesota had 330 registered teams, the second highest number in the nation. Only Pennsylvania (with 502 teams) had more.

American Legion State Champions (Division I)

2005 Eden Prairie; **2004** Eden Prairie; **2003** Rochester A's; **2002** Apple Valley; **2001** Coon Rapids; **2000** Tri-City Red (New Brighton); **1999** Tri-City Red (New Brighton); **1998** Excelsior; **1997** Tri-City Red (New Brighton); **1996** Rochester A's; **1995** New Ulm; **1994** Tri-City Red (New Brighton); **1993** Tri-City Red (New Brighton); **1992** New Ulm; **1991** Excelsior; **1990** St. Paul Hamline; **1989** Apple Valley; **1988** Moorhead; **1987** St. Louis Park; **1986** Waite Park; **1985** St. Paul Jacobsen; **1984** Waite Park; **1983** Edina; **1982** Edina; **1981** Rochester William T. McCoy; **1980** Minneapolis-Richfield; **1979** St. Paul Arcade-Phalen; **1978** New Ulm; **1977** St. Cloud; **1976** St. Cloud; **1975** Grand Rapids; **1974** St. Paul Attucks-Brooks; **1973** Minneapolis-Richfield; **1972** Minneapolis-Richfield; **1971** North St. Paul; **1970** Winona; **1969** Edina; **1968** St. Paul Attucks-Brooks; **1967** St. Paul Attucks-Brooks; **1966** North St. Paul; **1965** Rosetown Memorial; **1964** Mineapolis Grain Exchange; **1963** St. Paul Christie de Parcq; **1962** St. Paul Christie de Parcq; **1961** Minneapolis-Richfield; **1960** Fergus Falls;**1959** Minneapolis-Richfield; **1958** Minneapolis Grain Exchange; **1957** Mankato; **1956** St. Paul North End; **1955** Edina; **1954** St. Paul North End; **1953** Austin; **1952** St. Paul North End; **1951** St. Cloud; **1950** St. Paul North End; **1949** St. Paul North End; **1948** Austin; **1947** St. Paul Christie de Parcq; **1946** St. Paul Christie de Parcq; **1945** Minneapolis Fire & Police; **1944** Minneapolis-Richfield; **1943** Minneapolis-Richfield; **1942** St. Paul Hamline; **1941** New Ulm; **1940** Minneapolis Fire & Police; **1939** Minneapolis Fire & Police; **1938** St. Paul Midway; **1937** St. Paul Railroad; **1936** Minneapolis North Side; **1935** St. Paul Christie de Parcq; **1934** New Ulm; **1933** St. Paul Post 8; **1932** Minneapolis North Side; **1931** Winona; **1930** Minneapolis North Side; **1929** Cottonwood; **1928** St. Paul John de Parcq; **1927** St. Paul John de Parcq; **1926** Crosby

Minnesota American Legion Regional Champions

2004 Eden Prairie; **2003** Rochester A's; **1999** Tri-City Red (New Brighton); **1998** Excelsior; **1988** Moorhead; **1983** Edina; **1982** Edina; **1978** New Ulm; **1950** St. Paul North End; **1948** Austin; **1944** Minneapolis-Richfield; **1943** Minneapolis-Richfield; **1932** Minneapolis North Side

American Legion National Champions from Minnesota

2003 Rochester A's; **1999** Tri-City Red (New Brighton); **1983** Edina; **1943** Minneapolis-Richfield

Softball

Softball made its debut as an indoor sport. In 1887, a Chicago man invented the game, which was played in a local boat club. Eight years later, a member of the Minneapolis Fire Department created the outdoors version of the sport to help keep his co-workers in shape. Fireman Lewis Rober called his version of softball "Kitten League Ball," and the game quickly gained popularity nationwide. In 1922 the name of the game was changed to "Diamond Ball." The name "softball" was not used until 1926.

The first world championships were held in 1965 (for women) and 1966 (for men). Fastpitch softball debuted as an Olympic sport in 1996.

Johnny Vollmer

In 1937, 16-year-old Johnny Vollmer was the best pitcher in the top softball league in the Twin Cities. That year, a Cleveland company offered Vollmer $17,000 per year to pitch—an incredible wage for the era. But Vollmer's mother wouldn't let him take the deal, and he remained in St. Paul, where he dominated St. Paul softball into the 1960s.

Vollmer's fastball was once clocked at 102 miles per hour. His career record was 1,960 victories and 85 losses, with 60 no-hitters and five perfect games. Vollmer died in Ramsey County in 1984 at age 65.

Women's Professional Softball League

The short-lived Women's Professional Softball League debuted in 1997 and folded after the 2001 season. Four former University of Minnesota softball players played in the league—Shannon Beeler, Amber Hegland, Steph Klaviter and Wendy Logue.

Logue and Hegland played for the Georgia Pride in 1998. Beeler, Klaviter and Logue played for the Pride in 1999. In 2000 Beeler played with the Ohio Pride, and Klaviter played for the Florida Wahoos.

Klaviter played with the WPSL all-star team that toured the country in 2001. Klaviter was the league's pitcher of the year in 2000. She led her team to the WPSL championship and was the MVP of the championship series. In 1999 Klaviter led the league in earned run average.

University of Minnesota

The University of Minnesota fielded its first softball team in 1974. The Big Ten Conference offered its first official championship for softball in 1982. Going into the 2006 season, the Gophers have won or shared five Big Ten Conference titles.

In 1980 the Gophers won an unofficial championship by winning a conference tournament. They tied for first place in 1986 and then won the conference title in 1988. The Gophers also won conference titles in 1991 and in 1999, when they won the tournament title after finishing second in the regular season. (The Big Ten had started a conference tournament in 1995.)

The Gophers have advanced to the NCAA tournament seven times—1988, 1991, 1996, 1998, 1999, 2002 and 2003.

Three players have earned first-team All-American honors—Gretchen Larson (Association of Intercollegiate Athletics for Women in 1981, NCAA in 1993), Rachel Nelson (NCAA, 1996) and Shannon Beeler (NCAA, 1998).

Two Gophers have been the Big Ten MVP—Barb Drake (1986) and Kari Blank (co-player in 1997).

DID YOU KNOW ?

In January 2000 the University of St. Thomas baseball team traveled to Cuba for several exhibition games. The St. Thomas team was the first American college baseball team to visit Cuba since 1986. In 2001 the Tommies became the first Minnesota team to win the NCAA Division III baseball championship.

University of St. Thomas Repeats

The University of St. Thomas became the first softball team to repeat as NCAA Division III champions in 19 years when it won back-to-back titles in 2004 and 2005. (Eastern Connecticut State won consecutive titles in 1985 and 1986.)

The Tommies won the 2005 championship, with a 9–3 victory over Salisbury in Raleigh, N.C. The victory was the 20th consecutive in postseason play for the Tommies and the third national title for Tommies coach John Tschida, who also coached St. Mary's (Winona, Minnesota) to the championship in 2000.

St. Thomas second baseman Michelle Wong was named a first-team All-American. Wong finished her 173-game career as the MIAC's all-time leader in hits (241). That ranks 19th in Division III history. Nikki Conway, Wong's teammate, became the MIAC's all-time leader in home runs with 27 (in 124 games).

The national championship was the 12th for St. Thomas, which also won these national titles: women's cross country, in 1981, 1982, 1984, 1986, and 1987; men's cross country, in 1984 and 1986; women's basketball, in 1991; and men's indoor track, in 1985.

Slow-Pitch Softball

The United States had a professional slow-pitch softball league from 1977 to 1982. Minnesota had a team in the American Professional Slow Pitch League (APSPL) from 1977 to 1979.

In 1977 the Minnesota team was named the Minnesota Goofys; in 1978 and 1979, it became the Minnesota Norsemen. In 1978 the Norsemen reached the Pro Softball World Series. The Norsemen were swept by the Detroit Caesars, 4–0.

Football

3

Minnesota Vikings

THOUGH Minnesotans had tried to get the attention of the National Football League for years, it was not until late 1959 that two events in the Twin Cities made a lasting impression on the league, headquartered in New York. In November a group of businessmen who were frustrated by the NFL's unwillingness to expand its 12-team league announced the formation of a second professional football league. This upstart American Football League held its first meeting in Minneapolis on November 22, 1959. During that meeting, Minneapolis businessman Max Winter announced he planned to field a team, to begin play in 1960.

On the same day, a crowd of 26,625 gathered at Metropolitan Stadium in Bloomington to watch the New York Giants defeat the Chicago Cardinals, 30–20, in an NFL regular-season game. It was the second regular-season game the Cardinals, who were entertaining the idea of moving to the Twin Cities, played at Metropolitan Stadium in 1959.

In early January 1960, NFL owners convened in Miami with two major items on the agenda. After electing Pete Rozelle commissioner, the NFL, which had last expanded in 1950, turned to the "expansion question." Undoubtedly influenced by the threat of a competitive league moving into the Midwest, Chicago Bears' owner George Halas successfully convinced the other 11 owners to agree to expand, and on January 28, 1960, the league announced it would add two teams—Dallas (to begin play in 1960) and the Twin Cities (to begin in 1961).

On September 17, 1961, the Vikings played their first regular-season game. Before a crowd of 32,236 at Metropolitan Stadium, the team stunned the Chicago Bears, 37–13.

The Vikings quickly made the transition from a lowly expansion team to one of the league's best. The Vikings made the playoffs for the first time in 1968 under second-year coach Bud Grant.

Following the 1969 season, the Vikings earned the first of four Super Bowl berths (all in a seven-year span). The Vikings' last Super Bowl appearance came following the 1976 season.

The 1981 season was the Vikings' 21st and final season at Metropolitan Stadium. Starting in 1982, the Vikings joined the Twins baseball team and University of Minnesota football team in the Metrodome.

The Vikings made the playoffs in their first season in the Metrodome,

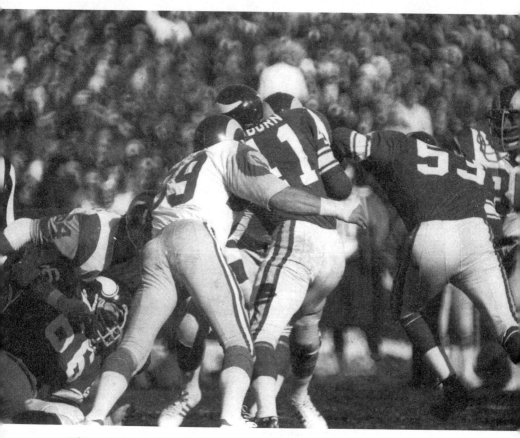

Vikings playing the Rams for the NFC title game, Met Stadium, 1974

but then missed the playoffs for four consecutive seasons (1983–86). Starting in 1987, the Vikings reached the playoffs for three consecutive seasons. Between 1992 and 2000 the Vikings missed the playoffs just once. Following a three-year drought, the Vikings returned to the playoffs in 2004.

Divison Assignment

After joining the NFL in 1961 as an expansion team, the Vikings were in the NFL's Western Conference from 1961 to 1966. From 1967 to 1969, the Vikings were in the NFL's Central Division.

Following the NFL/AFL merger in 1970, the Vikings were in the NFC's Central Division from 1970 to 2001. Since 2002, the Vikings have been in the NFC's North Division.

Vikings Year-by-Year

Season	Record	Coach
1961	3–11	Norm Van Brocklin
1962	2–11–1	Van Brocklin
1963	5–8–1	Van Brocklin
1964	8–5–1	Van Brocklin
1965	7–7	Van Brocklin
1966	4–9–1	Van Brocklin
1967	3–8–3	Bud Grant
1968	8–6	Grant
1969	12–2	Grant
1970	12–2	Grant
1971	11–3	Grant
1972	7–7	Grant
1973	12–2	Grant
1974	10–4	Grant
1975	12–2	Grant
1976	11–2–1	Grant
1977	9–5	Grant
1978	8–7–1	Grant
1979	7–9	Grant
1980	9–7	Grant
1981	7–9	Grant
1982	5–4	Grant
1983	8–8	Grant
1984	3–13	Les Steckel
1985	7–9	Grant
1986	9–7	Jerry Burns
1987	8–7	Burns
1988	11–5	Burns
1989	10–6	Burns
1990	6–10	Burns
1991	8–8	Burns
1992	11–5	Dennis Green
1993	9–7	Green
1994	10–6	Green
1995	8–8	Green
1996	9–7	Green
1997	9–7	Green
1998	15–1	Green

1999	10–6	Green
2000	11–5	Green
2001	5–11	Green (5–10), Mike Tice (0–1)
2002	6–10	Tice
2003	9–7	Tice
2004	8–8	Tice
2005	9–7	Tice

Division titles

1968, 1969, 1970, 1971, 1973, 1974, 1975, 1976, 1977, 1978, 1980, 1989, 1992, 1994, 1998, 2000

Vikings in the Super Bowl

Date	Site	Opponent	Result
Jan. 11, 1970	New Orleans	Kansas City	Lost, 23–7
Jan. 13, 1974	Houston	Miami	Lost, 24–7
Jan. 12, 1975	New Orleans	Pittsburgh	Lost, 16–6
Jan. 9, 1977	Pasadena	Oakland	Lost, 32–14

Vikings in the NFL/NFC Title Game

Date	Site	Opponent	Result
Jan. 4, 1970	Bloomington	Cleveland	Won, 27–7
Dec. 30, 1973	Irving, Texas	Dallas	Won, 27–10
Dec. 29, 1974	Bloomington	Los Angeles	Won, 14–10
Dec. 26, 1976	Bloomington	Los Angeles	Won, 24–13
Jan. 1, 1978	Irving, Texas	Dallas	Lost, 23–6
Jan. 17, 1988	Washington	Washington	Lost, 17–10
Jan. 17, 1999	Minneapolis	Atlanta	Lost, 30–27 (OT)
Jan. 14, 2001	E. Rutherford	N.Y. Giants	Lost, 41–0

Games Not on Sundays

The Vikings have played 63 games on days other than Sunday:

Monday (21–22); Thursday (10–5); Friday* (0–2); Saturday (3–0)

*The Vikings first played on a Friday on Sept. 22, 1967, when they lost to the Rams in Los Angeles, 39–3. On Friday, Dec. 24, 2004, the Vikings lost to the Green Bay Packers, 34–31, at the Metrodome.

The Vikings' Thursday record includes a 5–1 record on Thanksgiving Day:

Nov. 27, 1969, at Detroit	W, 27–0	
Nov. 26, 1987, at Dallas	W, 44–38 (OT)	

Nov. 24, 1988, at Dallas	W, 23–0
Nov. 23, 1995, at Detroit	L, 44–38
Nov. 26, 1998, at Dallas	W, 46–36
Nov. 23, 2000, at Dallas	W, 27–15

Games on Holidays

Date	Opponent	Result	Attendance
Dec. 25, 1971	Playoff vs. Dallas	L, 20–12	49,100
Jan. 1, 1978	Playoff at Dallas	L, 23–6	61,968
Dec. 31, 1978	Playoff at L.A. Rams	L, 34–10	69,631
Jan. 1, 1989	Playoff at San Francisco	L, 34–9	61,848
Dec. 25, 1989	R.S. vs. Cincinnati	W, 29–21	58,829
Dec. 31, 1993	R.S. at Washington	W, 14–9	42,836
Jan. 1, 1995	Playoff at Chicago	L, 35–18	60,347
Dec. 24, 1995	R.S. at Cincinnati	L, 27–24	34,568
Dec. 24, 2000	R.S. at Indianapolis	L, 31–10	56,672
Dec. 24, 2005	R.S. vs. Green Bay	L, 34–31	64,311

DID YOU KNOW ?

In 1992 former Vikings running back Herschel Walker competed on the U.S. Olympic bobsled team. Walker finished seventh in the two-man bobsled; he was cut from the U.S. four-man team.

First Games

Game	Date	Place	Attendance	Score
First preseason	Aug. 5, 1961	Sioux Falls, S.D.	4,954	Dallas 38, Vikings 13
First home preseason	Sept. 10, 1961	home	27,982	Rams 21, Vikings 17
First regular	Sept. 17, 1961	home	32,236	Vikings 37, Chicago 13
First regular road	Sept. 24, 1961	Dallas	12,992	Dallas 21, Vikings 7

Attendance

Largest preseason home crowd

Metropolitan Stadium	47,900 (five times, last on Aug. 12, 1972, vs. San Diego)
Metrodome	63,845, vs. Tennessee, Aug. 23, 2002

Vikings playing the Kansas City Chiefs in the last game at Met Stadium, 1981

Largest regular-season home crowd

Metropolitan Stadium   49,784 (nine times, last on Dec. 10, 1972, vs. Green Bay)
Metrodome   64,482, vs. Green Bay, Nov. 2, 2003

Largest postseason home crowd

Metropolitan Stadium   49,100, vs. Dallas, Dec. 25, 1971
Metrodome   64,060, vs. Atlanta, Jan. 17, 1999

Largest road crowds

Preseason   84,236 at Cleveland, Sept. 2, 1967 (vs. Atlanta)
Regular season   90,266 at Los Angeles Rams, Nov. 24, 1974
Postseason   103,438 at Pasadena, Calif., Jan. 9, 1977. Super Bowl XI vs. Oakland

Smallest preseason home crowd

Metropolitan Stadium   27,982, vs. Los Angeles Rams, Sept. 10, 1961
Metrodome   34,367, vs. San Diego, Aug. 3, 1996

Smallest regular-season home crowd

Metropolitan Stadium   26,728, vs. Los Angeles Rams, Nov. 25, 1962
Metrodome   13,911, vs. Green Bay, Oct. 4, 1987 (teams using replacement players)

Smallest postseason home crowd

Metropolitan Stadium   44,626, vs. St. Louis Cardinals, Dec. 21, 1974
Metrodome   57,353, vs. Washington, Jan. 2, 1993

Smallest road crowds

Preseason	4,954, at Sioux Falls, S.D. vs. Dallas, Aug. 5, 1961
Regular season	12,992, at Dallas, Sept. 24, 1961
Postseason	22,961, vs. Dallas at Miami, Jan. 5, 1969 (playoff bowl)

Highest home-season attendance

Metropolitan Stadium	367,259 in 8 games, 1980
Metrodome	513,437 in 8 games, 2003

Highest home-season average attendance

Metropolitan Stadium	49,246 for 7 home games, 1971
Metrodome	64,180 for 8 home games, 2003

DID YOU KNOW ?

The Vikings played two home games at the University of Minnesota's Memorial Stadium. On October 5, 1969, the Vikings defeated the Green Bay Packers, 19–7, before a crowd of 60,740. On August 8, 1971, the Vikings played a preseason game against the New England Patriots, who defeated the Vikings, 17–10, before 31,813 spectators.

Points in a Season

Record for most points scored and allowed

	Scored	Allowed
14-game	383 (1965)	410 (1962)
16-game	556 (1998)	484 (1984)

Record for fewest points scored and allowed

	Scored	Allowed
14-game	233 (1967)	133 (1969)
16-game	259 (1979)	233 (1988)

Coaching Records

Coach	Seasons	Overall	Playoffs
Bud Grant	18	158–96–5	10–12
Dennis Green	10	97–62	4–8

Jerry Burns	6	52–43	3–3
Mike Tice	4+	32–33	1–1
Norm Van Brocklin	6	29–51–4	—

Viking Players Records

Game

Rushing yards	200, by Chuck Foreman (Oct. 24, 1976)
Passing yards	490, by Tommy Kramer (Nov. 2, 1986)
Receiving yards	210, by Sammie White (Nov. 7, 1976)
Receptions	15, by Rickey Young (Dec. 16, 1979)
Touchdowns	4, by Chuck Foreman (Dec. 20, 1975) and by Ahmad Rashad (Sept. 2, 1979)
Touchdown passes	7, by Joe Kapp (Sept. 28, 1969)
Interceptions	3, many, most recently by Brian Williams (Nov. 23, 2003)

Single season

Rushing yards	1,521, by Robert Smith (2001)
Passing yards	4,717, by Daunte Culpepper (2004)
Receiving yards	1,632, by Randy Moss (2003)
Receptions	122, by Cris Carter (1995)
Touchdowns	22, by Chuck Foreman (1975)
Touchdown passes	39, by Daunte Culpepper (2004)
Interceptions	10, by Paul Krause (1975)

Career

Rushing yards	6,818, by Robert Smith
Passing yards	33,098, by Fran Tarkenton
Receiving yards	12,383, by Cris Carter
Receptions	1,004, by Cris Carter
Touchdowns	110, by Cris Carter
Touchdown passes	239, by Fran Tarkenton
Interceptions	53, by Paul Krause

Longest Plays

Run from scrimmage	85 yards, by Michael Bennett, Nov. 3, 2002, at Tampa Bay
Pass reception	89 yards, by Charley Ferguson (from Fran Tarkenton), Nov. 11, 1962, at Chicago
Kickoff return	101 yards, by Lance Rentzel, vs. Baltimore Colts, Nov. 14, 1965
Punt return	98 yards, by Charlie West, vs. Washington, Nov. 3, 1968
Interception return	97 yards, by Reggie Rutland, vs. Los Angeles Rams, Dec. 15, 1991
Fumble return	94 yards, by Dwayne Rudd, Dec. 6, 1998, vs. Chicago
Longest field goal	54 yards, by Jan Stenerud, Sept. 16, 1984, vs. Atlanta
Longest punt	84 yards, by Harry Newsome, Dec. 20, 1992, vs. Pittsburgh

Touchdown Returns (season and career)

	Season	Career
Kickoff	9 tied with one	9 tied with one
Punt	8 tied with one	2 by David Palmer
Interceptions	3 by Jimmy Hitchcock	7 tied with three

Defensive Stats (season and career)

	Season	Career
Fumble recoveries	9, by Don Hultz (1963)	29, by Jim Marshall
Tackles	230, by Scott Studwell (1981)	1,928, by Studwell
Blocked kicks	5, by Alan Page (1976)	20, by Matt Blair
Sacks	21, by Chris Doleman (1989)	130, by Carl Eller
Interceptions	10, by Paul Krause (1975)	53, by Krause
Interception return yards	242, by Jimmy Hitchcock (1998)	852, by Krause
Safeties	2, by Page (1971)	2.5, by Doleman

Single-game records

	Player	Date	Opponent
Fumble recoveries	3, by Joey Browner	Sept. 8, 1985	San Francisco
Tackles	24, by Studwell	Nov. 17, 1985	Detroit
Sacks	5, by Randy Holloway	Sept. 16, 1984	Atlanta
Interception return yards	97, by Reggie Rutland	Dec. 15, 1991	Los Angeles Rams

NOTE: Blocked kicks: 2, on seven occasions, three of them by Blair

Kicking (for extra-points, field goals and punting)

Field Goals

Single-game	7, by Rich Karlis, Nov. 5, 1989 vs. L.A. Rams
Season	35, by Gary Anderson, 1998
Career	282, by Fred Cox, 1963–77

Extra-point kicks

Single-game	7, by Cox (twice) and Chuck Nelson (once)
Season	59, by Gary Anderson, 1998
Career	519, by Fred Cox

Punting Average

Single-game	55.8, by Mitch Berger, vs. Cincinnati, Nov. 15, 1998
Season	46.4, by Bobby Walden (72 punts), 1964
Career	43.8, by Harry Newsome (308 punts), 1990–93

Consecutive Games

270 Jim Marshall (1961–79); **240** Mick Tingelhoff (1962–78); **210** Fred Cox (1963–77)

League Leaders

Scoring	Gary Anderson, 164 points in 1998; Fred Cox, 125 points in 1970
Touchdowns	Chuck Foreman, 14 (tied with Pittsburgh's Franco Harris), in 1976; Foreman, 15 in 1974
Quarterback rating (begun 1973)	Randall Cunningham, 106.0 rating in 1998; Tommy Kramer, 92.6 rating in 1986
Touchdown passes	Daunte Culpepper, 33 (tied with Indianapolis' Peyton Manning) in 2000; Fran Tarkenton, 25 (tied with Buffalo's Joe Ferguson) in 1975
Receptions	Cris Carter, 122 in 1994; Rickey Young, 88 in 1978; Chuck Foreman, 73 in 1975
Interceptions	Orlando Thomas, 9 in 1995; Audray McMillian, 8 (tied with Buffalo's Henry Jones) in 1992
Sacks	John Randle, 15½ in 1997; Chris Doleman, 21 in 1989; Doug Martin, 11½ in 1982

Vikings Voted NFL's MVP (Associated Press)

Alan Page, 1971
Fran Tarkenton, 1975

Vikings Postseason Honors

NFL MVP Alan Page (1971), Fran Tarkenton (1975), Randall Cunningham (1998)

NFC Player of the Year Chuck Foreman (1974), Tarkenton (1975), Cunningham (1998)

NFL Offensive Player of the Year Tarkenton (1975), Cunningham (1998)

NFL Defensive Player of the Year Page (1971, 1973), Keith Millard (1989)

NFC Defensive Player of the Year Chris Doleman (1992)

NFL Comeback Player of the Year Tommy Kramer (1986)

NFL Rookie of the Year Paul Flatley (1963), Foreman (1973), Sammy White (1976), Randy Moss (1998)

NFL Coach of the Year Bud Grant (1969), Dennis Green (1992, 1998)

Pro Bowl Honors

Most Pro Bowl Seasons

11 Randall McDaniel (1989–99); **9** Alan Page (1968–76); **8** Cris Carter (1993–2000); **7** Ron Yary (1971–77); **6** Joey Browner (1985–90), Matt Blair

(1977–82), Chris Doleman(1987–90, 92–93), Carl Eller (1968–71, 1973–74), Paul Krause (1969, 1971–75), Steve Jordan (1986–91), John Randle (1993–98), Mick Tinglehoff (1964–69)

Most Pro Bowl Starts

11 Randall McDaniel; **7** Alan Page, Ron Yary; **6** John Randle; **5** Chris Doleman

---

DID YOU KNOW ?

The Vikings have played 678 regular-season and 42 playoff games. Of those 720 games, 36 percent of their games (259) have been against three teams. The Vikings have played division rivals Chicago Bears and Green Bay Packers each 90 times. The Vikings have played the Detroit Lions 89 times.

The Vikings' record against the Bears is 48–40–2; against the Packers, 45–44–1; against the Lions, 58–29–2.

The Vikings and Tampa Bay Buccaneers met 49 times—the Vikings won 31 games—between 1976 and 2001, when the Buccaneers were in the NFC Central Division.

Vikings First-Round Draft Choices

1961 Tommy Mason; **1962** None; **1963** Jim Dunaway; **1964** Carl Eller; **1965** Jack Snow; **1966** Jerry Shay; **1967** Clint Jones, Gene Washington, Alan Page; **1968** Ron Yary; **1969** None; **1970** John Ward; **1971** Leo Hayden; **1972** Jeff Siemon; **1973** Chuck Foreman; **1974** Fred McNeill, Steve Riley; **1975** Mark Mullaney; **1976** James White; **1977** Tommy Kramer; **1978** Randy Holloway; **1979** Ted Brown; **1980** Doug Martin; **1981** None; **1982** Darrin Nelson; **1983** Joey Browner; **1984** Keith Millard; **1985** Chris Doleman; **1986** Gerald Robinson; **1987** D. J. Dozier; **1988** Randall McDaniel; **1989** None; **1990** None; **1991** None; **1992** None; **1993** Robert Smith; **1994** DeWayne Washington, Todd Steussie; **1995** Derrick Alexander, Korey Stringer; **1996** Duane Clemons; **1997** Dwayne Rudd; **1998** Randy Moss; **1999** Daunte Culpepper, Dimitrus Underwood; **2000** Chris Hovan; **2001** Michael Bennett; **2002** Bryant McKinnie; **2003** Kevin Williams; **2004** Kenechi Udeze; **2005** Troy Williamson, Erasmus James.

Retired Vikings Numbers

10   Fran Tarkenton
53   Mick Tingelhoff
70   Jim Marshall
77   Korey Stringer
80   Cris Carter
88   Alan Page

Playoff Games

The Vikings have played 42 playoff games in franchise history and have an 18–24 record. The team met a division rival only twice in the playoffs—losing to Chicago, 35–16, on January 1, 1995, and defeating the Green Bay Packers, 31–17, on January 9, 2005. During the 1994 regular season the Vikings defeated the Bears twice. In the 2004 regular season, the Packers won both games against the Vikings (each 34–31).

DID YOU KNOW ?

After the Vikings first reached the playoffs in their eighth season, they waited two weeks for their second game. On December 22, 1968, the Vikings lost to the Colts in Baltimore, 24–14, in the Western Conference championship game. Despite the loss, the Vikings played another playoff game two weeks later when they met the Dallas Cowboys in Miami in the Playoff Bowl Game. The Cowboys, who had lost to the Cleveland Browns on December 21 in the Eastern Conference championship game, defeated the Vikings, 17–13, before a crowd of 22,961.

The Vikings Outdoors

The Minnesota Vikings built a reputation for playing well in any conditions. From 1968 (the first season the team reached the playoffs) to 1981, the Vikings compiled an 82–28–1 record at the outdoor Met Stadium. In home games played after November 15, the Vikings were 28–9. That record included a 7–3 mark in the playoffs.

In *Once There Was a Ballpark,* Joe Soucheray writes about Vikings games played in memorable weather at Metropolitan Stadium. On December 4, 1966, it started snowing around 6:30 A.M. At least three inches of snow fell by the end of Atlanta's 20–13 victory over the Vikings. Only 20,206 of the 37,117 tickets sold for the game were used.

On December 14, 1969, about two inches of snow fell during the first half of the Vikings' 10–7 victory over the San Francisco 49ers.

On December 3, 1972, it was –2° at kickoff time (with the 11 mph breeze, the wind chill was –26°) for the Vikings game against the Chicago Bears. A crowd of 49,784 saw the Vikings win 23–10.

On November 22, 1970, it was 16° at game time for the Vikings and Packers. With gusts up to 40 mph and falling temperatures, the wind chill dropped to –25° and colder. The Vikings won the game 10–3.

Vikings in Milwaukee

From 1937 to 1994, the Green Bay Packers played three "home" games a year in Milwaukee, Wisconsin. Through the years, the Vikings have compiled a 22–23–1 record in Wisconsin: 16–14–1 in Green Bay and 6–9 in Milwaukee.

The Vikings played their first game in Milwaukee on October 29, 1961. The Packers won that game 28–10 before 44,112 fans. The two teams had just met seven days earlier in Bloomington where the Packers won 33–7. The Vikings played their final game in Milwaukee on December 19, 1993— winning the contest, 21–17, before a crowd of 54,773.

Bud Grant

Even before he became coach of the Minnesota Vikings, Bud Grant was well known in Minnesota. A native of Superior, Wisconsin, Grant was a two-sport standout at the University of Minnesota—a two-time All-Big Ten Conference selection in football and a three-year starter in basketball.

Grant played both professional football (in the National Football and the Canadian Football Leagues) and professional basketball (with the Minneapolis Lakers) before embarking on a coaching career with Winnipeg of the CFL.

In 1967 he became the coach of the Minnesota Vikings—a job that would eventually earn him a spot in the Pro Football Hall of Fame. In 1968, his second season as the Vikings coach, the team earned its first-ever playoff berth. Over the next 15 years, Grant coached the Vikings to 11 division titles, 12 playoff appearances, and four Super Bowls.

Bud Grant, Minnesota Vikings coach, about 1975

In January 1984 he announced his retirement. But following the team's disastrous 3–13 season in 1984, he returned to coach the Vikings in 1985. After a 7–9 season, he retired again.

Grant, who won 290 games in 28 seasons as a head coach, was the first person elected to both the Pro Football Hall of Fame and the Canadian Football League Hall of Fame. Grant was inducted into the Pro Football Hall of Fame in 1994.

Dennis Green

Late in the 1991 season, Jerry Burns announced he would retire as the Vikings coach following the season, his sixth as the team's coach. To find Burns's successor, the Vikings went outside the organization, something the team had not done since Bud Grant was hired in 1967.

On January 10, 1992, Dennis Green was introduced as the sixth Vikings coach in team history. The 42-year-old Green, who had spent the previous three seasons as the head coach at Stanford University, became just the second African American head coach in the NFL's modern era (following Art Shell of the Los Angeles Raiders).

Prior to his three seasons at Stanford, Green was a member of the San Francisco 49ers' staff for three seasons and head coach at Northwestern University for five seasons. Green told the media at his introductory press conference, "There's a new sheriff in town."

Green had an immediate impact on the team. The Vikings won the NFC Central Division title in his first season—the first of five playoff appearances in Green's first six seasons with the team.

The 1998 season—his seventh with the team—was extraordinary. The Vikings scored an NFL-record 556 points en route to a 15–1 record. After a bye in the first round of the playoffs, the Vikings defeated Arizona, 41–21, to earn a berth in the NFC championship game for the first time in 11 years.

The only team remaining between the Vikings and their first Super Bowl berth in 20 years was the Atlanta Falcons. The Falcons had enjoyed a tremendous turnaround in 1998—going 14–2 after winning just three games the previous season. The Falcons, 11-point underdogs to the Vikings, stunned the Vikings by rallying from a 20–7 deficit to tie the game and force it into overtime. In the overtime, the Falcons' Morten Anderson kicked a 38-yard field goal with 3:08 remaining to give Atlanta its first-ever Super Bowl berth.

The Vikings rebounded from the heartbreaking loss to reach the playoffs the next two seasons. Following the 2000 season, the Vikings again returned to the NFC championship game, where they lost to the New York Giants, 41–0.

The 2001 season was Green's 10th—and final—season as the Vikings coach. On January 4, 2002, with one game remaining in the 2001 regular season, Green was forced out despite two years remaining on his contract. The Vikings took a 5–10 record into their final game, which was coached by interim coach Mike Tice.

In 10 seasons under Green, the Vikings compiled a 101–70 record.

Purple People Eaters

The Los Angeles Rams had their "Fearsome Foursome." The Dallas Cowboys had a "Doomsday Defense." And the Vikings had their "Purple People Eaters."

For six seasons—from 1968 to 1973—the Vikings' defensive front four consisted of defensive ends Carl Eller and Jim Marshall and defensive tackles Gary Larsen and Alan Page. The foursome started 84 consecutive games, and the Vikings led the NFL in defense in 1969 and 1970. In 1971 Page became the first defensive player to be named the NFL's MVP. Page and Eller have been elected to the Pro Football Hall of Fame.

Midway through the 1974 season, Doug Sutherland replaced Larsen in the starting lineup. Sutherland, Eller, Marshall, and Page remained the starters through the 1977 season.

Two-point Conversions

Although college football began using the two-point conversion after touchdowns in 1958, the NFL held off until the 1994 season. The first two-point conversion in Vikings history came in the third game of the 1994 season. Cris Carter caught a pass from Warren Moon in the third quarter of the Vikings' 42–14 victory over the Bears in Chicago. The Vikings had three other two-point conversions that season.

Karl Kassulke

From 1963 to 1972, Kassulke started 117 games at safety for the Vikings. In his 131 career games, Kassulke, who had played college football at Drake, intercepted 16 passes. Kassulke's career was cut short when he was paralyzed from a motorcycle accident in July 1973.

Jim Marshall's Run

Jim Marshall played in the NFL for 20 seasons and in 282 consecutive games. He holds the NFL record for fumble recoveries (29) and is ninth in Vikings history with 988 tackles. He played in two Pro Bowls (following the 1968 and 1969 seasons) and played in four Super Bowls. Marshall is also known for one mistake: his wrong-way run.

On October 25, 1964, at Kezar Stadium in San Francisco, Marshall recovered a fumble by the 49ers quarterback and sprinted 66 yards to the wrong end zone. Marshall, who thought he had just scored a touchdown (it was actually a safety for the 49ers), was stunned when 49ers center Bruce Bosley arrived in the end zone and said "Thanks, Jim." Despite the mistake, the Vikings won the game, 27–22, in front of 31,845 fans.

Thirty years later, NFL Films produced a video titled "NFL's 100 Greatest Follies" and listed Marshall's gaffe as number one.

Korey Stringer

A 6-foot-5, 335-pound tackle, Korey Stringer was the Vikings' first-round draft choice in 1995. He moved into the starting lineup in the second game of the 1995 season and started 100 of the next 101 games for the Vikings. Following the 2000 season he was selected to play in the Pro Bowl.

On the second day of training camp of the 2001 season (his seventh in the league), Stringer became ill following the Vikings' morning workout in Mankato, Minnesota. He died from complications from heat stroke early in the morning of August 1, 2001, at the age of 27. His death was the first in an NFL training camp since 1979.

Stringer was inducted into the Vikings Ring of Honor on November 19, 2001.

Interceptions Thrown

The Vikings' single-game record for most interceptions thrown is five. It happened many times, most recently by Rich Gannon on October 28, 1990, against the Green Bay Packers in Milwaukee.

The Vikings' season record for most interceptions thrown is 32 by Fran Tarkenton in 1979. Tarkenton is the Vikings' career leader with 194 interceptions. As a team, the Vikings have intercepted six passes in a game on two occasions—at Tampa Bay on October 23, 1988, and at Atlanta on September 24, 1995. The Vikings' season record for passes intercepted is 36 in 1998.

Blockbuster Trade

On October 12, 1989, Vikings general manager Mike Lynn traded five players and eight draft choices to the Dallas Cowboys to acquire 27-year-old running back Herschel Walker. The *Minneapolis Star Tribune* called the trade, "the most-covered, if not the biggest story, in Minnesota sports history."

Walker helped immediately, leading the Vikings to the 1989 NFL Central title, their first division title in nine years. But the 1989 season ended with a first-round playoff loss, and the Vikings missed the playoffs following the 1990 and 1991 seasons. On May 29, 1992, Walker, who led the Vikings in rushing in each of his three years with the team, was released.

Other Memorable Trades

March 7, 1967 Acquired four draft choices (first-round in 1967 and 1968 and second-round in 1967 and 1969) from the New York Giants, in exchange for Vikings quarterback Fran Tarkenton. With the draft choices, the Vikings selected Clinton Jones and Bob Grim in 1967, Ron Yary in 1968, and Ed White in 1969.

January 28, 1972 Reacquired Tarkenton from the New York Giants in exchange for Norm Snead, Bob Grim, Vince Clements, and first-round draft choices in 1972 and 1973.

April 14, 1994 Acquired quarterback Warren Moon from the Houston Oilers in exchange for two draft choices.

What's It Worth?

In 1960 the NFL awarded an expansion franchise to a Minnesota group consisting of Max Winter, E. William Boyer, H. P. Skoglund, Ole Haugsrud, and Bernard H. Ridder Jr. The group paid an expansion "fee" of $1 million.

In December 1991, a group of owners—headed by former general manager Mike Lynn and owners Wheelock Whitney and Jaye Dyer—bought out the shares of another group of owners for $50 million. The group that sold its shares, which included Irwin Jacobs and Carl Pohlad, doubled its original $25 million investment in the team.

In August 1998, the Vikings' 10-person ownership group sold the franchise to Texan Red McCombs for $206 million in cash and the assumption of $40 million in debt.

On May 25, 2005, the NFL approved the sale of the Vikings from McCombs to a group headed by New Jersey real estate developer Zygmunt (Zygi) Wilf. Wilf's group paid $600 million for the franchise.

Tom Clancy

In October 1997, under pressure from the NFL to reorganize so that one person owned at least 30 percent of the team, the Vikings board of directors announced that the team was for sale. In February 1998 author Tom Clancy

Hubert H. Humphrey Metrodome, Minneapolis, 1982

agreed to buy the team for $200 million, but in May he withdrew his offer. Two months later, Red McCombs purchased the team.

Super Bowl XXVI

On January 26, 1992, the Metrodome played host to NFC champion Washington Redskins and AFC champion Buffalo Bills in the Super Bowl. The Redskins won the game, 37–24, before 63,130. Washington quarterback Mark Rypien was named the game's MVP. Rypien completed 18 of 33 passes for 292 yards and two touchdowns.

It was just the second time (in 26 years) that the Super Bowl had been held outside of the Sun Belt. On January 24, 1982, Super Bowl XVI was held in Pontiac, Michigan. The San Francisco 49ers defeated the Cincinnati Bengals, 26–21.

NFL Training Camps in Minnesota

Several NFL teams held training camps in Minnesota prior to 1960. The Chicago Cardinals trained in Duluth in 1939 and in nearby Superior, Wisconsin, in the 1940s. The Philadelphia Eagles trained in Hibbing in 1950 and 1951. The New York Giants trained at Gustavus Adolphus in St. Peter in 1952 and 1953. The Dallas Cowboys trained at St. Olaf in Northfield in 1961.

The Vikings' original training camp was in Bemidji. The team trained in the northern Minnesota town for four years before moving to Mankato.

NFL Work Stoppages

NFL players have gone on strike twice in NFL history. In 1982 a 56-day strike by players shortened the 16-game regular season to nine games. The Vikings went 5–4 that season. In 1987 a 24-day strike by players shortened the 16-game regular season to 15 games. NFL owners voted to use replacement players instead of canceling games. Prior to the 1987 strike, the Vikings had opened the season with victories over Detroit and the Los Angeles Rams.

The Vikings went 0–3 (losses to Green Bay, Chicago and Tampa Bay) in the games involving replacement players. In one of these games, on Octrober 4, the Vikings lost to the Green Bay Packers, 23–16, before 13,911 fans at the Metrodome. It is the smallest crowd in team history. The Vikings went 8–7 in 1987 and missed the playoffs.

Catholic Welfare Charities Exhibitions

While Minnesota had no professional football between 1931 and 1961, the state did get a glimpse of the NFL from 1949 to 1960. An annual event in Minnesota during that time was an NFL exhibition game, which benefited Catholic Welfare Charities. The first exhibition was played at St. Paul Central High School on September 18, 1949. A crowd of 7,000 watched the Detroit Lions defeat the New York Giants, 21–6.

In the early 1950s, the game was played at Parade Stadium in Minneapolis, drawing crowds of 20,000. In 1956 the game was moved to Metropolitan Stadium.

Charities Exhibition Games

Date	Site	Attendance	Result
Sept. 18, 1949	St. Paul Central	7,000	Detroit 21, N.Y. Giants 6
Sept. 12, 1951	Parade	19,021	San Francisco 20, Green Bay 0

Sept. 17, 1952	Parade	20,000	Green Bay 23, Pittsburgh 10
Aug. 22, 1953	Parade	20,560	Green Bay 31, N.Y. Giants 7
Aug. 14, 1954	Parade	19,950	Chicago Cardinals 27, Green Bay 10
Sept. 6, 1955	Parade	20,000	N.Y. Giants 17, Baltimore 14
Sept. 15, 1956	Met Stadium	17,752	Pittsburgh 14, Philadelphia 12
Sept. 21, 1957	Met Stadium	17,226	Pittsburgh 10, Green Bay 10
Sept. 21, 1958	Met Stadium	18,520	Chicago Cardinals 31, Green Bay 24
Sept. 20, 1959	Met Stadium	18,081	Green Bay 13, Pittsburgh 10
Sept. 11, 1960	Met Stadium	20,151	Green Bay 28, Dallas 23

Other Professional Football

The history of professional football dates to 1892. Minneapolis native William W. "Pudge" Heffelfinger, a three-time All-American at Yale considered to be one of the greatest linemen in college football history, became the first professional player when he was paid $500 by the Allegheny (Pennsylvania) Athletic Association to play against its rival, the Pittsburgh Athletic Club. The money turned out to be a good investment for Allegheny—Heffelfinger caused a fumble, recovered it and returned it for the game-winning touchdown.

For the most part, though, professional football in the late 19th century and early 20th century was a disorganized affair, with team rosters and schedules changing weekly. Finally, in 1920, the leaders of 10 "independent" professional teams formed the American Pro Football Association (the forerunner of the National Football League). Following its inaugural 1920 season, APFA members decided to admit 11 more teams. One of those expansion teams, which would begin play in 1921, was the Minneapolis Marines.

Minneapolis Marines

The Marines were well known across the Upper Midwest. Formed in 1905, they quickly became the region's strongest "independent" football team. In a five-season span from 1913 to 1917, the Marines won 34 consecutive regular-season games (losing twice in postseason all-star games). By 1917, the team's record made it difficult to find other teams willing to play them.

Most of the "independent" teams did not play in 1918 because of the influenza pandemic. By the time the Marines reformed in 1919, several of their star players had joined the Rock Island Independents, who would go on to win the professional football championship in 1919. The Marines regrouped by going 5–2–1 in 1919 and 5–1–2 in 1920.

In August 1921, the Marines joined the APFA. The Marines were coached by Johnny Dunn and quarterbacked by Rube Ursella, considered one of the top professional football players ever produced in Minnesota. The 5-foot-9, 170-pound Ursella, who also played minor league baseball for several seasons, played professional football for 22 seasons.

The Marines's 15-man roster also included former University of Minnesota players Peter Regnier and Ben Dvorak.

On October 2, 1921, the Marines made their APFA debut against the Chicago Cardinals, coached by Paddy Driscoll, in Chicago. In front of 4,000 fans, the Cardinals dominated the Marines, 20–0.

After two nonleague games—against the Ideals and the Knights of Columbus—the Marines traveled to Green Bay, Wisconsin, to take on the Packers. In front of 6,000 spectators, the Marines forged a 6–0 lead on a touchdown by Dvorak. But the Marines's kicker missed the extra point, which allowed the Packers to tie the score on a touchdown by Art Schmaehl. The Packers won the game on an extra-point kick by a substitute running back named Curly Lambeau.

The following Sunday, the Marines played their first APFA home game when they played host to the Columbus Panhandles. In front of a large crowd at Nicollet Park, the Marines's Eber Sampson redeemed himself for the missed extra-point kick at Green Bay by scoring two touchdowns in the Marines's 28–0 victory.

The Marines played their fourth and final game of the APFA season the following Sunday when they traveled to Rock Island, Illinois, and suffered a 14–3 loss to the Independents. The Marines finished a 3–4 record—1–3 in the APFA.

In 1922 the Marines again went 1–3, and in 1923 they went 2–5–2. After going 0–6 in 1924, the Marines franchise suspended operations.

The team was reformed in 1929 and renamed the Red Jackets, But the team had little success, winning just one of 10 games. There was only slight improvement in 1930, when the Red Jackets went 1–7–1. Following the 1930 season, the franchise folded.

Football in Duluth

In 1926 the National Football League's fifth season, the league was struggling financially. Its teams—primarily based in the East and Midwest—were hampered by months of poor weather that had greatly affected attendance. The league also faced a serious challenge from the American Football League, which was competing head-to-head against the NFL in at least four cities.

The league would get a much-needed boost from the Duluth Eskimos. The Eskimos were run by Ole Haugsrud, who had assumed control of the struggling franchise in 1924. The franchise was originally known as the Duluth Kelleys—the team was formed by the manager of the sporting goods department of the Kelley-Duluth Hardware Store. The team secured a spot in the NFL in 1923. In 1924 and 1925 the team primarily played teams in the Twin Cities and on the Iron Range.

In 1926, to ease the team's financial situation, Haugsrud enlisted the services of one of his high school friends—Ernie Nevers. Born in Willow River, Minnesota, Nevers was one of the greatest college football players and all-around athletes of all time. (He earned 11 letters in four sports at Stanford.)

In the summer of 1926, Nevers was playing professional baseball for the St. Louis Browns of the American League. In August he agreed to join the Kelleys for the sum of $15,000 and a percentage of gate receipts. Haugsrud renamed the team "Ernie Nevers' Eskimos."

In early September 1926, the team embarked on a remarkable road trip. Over the next 117 days, the team reportedly played 29 games. On that road trip, the team, which included future Pro Football Hall of Famers Walt Kiesling and Johnny "Blood" McNally, played 13 league games and exhibitions in most of the NFL cities and the West Coast. In one eight-day stretch, the Eskimos played five games. In its recap of the 1926 season, *The Football Encyclopedia* said, "Nevers gave the NFL a needed heroic image and some gate pull in a season of rain and red ink."

That red ink continued in 1927, as 10 of the league's 22 teams folded prior to the season. The Eskimos played all nine of their games on the road and then folded after the 1927 season. The team did not operate in 1928, and in 1929, Haugsrud sold it to a group in Orange, New Jersey.

As part of that sales agreement, Haugsrud was promised he would receive a share of the next NFL franchise in Minnesota. In 1960 Haugsrud was part of the ownership group that was awarded an expansion team.

Women's Professional Football

The Women's Professional Football League was established in 2000. Since that year, the Minnesota Vixens have been an affiliate of the league.

In 2004 the Vixens played six league games against the Wisconsin Northern Ice, Indiana Speed and Toledo Reign. The Northern Ice was league champion in 2003 and league runner-up in 2004. The Vixens also played four nonleague games and finished with a 6–4 record in 2004. The team, with a

30-player roster, played home games at Augsburg College, St. Paul Central High School, and Farmington High School.

Arena Football League

The Arena Football League was formed in June 1987. In the 18-year history of the league, there have been 47 franchises. There are currently 19.

Minnesota's only franchise in the league was the Minnesota Fighting Pike, which played at the Target Center in 1996. The Pike, coached by Ray Jauch, compiled a 4–10 record in its only season (April to August) in Minnesota. The Pike was quarterbacked by former Gophers quarterback Rickey Foggie.

The league disbanded the Pike in November 1996, after it reportedly lost $450,000 in its lone season in Minnesota. The Pike averaged 8,894 fans for seven home games, the largest being 14,840 for the season opener against Iowa. That was the only crowd larger than 8,728.

DID YOU KNOW ?

Six native Minnesotans have been inducted into the Pro Football Hall of Fame in Canton, Ohio: Dave Casper (Bemidji), Sid Gillman (Minneapolis), Joe Guyon (White Earth Indian Reservation), Walt Kiesling (St. Paul), Jim Langer (Little Falls), and Ernie Nevers (Willow River).

College Football—University of Minnesota

A contest between Rutgers and Princeton played in New Jersey on November 6, 1869, is considered the nation's first intercollegiate football game. Rutgers won that game, which resembled soccer more than football, 6–4. Several other eastern colleges began playing the sport in the next few years. In 1875 Harvard and Yale played a contest, which more resembled rugby.

The first mention of "football" at the University of Minnesota was in the October 19, 1878, issue of *Ariel,* a student publication, which noted, "Football has been the all-absorbing amusement for the past few weeks." Intramural contests occupied university students for four years because challenges sent to Carleton College in Northfield for an intercollegiate contest were rejected.

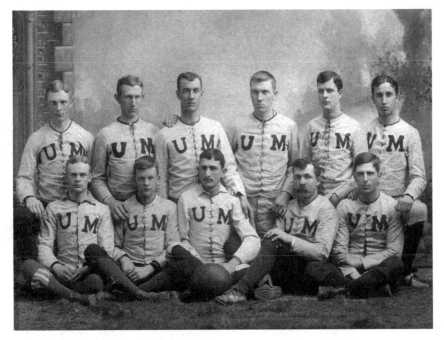

Early Gophers football team, 1888

Finally, the university found an opponent. On September 30, 1882, at the Colonel King Fairgrounds in South Minneapolis, the university and Hamline played the first intercollegiate athletic contest in state history. (Carleton had also been invited but declined.) Captain A. J. Baldwin scored the first points in Gophers history as the Gophers went on to defeat Hamline, 4–0.

Top Gophers Football Games

The 1981 season was the 100th season of University of Minnesota football. In its homecoming issue on October 5, 1981, the *Minnesota Daily* (student newspaper) picked these top 10 games in Gophers football history.

Date	Scores
Oct. 31, 1903	Gophers 6, Michigan 6 (first Little Brown Jug game)
Nov. 15, 1924	Gophers 24, Illinois 7 (the Gophers stop Red Grange)
Nov. 5, 1927	Gophers 7, Notre Dame 7
Oct. 20, 1934	Gophers 13, Pittsburgh 7 (key victory en route to first national title)
Nov. 9, 1935	Gophers 13, Iowa 6 (first Floyd of Rosedale game)
Oct. 25, 1941	Gophers 7, Michigan 6 (two legends—Gophers' Bruce Smith and Michigan's Tom Harmon)

Oct. 24, 1953	Gophers 22, Michigan 0 (Paul Giel rushed for 112 yards, passed for 169 yards and intercepted two passes)
Nov. 5, 1960	Gophers 27, Iowa 10 (Gophers upset No. 1 Iowa)
Jan. 1, 1962	Gophers 21, UCLA 3 (Gophers' first bowl victory)
Oct. 22, 1977	Gophers 16, Michigan 0 (No. 1 Michigan's first shutout in 112 games)

Gopher Bowl Games

Bowl Game	Site	Date	Result
Rose	Pasadena, Calif.	Jan. 2, 1961	Washington 17, Gophers 7
Rose	Pasadena, Calif.	Jan. 1, 1962	Gophers 21, UCLA 3
Hall of Fame	Birmingham, Ala.	Dec. 22, 1977	Maryland 17, Gophers 7
Independence	Shreveport, La.	Dec. 21, 1985	Gophers 20, Clemson 13
Liberty	Memphis, Tenn.	Dec. 29, 1986	Tennessee 21, Gophers 14
Sun	El Paso, Texas	Dec. 31, 1999	Oregon 24, Gophers 20
Micronpc.com	Opa-Locka, Fla.	Dec. 28, 2000	N. C. State 38, Gophers 30
Music City	Nashville, Tenn.	Dec. 30, 2002	Gophers 29, Arkansas 14
Sun	El Paso, Texas	Dec. 31, 2003	Gophers 31, Oregon 30
Music City	Nashville, Tenn.	Dec. 31, 2004	Gophers 20, Alabama 16
Music City	Nashville, Tenn.	Dec. 30, 2005	Virginia 34, Gophers 31

Alumni Games

In the 1950s and 1960s, a highlight on the Gophers' football schedule was their annual exhibition game against an alumni team. These games were very competitive—for example, in 1960, the Gophers opened their season with a 19–7 loss to the alumni. The Gophers recovered to earn their first-ever berth in the Rose Bowl following the season.

The most memorable alumni game may have been the 1958 game. The alumni team featured a host of Gopher legends—Bud Grant, Gordy Soltau, Geno Cappelletti, Verne Gagne, and college football Hall of Fame members Clayton Tonnemake and Leo Nomellini. But the most recognizable member of the alumni squad was College Football Hall of Fame and future Pro Football Hall of Fame member Bronko Nagurski.

Nagurski, who was 50 years old and had last played for the Gophers 29 years earlier, had not played football since retiring from the NFL's Chicago Bears in 1943 and settling in International Falls. Although not expected to play, he suited up and carried the ball three times—gaining six yards. The crowd of 14,129 gave him the loudest ovation of the day. The alumni won the game, 26–2.

Rivals and Trophies

The University of Minnesota football team and rivals play for several well-known trophies in college football.

Gophers and Michigan

Since 1903, the Gophers and Michigan have competed for the Little Brown Jug. On October 31, 1903, Michigan came to Minneapolis riding a 29-game winning streak. The Wolverines, coached by Fielding Yost, had outscored

Gophers coach Doc Spears with team at Memorial Stadium, 1926

U of M equipment manager Oscar Munson with the Little Brown Jug trophy, 1933

their opponents 447–0 in their first seven games of the 1903 season. In front of a crowd of about 20,000 at Northrop, the Gophers and Michigan played to a 6–6 tie. The *Minneapolis Sunday Tribune* credited the Gophers with a "Victory, though the score is tied." In their haste to leave the field, the Wolverines left behind a water jug, which was found by University of Minnesota equipment manager Oscar Munson. L. J. Cooke, the University of Minnesota athletic director, informed Yost that if he wanted the jug returned, the Wolverines would have to win it. The Gophers kept the jug for six years because the teams didn't play again until 1909.

Michigan leads the all-time series for the jug, 63–22–3. In 2005, the Gophers ended a 16-game losing streak to Michigan with a 23–20 victory in Ann Arbor.

Gophers and Iowa

Since 1935, the Gophers and Iowa have played for a bronzed pig called Floyd of Rosedale. In 1934 the Gophers defeated the Hawkeyes, 48–12. Following the game, several Iowa newspapers suggested that the Gophers had intentionally tried to rough up Iowa's star running back Oz Simmons. On the eve of the 1935 game, which was to be played in Iowa City, Iowa governor Clyde

Herring told an Associated Press reporter that "if the officials stand for any rough tactics like Minnesota used last year, I'm sure the crowd won't."

Gophers football coach Bernie Bierman said Herring's comment, published nationwide, was "inflammatory" and encouraged the Hawkeye crowd to take charge if it thought the Hawkeyes were not being treated fairly. Minnesota Governor Floyd B. Olson used tact and diplomacy to diffuse the situation. He sent Herring a telegram, which suggested a friendly bet to settle the differences. Olson's suggestion was the winning team should receive a hog.

Several days after the Gophers' 13–7 victory, Herring had "Floyd" delivered to Olson's office. Through the 2004 season, the Gophers lead the all-time series, 58–38–2. Iowa's victory in 2004 was its fourth consecutive in the series.

DID YOU KNOW ?

In 1898 University of Minnesota student Johnny Campbell volunteered to lead organized cheers at football games. His offer came after the Gophers had lost three consecutive games and a subsequent editorial in the school paper pleaded, "Any plan that would stir up enthusiasm would be helpful." Campbell began leading cheers at the Minnesota–Northwestern football game on November 12. The Gophers won the game, 17–6, and much of the credit went to Campbell and his "yell leaders."

Gophers and Wisconsin

The Gophers and Badgers have played for two trophies. During the 1930s and 1940s, the teams played for the Slab of Bacon. But the trophy was misplaced in 1945 and wasn't rediscovered until 1994, when it was found in a storage room at Camp Randall Stadium in Madison. Even though the Slab had been missing since the mid-1940s, each score in the series from 1930 to 1970 was somehow printed on the trophy.

Since 1948, the teams have played for Paul Bunyan's Axe, a trophy suggested by Wisconsin's W Club. Through the 2004 season, Wisconsin leads the series, 31–23–3.

The Gophers and Wisconsin have played each other in football since 1890, making their series of 114 games a record in NCAA Division I-A football.

Gophers and Penn State

The Gophers and Penn State play for a trophy called the Victory Bell. The trophy, suggested by acting Pennsylvania Governor Mark Singel and Minnesota Governor Arne Carlson, was established for the first meeting between the two teams on September 4, 1993. That inaugural meeting was also Penn State's first Big Ten conference game.

Through the 2005 season, Penn State leads the series, 5–4. Penn State won the first four meetings, but the Gophers' 16–7 victory in 2004 was their fourth consecutive over the Nittany Lions. Penn State defeated the Gophers 44–14 in 2005.

DID YOU KNOW ?

The Gophers football team was offered a postseason game following the 1941 season. The Board of Regents responded that they wouldn't consider the invitation for either "commercial or charitable purposes." The Gophers played in their first bowl game following the 1960 season.

Gopher Football Titles

The University of Minnesota football team has won six national titles and 18 Big Ten Conference titles. Under coach Bernie Bierman, the Gophers won national titles in 1934, 1935, 1936, 1940, and 1941. The Gophers won the 1960 national title under coach Murray Warmath.

The Gophers won or shared 16 conference titles between 1900 and 1941. Since 1941, the team has shared in two titles (1960 and 1967).

Bierman is the second-winningest coach in school history. In 16 seasons, Bierman led the Gophers to a 93–35–6 record. Dr. Henry L. Williams is the winningest coach in school history. Williams compiled a 136–33–11 record in 22 seasons (1900–21).

Outland Trophy

Two Gophers have won the Outland Trophy, given annually to the top lineman in college football. Tom Brown received it in 1960; he was also the runner-up in the Heisman voting. Bobby Bell won it in 1962.

Coach Bernie Bierman with Gopher team members, 1930s

Heisman Trophy

Only one University of Minnesota football player has won the Heisman Trophy, which is given annually to college football's top player: running back Bruce Smith in 1941.

Paul Giel of the Gophers was third in Heisman voting in 1952 (won by Oklahoma's Billy Bessels) and finished second in 1953 (won by Notre Dame's John Lattner).

One other player with Minnesota connections won the Heisman. In 2000 Florida State quarterback Chris Weinke received the award at the age of 28, making him the oldest player to win the trophy. Weinke, who had played high school football at Cretin–Derham Hall in St. Paul, had played six seasons of professional baseball in the Toronto Blue Jays organization before enrolling at Florida State.

In 2003 Minneapolis native Larry Fitzgerald Jr., who played high school football at Holy Angels Academy in Richfield and in college for the University of Pittsburgh, was the runner-up in the Heisman voting. Fitzgerald, who earned All-American honors at wide receiver, was second to Oklahoma quarterback Jason White.

DID YOU KNOW ?

On September 10, 1939, the Gophers team was the first college football team to be seen on TV, when KSTP broadcast a Gophers practice as an experiment. The first televised Gophers football game was on October 31, 1953, when the Gophers hosted Pittsburgh.

Coaching Legends

Bernie Bierman retired as the Gophers coach following the 1950 season. The first two men that university athletic director Ike Armstrong interviewed to replace him were Bear Bryant, the coach at Kentucky, and Bud Wilkinson, a Minneapolis native who was coaching at Oklahoma. Both elected to remain in their current positions, and Armstrong eventually hired former Ohio State coach Wes Fesler. Fesler coached the Gophers three seasons while Bryant and Wilkinson went on to Hall of Fame coaching careers.

Gophers playing Ohio State in Memorial Stadium, 1945

William W. "Pudge" Heffelfinger

Heffelfinger, a Minneapolis native, started his college football career while he was still in high school. In 1887, while he was a senior at Minneapolis Central High School, the Gophers, who were one player short, recruited the 6-foot-3, 195-pound Heffelfinger to play for them. The next year, Heffelfinger enrolled at Yale.

From 1889 until 1891, Heffelfinger was named an All-American. In 1892 Heffelfinger, who is in the College Football Hall of Fame, became the first "professional" football player when he was paid $500 to play for the Allegheny (Pennsylvania) Athletic Association team.

In 1893 Heffelfinger coached the University of California team, and in 1895 he coached the Gophers, before embarking on a business career.

But Heffelfinger wasn't done playing football. In 1916, at the age of 49, he scrimmaged against the Yale varsity to help the Elis prepare for their game against rival Harvard. In 1920, at age 53, he played 50 minutes for the East All-Stars against the Ohio State All-Stars in Columbus, Ohio. Ten years later, at age 63, he donned a football uniform for the last time when he played in an all-star game in Minneapolis.

DID YOU KNOW ?

In a year-long series on in the history of Minnesota sports in 1999, the *Minneapolis Star Tribune* named this All-time Gophers' football team:
    Coach: Bernie Bierman. Players: Bobby Marshall, Aaron Brown, Bobby Bell, Ed Widseth, Tom Brown, Leo Nomellini, Clayton Tonnemaker, Sandy Stephens, Bruce Smith, Paul Giel, Bronko Nagurski.

College Football Hall of Fame

The College Football Hall of Fame includes 16 former University of Minnesota athletes and three former coaches.

Players

Ed Rogers, Bobby Marshall, John McGovern, Bert Baston, Herb Joesting, Bronko Nagurski, Francis "Pug" Lund, Ed Widseth, George Franck, Bruce Smith, Dick Wildung, Clayton Tonnemaker, Leo Nomellini, Paul Giel, Tom Brown and Bobby Bell.

Coaches

Henry Williams, Fritz Crisler and Bernie Bierman.

Retired Gophers Football Numbers

10	Paul Giel
54	Bruce Smith
72	Bronko Nagurski

NOTE: On Nov. 18, 2000, the University of Minnesota retired the football jersey of former quarterback Sandy Stephens. Stephens wore number 15 during his three-year career (1959–61) with the Gophers.

University of Minnesota football crowd at Memorial Stadium, 1939

Weather

November 8, 1890 The University of Minnesota played its first out-of-state opponent when it hosted Grinnell College of Iowa. The Gophers won the game, 18–13, in front of the 300 fans who weathered a snowstorm.

November 25, 1933 The Gophers closed out their season with a 6–3 victory over Wisconsin before a crowd of 25,000 at Memorial Stadium. At 2 P.M. kickoff, it was 40° (it had been 50° at noon) and raining. By the third quarter, it was snowing, with a 29 mph wind. By 5 P.M., it was 31°.

November 8, 1947 Despite cold (28°) and windy conditions, a then Memorial Stadium record-crowd of 63,659 turned out to watch the Gopher football team rally for a 26–21 victory over Purdue.

October 29, 1955 In a game the *Minneapolis Tribune* said was played "in perhaps the worst weather ever for a Gophers football game," the Gophers upset Southern California and its star running back Jon Arnett, 25–19. A crowd of 64,592 watched at Memorial Stadium in the wind, snow, and sleet and 34° temperature. The Gophers never trailed after taking a 6–0 lead late in the first quarter on a 14-yard touchdown run by Bob "Snowshoes" Schultz. Schultz also intercepted a pass for the Gophers.

DID YOU KNOW ❓

The phrase "Ski-U-Mah" was first heard at a Gopher athletic event in 1884. Pronounced SKY-YOU-MAH, the phrase was conceived by two rugby players, John W. Adams and Win Sargent, who used the word "Ski," supposedly a Siouan word meaning victory, and "U-Mah" (representing the University of Minnesota and rhyming with "rah") to create a cheer.

The phrase was eventually incorporated into both official school songs, "Hail Minnesota" and the "Minnesota Rouser."

Gophers in the NFL Draft

The National Football League held its first player draft in 1936. Between 1936 and 2004, the University of Minnesota saw 249 of its athletes selected in the draft. The Gophers had at least one player selected every year between 1936 and 1992.

On seven occasions, the Gophers have had at least eight players taken in one year: 1942 (8), 1943 (8), 1944 (11), 1950 (13), 1957 (8), 1958 (8), and 1969 (9). Since 1936, there have been only five years—1993, 1994, 1995, 1997, and 1999—in which a Gopher was not selected in the draft.

Gophers in the First Round of the Draft

Sixteen Gophers have been selected in the first round of the draft: **1937** Ed Widseth; **1939** Larry Butler; **1940** Harold Van Every; **1941** George Franck; **1942** Urban Odson; **1943** Bill Daley, Dick Wildung; **1950** Clayton Tonnemaker, Leo Nomellini, Bud Grant; **1964** Carl Eller; **1966** Gale Gillingham;

1968 John Williams; **1989** Brian Williams; **1990** Darrell Thompson; **2001** Willie Middlebrooks.

Big Ten in the NFL Draft

According to the *Complete Pro Football Draft Encyclopedia* (Sporting News), Ohio State has had the most players—369—selected in the NFL draft. Other conference schools had the following number of players: **311** Michigan; **299** Penn State; **270** Michigan State; **254** Purdue; **249** Minnesota; **225** Wisconsin; **216** Illinois; **202** Iowa; **163** Northwestern; **150** Indiana; **2** University of Chicago.

Notre Dame has had the most players—446—selected in the history of the draft. University of Southern California, with 416, is second.

A girls football game at Gustavus Adolphus, St. Peter, about 1920

College Football—Other Conferences

Minnesota Intercollegiate Athletic Conference

The Minnesota Intercollegiate Athletic Conference was formed in 1920 when Carleton, Gustavus Adolphus, Hamline, Macalester, St. John's, St. Olaf, and St. Thomas adopted a constitution. The MIAC named its first champion that fall.

MIAC titles won or shared:

27 St. John's; **22** Gustavus; **18** Concordia; **14** St. Thomas; **6** St. Olaf; **5** Hamline; **3** Minnesota–Duluth*; **2** Augsburg, Bethel, Carleton, Macalester**; **1** St. Mary's.

*no longer in MIAC; **no longer competes in MIAC football.

DID YOU KNOW ?

Each year since 1975, a group in Newport Beach, California, has honored the last player selected in the NFL draft with a weeklong celebration and an award titled "Mr. Irrelevant." In 2003 Ryan Hoag of Gustavus Adolphus earned the award by being the 262nd player selected in the draft. Hoag was drafted by the Oakland Raiders.

John Gagliardi

Twenty-three of the 27 conference titles won by St. John's in Collegeville have been under the direction of Coach John Gagliardi. In 2004 Gagliardi completed his 56th season as a college football coach—his 52nd season with the Johnnies. Gagliardi is the winningest coach in college football history, with a 421–117–11 record. Gagliardi, who began his coaching career at Carroll College (Montana) in 1949, took over at St. John's in 1953.

Football at Macalester

On October 11, 1974, Macalester defeated Gustavus Adolphus, 21–20. The victory would be the last of the decade for the Scots. The Scots' next victory was September 6, 1980, when they edged Mount Senario (a now-closed school from Ladysmith, Wisconsin). Between the two victories, the Scots lost 50 consecutive games.

During the 1978 season, the Scots lost to St. Thomas, 28–0, their 39th consecutive loss, tying an NCAA record for Division I, II, or III for the longest losing streak. The next week, the Scots lost to St. John's, 44–0, to break the NCAA record. The Scots lost their final two games of the 1978 season to extend their losing streak to 42 games.

The Scots were scheduled to open the 1979 season against University of Wisconsin–La Crosse, but the game was cancelled. In 1978 La Crosse had defeated the Scots, 61–0, in a game that was shortened because of heat and injuries to Scots' players. The Scots went winless in 1979 to extend their losing streak to 50 games.

John Gagliardi of St. John's University,
the winningest coach in college football history

The Scots opened the 1980 season against Mount Senario. With 11 seconds remaining, Macalester's Bob Kaye kicked a 50-yard field goal—the first and only field goal of his college career—to lift the Scots to a 17–14 victory. It was Mount Senario's only loss of the season and the Scots' only victory of the season. And the Scots ended their losing streak in the MIAC when they tied St. Thomas, 0–0. The Scots tied another game to finish the season 1–6–2.

The Scots opened the 1981 season with a 22–6 victory over Mount Senario. In their third game of the season, the Scots rallied from a 24–7 deficit for a 27–24 victory over Augsburg. It was their first conference victory since 1974 and ended a 45-game winless streak in conference games. The Scots won two more games in 1981 for four victories—the most since 1969.

The Scots put together four consecutive winning seasons in the 1980s, but fell upon difficult times again in the 1990s. The Scots won just six of 126 games between 1989 and 2001, and the football team dropped out of the MIAC after the 2001 season to play an independent schedule.

Local Rivals

Macalester and Hamline, schools located about two miles apart in St. Paul, have played each other in football since the late 19th century. The teams have met 105 times, making this the oldest rivalry between two Minnesota schools.

North Central Conference

The North Central Conference was formed in 1921 by four schools in North and South Dakota. The University of Minnesota–Duluth, Minnesota State University–Mankato and St. Cloud State University are currently members of the seven-team league. Two Minnesota schools won league football titles: Mankato State in 1987 and 1993 and St. Cloud State in 1989.

University of Minnesota–Morris

Another Minnesota college football program that suffered through a long losing streak is the University of Minnesota–Morris. On November 14, 1998—in their season finale—the Cougars defeated Mayville State, 25–22, at the Metrodome, but it was the Cougars' last victory for nearly five years. The Cougars went 0–11 in each of the next four seasons, and their 44-game losing streak was the longest in NCAA Division II history. The Cougars dropped out of the Division II NSIC following the 2001–02 school year and joined the NCAA Division III Upper Midwest Athletic Conference. The Cougars lost their first two games of the 2003 season to stretch their losing streak to 46 games.

On September 20, 2003, the Cougars traveled to Elsah, Illinois, where they defeated Principia College, 61–28, to end their losing streak.

Northern Sun Intercollegiate Conference

The Northern Sun Intercollegiate Conference, originally known as the Northern Teachers Athletic Conference, began in 1932 with five members—Bemidji State, Mankato State, Moorhead State, St. Cloud State and Winona State.

DID YOU KNOW ?

The National Football Foundation and College Football Hall of Fame's divisional class for 2005 included legendary small-college coach Frosty Westering. Westering compiled a 305–96–7 record in 40 seasons as a college football coach. Before spending the final 32 seasons of his career at Pacific Lutheran in Tacoma, Washington, Westering was the athletic director and football coach at Lea College in Albert Lea, Minnesota. In six years at Lea (1966–72), his teams compiled a 29–22–2 record. Westering also spent two seasons at Parsons College in Keokuk, Iowa.

NSIC titles won or shared:

16 Winona State; **14** Moorhead State, St. Cloud State*; **13** Mankato State*, Minnesota–Duluth*; **8** Minnesota–Morris*; **7** Michigan Tech*; **4** Bemidji State; **3** Northern State (Aberdeen, SD); **1** Southwest Minnesota State, Concordia (St. Paul).

*no longer a member of the NSIC.

Minnesota Schools in the NFL Draft

Gustavus Adolphus College in St. Peter has had 13 players selected in the NFL draft. Cal Roberts was selected in the third round in 1953, making him the highest pick.

Four other Minnesota college football players have been selected in the first four rounds of the draft: Hamline's Dick Donlin (second, 1956), Minnesota–Duluth's Ted McKnight (second, 1977), St. Cloud State's John Kimbrough (third, 1977) and Concordia at Moorhead's Dave Klug (fourth, 1980).

Minnesota colleges have had the following number of players drafted: **8** Concordia (Moorhead); **5** Hamline, Minnesota–Duluth; **4** Mankato State; **3** Moorhead State, St. Olaf; **2** Bemidji State, Macalester, Southwest State, St. Cloud State, Winona State.

Basketball

After Minneapolis businessmen Ben Berger and Morris Chalfen purchased the Detroit Gems and moved them to Minneapolis in 1947, the new team needed a new name. While a naming contest was under way, general manager Max Winter reportedly decided he wanted the basketball team to be called the "Minnesota Vikings." The radio station running the contest caught wind of Winter's preference and convinced him it would be bad for the team and his reputation if the contest seemed to be fraudulent.

On October 2, 1947, the *Minneapolis Times* reported the team would be the "Lakers," crediting Minneapolitan Ben Frank as the "first to enter the winning name." Frank was given a $100 savings bond. Winter's name, the "Vikings," found a team in 1960 when the National Football League granted the Twin Cities an expansion team.

Minnesota Timberwolves

ALTHOUGH the Twin Cities had been instrumental in the early success of the fledgling National Basketball Association (NBA) in the 1950s, Minnesota had no NBA team after the Minneapolis Lakers relocated to Los Angeles in 1960.

When the NBA announced in the mid-1980s that it wanted to expand, Minnesotans eagerly tried to lure it back. In October 1986, after preparing for more than a year, Marv Wolfenson and Harvey Ratner made their presentation to the NBA expansion committee. In early April 1987 the committee recommended that Minnesota be awarded a team, and on April 22, 1987, the league's Board of Governors voted unanimously to grant a franchise to Minnesota. Play would begin in the 1989–90 season.

On November 8, 1989, the NBA officially returned to Minneapolis after a 29-year absence. A crowd of 35,427 gathered at Minneapolis's Hubert H. Humphrey Metrodome and watched the Timberwolves lose to the Chicago Bulls, 96–84, in the regular-season opener. Michael Jordan scored 45 points for the Bulls.

On April 17, 1990, the third-largest crowd in NBA history—49,551— showed up at the Metrodome for Fan Appreciation Night. The crowd made the Timberwolves the league's all-time single-season attendance champions. The team's season total was 1,072,572—an average of 26,160 per game.

The next season, the Timberwolves moved into their new home—Target Center in downtown Minneapolis. On November 2, 1990, the team had its first regular-season contest in the arena, beating the Dallas Mavericks, 98–85, before a sellout crowd of 19,006.

By the end of their fifth season in Minnesota, it appeared the Timberwolves would move. During the 1993–94 season, team owners Marv Wolfenson and Harvey Ratner put the franchise up for sale and set a deadline of May 20, 1994, for a local buyer. When that deadline passed, a group from New Orleans offered $152.5 million for the franchise. The move was stopped when the NBA relocation committee rejected the group's offer. The team was eventually sold to Mankato businessman Glen Taylor for $88.5 million, a sale approved in October 1994.

In the first seven seasons in the league, the Timberwolves averaged just 20 victories per season and weathered four coaching changes. The franchise's fortunes started changing in 1995, when the team selected 19-year-old Kevin

Garnett in the first round of the NBA draft. The Timberwolves won 26 games in 1995–96, the most victories in five seasons.

The 1996–97 season saw a breakthrough for the Timberwolves. The team won 40 games and finished third in the Midwest Division to make the playoffs for the first time. It reached the playoffs in each of the next five seasons but never advanced past the first round.

In the 2003–04 season the Timberwolves won the Midwest Division and accomplished a first by winning a playoff series. The Timberwolves won two series to reach the Western Conference finals, where they lost to the Los Angeles Lakers.

Picked by many observers to contend for the NBA championship in 2004–05, the Timberwolves instead suffered through a disappointing season. After winning 13 of their first 19 games, the Timberwolves stumbled to just 12 victories in their next 32 games. On February 12, 2005, one day after a 100–82 loss in Utah dropped the team's record to 25–26, Flip Saunders was relieved of his coaching duties. Saunders had coached the team since early in the 1995–96 season. Kevin McHale took over as coach for the remainder of the season. The Timberwolves went 19–12 in their final 31 games but missed the playoffs for the first time in nine seasons. The Timberwolves were just the eighth team in NBA history to play in the conference finals one year and miss the playoffs entirely the next.

In June 2005 Dwane Casey was hired as the seventh head coach in the franchise's 16-season history. Casey spent the previous 11 seasons as an assistant with the Seattle Supersonics. Casey, who played college basketball at the University of Kentucky, started his coaching career as an assistant at Western Kentucky University and the University of Kentucky.

Timberwolves Year-by-Year

Season	Record	Playoffs	Coach
1989–90	22–60	None	Bill Musselman
1990–91	29–53	None	Musselman
1991–92	15–67	None	Jimmy Rodgers
1992–93	19–63	None	Rodgers (6–23), Sidney Lowe (13–40)
1993–94	20–62	None	Lowe
1994–95	21–61	None	Bill Blair
1995–96	26–56	None	Blair (6–14), Flip Saunders (20–42)
1996–97	40–42	0–3	Saunders
1997–98	45–37	2–3	Saunders
1998–99	25–25	1–3	Saunders

1999–2000	50–32	1–3	Saunders
2000–01	47–35	1–3	Saunders
2001–02	50–32	0–3	Saunders
2002–03	51–31	2–4	Saunders
2003–04	58–24	10–8	Saunders
2004–05	44–38	None	Saunders (25–26), McHale (19–12)

Timberwolves Coaching Records

Coach	Seasons	Record
Bill Musselman	2	51–113
Jimmy Rodgers	1+	21–90
Sidney Lowe	1+	33–102
Bill Blair	1+	27–75
Flip Saunders	9+	411–326
Kevin McHale	1	19–12

Timberwolves Players Records

Single game through 2004–05

Field goals made	19, by Wally Szczerbiak, vs. Chicago, Apr. 13, 2003, and by Kevin Garnett, vs. Phoenix, Jan. 4, 2005
Field goals attempted	33, by Kevin Garnett, vs. New Jersey, Feb. 20, 2000
Free throws made	18, by Christian Laettner, vs. Sacramento, Feb. 18, 1993
Free throws attempted	23, by Tony Campbell, vs. L.A. Clippers, Mar. 8, 1990
Three-point field goals made	8, by Stephon Marbury, vs. Seattle, Dec. 23, 1997
Three-point field goals attempted	14, by James Robinson, vs. Utah, Apr. 19, 1997
Points	47, by Garnett, vs. Phoenix, Jan. 4, 2005
Total rebounds	25, by Garnett twice, most recently vs. Orlando, Jan. 12, 2005
Offensive rebounds	11, by Felton Spencer, vs. L.A. Clippers, Dec. 11, 1990, and by Garnett, vs. Phoenix, Dec. 3, 2004
Defensive rebounds	23, by Garnett twice, most recently vs. Orlando, Jan. 12, 2005
Assists	17, most recently by Chauncey Billups, vs. Dallas, Mar. 25, 2002
Blocked shots	9, by Randy Breuer, vs. Orlando, Apr. 13, 1990, and by Rasho Nesterovic, vs. Dallas, Mar. 10, 2003
Turnovers	10, by Laettner, twice, most recently vs. Golden State, Feb. 27, 1994
Minutes played (regulation game)	48, most recently by Terrell Brandon, vs. Seattle, Dec. 23, 1999
Minutes played (overtime)	58, by Sam Mitchell, vs. Philadelphia, Feb. 3, 1991
Steals	8, by Tyrone Corbin, vs. Dallas, Mar. 30, 1990, and by Terrell Brandon, vs. New Jersey, Mar. 24, 2000

Season through 2004–05

Games played	82, most recently by Kevin Garnett and Trenton Hassell, 2004–05
Minutes played	3,321, by Garnett, 2002–03
Field goals made	804, by Garnett, 2003–04
Field goals attempted	1,611, by Garnett, 2003–04
Free throws made	464, by Tom Gugliotta, 1996–97
Free throws attempted	569, by Tony Campbell, 1989–90
Three-point field goals made	139, by Isaiah Rider, 1994–95
Three-point field goals attempted	396, by Rider, 1994–95
Points	1, 987, by Garnett, 2003–04
Total rebounds	1,139, by Garnett, 2003–04
Offensive rebounds	272, by Felton Spencer, 1990–91
Defensive rebounds	894, by Garnett, 2003–04
Assists	734, by Pooh Richardson, 1990–91
Blocked shots	178, by Garnett, 2003–04
Steals	175, by Tyrone Corbin, 1989–90
Turnovers	293, by Gugliotta, 1996–97
Fouls	338, by Sam Mitchell, 1990–91
Most disqualifications	14, by Spencer, 1990–91
Double-doubles	71, by Garnett, 2003–04
Triple-doubles	6, by Garnett, 2003–04

Career (through 2004–05)

Games played	775, by Garnett, 1995–2005
Minutes played	29,583, by Garnett, 1995–2005
Field goals made	6,311, by Garnett, 1995–2005
Field goals attempted	12,882, by Garnett, 1995–2005
Free throws made	2,915, by Garnett, 1995–2005
Free throws attempted	3,794, by Garnett, 1995–2005
Three-point field goals made	465, by Anthony Peeler, 1998–2003
Three-point field goals attempted	1,226, by Peeler, 1998–2003
Points	14,681, by Garnett, 1995–2005
Total rebounds	8,605, by Garnett, 1995–2005
Offensive rebounds	2,174, by Garnett, 1995–2005
Defensive rebounds	6,431, by Garnett, 1995–2005
Assists	3,525, by Garnett, 1995–2005
Blocked shots	1,343, by Garnett, 1995–2005
Steals	1,089, by Garnett, 1995–2005
Turnovers	2,002, by Garnett, 1995–2005

Fouls	1,965, by Garnett, 1995–2005
Most disqualifications	31, by Felton Spencer, 1990–93
Double-doubles	479, by Garnett, 1995–2005
Triple-doubles	16, by Garnett, 1995–2005

Timberwolves Streaks (going into 2004–05 season)

Longest winning streak	11, from Jan. 17 to Feb. 7, 2001
Longest home winning streak	17, from Jan. 8 to Mar. 2, 2003
Longest road winning streak	6, from Jan. 8 to Jan. 25, 2000, and from Dec. 3 to Dec. 23, 2003
Longest losing streak	16, from Feb. 29 to Mar. 29, 1992
Longest home losing streak	14, from Apr. 9 to Dec. 14, 1994
Longest road losing streak	22, from Dec. 9, 1989, to Mar. 23, 1990
Largest margin of victory	53, vs. Chicago, Nov. 8, 2001 (127–74)
Largest margin of victory on the road	31, at L.A. Clippers, Jan. 15, 2003 (95–64)
Largest margin of defeat	41, at Miami, Mar. 5, 1996 (113–72)
Largest margin of defeat at home	38, vs. Philadelphia, Nov. 25, 1994 (109–71)
Biggest comeback	25, vs. Charlotte, Mar. 1, 1996 (trailed 41–16, won 105–101)
Biggest lead squandered	22, vs. Dallas, Dec. 18, 2001 (led 80–58, lost 107–103)

Awards and Honors

NBA MVP

Kevin Garnett, 2003

All-NBA Team

Kevin Garnett*, 2000, 2003, 2004

*selected by media

NBA All-Rookie Team

Pooh Richardson, 1990
Christian Laettner, 1993
Isaiah Rider, 1994
Stephon Marbury, 1997
Wally Szczerbiak, 2000

NBA All-Stars

Tom Gugliotta, 1997
Kevin Garnett, 1997, 1998, 2000, 2001, 2002, 2003, 2004
Wally Szczerbiak, 2002
Sam Cassell, 2004

NOTE: No NBA All-Star game played in 1999

Timberwolves First-Round Draft Choices

Year	Name and school	Overall	Games with team
1989	Pooh Richardson, UCLA	10	246
1990	Felton Spencer, Louisville	6	213
1991	Luc Longley, New Mexico	7	170
1992	Christian Laettner, Duke	3	276
1993	J. R. Rider, UNLV	5	229
1994	Donyell Marshall, Connecticut	4	40
1995	Kevin Garnett, high school	5	775*
1996	Ray Allen, Connecticut	5	0
1997	Paul Grant, Wisconsin	20	4
1998	Rasho Nesterovic, none	17	316
1999	Wally Szczerbiak, Miami OH	6	398*
2000	None		
2001	None		
2002	None		
2003	Ndudi Ebi, high school	26	19*
2004	None		
2005	Rashad McCants, No.Car.	14	—

* Still with the team at the end of the 2004–05 season.

NOTE: The Timberwolves did not have a first-round selection in 2000 because of a three-way trade in January 1999, when they acquired Bobby Jackson and Dean Garrett. Because of a salary-cap violation, the Timberwolves forfeited their No. 1 draft pick for five consecutive seasons, 2001–05. Two of those first-round draft choices (2003 and 2005) were later reinstated.

Memorable Timberwolves Trades

February 22, 1996 Timberwolves acquired Andrew Lang and Spud Webb from Atlanta in exchange for Christian Laettner and Sean Rooks.

June 26, 1996 Acquired Connecticut guard Ray Allen with the fifth selection in the NBA draft. The Timberwolves immediately traded Allen and a future first-round draft pick to the Milwaukee Bucks for Georgia Tech guard Stephon Marbury, who had been selected by the Bucks with the fourth pick. Marbury was a starter for the Timberwolves before being traded to New Jersey in March 1999.

July 23, 1996 Acquired James Robinson, Bill Curley and a first-round draft pick in 1997 from Portland in exchange for J. R. Rider.

March 11, 1999 Acquired Terrell Brandon from the Milwaukee Bucks and Brian Evans and future considerations from the New Jersey Nets in a three-team trade. Sent Stephon Marbury, Chris Carr and Bill Curley to the Nets and Paul Grant to the Bucks.

June 27, 2003 Acquired Sam Cassell and Ervin Johnson from Milwaukee in exchange for Joe Smith and Anthony Peeler.

July 23, 2003 Acquired Latrell Sprewell from the New York Knicks in a four-team trade. Sent Terrell Brandon to Atlanta and Marc Jackson to Philadelphia.

Kevin Garnett

The Minnesota Timberwolves averaged 61 losses per season in their first six seasons in the NBA. In the spring of 1995, several key moves were made by new franchise owner Glen Taylor, who officially took over the team on March 23, 1995. He promoted Kevin McHale to executive vice president and Flip Saunders to general manager. Three months later, McHale and Saunders made the most important decision in the history of the franchise.

At the NBA's annual draft in June, the Timberwolves were scheduled to select fifth. Most experts agreed that the top five players available for the draft were Maryland forward Joe Smith, North Carolina guard Jerry Stackhouse, Alabama forward Antonio McDyess, North Carolina forward Rasheed Wallace and a high school senior from Chicago named Kevin Garnett. McHale and Saunders decided that Garnett's potential outweighed the risks of drafting the 6-foot-11 nineteen year old.

Garnett, who had been South Carolina's Mr. Basketball as a high school junior and Illinois's Mr. Basketball as a high school senior, was the first player in more 20 years to go directly from high school to the NBA. Twenty games into his rookie season, Garnett moved into the Timberwolves' starting lineup. As a rookie, he averaged 10.4 points and 6.3 rebounds per game. In his second season, Garnett averaged 17 points per game and helped the Timberwolves make the playoffs for the first time.

In October 1997 the 21-year-old Garnett signed a six-year contract with the Timberwolves worth $125 million. On October 1, 2003, Garnett signed a five-year contract extension with the Timberwolves worth $100 million.

During the 2003–04 season, Garnett became the first player in 29 years (fifth in league history) to lead the league in points scored and rebounding in the same season. Garnett was named the league's MVP following the season. Going into the 2004–05 season, Garnett and Larry Bird were the only players in league history to average at least 20 points, 10 rebounds and 5 assists per game for five consecutive seasons.

In his first nine seasons in the league, Garnett was a seven-time all-star and a three-time All-NBA player.

Malik Sealy

The Timberwolves signed Malik Sealy as a free agent on January 22, 1999, just prior to the league's shortened 1998–99 season that began on February 5.

In 33 games with the Wolves during 1998–99, he averaged 8.1 points per game. The next season, Sealy, a 6-foot-8 guard-forward who had played collegiately at St. John's (N.Y.), started 61 games for the Timberwolves and averaged 11.3 points and 4.3 rebounds per game.

In the early morning hours on May 20, 2000, Sealy was killed in an auto accident on Highway 100 in St. Louis Park. He was on his way home after a birthday party for teammate Kevin Garnett.

Sealy's No. 2 jersey is the only one to have been retired by the Timberwolves.

Joe Smith

Joe Smith, a 6-foot-10 forward from Maryland, was the first player selected in the 1995 draft (by the Golden State Warriors). He was signed by the Timberwolves as a free agent prior to the 1998–99 season. That contract would turn out to be very costly for the franchise. Smith's agent negotiated a multi-year contract with team owner Glen Taylor that violated the league's collective bargaining agreement. In October 2000, just days before the 2000–01 season opened, the league learned of the secret deal and imposed severe penalties on the team.

On October 25, 2000, the NBA commissioner handed out the following sanctions: Smith's contract with the Timberwolves for the 2000–01 season was voided, the franchise was fined $3.5 million for the violation, and the team was ordered to forfeit its first-round draft picks for the next five years. Two of those first-round draft choices (2003 and 2005) were later reinstated.

Smith, who had averaged 13.7 points and 9.9 points per game, respectively, in his two seasons with the Timberwolves, signed with the Detroit Pistons for 2000–01. On July 30, 2001, Smith was re-signed by the Wolves, and he spent the next two seasons with the team before being traded to Milwaukee on July 23, 2003.

In 247 games with the Timberwolves, Smith averaged 10.3 points per game.

NBA Work Stoppages

There have been three lockouts in NBA history, but only one has involved a work stoppage.

The league imposed its first lockout on July 1, 1995. That lasted until August 8, when players agreed to a new contract.

The second lockout lasted just a few hours on July 11, 1996.

The third lockout was significant. In March 1998, NBA owners voted to re-open negotiations on the contract, which was set to expire following the 2000–01 season. On July 1, 1998, the league imposed a lockout. It lasted until January 1999 and threatened the cancellation of the 1998–99 season. On January 6, 1999—one day before the league's deadline for canceling the entire season—the players association and the league reached an agreement on a new contract. The 1998–99 season, which was shortened to 50 games, began on February 5, 1999. The lockout lasted 191 days.

What's It Worth?

On April 22, 1987, the NBA's Board of Governors awarded an expansion franchise—to begin play in 1989–90—to Minnesota businessmen Marv Wolfenson and Harvey Ratner. The fee for the expansion franchise was $32.5 million.

In May 1994 Wolfenson and Ratner announced they had agreed to sell the franchise to a group from New Orleans for $152.5 million. The sale was not approved by the league's Board of Governors, however, and on October 5, 1994, the league approved the sale of the franchise to Mankato businessman Glen Taylor for $88.5 million.

In December 2004, *Forbes Magazine* estimated the value of the Timberwolves franchise as $291 million.

Minneapolis Lakers

In 1946 young newspaper reporter Sid Hartman helped convince Minneapolis businessman Ben Berger that the area could support a professional basketball team. After that conversation, Berger agreed to sponsor an exhibition game between two teams from the National Basketball League. On December 1, 1946, a crowd of 5,500 gathered at the Minneapolis Auditorium to watch Oshkosh defeat Sheboygan, 56–42.

Satisfied that Minneapolis was ready for a professional basketball team, a group of investors began looking for a team to buy. Hartman and the group focused on the lowly Detroit Gems of the National Basketball League. The Gems won just four of 44 games (just one of their final 28 games) during the 1946–47 season, and the team's owner decided to cut his losses (one home game was played in front of six fans).

During the summer of 1947, the Minneapolis group purchased the Gems for $15,000. Because of the Gems' dismal record, the Minneapolis group was guaranteed the first selection in the league's draft.

Again the group did its homework and set its sights on one player—George Mikan, who was playing for the Chicago American Gears. The Gears had won the National Basketball League in 1947 but joined the new Pro Basketball League of America for the 1947–48 season. The league folded just two weeks into its first season, making Mikan available to be drafted by the Lakers.

DID YOU KNOW ?

For three years, Fort Wayne Pistons coach Murray Mendenhall had been trying to figure out a way to stop the Lakers' George Mikan. On November 22, 1950, Mendenhall came up with a solution. Before a crowd of 7,021 at the Minneapolis Auditorium, Mendenhall ordered his team to stall. Holding the ball for as much as three minutes at a time, the Pistons finally defeated the Lakers, 19–18, in the lowest-scoring game in NBA history.

The game eventually spurred the league to institute a "shot clock" to prevent teams from stalling. Before the 1954–55 season, the league introduced a 24-second shot clock.

On November 19, 1947, only 18 days after the Lakers had played their first game, Mikan signed a contract and joined the team. The Lakers started slowly with Mikan in the lineup but went on to win the league title in their first season.

Following the season, the Lakers and three other teams (Rochester, Indianapolis and Fort Wayne) left the National Basketball League and joined the Basketball Association of America. In the first season in the BAA (1948–49), the Lakers won the title. Following that season, the league renamed itself the National Basketball Association. The Lakers would earn another title in the 1949–50 season—their third consecutive (in three different leagues).

Minneapolis Lakers, including Hall of Famers Vern Mikkelsen, Jim Pollard (All-NBA), Slater Martin, Bud Grant, and George Mikan (All-NBA), 1950

The Lakers did not reach the finals of the NBA playoffs in 1951, but starting in 1952, they won three more consecutive titles.

On April 13, 1954, one day after the Lakers had defeated the Syracuse Nationals for their sixth league title in seven seasons, more than 400 people gathered at a luncheon at the Nicollet Hotel to honor the team. The *Minneapolis Tribune* reported NBA President Maurice Podoloff's remarks to the crowd: "One can only deal with superlatives in discussing this team. I will say that it is the greatest team in the history of basketball and deserves a place not earned by a team in any type of athletics. The Lakers have been the greatest contributing factor to the success of the NBA. Names of the players are a household word all over the nation. The record of the Minneapolis Lakers—winning six world titles in seven years—will remain unchallenged for years to come."

While the team was enjoying success on the court, financial problems were building. The Lakers were unable to call one arena "home." They shuttled their games among facilities—the Minneapolis Auditorium, the Minneapolis Armory and the St. Paul Auditorium. In the late 1950s, as financial problems grew more serious, the team frequently took a back seat to conventions and

expositions at the Minneapolis Auditorium. In 1960 Bob Short, who had purchased the team in 1957, announced he was going to move the team because
of his inability to solve the franchise's arena problems. On April 27, 1960,
the league's board of governors voted to allow Short to move the franchise
to Los Angeles.

Minneapolis Lakers playing Boston, 1954

Minneapolis Tribune columnist Dick Cullum was sympathetic to Short: "We must face the fact that the Lakers did not have a fair chance here. They were denied suitable facilities. It has been nobody's fault, only a case of the town lacking suitable facilities. On a comparison of facilities alone, the move is justified."

Minneapolis Lakers Year-by-Year

Season	Record	Playoffs	Coach
1947–48 (NBL)	43–17	8–2*	Kundla
1948–49 (BAA)	44–16	8–2*	Kundla
1949–50 (NBA)	51–17	10–2*	Kundla
1950–51 (NBA)	44–24	3–4	Kundla
1951–52 (NBA)	40–26	9–4*	Kundla
1952–53 (NBA)	48–22	9–3*	Kundla
1953–54 (NBA)	46–26	9–4*	Kundla
1954–55 (NBA)	40–32	3–4	Kundla
1955–56 (NBA)	33–39	1–2	Kundla
1956–57 (NBA)	34–38	2–3	Kundla
1957–58 (NBA)	19–53	—	Mikan (9–30), Kundla (10–23)
1958–59 (NBA)	33–39	6–7	Kundla
1959–60 (NBA)	25–50	6–6	Castellani (11–25), Pollard (14–25)

*League champions

Minneapolis Lakers Records

NOTE: Assists did not become an official statistic until the 1948–49 season; rebounds, 1950–51 season; minutes, 1951–52 season; and steals and blocks, 1973–74 season.

Single-game

Points: 64 by Elgin Baylor, vs. Boston, Nov. 8, 1959; 61 by George Mikan, vs. Rochester, Jan. 20, 1952

Season

Games played: 75 by Jim Krebs, 1959–60
Points: 2,074 by Baylor, 1959–60
Rebounds: 1,150 by Baylor, 1959–60

Career

Games played: 699 by Vern Mikkelsen
Games disqualified (fouled out): 127* by Mikkelsen.
Points: 11,351 by Mikan; 10,063 by Mikkelsen; 6,522 by Jim Pollard

*An NBA record. Mikkelsen led the league in games fouled out three consecutive times: 17 in 1955–56, 18 in 1956–57 and 20 in 1957–58.

League Leaders

George Mikan   scoring, 1949, 1950 and 1951; rebounding, 1953; and personal fouls, 1950, 1951 and 1952

Slater Martin   minutes played, 1956

Vern Mikkelsen   most personal fouls, 1955, 1956 and 1957

Awards and Honors

In 1959 the Lakers' Elgin Baylor won the Rookie of the Year award (begun in 1953). The NBA's Coach of the Year award began in 1963, too late for the Minneapolis Lakers' John Kundla. No Lakers won the NBA's Most Valued Player award (begun in 1956).

All-Star Players

Vern Mikkelsen   1951, 1952, 1953, 1955, 1956 and 1957
Slater Martin   1953, 1954, 1955 and 1956
George Mikan   1951, 1952, 1953 and 1954
Jim Pollard   1951, 1952, 1954 and 1955
Elgin Baylor   1959 and 1960

All-NBA

George Mikan   1949, 1950, 1951, 1952, 1953 and 1954
Jim Pollard   1949 and 1950
Elgin Baylor   1959 and 1960

Minneapolis Lakers First-Round Draft Choices

1947 none; **1948** Arnie Ferrin, Utah; **1949** Vern Mikkelsen, Hamline; **1950** Kevin O'Shea, Notre Dame; **1951** Whitey Skoog, Minnesota; **1952** Clyde Lovellette, Kansas; **1953** Jim Fritsche, Hamline; **1954** Ed Kalafat, Minnesota; **1955** Dick Garmaker, Minnesota; **1956** Jim Paxson, Dayton; **1957** Jim Krebs, SMU; **1958** Elgin Baylor, Seattle*; **1959** Tom Hawkins, Notre Dame

*first overall pick

George Mikan

When George Mikan was a 12-year-old growing up in Joliet, Illinois, he needed glasses. Two years later as a freshman at Joliet Catholic High School, he was cut from the basketball team because school officials thought he couldn't play basketball while wearing glasses. After high school, he wanted to play basketball for Notre Dame, but Notre Dame Coach George Keogan, a Minnesota native, wasn't interested because he was too awkward—and wore glasses.

The 6-foot-10 Mikan enrolled at DePaul, where he met a young coach named Ray Meyer. Under Meyer's patient direction, Mikan blossomed into a tremendous basketball player. Mikan was a three-time All-American for the Blue Demons, and in 1946, he was named the national player of the year.

Slater Martin, Laker guard and Basketball Hall of Famer

Mikan began his professional career in 1946 with the Chicago Gears of the National Basketball League. As a rookie, he helped lead the Gears to a league title. In late 1947, the Gears folded, making Mikan available.

In November 1947, Mikan reached a contract agreement with the Minneapolis Lakers. The Lakers and Mikan would become professional basketball's first "dynasty." The Lakers won six league titles in their first seven seasons with Mikan.

Mikan, who led the league in scoring six consecutive seasons, retired as a player following the Lakers' championship in 1954. He returned to play 37 games in the 1955–56 season.

In 1951 he was named the "Greatest Player of the First Half-Century" by the Associated Press, and in 1959 he was elected to the Naismith Memorial Basketball Hall of Fame.

In 1970 he was named to the NBA's 25th anniversary team. In 1980 he was named to the NBA's 35th anniversary team, and in 1996 he was named one of the top 50 players in NBA history.

In 1984 Governor Rudy Perpich formed a task force to see if an NBA team could succeed in the Twin Cities—with Mikan in the lead. Two years later, the NBA awarded an expansion franchise to a Minnesota group.

In retirement, Mikan campaigned to improve pension benefits for the NBA players who retired before 1965, the year a pension plan had been put in place. Mikan died on June 1, 2005, in Scottsdale, Arizona. He was 80.

Lakers and Globetrotters

In the early 1950s, the two best professional basketball teams were the Minneapolis Lakers and the Harlem Globetrotters. In a four-year span between 1948 and 1952, the two teams met seven times.

The first meeting came on February 19, 1948. The Lakers, in their first season in Minneapolis, were en route to the National Basketball League championship. The Globetrotters had a 103-game winning streak going into the game. A Chicago Stadium crowd of 17,823 watched the Globetrotters edge the Lakers, 61–59, on a shot at the buzzer by Ermer Robinson. George Mikan had scored 24 for the Lakers.

A year later, a crowd of 20,046 showed at Chicago Stadium to watch the Globetrotters defeat the Lakers, 49–45. Goose Tatum scored 14 for the Globetrotters while Mikan had 19 for the Lakers. Two weeks later, on March 14, 1949, the teams met in Minneapolis. A crowd of 10,122—a record for the Minneapolis Auditorium—watched Mikan score 32 points to lead the Lakers to a 68–53 victory.

On February 21, 1950, the Lakers evened the series, 2–2, when Mikan scored 36 to lead the Lakers to a 76–60 victory over the Globetrotters before a crowd of 21,666 at Chicago Stadium. A month later, on March 20, the teams met in St. Paul. Mikan scored 21 and Vern Mikkelsen scored 18, to lead the Lakers to a 69–54 victory over the Globetrotters before 9,807 at the St. Paul Auditorium. The loss was just the second (both to the Lakers) in 141 games for the Globetrotters.

On February 23, 1951, Mikan scored 47 to lead the Lakers to a 72–68 victory over the Globetrotters before 16,963 at Chicago Stadium. The loss ended a 116-game winning streak for the Globetrotters. On January 2, 1952, Mikan and Mikkelsen each scored 25 to lead the Lakers to a 84–60 victory over the Globetrotters before 20,004 at Chicago Stadium.

The teams met just one more time, six years later. On January 3, 1958, the Lakers defeated the Globetrotters, 111–100 at Chicago Stadium.

DID YOU KNOW ?

The Harlem Globetrotters are owned by a Minnesotan. In August 1992, Mannie Jackson, a senior vice president for then Minneapolis-based Honeywell, purchased the Globetrotters. Jackson, the first African American to own a major sports franchise, was born in Missouri and played for the Globetrotters in the early 1960s after playing college basketball at the University of Illinois.

Lakers and Royals Rivalry

In the six seasons between 1949 and 1954, the biggest rivalry in the NBA was between the Minneapolis Lakers and the Rochester Royals. During the six seasons, the Lakers won 273 regular-season games while the Royals won 266. The Royals finished ahead of the Lakers in the standings twice.

The Lakers, however, won 38 of the 66 meetings (including playoffs) between the teams. The Lakers' advantage was their front line—6-foot-10 George Mikan, 6-foot-7 Vern Mikkelsen and 6-foot-5 Jim Pollard.

The Lakers, despite winning just seven more regular-season games than the Royals, won five league titles during that time. The Royals won one title in 1951.

Lakers' Final Season in Minnesota

The 1959–60 season, the Minneapolis Lakers' 13th and final season, almost ended prematurely. On Sunday afternoon, January 17, 1960, the Lakers played in St. Louis, where they lost to the Hawks, 135–119. Following the game, the Lakers headed to Lambert Field in St. Louis for their charter flight back to Minneapolis. When the Lakers got to the airport, an ice storm had grounded flights. At 8:30 P.M., the Lakers' DC-3, a converted World War II cargo plane, was able to take off for the flight home. Shortly after takeoff, the plane's generators failed, and the plane lost its electrical system and radio. Pilot Vern Ullman tried to climb above a snowstorm to navigate by the stars. After five hours in the air, and with no idea of how much fuel the plane had left, Ullman finally landed the plane in a cornfield near Carroll, Iowa. None of the 23 on board was injured.

Lakers Pricetag

In the summer of 1947, a Minneapolis group headed by Ben Berger purchased the Detroit Gems for $15,000 and relocated the basketball franchise to the Twin Cities. In February 1957 Berger sold the team to a local group of 100 investors. After the sale, Bob Short became the president of the franchise.

In April 1960 Short announced he was moving the franchise to Los Angeles. Shortly after the move, Short sold it to Jack Kent Cooke for $5 million. Jerry Buss eventually purchased the team for $60 million. In December 2004 *Forbes Magazine* estimated the value of the Lakers franchise as $510 million.

All-Star Games

The NBA began holding an in-season All-Star game in 1951. The Minneapolis Lakers never hosted the game.

The Minnesota Timberwolves have hosted the All-Star game once—on February 13, 1994. The East All-Stars, coached by Lenny Wilkens, defeated the West All-Stars, coached by George Karl, 127–118. Scottie Pippen of the Chicago Bulls was named the game MVP. He scored 29 points for the East.

Other Professional Basketball

Seven years after the Lakers left Minnesota for Los Angeles, professional basketball returned to the state. But it wasn't the NBA, which had only 10 teams in the mid-1960s. In February 1967 a rival 10-team league, the new American Basketball Association, selected former Lakers great George Mikan as its commissioner and awarded a franchise to Minnesota. The franchise, known as the Minnesota Muskies, cost $30,000.

On October 22, 1967, nine days after the Oakland Oaks and Anaheim Amigos played the first game in league history, the Muskies made their debut. The Muskies lost to the Kentucky Colonels, 104–96, before 8,104 at Met Center in Bloomington. Led by Mel Daniels, who would earn the league's rookie of the year award, the Muskies closed out the regular season with a 104–101 victory over New Orleans before 4,229 at Met Center. The victory gave the Muskies a 50–28 record, good for second place in the Eastern Division.

In the playoffs, the Muskies defeated the Colonels in the first round of the playoffs before being defeated by the Pittsburgh Pipers in the Eastern Division finals. The Pipers, who would go on to win the league title, closed out the series on April 14 with a 114–105 victory over the Muskies in Pittsburgh.

A month later, the franchise's owners, citing low attendance (the Muskies had averaged about 2,500 fans per game) and losses of $400,000, announced they would move the team to Miami.

DID YOU KNOW ?

In 1967 the Minnesota Muskies drafted a tall player out the University of North Dakota, but the player, Phil Jackson, signed with the New York Knicks of the NBA. He eventually embarked on a successful coaching career.

In 1968 the Muskies signed University of Minnesota product Lou Hudson, who was playing with the Atlanta Hawks of the NBA. A court ruled the contract "invalid," saying the Muskies did not have "clean hands" in dealing with Hudson, who remained with the Hawks.

Minnesota Pipers

After the Muskies left, the Twin Cities was without pro basketball for only one month. On June 24, 1968, William J. Erickson purchased a majority interest in the Pittsburgh Pipers and announced he would move the team to Minnesota. The team—which had just won the league title and claimed one of the

Minnesota Muskies game, 1967

league's best players, Connie Hawkins—had lost $250,000 in its first season in Pittsburgh. Owner Gabe Rubin sold 85 percent of the team to Erickson.

Erickson named former Minneapolis Lakers great Vern Mikkelsen as the team's general manager and Jim Harding as coach. The Pipers opened the 1968–69 season at home against the team they had replaced in Minnesota. On October 27, 1968, the Pipers defeated the Miami Floridians (formerly the Muskies), 126–94, before only 1,943 at Met Center. It was a stormy season, however, and Harding was fired as coach after getting into a fight with Rubin at the league's all-star game in Louisville on January 28, 1969.

Connie Hawkins was brilliant when healthy, but played in only 47 games because of a knee injury. On November 27, he scored 57 points in the Pipers' 110–101 victory over the New York Nets in New York. Eight days later, he scored 53 in a 119–108 loss to Denver.

The Pipers tried to increase interest in the team regionally by playing eight "home" games in Duluth but never generated much fan support. In November only 652 watched the Pipers lose to Denver, 126–121, in Duluth. On January 12 only 878 showed up at Met Center to see the Pipers defeat the Dallas Stars. The largest home crowd of the season was 7,162 on December 10, when the Pipers defeated the Floridians, 112–105, at Met Center.

For their final home game on April 15, 1969, only 1,345 showed up to see the Pipers defeat the Floridians, 105–100, in a playoff game. Four days later, the Pipers' season came to end after a 137–128 loss in Miami. Shortly after the season, which saw the team lose $400,000, the team announced it would move back to Pittsburgh.

DID YOU KNOW ?

Minnesota has had several franchises in "minor" professional basketball leagues. Rochester had two stints in the Continental Basketball Association (1987–89 and 1992–94), while Fargo-Moorhead also had a stint in the league (1992–94).

When the International Basketball Association formed in 1995, Fargo-Moorhead and St. Cloud fielded teams. After one season, the St. Cloud team moved to St. Paul. After two seasons there, the team moved again—to Rochester.

In 2001 the CBA folded. Teams from the IBA and several CBA teams formed a new CBA. Fargo-Moorhead fielded a team in the merged league.

First and Last Games
Minneapolis Lakers

First game	Nov. 1, 1947	Lakers 49, Oshkosh 47
Last home game	Mar. 24, 1960	St. Louis 117, Lakers 96
Last game	Mar. 26, 1960	St. Louis 97, Lakers 86

Minnesota Muskies

First game	Oct. 22, 1967	Kentucky 104, Muskies 96
Last home game	Apr. 13, 1968	Pittsburgh 117, Muskies 98
Last game	Apr. 14, 1968	Pittsburgh 114, Muskies 105

Minnesota Pipers

First game	Oct. 27, 1968	Pipers 126, Miami 94
Last home game	Apr. 15, 1969	Pipers 105, Miami 100
Last game	Apr. 19, 1969	Miami 137, Pipers 128

St. Paul Lights

In late 1950 the Twin Cities briefly claimed two professional basketball teams. As the Minneapolis Lakers were beginning their fourth season, a St. Paul team called the Lights began its first season in the eight-team National Professional Basketball League. The league was made up of teams primarily in the Midwest that had been in the former National Basketball League and did not go on to join the National Basketball Association.

The Lights were owned by Dick Headley and coached by Howie Schultz, who had played basketball at Hamline before playing professional baseball and basketball. The Lights' first game was November 1, 1950, when they defeated Louisville, 60–48, in St. Paul.

On November 17, 1950, the Lights issued a press release challenging the Minneapolis Lakers to a game or series of games. In the release, Headley, who was also the team's president and general manager, said, "We the management feel that our boys are capable of playing any other team in the country." Minneapolis Lakers general manager Max Winter told the *Minneapolis Tribune* that his team had "received no challenge" and therefore, had "no comment."

Less than two weeks later, rumors about the Lights' financial problems surfaced. On December 5, the *Minneapolis Tribune* mentioned the Lights were using a pro wrestling match on the same program to attract more fans. Ten days later, the National Basketball Association announced that it had rejected a franchise application from the Lights. On December 19, the Lights defeated Waterloo, 76–70, before a crowd of 972 at the St. Paul Auditorium. The victory, which improved the Lights' record to 12–8, was their last. Two days later, Headley told the *Minneapolis Tribune* that the club had decided to quit after losing $40,000. "We were forced out of basketball by a combination of factors," Headley said. "We dropped a bundle of cash, but if we could have seen something bright in the future we would have stayed in business. But with the (Korean) war conditions, we couldn't see any sense of continuing."

Three other league teams—Kansas City, Louisville and Grand Rapids—disbanded during the season. A Denver team relocated to Evansville during the season.

Stan Miasek, who started the season with the Lights, finished the season with Louisville and was named to the All-League team. Wally Osterkorn, a rookie out of Illinois, joined Sheboygan after the Lights folded and was named second team All-League. Three other players—Gene Berce, former Hamline star Hal Haskins and Joe Nelson—caught on with other NPBL teams after the Lights folded. St. Paul also had a pro team in 1947.

DID YOU KNOW ?

Susan King Borchardt, who played high school basketball at Academy of Holy Angels in Richfield, was the Ms. Basketball winner for Minnesota in 2000. She and her husband, Curtis Borchardt, are the first husband and wife pair to play in the WNBA and NBA. She played briefly for the Lynx in 2005 while her husband played for the Utah Jazz. They met at Stanford.

Women's Professional Basketball—Lynx

Major women's professional basketball returned to the Twin Cities in 1999 under vastly improved circumstances. The Women's National Basketball Association (WNBA), which was backed by the owners of the NBA, debuted in 1998. The WNBA, which played its season during the summer, announced it would expand for its second season and awarded a franchise to Minnesota.

On June 12, 1999, the Minnesota Lynx made its regular-season debut with a 68–51 victory over the Detroit Shock before 12,122 at Target Center.

The Lynx—with one of the league's top players, Katie Smith—reached the playoffs in 2003, its fourth season. On July 13, 2005, Smith became the first American woman to score 5,000 points in her professional career. Smith, 31, an Ohio State graduate, scored 11 points in Minnesota's 71–61 victory over Detroit. The 11 points left her with exactly 5,000 points in her nine-season professional career.

Katie Smith, Minnesota Lynx guard and Olympic gold medalist, 2004

On July 30, 2005, the Lynx traded Smith, who held 19 franchise records, to the Detroit Shock. In exchange for Smith and a second-round draft choice, the Lynx acquired Chandi Jones, Stacey Thomas and Detroit's first-round draft pick in 2006.

Lynx Year-by-Year

Season	Record	Playoffs	Coach
1999	15–17		Brian Agler
2000	15–17		Agler
2001	12–20		Agler
2002	10–22		Agler (6–13), Heidi VanDerveer (4–9)
2003	18–16	1–2	Suzie McConnell Serio
2004	18–16	0–2	McConnell Serio
2005	14–20		McConnell Serio

Lynx Records through 2004 Season

Single game

Field goals made	3, by Katie Smith, at Detroit, Jun. 17, 2001
Field goals attempted	23, three times, most recently by Svetlana Abrosimova, Jul. 30, 2001
Free throws made	18, by Smith, at Los Angeles, Jul. 8, 2001 (OT)
Free throws attempted	19, by Smith, at Los Angeles, Jul. 8, 2001 (OT)
Three-point field goals made	7, by Smith, at Seattle, Jun. 14, 2003
Three-point field goals attempted	13, by Smith, at Los Angeles, Jun. 3, 2000
Points	46, by Smith, at Los Angeles, Jul. 8, 2001 (OT)
Total rebounds	15, by Abrosimova, vs. Sacramento, Aug. 5, 2001 (OT)
Offensive rebounds	10, by Tamika Williams, at Phoenix, Jun. 23, 2003
Defensive rebounds	13, by Abrosimova, vs. Sacramento, Aug. 5, 2001
Assists	11, by Andrea Lloyd Curry, at Charlotte, Jul. 21, 1999
Blocked shots	5, by Janell Burse, at Indiana, Jul. 26, 2003
Turnovers	11, by Betty Lennox, at Houston, Aug. 9, 2000
Steals	6, most recently by Teresa Edwards, vs. Sacramento, Jul. 8, 2003
Minutes played (regulation game)	40, most recently by Smith, Aug. 9, 2003
Minutes played (overtime)	49, by Sonja Tate, vs. Los Angeles, Jul. 1, 1999 (2OT)

Season

Minutes played	1,234, by Katie Smith, 2001
Field goals made	208, by Smith, 2001
Field goals attempted	519, by Smith, 2001
Free throws made	246, by Smith, 2001
Free throws attempted	275, by Smith, 2001
Three-point field goals made	88, by Smith, 2000

Three-point field goals attempted	240, by Smith, 2001
Points	739, by Smith, 2001
Total rebounds	229, by Tamika Williams, 2002
Offensive rebounds	96, by Williams, 2002
Defensive rebounds	133, by Williams, 2002
Assists	148, by Teresa Edwards, 2003
Blocked shots	45, by Nicole Ohlde, 2004
Steals	53, by Betty Lennox, 2000
Turnovers	97, by Lennox, 2000
Fouls	112, by Lennox (2000) and Smith (2003)
Most disqualifications	6, by Tonya Edwards, 1999

Career

Games	182, by Katie Smith
Minutes played	6,521, by Smith, 1999–2004
Field goals made	1,027, by Smith, 1999–2004
Field goals attempted	2,467, by Smith, 1999–2004
Free throws made	820, by Smith, 1999–2004
Free throws attempted	949, by Smith, 1999–2004
Three-point field goals made	425, by Smith, 1999–2004
Three-point field goals attempted	1,135, by Smith, 1999–2004
Points	3,299, by Smith, 1999–2004
Total rebounds	643, by Tamika Williams, 2002–04
Offensive rebounds	270, by Williams, 2002–04
Defensive rebounds	426, by Smith, 1999–2004
Assists	435, by Smith, 1999–2004
Blocked shots	58, by Vanessa Hayden, 2004–05
Steals	166, by Smith, 1999–2004
Turnovers	406, by Smith, 1999–2004
Fouls	533, by Smith, 1999–2004

Lynx Awards

WNBA Rookie of the Year	Betty Lennox, 2000
WNBA Coach of the Year	Suzie McConnell Serio, 2004
First-team All-WNBA	Katie Smith, 2001, 2003

Lynx First-Round Draft Choices

1999 Tonya Edwards; **2000** Grace Daley, Betty Lennox; **2001** Svetlana Abrosimova; **2002** Tamika Williams; **2003** none; **2004** Nicole Ohlde, Vanessa Hayden; **2005** Kristen Mann; **2006** Seimone Augustus

Minnesota Fillies player Brenda Chapman and Iowa Cornets player Joan Uhl during Fillies debut game, Met Center, 1978

Fillies

Through the 1970s women could play professional basketball in Europe but not in the United States. That changed in 1978, when the U.S. Women's Professional Basketball League (WBL) formed. The WBL was the brainchild of Bill Byrne, who had been involved with the creation of the World Football League. Byrne thought that the WBL would take advantage of the new interest in college basketball, international basketball and the upcoming 1980 Summer Olympic games.

A Minnesota franchise was one of the league's original eight franchises. Other areas to pay the $50,000 franchise fee were Iowa, New Jersey, Milwaukee, Chicago, Dayton, New York and Houston.

The Minnesota team, owned by a group of investors led by Gordon Nevers, played its first game on December 15, 1978. The Fillies lost their debut to the Iowa Cornets, 103–81, before a crowd of 4,102 at the Met Center.

The Fillies team, which included Trish Roberts, a member of the 1976 U.S. Women's Olympic team and captain of the 1977 U.S. national team, compiled a respectable 17–17 record in their first season. In their second season, the Fillies earned a 22–12 record and reached the semifinals of the league's playoffs.

Their third season, 1980–81, proved to be a nightmare for the Fillies and the league. The league had failed to receive any promotional benefit from the 1980 Olympics because the United States boycotted the games held in Moscow. The Fillies were plagued by severe financial problems and low attendance while winning just seven of 35 games. The league folded following the season.

The Fillies had played at Met Center in Bloomington during the 1978–79 and 1979–80 seasons. The 1980 playoffs were at the University of Minnesota's Williams Arena. During the 1980–81 season, the team played at the Minneapolis Auditorium.

Fillies Year-by-Year

Season	Record	Playoffs
1978–79	17–17	
1979–80	22–12	3–3 (defeated New Orleans, 2–1; lost to Iowa, 2–1)
1980–81	7–28	

Coaches

1978–79   Dee Hopfenspirger (resigned before season started), Julia Yeater, Lou Mascari, Gordon Nevers, Trish Roberts
1979–80   Terry Kunze
1980–81   Kunze, Mark DeLapp

Minnesota Stars

Women's professional basketball briefly returned to the Twin Cities in 1995, when the Indiana Stars franchise of the Women's Basketball Association, a league founded in 1993, relocated to Minnesota. The Minnesota Stars lasted one season, and the league folded following the 1995 season. Former University of Minnesota standout Molly Tadich was the Stars' top player.

Gophers men's basketball team, 1903

College Basketball

In 1891, Dr. James Naismith, the director of the YMCA in Springfield, Massa-chusetts, needed a winter activity to fill the void between the football and baseball seasons. His invented game—basketball—quickly spread to Minne-sota, when Max Exner, Naismith's former roommate, introduced the sport to students at Carleton College in Northfield.

On February 8, 1895, the University of Minnesota Agricultural School and Hamline College played Minnesota's first intercollegiate basketball game. The Agricultural School won the game, played at the Minneapolis YMCA, 9–3. Two years later—on March 13, 1897—the University of Minnesota played its first game against an outside team, defeating a YMCA team, 11–5.

The Gopher men's team, under the direction of Dr. L. J. Cooke, was one of the top teams in the country during the first 25 years of the 20th century. The Gophers were named national champions by the Helms Foundation follow-ing unbeaten seasons in 1901–02 and 1918–19. In 1928 the Gophers began playing their games in their new fieldhouse—now called Williams Arena.

During the mid-20th century, another Twin Cities college basketball team gained major attention. Hamline's team, coached by Joe Hutton Sr., won three national small-college championships in a 10-year span—in 1942, 1949 and 1951. Hutton, born in Minneapolis in 1899 and a graduate of Excelsior High School, coached the Pipers for 35 seasons before retiring after the 1964–65 season.

Hutton had lettered four years in basketball at Carleton and coached high school basketball for five years before taking over as athletic director and coach at Hamline in 1931. During his tenure there, the Pipers compiled a 591–208 record and won 19 conference championships. Hutton coached future professional basketball players Hal Haskins, Vern Mikkelsen, Howie Schultz and Rollie Seltz.

While federal legislation—known as Title IX—was passed in 1972 to force greatly expanded college athletic opportunities for women, Mary Willerscheidt had already been doing that for the women of Mankato State College (now Minnesota State University–Mankato) since 1966, when Mankato State decided to field an intercollegiate basketball team for women. After searching for a coach, Mankato found a candidate on campus: Willerscheidt, who was a graduate assistant in the physical education department.

In Willerscheidt's early years of coaching, only a few other schools in the state claimed women's basketball teams: St. Olaf, Carleton and the University of Minnesota. Willerscheidt guided the program into the modern era, coaching the program from 1966 to 1985. She compiled a 246–158 record and won three state championships—in 1972, 1973 and 1975—before retiring from coaching in 1985. She continued to teach until 1998.

University of Minnesota Basketball Gophers—Men

Seasons Winning 20 Games

In the 109 seasons since first playing in 1896, the Gophers have won at least 20 games on 12 occasions.

Season	Coach	Record
1972–73	Bill Musselman	21–5
1976–77*	Jim Dutcher	24–3
1979–80	Dutcher	21–11
1981–82	Dutcher	23–6
1989–90	Clem Haskins	23–9
1992–93	Haskins	22–10

1993–94**	Haskins	21–12
1994–95**	Haskins	20–10
1995–96**	Haskins	20–12
1996–97**	Haskins	31–4
1997–98**	Haskins	20–15
2004–05	Dan Monson	21–11

NOTE: The NCAA ordered that some Gophers records be recalculated because of ineligible student-athlete participation, in violation of NCAA rules.

* The NCAA declared all games from the 1976–77 season forfeited because of an ineligible player. The Big Ten Conference lists the Gophers' record as 0–27 that season. The Gophers' only losses were to Purdue (in overtime) and twice to Michigan. On December 12, 1976, the Gophers defeated Marquette, 66–59, in Milwaukee; Marquette went on to win the 1977 NCAA title. The Gophers' starting five that season included Kevin McHale, Ray Williams, Mychal Thompson, Osborne Lockhart and Flip Saunders.

**records vacated

DID YOU KNOW ?

As part of a year-long series in 1999 on Minnesota sports history, the *Minneapolis Star Tribune* named this all-time Gophers men's basketball team: Dick Garmaker, Lou Hudson, Ron Johnson, Kevin McHale and Mychal Thompson.

Gophers Coaching Records Since 1897

Coach	Seasons	Overall	Big Ten
L. J. Cooke	27	244–135	103–100
Dave MacMillan	18	196–157	114–106
Jim Dutcher	11	190–113	98–89
Ozzie Cowles	11	147–93	86–68
Clem Haskins*	13	111–100	48–78
John Kundla	9	110–105	67–59
Dan Monson	6	100–86	39–57
Bill Musselman	4	65–32	38–22
Bill Fitch	2	25–23	13–15
Harold Taylor	3	19–30	12–24
Carl Nordly	2	17–23	7–17

George Hanson	1	11–13	5–9
Weston Mitchell	1	8–13	4–8
Jimmy Williams	1	2–9	2–9

*The NCAA ordered the Gophers' won-lost records for six seasons (1993–99) vacated. If included, Haskins's record was 240–165 overall and 108–122 in the Big Ten.

Gophers Men's Players Records

Single game (through 2004–05 season)

Field goals made	18, by Ron Johnson, at Ohio State, Jan. 31, 1959
Field goals attempted	42, by Ollie Shannon, vs. Wisconsin, Mar. 6, 1971
Free throws made	17, by Larry Mikan, vs. Purdue, Jan. 25, 1969
Free throws attempted	20, by Tony Jaros (vs. Wisconsin, Mar. 3, 1946) and Mikan (vs. Purdue, Jan. 25, 1969)
Three-point field goals made	7, most recently by Terrance Simmons, vs. Michigan State, Feb. 10, 2001
Three-point field goals attempted	13, by Simmons, vs. Tulsa, Mar. 19, 2002
Points	42, by Shannon (vs. Wisconsin, Mar. 6, 1971) and Eric Magdanz (at Michigan, Mar. 5, 1962)
Rebounds	28, by Mikan, vs. Michigan, Mar. 3, 1970
Assists*	16, by Arriel McDonald, vs. Wisconsin, Jan. 12, 1994
Blocked shots	12, by Mychal Thompson, vs. Ohio State, Jan. 26, 1976
Steals	9, by Melvin Newbern, vs. Rider, Jan. 3, 1990

Season (through 2004–05 season)

Field goals made	264, by Mychal Thompson, 1975–76
Field goals attempted	531, by Tom Kondla, 1966–67
Free throws made	187, by Kris Humphries, 2003–04
Free throws attempted	251, by Dick Garmaker, 1953–54
Three-point field goals made	71, by Michael Bauer, 2002–03
Three-point field goals attempted	190, by Bauer, 2002–03
Points	647, by Thompson, 1975–76
Rebounds	349, by Larry Mikan, 1969–70
Assists*	179, by Arriel McDonald, 1993–94
Blocked shots	87, by Randy Breuer, 1982–83
Steals	101, by Melvin Newbern, 1988–89
Double-doubles	21, by Thompson, 1975–76

Career (through the 2004–05 season)

Games played	130, by Sam Jacobson, 1995–98
Field goals made	823, by Mychal Thompson, 1975–78

Gopher Jim Brewer (#52) playing Ohio State, 1972

Field goals attempted	1,635, by Chuck Mencel, 1952–55
Free throws made	426, by Willie Burton, 1987–90
Free throws attempted	569, by Burton (1987–90) and Randy Breuer (1980–83)
Three-point field goals made	191, by Michael Bauer, 2000–04
Three-point field goals attempted	535, by Bauer, 2000–04
Points	1,992, by Thompson, 1975–78

(NOTE: Voshon Lenard scored 2,103 points in 127 games for the Gophers; the NCAA officially recognized 1,097 points in 74 games).

Rebounds	956, by Thompson
Assists*	547, by Arriel McDonald, 1991–94
Blocked shots	235, by Kevin McHale, 1977–80
Steals	215, by Melvin Newbern, 1988–90

*Assists became an official statistic during 1974–75 season.

Margins

Largest margin of victory: 68, vs. Rider, Jan. 3, 1990 (116–48)
Largest margin of defeat: 46, at No. 10 Indiana, Jan. 9, 1992 (96–50)

Streaks

Longest winning streak: 34, from Feb. 9, 1901, to Jan. 23, 1904
Longest losing streak: 17, from Jan. 10, 1987, to Nov. 29, 1987

Gophers Awards

First-team All-Americans

George Tuck (1905), Garfield Brown (1906), Frank Lawler (1911), Francis Stadsvold (1917), Harold Gillen (1918), Erling Platou (1919), Arnold Oss (1919, 1921), Martin Rolek (1937, 1938), Jim McIntyre (1948, 1949), Whitey Skoog (1950, 1951), Dick Garmaker (1955), Chuck Mencel (1955), Ron Johnson (1960), Lou Hudson (1965), Tom Kondla (1967), Jim Brewer (1973), Ron Behagen (1973), Roy Williams (1977), Mychal Thompson (1977, 1978) and Trent Tucker (1982)

First-team All-Big Ten

Jim McIntyre (1948, 1949), Whitey Skoog (1950, 1951), Chuck Mencel (1953, 1955), Dick Garmaker (1954, 1955), George Kline (1957, 1958), Ron Johnson (1959, 1960), Lou Hudson (1965), Archie Clark (1966), Tom Kondla (1967), Clyde Turner (1972), Ron Behagen (1973), Jim Brewer (1973), Mychal Thompson (1976, 1977, 1978), Kevin McHale (1980), Darryl Mitchell (1982), Randy Breuer (1982, 1983), Tommy Davis (1985), Willie Burton (1990), Quincy Lewis (1999), Rick Rickert (2003), and Kris Humphries (2004)

Retired Gophers Basketball Numbers

14   Lou Hudson
43   Mychal Thompson
44   Kevin McHale
52   Jim Brewer

Gophers in the Postseason

In March 1936 the Gophers appeared in the postseason for the first time when they played in the district Olympic tournament. They were competing for the right to enter the U.S. Olympic trials, to be held in New York in April.

The Gophers opened the postseason with a 36–19 victory over Drake. The team then advanced to the district finals, where they would play a best-of-three series against DePaul in Chicago. DePaul defeated the Gophers, 36–30, on March 26 and 33–27 on March 27 to win the series. The Blue Demons had defeated the Gophers, 48–17, during the regular season three months earlier.

The NCAA held its first men's basketball championship in 1939. The Gophers made their first appearance in the NCAA tournament in 1970. Since then, the Gophers have appeared in the NCAA tournament seven other times, although the Gophers games in the 1994, 1995, 1997 and 1999 NCAA tournaments were ordered vacated by the NCAA due to an ineligible student-athlete. The NCAA does not recognize the Gophers appearance in the 1997 Final Four.

The NCAA has vacated the appearance of several other teams in the Final Four—St. Joseph's (1961), Villanova and Western Kentucky (1971), and UCLA (1980).

The Gophers have also appeared in the National Invitation Tournament (NIT) 11 times—reaching the NIT Final Four (in New York) four times. The team played in the championship game three times—1980, 1993 and 1998—and the third-place game in 2003. The Gophers won the championship in 1993 and 1998. The NCAA vacated the Gophers' records in the 1996 and 1998 NIT tournaments.

Gophers in the NCAA

Year	Record	Results
1972*	1–1	lost to Florida State, 70–56; defeated Marquette, 77–72, in regional consolation game
1982	1–1	defeated Tenn.-Chattanooga, 62–61; lost to Louisville, 67–61

1989	2–1	defeated Kansas State, 86–75; defeated Siena, 80–67; lost to Duke, 87–70
1990	3–1	defeated UTEP, 67–61 (OT); defeated Northern Iowa, 81–78; defeated Syracuse, 82–75; lost to Georgia Tech, 93–91
1994*	1–1	defeated Southern Illinois, 74–60; lost to Louisville, 60–55
1995*	0–1	lost to St. Louis, 64–61 (OT)
1997*	4–1	defeated SW Texas St., 78–46; defeated Temple, 78–67; defeated Clemson, 90–84 (2OT); defeated UCLA, 80–72; lost to Kentucky, 78–69
1999*	0–1	lost to Gonzaga, 75–63
2005	0–1	lost to Iowa State, 64–53

*records vacated

Gophers in the NIT

Year	Record	Results
1973	1–1	defeated Rutgers, 68–59; lost to Alabama, 69–65
1980	4–1	defeated Bowling Green, 64–50; defeated Mississippi, 58–56; defeated SW Louisiana, 94–73; defeated Illinois, 65–63; lost to Virginia, 58–55
1981	2–1	defeated Duke, 90–77; defeated Connecticut, 84–66; lost to West Virginia, 80–69
1983	0–1	lost to DePaul, 76–73
1992	0–1	lost to Washington St., 72–70
1993	5–0	defeated Florida, 74–66; defeated Oklahoma, 86–72; defeated USC, 76–58; defeated Providence, 76–70; defeated Georgetown, 62–61
1996*	1–1	defeated St. Louis, 68–52; lost to Tulane, 84–65
1998*	5–0	defeated Colorado State, 77–65; defeated Ala.-Birmingham, 79–66; defeated Marquette, 73–71; defeated Fresno State, 91–89 (OT); defeated Penn State, 79–72
2001	1–1	defeated Villanova, 87–78; lost to Tulsa, 76–73 (OT)
2002	1–1	defeated New Mexico, 96–62; lost to Richmond, 67–66
2003	3–2	defeated St. Louis, 62–52; defeated Hawaii, 84–70; defeated Temple, 63–58 (OT); lost to Georgetown, 88–74; lost to Texas Tech, 71–61

*records vacated

Gophers in the NBA Draft

The number of Gophers selected in the annual NBA totals 54. Eighteen were first-round selections:

Whitey Skoog (Minneapolis Lakers, 1951), Ed Kalafat (Minneapolis, 1951), Dick Garmaker (Minneapolis, 1955), Lou Hudson (St. Louis, 1966), Jim Brewer (Cleveland, 1973), Ron Behagen (Kansas City–Omaha, 1973), Ray Williams (New York, 1977), Mychal Thompson* (Portland, 1978), Kevin

McHale (Boston, 1980), Trent Tucker (New York, 1982), Randy Breuer (Milwaukee, 1983), Willie Burton (Miami, 1990), Bobby Jackson (Seattle, 1997), John Thomas (New York, 1997), Sam Jacobson (Los Angeles Lakers, 1998), Quincy Lewis (Utah, 1999), Joel Przybilla (Houston, 2000), and Kris Humphries (Utah, 2004).

*Thompson is the only Gopher to be the first player selected overall. Brewer was the second player selected, McHale was the third and Hudson was the fourth.

Gophers in the ABA Draft

Nine Gophers were selected in the annual ABA draft. Two were first-round selections:

Jim Brewer (New York, 1973) and Mark Olberding (San Antonio, 1975).

Gophers three-sport star Dave Winfield was a supplementary draft pick of the Utah Stars in the 1973 ABA draft. Winfield was selected by four teams in three sports in 1973: the Minnesota Vikings (NFL, 17th round), Atlanta Hawks (NBA, 5th round), and the San Diego Padres (major league baseball, 1st round).

Hall of Fame

Three members of the Naismith Memorial Basketball Hall of Fame in Springfield, Massachusetts, were born in Minnesota. John Kundla and Vern Mikkelsen are also members.

George Keogan was inducted as a coach in 1961. Born in Minnesota Lake in 1890, he graduated from Detroit Lakes High School in 1909 and started his coaching career at Lockport (Ill.) High School in 1910. Over the next 13 years, Keogan had nine coaching jobs—including one season (1915–16) at St. Thomas College.

In 1923 Keogan was named the Notre Dame head baseball and basketball coach and an assistant football coach (to Knute Rockne). Over the next 20 years, Keogan directed the Irish basketball team to a 327–96 record. The Irish were named the Helms Foundation National Champions in 1927 and 1936. The Irish did not have a losing season under Keogan.

In 28 seasons as a college basketball coach, Keogan had a 412–124 record. In seven seasons as Notre Dame's baseball coach, he had a 68–57 record.

Keogan died on February 17, 1943, at age 53, two days after the Irish had defeated Canisius, 55–37, to improve to 12–1.

Cliff Fagan was inducted as a contributor in 1984. Born in Mankato in 1911, he graduated from high school in Wisconsin in 1928. A basketball official for 16 years, he then served for 10 years as the executive secretary of the Wisconsin Interscholastic Athletic Association. He joined the National Federation of High School Athletic Associations and served as the organization's executive director from 1959 to 1977. He also served as the president of the Basketball Hall of Fame from 1963 to 1969. He was on the U.S. Olympic Committee's board of directors for 15 years.

Kevin McHale was inducted as a player in 1999. Born in Hibbing in 1957, he was a member of two Hibbing teams that played in the boys state basketball tournament. In 1976 Hibbing lost to Bloomington Jefferson in the Class AA championship game.

DID YOU KNOW ❓

In a span of nine days in 1967, the Gophers basketball team played No. 1 UCLA and No. 2 Houston. On December 18, the Gophers lost to Houston, 103–65, which was led by future NBA great Elvin Hayes. On December 27, Lew Alcindor, who later changed his name to Kareem Abdul-Jabbar, scored 28 points and grabbed 15 rebounds to lead UCLA to a 95–55 victory over the Gophers in Los Angeles. Three weeks later, UCLA and Houston played in front of 52,693 fans at the Astrodome in Houston. Houston won the game to end UCLA's 47-game winning streak. The loss was the only one of the season for the Bruins, who went on to win the NCAA championship that season—their second of seven consecutive titles.

The 6-foot-10 McHale went on to be a four-year starter for the University of Minnesota. Following his Gophers career, he was selected by the Boston Celtics in the first round of the 1980 NBA draft. McHale was the third player selected in the draft (behind Purdue's Joe Barry Carroll and Louisville's Darrell Griffith).

In his 13-year career with the Celtics, McHale was a seven-time all-star who played on three NBA championship teams (1981, 1984 and 1986). McHale retired following the 1992–93 season. In 1996 McHale was named one of the 50 Greatest Players in NBA History.

Gophers Coach John Wooden?

Legendary Hall of Fame coach John Wooden almost became the Gophers basketball coach in 1948. The University of Minnesota sought a basketball coach after Dave McMillan had resigned following 18 seasons as coach. At the same time, Wooden, who had just finished his second year coaching at Indiana State, was looking for a new job. Both Minnesota and UCLA were interested in Wooden.

Both schools were looking for an answer from Wooden. Both were to call him—an hour apart—but Minnesota didn't call. Wooden accepted UCLA's offer to become the Bruins' coach, and shortly after, Minnesota called to offer Wooden the job. Wooden told Jim Souhan of the *Minneapolis Star Tribune* years later, "I had accepted UCLA's offer and I couldn't break my word. They said a snowstorm had downed the wires. Otherwise, I would have been there for the 1948–49 season."

Over the next 27 seasons, Wooden coached the Bruins to 10 national championships and a 620–147 record. In the same span, the Gophers had five coaches.

Bob Knight

In 1970 Bill Fitch resigned after two seasons as the Gophers basketball coach to accept a position with the expansion Cleveland Cavaliers of the NBA. According to *Minneapolis Tribune* columnist Sid Hartman, one person interviewed to replace Fitch was a young coach named Bob Knight. Knight, who was 30, had just completed his fifth season as the head coach at Army. The University of Minnesota eventually promoted assistant coach George Hanson to replace Fitch, but after just one season, Hanson resigned, and in 1971 the university was looking for a coach again. Hartman said he called Knight to see if he would be interested in coaching, but Knight had committed to the job at Indiana. Minnesota eventually hired Bill Musselman, who lasted four seasons at the university, while Knight won three national titles and 11 Big Ten titles in 29 seasons at Indiana. Knight, currently the coach at Texas Tech, has won 854 games in 39 seasons as a Division I coach.

Gophers Academic Scandal

On March 10, 1999, the *St. Paul Pioneer Press* published a five-page report alleging a widespread academic scandal in the University of Minnesota men's basketball program. The report ran one day before the Gophers were scheduled to play Gonzaga in the first round of the NCAA Division Tournament in Seattle. The story had an immediate impact. Four current Gophers—including two starters—were named in the report. On March 11, the University of Minnesota administration suspended the four players for the game against Gonzaga.The Gophers lost to Gonzaga, 75–63.

Three months later, the school bought out coach Clem Haskins's contract for $1.5 million. In July 1999, Dan Monson, who had coached Gonzaga to the victory over the Gophers, was named the Gophers' new coach.

In November, University of Minnesota President Mark Yudof announced that the school's internal investigation showed the allegations were true. In October 2000, the NCAA placed the Gophers basketball program on probation for four years.

Among the sanctions was the order to remove the championship banner for the Big Ten title in 1997 and to vacate all records for six seasons (1993–99).

The *St. Paul Pioneer Press* won a Pulitzer Prize for its reporting.

Minneapolis and NCAA Men's Finals

Minneapolis has been the site of the NCAA men's championship games on three occasions—1951, 1992 and 2001.

On March 27, 1951, Kentucky, coached by Adolph Rupp, defeated Kansas State, 68–58, before 15,348 at Williams Arena. Kentucky's Bill Spivey had 22 points and 21 rebounds and received the Outstanding Player Award.

On April 6, 1992, Duke, coached by Mike Krzyzewski, defeated Michigan, 71–51, before 50,379 at the Metrodome. Duke's Bobby Hurley, who had nine points and seven assists in the championship game, was named the Outstanding Player of the Final Four.

On April 4, 2001, Duke, coached by Krzyzewski, defeated Arizona, 82–72, before, 45,994 at the Metrodome. Duke's Shane Battier had 18 points and 11 rebounds in the championship game and was named the Outstanding Player. Arizona was coached by Lute Olson, who graduated from Augsburg College in Minneapolis and coached high school basketball in Minnesota for five years before moving to college coaching.

Williams Arena Honors

Eight former University of Minnesota basketball players (four men and four women) are honored with banners hanging from the rafters of Williams Arena: Jim Brewer, Lou Hudson, Kevin McHale, Mychal Thompson, Laura

Coenen, Carol Ann Shudlick, Lindsey Whalen and Linda Roberts. Former announcer Ray Christensen has also been honored with a banner.

University of Minnesota Basketball Gophers— Women

Gopher women first formed a women's basketball association in 1897. Three years later, on February 24, 1900, the University of Minnesota women's varsity played its first game against an outside opponent, Stanley Hall, which was a Minneapolis female prep school. The university won, 12–6. Over the next eight seasons, the university's women's team was one of the top teams in the country—winning 36 of 37 games in one stretch.

Despite this success, women's varsity basketball at the university quickly disappeared in the early years of the 20th century. The last official intercollegiate game for women took place on April 24, 1908. It would be 60 years before intercollegiate basketball for women reappeared on campus.

DID YOU KNOW ?

Between 1985 and 2001, the Gophers women's basketball team compiled a 58–200 record (.224 winning percentage) in Big Ten Conference games. Since 2001, the Gophers have a 55–25 record (.687 winning percentage) in Big Ten games.

Coaching records (1977 through 2004–05)

Coach	Seasons	Overall	Big Ten
Ellen Mosher Hanson	10	172–125	52–38
Pam Borton	3	76–23	33–15
Linda Hill-MacDonald	7	66–126	32–88
Cheryl Littlejohn	4	29–81	7–57
LaRue Fields	3	24–60	12–42
Brenda Oldfield	1	22–8	11–5

20-Victory Seasons

1977–78	24–10, coached by Ellen Mosher Hanson
1980–81	28–7, coached by Mosher Hanson
1982–83	20–7, coached by Mosher Hanson
2001–02	22–8, coached by Brenda Oldfield
2002–03	25–6, coached by Pam Borton
2003–04	25–9, coached by Borton
2004–05	26–8, coached by Borton

Gophers Women's Players Records

Top ten scorers (through 2004–05 season)

Lindsay Whalen	2,285
Carol Ann Shudlick	2,097
Laura Coenen	2,044
Linda Roberts	1,856
Janel McCarville	1,835
Molly Tadich	1,706
Carol Peterka	1,441
Deb Hunter	1,363
Marty Dahlen	1,345
Ellen Kramer	1,336

Single game (through 2004–05)

Field goals made	18, by Carol Ann Shudlick, vs. Texas Tech, Dec. 18, 1993
Field goals attempted	33, by Shudlick, vs. Marquette, Dec. 21, 1991
Free throws made	21, by Linda Roberts, vs. Rhode Island, Dec. 1, 1979
Free throws attempted	25, by Roberts, vs. Rhode Island, Dec. 1, 1979
Three-point field goals made	9, by Stacy Carver, vs. Boise State, Dec. 20, 1992
Three-point field goals attempted	17, by Carver, vs. Boise State, Dec. 20, 1992; by Jodi Olson, vs. Iowa, Feb. 12, 1988
Points	44, by Shudlick, vs. Marquette (Dec. 21, 1991) and vs. Texas Tech (Dec. 18, 1993)
Rebounds	25, by Angie Iverson, vs. Colorado State, Dec. 3, 1996
Assists	15, by Deb Hunter, vs. Illinois, Mar. 12, 1983
Steals	12, by Hunter, vs. Northwestern, Jan. 31, 1981
Blocked shots	8, by Mary Manderfeld, vs. Northwestern, Jan. 31, 1981

Season (through 2004–05)

Field goals made	275, by Laura Coenen, 1984–85
Field goals attempted	542, by Carol Ann Shudlick, 1993–94

Lindsay Whalen, Gophers top scorer and All-American

Free throws made	158, by Coenen, 1984–85
Free throws attempted	209, by Coenen, 1984–85
Three-point field goals made	73, by Lindsay Lieser, 2001–02, and Shannon Schonrock, 2004–05
Three-point field goals attempted	209, by Cassie Vanderheyden, 1999–2000
Points	708, by Coenen, 1984–85
Total rebounds	387, by Linda Roberts, 1977–78
Assists	241, by Deb Hunter, 1980–81
Steals	139, by Hunter, 1980–81
Blocked shots	65, by Janel McCarville, 2003–04
Double-doubles	17, by McCarville, 2003–04

DID YOU KNOW ❓

St. John's coach Jim Smith is the winningest basketball coach in state history. The 2005–06 season was Smith's 42nd as the Johnnies coach. Smith has a 650–455 career record.

Career (through 2004–05)

Games played	129, by Linda Roberts, 1977–81
Field goals made	854, by Carol Ann Shudlick, 1990–94
Field goals attempted	1,682, by Shudlick, 1990–94
Free throws made	557, by Lindsay Whalen, 2000–04
Free throws attempted	850, by Roberts, 1977–81
Three-point field goals made	216, by Lindsay Lieser, 1999–2003
Three-point field goals attempted	567, by Lieser, 1999–2003
Points	2,285, by Whalen, 2000–04
Total rebounds	1,413, by Roberts, 1977–81
Assists	632, by Deb Hunter, 1979–83
Steals	413, by Hunter, 1979–83
Blocked shots	200, by Janel McCarville, 2001–05
Double-doubles	49, by McCarville, 2001–05

Awards and Honors

Wade Trophy

The Wade Trophy is given annually to the top player in women's college basketball. Only one Gophers player has won the award.

Carol Ann Shudlick   1994

All-Americans

Lindsay Whalen	2002, 2003, 2004
Carol Ann Shudlick	1993, 1994
Laura Coenen	1982, 1985
Janel McCarville	2004, 2005
Deb Hunter	1982
Linda Roberts	1981
Laura Gardner	1979
Elsie Ohm	1978

First-Team All-Big Ten

Lindsay Whalen	2002, 2003, 2004
Janel McCarville	2003, 2004, 2005
Carol Ann Shudlick	1993, 1994
Laura Coenen	1983, 1985
Deb Hunter	1983

Retired Gopher Women's Basketball Numbers

13	Lindsay Whalen
42	Carol Ann Shudlick
44	Laura Coenen

Gopher Women in the Postseason

The NCAA began offering a women's basketball tournament in 1982, but the Gophers appeared in postseason play five times before that year. In 1978 and 1979, the team played in the Women's NIT tournament in Amarillo, Texas. In 1977, 1981 and 1982, the Gophers played in the AIAW national tournament. The Gophers reached the NCAA tournament for the first time in 1994 and made four consecutive appearances in 2002, 2003, 2004, and 2005.

Gopher Women in the NCAA

Year	Record	Results
1994	1–1	Defeated Notre Dame, 81–76; lost to Vanderbilt, 98–72
2002	1–1	Defeated UNLV, 71–54; lost to North Carolina, 72–69
2003	2–1	Defeated Tulane, 68–48; defeated Stanford, 68–56; lost to Texas, 73–60
2004	4–1	Defeated UCLA, 92–81; defeated Kansas State, 80–61; defeated Boston College, 76–63; defeated Duke, 82–75; lost to Connecticut, 67–58
2005	2–1	Defeated St. Francis (Pa.) 64–33; defeated Virginia, 73–58; lost to Baylor, 64–57

Gopher Women in the Big Ten

The Gophers did not officially join the Big Ten Conference in women's basketball until the 1982–83 season, although the team first played Big Ten opponents during the 1974–75 season. The Gophers have won one Big Ten title—the "unofficial" title in 1981.

DID YOU KNOW ?

St. Thomas coach Steve Fritz has been involved in more than 1,000 consecutive Tommies basketball games over the past 39 years. Fritz spent four seasons as a player and nine seasons as an assistant coach with the Tommies before becoming the Tommies' head coach in 1980. In 25 seasons, Fritz has a 464–228 record.

McCarville Top Draft Choice

Janel McCarville made University of Minnesota and Big Ten Conference history in April 2005 when the Charlotte Sting selected her with the first choice in the WNBA draft. McCarville, the seventh Big Ten Conference player selected in the first round of the WNBA draft, replaced her former teammate, Lindsay Whalen, as the highest draft pick in conference history. Whalen was selected with the fourth overall pick in the 2004 WNBA draft by Connecticut.

McCarville, the only player in school history to play in four NCAA tournaments, finished her Gophers career as the only player to rank in the top five in school history in the five major statistical categories: points (5th, 1,835), rebounds (2nd, 1,217), assists (5th, 310), blocks (1st, 200) and steals (3rd, 274).

McCarville became the second player in Minnesota history to be selected as the No. 1 pick overall in any professional sport. In 1978 the Portland Trail Blazers selected Mychal Thompson with the first pick in the NBA draft.

Women's Final Four

Minneapolis was the host to the 1995 NCAA Women's Final Four. Playing were Connecticut, Georgia, Stanford and Tennessee. On April 2, Connecticut

Hamline vs. Macalester College, 1942

defeated Tennessee, 70–64, to win the national championship before 18,038 at the Target Center. The Gophers hosted the AIAW tourney in 1977.

College Basketball—Other Conferences

MIAC Men's Basketball

The Minnesota Intercollegiate Athletic Conference (MIAC) was formed in 1920. St. Thomas has won the most men's conference titles (20), followed by Hamline (19), Gustavus Adolphus (16), Augsburg (13), St. John's (7), University of Minnesota–Duluth* (4), St. Olaf (3), Concordia (Moorhead) (3), Carleton (3), Macalester (2) and St. Mary's (2).

Gustavus has made the most appearances (12) in the NCAA Division III men's playoffs, followed by St. John's (7) and St. Thomas (6).

*no longer a member of the conference.

MIAC Leading Scorers—Men

St. John's Frank Wachlarowicz is the MIAC's all-time men's leading scorer. Wachlarowicz, who helped Little Falls to the 1975 Class AA state high school championship, scored 2,357 points in four seasons with the Johnnies (1975–79).

Devean George scored 2,258 points in his four-year Augsburg career (1995–99). George, who played for Benilde–St. Margaret's High School in St. Louis Park, was the Los Angeles Lakers' first-round draft choice in the 1999 draft.

DID YOU KNOW ?

The Amateur Athletic Union (AAU) conducted its first national basketball tournament in 1897. The tournament shifted around for a few years before moving to Kansas City, Missouri, in 1921. Between 1921 and 1968, only one team from Minnesota reached the quarterfinals (final eight) of the tournament. In 1923, the Two Harbors All-Stars lost in the semifinals of the popular tournament before taking third place.

MIAC Women's Basketball

St. Thomas has won the most conference titles (10) since 1981, followed by St. Benedict (7), Concordia (Moorhead) (6), Carleton (3), St. Mary's (2), and St. Olaf and Gustavus Adolphus (1).

St. Thomas has made the most appearances (16) in the NCAA Division III playoffs, followed by Concordia (14) and St. Benedict (13).

Concordia and St. Thomas have won NCAA Division III championships in 1988 and 1991, respectively.

Concordia reached the NCAA Division III championship game in 1987, as did St. Benedict in 1999. St. Benedict coach Mike Durbin has a 428–89 record in 19 seasons as the Blazers' coach through the 2004–05 season.

The all-time leading scorer in MIAC women's history is Laurie Trow, who scored 1,804 points in four seasons for St. Thomas (1989–93). Trow (now Laurie Kelly) is the head coach of the Northern Arizona women's program.

Crowd watching basketball game at the Minneapolis Auditorium, 1941

Northern Sun Intercollegiate Conference

The conference was formed in 1932 as the Northern Intercollegiate Conference. St. Cloud State has won the most men's conference basketball championships (17), followed by University of Minnesota–Duluth (15), Mankato State (13), Northern State (10), Winona State (9), Bemidji State (9), Moorhead State (4), University of Minnesota–Morris (3), Michigan Tech (2), Wayne State (1) and Southwest State (1).

St. Cloud State, Mankato State, Minnesota–Duluth, Minnesota–Morris and Michigan Tech are no longer members of the conference.

North Central Conference

St. Cloud State has won four North Central Conference men's basketball titles: 1986, 1987, 1988 and 2003. Mankato State won the 1976 title.

Hockey

Minnesota Wild

MINNESOTA'S professional hockey team, the Minnesota Wild, has been at home in the state since 2000. This reflects a successful and timely local effort to secure a National Hockey League (NHL) team to replace the Minnesota North Stars, the team moved by owner Norm Green to Dallas in 1993 after more than two dozen years in the state.

Initially, Minnesota's efforts centered on acquiring an existing franchise, and over the next four years, several franchises—Edmonton, Winnipeg and Hartford—entertained the idea of moving to the Twin Cities. In November 1996, after being spurned by Edmonton and Winnipeg, a Minnesota group formally applied for an NHL expansion franchise. In June 1997 the NHL Board of Governors approved Robert Naegele Jr.'s investment group for an expansion team, to begin play in the 2000–01 season.

On October 11, 2000, after a 7½-year absence, the NHL officially returned to the Twin Cities when the Minnesota Wild hosted the Philadelphia Flyers before a crowd of 18,827 at the Xcel Energy Center in downtown St. Paul. The teams played to a 3–3 tie.

The Wild quickly developed into a solid hockey team. In its third season (2002–03), the Wild qualified for the playoffs. This was only the third time since 1970 that an NHL team had reached the playoffs in its third season. The Wild, with the lowest payroll in the league, advanced to the Western Conference finals.

In their fourth season, the Wild missed the playoffs by eight points.

The entire 2004–05 season was not played because of a labor dispute after the league locked out the players. This was the second work stoppage in the NHL in 10 years. On July 13, 2005, the NHL and the players' association reached an agreement to end the lockout.

When the Wild and the NHL returned to the ice in October 2005, the fans returned to the Xcel Energy Center. The Wild has sold out every home game, including the preseason, in its history.

Wild Year-by-Year

Season	Record	Points	Playoffs	Coach
2000–01	25–39–13–5	68	None	Jacques Lemaire
2001–02	26–35–12–9	73	None	Lemaire
2002–03	42–29–10–1	95	Conf. finals	Lemaire
2003–04	30–29–20–3	83	None	Lemaire

North Stars playing the Los Angeles Kings, 1967

Minnesota North Stars

For 25 seasons—from 1942 to 1967—the National Hockey League main-
tained the same six franchises. With the 1967–68 season, the NHL doubled
in size with six more franchises. One of these was the Minnesota North
Stars, a team that would call Bloomington's Met Center home for the next
26 seasons.

The North Stars' first season was marred by tragedy when 29-year-old
rookie Bill Masterton died from head injuries suffered in a game on January

13, 1968. Masterton was the first player to die from game injuries in the 51-year history of the league. Following the 1967–68 season, the NHL established an award named after Masterton and given annually to the player who most fits the description "unsung hero."

The North Stars reached the Stanley Cup finals twice—in 1981 and 1991. Financial difficulties, however, began developing in the late 1980s. In 1990 the league blocked attempts by the team's owners to move the franchise. The franchise was eventually sold to Norm Green, a Canadian real-estate developer.

The success of reaching the 1991 Stanley Cup finals was short-lived. In 1992 the North Stars failed to advance past the first round of the playoffs. In October 1992, Green signed 22-year-old center Mike Modano to a four-year, $6.75 million contract—the fifth-richest agreement in league history at that point. Shortly after Modano signed the new contract, Green started emphasizing his team's financial problems.

DID YOU KNOW ?

In 1999, in its year-long series on sports in the *Minneapolis Star Tribune*, Al Shaver, the Minnesota North Stars' radio announcer from 1967 until 1993, named this all-time North Stars team: goalie, Gilles Meloche; defense, Craig Hartsburg, Ted Harris; left wing, J. P. Parise; center, Neal Broten; right wing, Bill Goldsworthy.

After Green's proposal to remodel Metropolitan Sports Center in Bloomington was turned down and after he heard bids from arenas in downtown Minneapolis and St. Paul, Green announced on March 10, 1993 (with a month remaining in the regular season) that he would be moving the team to Dallas. On April 13, 1993, the North Stars played their final home game, a 3–2 loss to the Chicago Blackhawks. The North Stars closed out the season with two road games and missed the playoffs by one point. Ironically, their 36–36–10 record and 82 points were their best marks in 10 seasons.

The North Stars, renamed simply the Stars, flourished in Dallas. They won the Stanley Cup in 1999 and reached the finals in 2000. Led by Modano, the team finished first in their division six times in a seven-year span.

North Stars Year-by-Year

Season	Record	Points	Playoffs	Coach
1967–68	27–32–15	69	Semifinals	Wren Blair
1968–69	18–43–15	51	None	Blair, John Muckler
1969–70	19–35–22	60	Quarterfinals	Blair, Charlie Burns
1970–71	28–34–16	72	Semifinals	Jack Gordon
1971–72	37–29–12	86	Quarterfinals	Gordon
1972–73	37–30–11	85	Quarterfinals	Gordon
1973–74	23–38–17	63	None	Gordon, Parker MacDonald
1974–75	23–50–7	53	None	Gordon, Burns
1975–76	20–53–7	47	None	Ted Harris
1976–77	23–39–18	64	Preliminary	Harris
1977–78	18–53–9	45	None	Harris, Andre Beaulieu, Lou Nanne
1978–79	28–40–12	68	None	Harry Howell, Glen Sonmor
1979–80	36–28–16	88	Semifinals	Sonmor
1980–81	35–28–17	87	Finals	Sonmor
1981–82	37–23–20	94	Div. Semifinals	Sonmor, Murray Oliver
1982–83	40–24–16	96	Div. Finals	Sonmor, Oliver
1983–84	39–31–10	88	Conf. Finals	Bill Mahoney
1984–85	25–43–12	62	Div. Finals	Mahoney, Sonmor
1985–86	38–33–9	85	Div. Semifinals	Lorne Henning
1986–87	30–40–10	70	None	Henning, Sonmor
1987–88	19–48–13	51	None	Herb Brooks
1988–89	27–37–16	70	Div. Semifinals	Pierre Page
1989–90	36–40–4	76	Div. Semifinals	Page
1990–91	27–39–14	72	Finals	Bob Gainey
1991–92	32–42–6	70	Div. Semifinals	Gainey
1992–93	36–38–10	82	None	Gainey

North Stars in the Playoffs

1968 7–7; **1970** 2–4; **1971** 6–6; **1972** 3–4; **1973** 2–4; **1977** 0–2; **1980** 8–7; **1981** 12–7; **1982** 1–3; **1983** 4–5; **1984** 7–9; **1985** 5–4; **1986** 2–3; **1989** 1–4; **1990** 3–4; **1991** 14–9; **1992** 3–4. **Total:** 80–86

NOTE: The team had an 11–15 record in the 26 playoff games decided in overtimes. The longest playoff game came in the North Stars' first season: in the seventh game, they lost to the St. Louis Blues, 2–1, in St. Louis. Overtime lasted 22 minutes, 50 seconds.

North Stars in the Stanley Cup

1981	Site	Score
May 12	New York	Islanders 6, North Stars 3
May 14	New York	Islanders 6, North Stars 3
May 17	Minnesota	Islanders 7, North Stars 5
May 19	Minnesota	North Stars 4, Islanders 2
May 21	New York	Islanders 5, North Stars 1

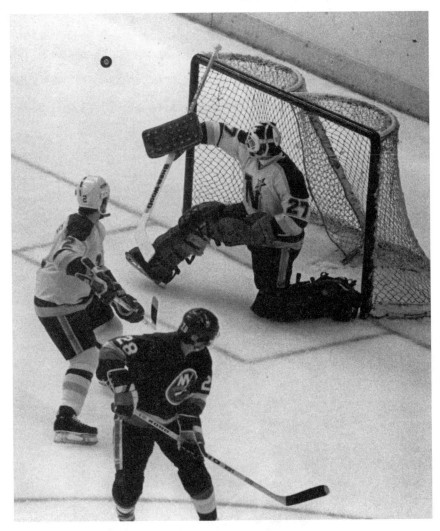

North Stars vs. New York Islanders in Stanley Cup action at Met Sports Center, 1981

1991	Site	Score
May 15	Pittsburgh	North Stars 5, Penguins 4
May 17	Pittsburgh	Penguins 4, North Stars 1
May 19	Minnesota	North Stars 3, Penguins 1
May 21	Minnesota	Penguins 5, North Stars 3
May 23	Pittsburgh	Penguins 6, North Stars 4
May 25	Minnesota	Penguins 8, North Stars 0

North Stars Coaching Records

Coach	Seasons	Record
Glen Sonmor	7	174–161–82
Jack Gordon	5	116–123–50
Bob Gainey	3	95–119–30
Lorne Henning	2	68–72–18
Pierre Page	2	63–77–20
Wren Blair	3	48–65–34
Ted Harris	3	48–104–27
Bill Mahoney	2	42–39–12
Charlie Burns	2	22–50–14
Murray Oliver	2	21–12–8
Parker McDonald	1	20–30–11
Herb Brooks	1	19–48–13
Lou Nanne	1	7–18–4
John Muckler	1	6–23–6
Andre Beaulieu	1	6–23–3
Harry Howell	1	3–6–2

North Stars Players Records

Game

Goals	5, by Tim Young, Jan. 15, 1979
Assists	5, by Murray Oliver, Oct. 24, 1971, and Larry Murphy, May 17, 1989
Points	7, by Bobby Smith (four goals, three assists), Nov. 11, 1981

Season

Goals	55, by Dino Ciccarelli, 1981–82, and Brian Bellows, 1989–90
Assists	76, by Neal Broten, 1985–86
Points	114, by Bobby Smith, 1981–82
Penalty minutes	382, by Basil McRae, 1987–88
Wins (by goalie)	31, by Jon Casey, 1989–90
Shutouts (by goalie)	6, by Cesare Maniago, 1967–68

Career

Seasons	13, by Neal Broten
Games played	876, by Broten
Consecutive games played	442, by Danny Grant (Dec. 4, 1968–Apr. 7, 1974)
Goals	342, by Brian Bellows
Assists	547, by Broten
Points	796, by Broten
Penalty minutes	1,567, by Basil McRae
Games played (by goalie)	420, by Cesare Maniago
Wins (by goalie)	143, by Maniago

Team

Longest losing streak	10 games, Feb. 1–20, 1976
Longest winless streak	20 games (0–15–5), Jan. 15–Feb. 28, 1970

Retired North Stars Numbers

7   Neal Broten*
8   Bill Goldsworthy
19 Bill Masterton

*Retired by the Dallas Stars in 1998

North Stars First-Round Draft Choices

1967 Wayne Cheesman, Whitby Junior B; **1968** Jim Benzelock, Winnipeg; **1969** Dick Redmond, St. Catherines; **1970** none; **1971** none; **1972** Jerry Byers, Kitchenor; **1973** none; **1974** Doug Hicks, Flin Flon; **1975** Bryan Maxwell, Medicine Hat; **1976** Glen Sharpley, Hull; **1977** Brad Maxwell, New Westminster; **1978** Bobby Smith, Ottawa; **1979** Craig Hartsburg, Sault Ste. Marie; **1980** Brad Palmer, Victoria; **1981** Ron Meighan, Niagara Falls; **1982** Brian Bellows, Kitchenor; **1983** Brian Lawton, Mt. St. Charles; **1984** David Quinn, Kent H.S.; **1985** none; **1986** Warren Babe, Lethbridge; **1987** Dave Archibald, Portland; **1988** Mike Modano, Prince Albert; **1989** Doug Zmolek, Rochester John Marshall; **1990** Derian Hatcher, North Bay; **1991** Richard Matvichuk, Saskatoon.

NOTE: Bobby Smith, Brian Lawton and Mike Modano were the first players selected overall in the draft.

All-Time Points Leaders

St. Paul native Phil Housley, who played 21 seasons in the NHL before retiring after the 2002–03 season, is the NHL's all-time American-born leader in points. In 1,495 games, Housley had 1,232 points. A first-round draft pick (sixth overall) by the Buffalo Sabres in 1982 out of South St. Paul High School, Housley ranks tenth in goals scored (338) by an American-born player.

Warroad native Dave Christian is ninth in goals scored (340) by an American-born player, while Roseau native Neal Broten is seventh in points (923). Former North Star Mike Modano is third in points (1,106).

NHL Draft in Minnesota

The NHL began conducting a draft in 1963. The first U.S. college player selected in a first round of the draft was the University of Minnesota's Mike Ramsey. He was the 11th overall pick, chosen by the Buffalo Sabres in 1979.

The first U.S. high school player ever drafted by the NHL after the league allowed 18-year olds to be picked was Jay North, from Bloomington Jefferson High School. North was taken 62nd overall by Buffalo in 1980. In 1983 Minnesota's North Stars picked the first U.S.–born player selected first overall in the draft, Brian Lawton of Mount St. Charles High School in Rhode Island.

DID YOU KNOW ?

Gord Gallant of the Fighting Saints, who led the WHA in penalty minutes, punched out his coach, Harry Neale, after the Fighting Saints had opened the 1975 playoffs with a 6–5 victory over New England. Gallant was suspended immediately by the team and traded during the off-season.

High Schools and the NHL Entry Draft

Between 1980 and 2004, 15 U.S. high schools and prep schools had at least 10 players selected in the NHL Entry Draft. Three of the high schools are in Minnesota—Edina (tied for third with 16 players drafted), Hill-Murray (fifth with 15) and Roseau (tied for twelfth with 10). In the same period the University of Minnesota had 65 players selected in the draft—the most of any U.S. college. Minnesota–Duluth had 13 players selected in that time.

On June 17, 1989, the NHL held its annual Entry Draft at the Met Center in Bloomington. It was just the second time in the 26-year history of the draft that it was held in the United States. In 1987 the draft had been held in Detroit.

First Primetime NHL Game

On December 29, 1972, a crowd of 15,601 at the Met Center watched the Boston Bruins defeat the North Stars, 2–0. Losing to the Bruins wasn't significant—the North Stars won just three of the first 28 meetings between the two teams.

What made the game significant was that it was the first NHL game carried on network television in primetime hours. NBC spent $60,000 to bring the game to 185 stations nationwide and Puerto Rico. It was the first of 15 NHL games that NBC telecast that season.

Fighting Saints

Twenty years before the Minnesota Wild brought professional hockey to downtown St. Paul, the capital city had another big-league hockey team.

When the World Hockey Association was formed in August 1971, St. Paul was granted a charter franchise in the 12-team league, which began play the following year. The Minnesota Fighting Saints debuted on October 13, 1972, losing to the Winnipeg Jets, 4–3, before 7,892 viewers at the St. Paul Auditorium.The Fighting Saints played in the Auditorium for three months while the St. Paul Civic Center was being constructed next door.

For three seasons, the Saints provided a high-scoring, exciting brand of hockey, but by their fourth season, financial problems surfaced. On February 27, 1976, the Saints folded.

Following the 1975–76 season, the financially troubled Cleveland Crusaders were considering a move to the vacant St. Paul Civic Center. The Crusaders, owned by Nick Mileti, were squeezed out in Cleveland when the NHL's California Seals moved to Cleveland. (Ironically, the renamed Barons would last just two NHL seasons in Cleveland. Following the 1977–78 season, the Barons were merged with the Minnesota North Stars.)

In July 1976, after briefly considering a move to Florida, the Crusaders relocated to St. Paul and were reborn as the "new" Minnesota Fighting Saints. This version of the Saints would last less than one season. Despite a respectable 19–18–5 record, financial problems plagued the team, and on January 17, 1977, the Saints folded again.

The league lasted two more seasons before it was announced in March 1979 that four teams—Edmonton, New England (later renamed Hartford), Quebec and Winnipeg—would join the NHL.

Fighting Saints Year-by-Year

Coach	Season	Record	Points	Playoffs
Glen Sonmor (28–28–3) Harry Neale (10–9–0)	1972–73	38–37–3	79	1–4
Neale (42–32–2) Jack McCartan (2–0)	1973–74	44–32–2	90	6–5
Neale (42–32–3) McCartan (0–1)	1974–75	42–33–3	87	6–6
Neale	1975–76*	30–25–4	65	—
Sonmor	1976–77**	19–18–5	43	—

*folded Feb. 27, 1976; **folded Jan. 17, 1977

DID YOU KNOW ?

Prior to the 1975–76 season, the Minnesota Fighting Saints tried to sign future Hall of Famer Bobby Orr, but Orr remained with the Boston Bruins. The Saints folded in January 1976.

Fighting Saints Records

Mike "Shakey" Walton holds most Fighting Saints' single-season and career scoring records. In the 1973–74 season, Walton had 57 goals, 60 assists and 117 points (each a team record). His career totals of 136 goals, 145 assists and 281 points are also team records.

The team single-season leader for penalty minutes is Curt Brackenbury, with 254 in the 1975–76 season. John Arbour is the team's career leader with 461 penalty minutes.

John Garrett and Mike Curran share the franchise's goaltending records. Garrett holds the records for victories in a season (30 in 1974–75), career victories (77, from 1973–76), and career goals-against average (3.38). Curran holds the single-season (4) and career (7) record for shutouts and had the best single-season goals-against average (3.09).

Professional Minor League Hockey Teams

Professional minor league hockey has existed in Minnesota since 1926. Teams from Minneapolis, St. Paul and Duluth played in four professional leagues from 1926 to 1996.

American Hockey Association

Duluth Hornets (1926–33), St. Paul Saints (1926–30, 1932–33, 1935–42), Minneapolis Millers (1926–31, 1936–42)

United States Hockey League

St. Paul Saints (1945–51), Minneapolis Millers (1945–50)

International Hockey League

St. Paul Saints and Minneapolis Millers (1959–63), Minnesota Moose (1994–96)

Central League

Minneapolis Bruins (1963–65), St. Paul–Minnesota Rangers (1963–66).

Olympic Hockey

Men's Olympic Hockey

Minnesotans have made substantial contributions to Olympic hockey. The 1920 U.S. team, the first to represent the United States, included four Minnesotans on its 11-player roster: Anthony Conroy, Moose Goheen, Eddie Fitzgerald and Cyril Weidenborner. The four teammates from the St. Paul Athletic Club team helped the U.S. win a silver medal at the games in Antwerp.

At least seven players with Minnesota connections—Rueben Bjorkman, Andre Gambucci, John Noah, Arnie Oss, Robert Rompre, James Sedin and Ken Yackel Sr.—were on the 1952 team that won a silver medal.

The 1956 team, coached by Minnesota legend John Mariucci, also had at least seven Minnesotans, including future Governor Wendell Anderson.

The 1960 team, which included eight Minnesotans, avenged a 4–0 loss to Russia in the 1956 gold medal game by defeating the Russians, 3–2, in the semifinals. The U.S. team then defeated Czechoslovakia for the gold medal. Goalie Jack McCartan, who played baseball and hockey at the University of Minnesota, made 31 saves in the gold medal game and was named Most Outstanding Player of the games.

U.S. Olympic hockey team celebrating an upset victory over Soviet team, 1980

In 1972 the U.S. team, including 10 Minnesotans, won the silver medal.

The 1980 team, coached by Herb Brooks, who was on leave from coaching the University of Minnesota hockey team, included 12 Minnesotans. The team would accomplish what *Sports Illustrated* two decades later called, "the greatest sports moment of the 20th century." On February 24, 1980, in Lake Placid, N.Y., the U.S. team rallied to defeat the heavily favored Russian team, 4–3, in the semifinals. The victory was stunning. The Russians had not lost in Olympic competition in 12 years and had won all but one of the gold medals in the previous 24 years. Two weeks before the start of the Olympics, the Russians had defeated the U.S., 10–3, in an exhibition game in New York City.

Between 1984 and 1998, the U.S. Olympic team finished no higher than fourth at the Olympics. The 2002 team won the silver medal at the Salt Lake games. At the Turin Olympics in 2006, the U.S. team reached the quarter-finals but did not medal.

Women's Olympic Hockey

In 1998 women's hockey debuted at the Winter Olympics. Two Minnesotans—Alana Blahoski and Jenny Schmidgall—helped lead the Americans to the gold medal.

In 2002 Minnesotans Natalie Darwitz, Jennifer Schmidgall, and Krissy Wendell led the United States to a silver medal. Courtney Kennedy and Lyndsay Wall—teammates of Darwitz and Wendell at the University of Minnesota—were also on the team.

The 2006 team earned a bronze medal at the Turin Olympics.

DID YOU KNOW ?

Four Minnesota natives—Frank Brimsek, Walter Bush, Francis Goheen, and Robert Johnson—are in the Hockey Hall of Fame in Toronto, Ontario.

Amateur Hockey

Eveleth

Any conversation about hockey in Minnesota can begin with Eveleth, the birthplace of American hockey. The United States Hockey Hall of Fame is headquartered in Eveleth, and 12 members of the hall hail from Eveleth.

The first recorded game in Eveleth dates to 1903, when an Eveleth team played a team from Two Harbors. In 1921 the state's first indoor hockey rink was constructed in Eveleth.

Eveleth fielded a high school team in 1920, some 25 years before the first boys' state hockey tournament. Eveleth Junior College had one of the top college teams in the United States in the 1920s. Cliff Thompson coached both teams.

From 1926 to 1935, Mike Karakas, Frankie Brimsek and Sam LoPresti served as goalies for the Eveleth High School team. Each eventually became a

Francis "Moose" Goheen (age 21),
U.S. Hockey Hall of Famer

starting goalie in the National Hockey League at a time when there were only six teams and few Americans playing in the NHL.

In 1956 the U.S. Olympic hockey team that won a silver medal included three players from Eveleth—Willard Ikola, John Mayasich and John Matchefts. It was coached by another Eveleth legend, John Mariucci.

U.S. Hockey Hall of Fame

The United States Hockey Hall of Fame opened in Eveleth in 1973. Since then, 125 individuals and two teams have been inducted. Twelve members are Eveleth natives. Nearly 40 percent (47 members) are Minnesota natives. The 1960 and 1980 U.S. Olympic teams have also been inducted into the hall.

Minnesota Natives in the U.S. Hockey Hall of Fame

Oscar Almquist, Henry Boucha, Herb Brooks, Neal Broten, Frank Brimsek, Walter Bush, Dave Christian, Roger Christian, William Christian, James Claypool, Anthony Conroy, Mike Curran, Carl Dahlstrom, Bob Dill, Richard Dougherty, Serge Gambucci, Francis Goheen, Wally Grant, Phil Housely, Willard Ikola, Mark Johnson, Paul Johnson, Robert Johnson, Virgil Johnson, Michael Karakas, Dave Langevin, Reed Larson, Sam LoPresti, John Mariucci, Cal Marvin, John Matchefts, John Mayasich, Jack McCartan, Hubert Nelson, Doug Palazzari, Bob Paradise, John Pleban, Mike Ramsey, Elwyn Romnes, Larry Ross, Charles Schulz, Cliff Thompson, Harold Trumble, Thomas Williams, Frank Winters, Doug Woog, Ken Yackel.

Cal Marvin

John Mariucci may be the "Godfather of Minnesota hockey," but it is doubtful anyone did more for hockey in the state than Cal Marvin. Marvin, the youngest of five sons of lumber baron George Marvin, is a member of the United States Hockey Hall of Fame. In 1948 Marvin, who helped develop the

1919–20 St. Paul Athletic Club team, including Francis Goheen (seated, 3rd from left), co-winners of the MacNaughton Cup

hockey program at the University of North Dakota, founded a senior men's amateur team named the Warroad Lakers. The Lakers played host to national teams from Canada, Finland and Sweden and won the Allan Cup (senior hockey's equivalent of the Stanley Cup) several times. Marvin, the patriarch of Warroad (known as "Hockeytown USA"), died on September 5, 2004, at age 80.

Warroad, a town of 1,600 in northwestern Minnesota near the Canadian border, boasts six Olympic hockey medal winners—including gold medalists Billy Christian and Roger Christian in 1960 and Dave Christian (Billy's son) in 1980.

St. Paul Athletic Club

A half-century before Minnesota fielded a team in the NHL, the North Star state was home to a prominent "amateur" team. The St. Paul Athletic Club, led by the legendary Francis "Moose" Goheen, won the MacNaughton Cup—given to the winner of the American Amateur Hockey Association—in 1916 and shared the cup in 1920. The St. Paul Athletic Club reached the finals of the United States Amateur Hockey Association twice—in 1922 and 1923.

When Boston joined the NHL for the 1924–25 season as the league's first American franchise, it spelled the demise of "major league" amateur hockey in the United States.

Between 1926 and the arrival of the NHL Minnesota North Stars in 1967, Minnesota was home to significant minor league hockey. Teams mainly from Minneapolis and St. Paul successfully participated in the American Hockey Association, Central Hockey League, United States Hockey League, International Hockey League, and Central Professional Hockey League. The first Central League is particularly noteworthy because the players were overwhelmingly native Minnesotan.

College Hockey

Gopher Men

College hockey in Minnesota dates to 1895, when, on February 16, the University of Minnesota and Minneapolis hockey teams played each other at a rink at 4th Avenue South and South 11th Street. The purpose of the game was to decide the championship of the Northwest and to raise funds to meet expenses for a game with the Winnipeg Victorias, frequently called the "champions of the world." The university and Minneapolis teams skated to a 3–3 tie, and the best players from those teams played the Victorias about a week later. The Victorias won that game, 11–3; it was played at Athletic Park in downtown Minneapolis.

The Gophers played their first full official season in 1921–22. In the 1939–40 season, the Gophers went unbeaten (18–0) and won the National AAU tournament (the predecessor to the NCAA tournament).

The Gophers finished second at the NCAA tournament in 1953, 1954 and 1971 before winning their first NCAA championship in 1974 under Herb Brooks. The Gophers won two more championships under Brooks (1976 and 1979). The Gophers reached the NCAA Frozen Four eight times between 1981 and 1995 without winning another NCAA title. The Gophers ended a 23-year championship drought by winning back-to-back NCAA championships under Don Lucia in 2002 and 2003. This was the first time an NCAA Division I men's hockey champion had repeated in 31 years.

The Gophers are tied for fourth among NCAA Division I men's hockey programs with five NCAA titles. The top five title holders are: Michigan 9, North Dakota 7, Denver U. 6, Gophers 5 and Wisconsin 5.

The Gophers have won 13 WCHA playoff championships: 1961, 1971, 1974, 1975, 1976, 1979, 1980, 1981, 1983, 1994, 1996, 2003 and 2004.

Gophers Coaching Records (through the 2005–06 season)

Coach	Seasons	Record
Doug Woog	13	390–187–40
John Mariucci	13	197–138–18
Don Lucia	7	189–86–26
Brad Buetow	5	171–75–8
Herb Brooks	7	167–97–18
Larry Armstrong	11	123–53–10
Glen Sonmor	4+	77–80–6

Gopher hockey team with its first NCAA trophy, 1973–74 (Herb Brooks at right, kneeling)

Emil Iverson	6	75–21–10
Doc Romnes	4	53–59–0
Frank Pond	4	46–22–4

Gopher 30-Victory Seasons

Season	Coach	Record
1985–86	Woog	35–13
1986–87	Woog	34–14–1
1987–88	Woog	34–10–0
1988–89	Woog	34–11–3
1980–81	Buetow	33–12–0
1991–92	Woog	33–11–0
2001–02	Lucia	32–8–4
1978–79	Brooks	32–11–1
1982–83	Buetow	32–12–1
1974–75	Brooks	31–10–1
1984–85	Buetow	31–13–3
1995–96	Woog	30–10–2
1990–91	Woog	30–10–5

Gopher Players Records

Individual single-game

Goals	6, by John Mayasich, vs. Winnipeg, Dec. 10, 1954
Assists	5, 11 times, most recently by Gino Guyer, vs. Mercyhurst, Mar. 27, 2003
Points	8, by Mayasich (4 goals, 4 assists), at Michigan, Jan. 14, 1955
Penalty minutes	27, by Mike Crupi, at Michigan, Jan. 13, 1967
Goalie saves (regulation)	61, by Don Vaia, vs. Michigan, Feb. 19, 1957 (lost 4–3)
Goalie saves (overtime)	72, by Jeff Tscherne, at Michigan State, Mar. 14, 1976 (3 overtimes, won 7–6)

Team single-game

Goals	16, vs. Brown (Dec. 21, 1979) and vs. Maine (Jan. 14, 1986)
Shots on goal	75, vs. U.S. International, Oct. 23, 1981 (won 7–0)
Penalty minutes	109, at Minnesota-Duluth, Mar. 14, 1998 (won 5–0)

Individual single-season

Goals	53, by Tim Harrer, 1979–80
Assists	59, by Aaron Broten, 1980–81
Points	106, by Broten, 1980–81

Penalty minutes	154, by Pat Micheletti, 1984–85
Appearances by a goalie	44, by Robb Stauber, 1987–88
Shutouts by a goalie	5, by Stauber, 1987–88
Goals against average by a goalie	2.36, by Jim Mattson, 1952–53
Victories by a goalie	34, by Stauber, 1987–88

Career

Games	182, by Larry Olimb, 1988–92
Goals	144, by John Mayasich, 1951–55
Assists	159, by Olimb, 1988–92
Points	298, by Mayasich, 1951–55
Penalty minutes	473, by Matt DeMarchi, 1999–2003
Appearances by a goalie	151, by Adam Hauser, 1998–2002
Goals against average by a goalie	2.36, by Jim Mattson, 1951–54
Victories by a goalie	83, by Hauser, 1998–2002
Shutouts by a goalie	8, by Hauser, 1998–2002

DID YOU KNOW ?

In 1999, as part of a series on a history of sports in the *Minneapolis Star Tribune,* Glen Sonmor named his all-time Gophers' hockey squad: goalie, Robb Stauber (1986–89); defense, John Mariucci (1937–40), Mike Crowley (1994–97); forwards, John Mayasich (1951–55), Neal Broten (1978–79, 1980–81), Brian Bonin (1992–96).

Retired Gophers Hockey Number

8   John Mayasich

Gopher First Team All-Americans

1940 John Mariucci, Harold Paulson; **1951** Gordon Watters; **1952** Larry Ross; **1954** Ken Yackel Sr., Jim Mattson, Dick Daugherty, John Mayasich; **1955** John Mayasich; **1958** Jack McCartan, Dick Burg, Mike Pearson; **1959** Murray Williamson; **1963** Lou Nanne; **1964** Craig Falkman; **1965** Doug Woog; **1968** Gary Gambucci; **1970** Murray McLachlan, Wally Olds; **1975** Les Auge, Mike Polich; **1979** Bill Baker; **1980** Tim Harrer; **1981** Neal Broten,

Steve Ulseth; **1985** Pat Micheletti; **1988** Robb Stauber; **1995** Brian Bonin; **1996** Brian Bonin, Mike Crowley; **1997** Mike Crowley; **2001** Jordan Leopold; **2002** Jordan Leopold, John Pohl; **2004** Keith Ballard. Total: 34

Gophers in the NHL Draft

Eight Gophers have been selected in the first round of the NHL entry draft:
Kris Chucko (2004, by Calgary); Thomas Vanek (2003, by Buffalo); Keith Ballard (2002, by Buffalo); Jeff Taffe (2000, by St. Louis); Erik Rasmussen (1996, by Buffalo); Doug Zmolek (1989, by Minnesota); Tom Chorske (1985, by Montreal) and Mike Ramsey (1979, by Buffalo).

Dick Spannbauer was a first-round selection in the 1974 WHA draft by Houston.

Frozen Four

The Gophers have competed in the NCAA Division I Frozen Four a total of 19 times: 1953, 1954, 1961, 1971, 1974, 1975, 1976, 1979, 1981, 1983, 1986, 1987, 1988, 1989, 1994, 1995, 2002, 2003, and 2005.

In the 19 trips to the Final Four, the Gophers have made 11 appearances in the championship game. The Gophers have a 5–6 record in championship games:

1953	Michigan 7, Gophers 3
1954	RPI 5, Gophers 4 (OT)
1971	Boston U. 4, Gophers 2
1974	Gophers 4, Michigan Tech 2
1975	Michigan Tech 6, Gophers 1
1976	Gophers 6, Michigan Tech 3
1979	Gophers 4, North Dakota 3
1981	Wisconsin 6, Gophers 3
1989	Harvard 4, Gophers 3 (OT)
2002	Gophers 4, Maine 3 (OT)
2003	Gophers 5, New Hampshire 1

Gopher Women

The University of Minnesota is home to two championship hockey teams. The Gophers women's team has earned two national championships: AWCHA in 2000 and NCAA in 2004 and 2005, both under coach Laura Halldorson.

Gopher women's hockey team after winning the 2000 national championship

Announcing on October 31, 1995, that it would add hockey as a varsity sport for women, the university fielded its first team in the 1997–98 season. The first game, played against Augsburg at Mariucci Arena on November 2, 1997, was watched by 6,854 fans, a national record for women's college hockey.

In its first seven seasons (through 2005–06), the Gophers compiled a 261–50–22 record. The Gophers won their first national championship at the AWCHA tournament in 2000. The NCAA sponsored its first tournament in 2001, and the Gophers won the NCAA title in 2004 and 2005. In 2005 Gophers junior Krissy Wendell received the Patty Kazmaier Award as the top player in NCAA Division I women's hockey. In 2006, the Gophers reached the NCAA championship game, where they lost to WCHA rival Wisconsin.

Gopher Players Records (through 2004–05)

Single-game

Goals	5, by Nadine Muzerall, vs. Bemidji State, Jan. 22, 2000
Assists	5, six times, most recently by Natalie Darwitz, vs. North Dakota, Nov. 30, 2003
Points	7, by Muzerall, vs. Bemidji State, Jan. 22, 2000
Saves by a goalie	51, by Erica Killewald, at Minnesota-Duluth, Feb. 12, 2000

Season

Goals	49, by Nadine Muzerall, 1999–2000
Assists	72, by Natalie Darwitz, 2004–05
Points	114, by Darwitz, 2004–05
Victories by a goalie	24, by Jody Horak, 2004–05
Goals against average by a goalie	1.24, by Erica Killewald, 1998–99

Career

Games	148, by Kelly Stephens, 2001–05
Goals	139, by Nadine Muzerall, 1997–2001
Assists	144, by Natalie Darwitz, 2002–05
Points	246, by Darwitz, 2002–05
Victories by a goalie	83, by Jody Horak, 2001–05
Goals against average by a goalie	1.59, by Horak, 2001–05
Shutouts by a goalie	21, by Erica Killewald, 1998–2001

University of Minnesota–Duluth Men's Hockey

The University of Minnesota–Duluth fielded its first men's hockey team in 1930–31. After just two seasons, the sport was dropped. The school reinstated hockey in 1946. After two seasons as an independent, the Duluth Bulldogs joined the MIAC in 1949.

From 1949 to 1961, the Bulldogs dominated the MIAC. In February 1961 the Bulldogs played their final MIAC game, defeating Augsburg, 19–0. That victory was the 56th consecutive in league play and gave the Bulldogs their sixth consecutive league title.

In August 1961 the Bulldogs decided to upgrade their program to Division I, and the Bulldogs spent four seasons as an independent. The Bulldogs joined the WCHA in 1965.

The Bulldogs have reached the NCAA Division I Frozen Four on three occasions: 1984, 1985 and 2004. In 1984 the Bulldogs reached the championship game, where they lost to Bowling Green, 5–4, in four overtimes. Bulldogs goalie Rick Kosti made a tournament-record 55 saves in the game. The next year, the Bulldogs lost to RPI, 6–5, in three overtimes in the semifinals. In 2004 Denver U. defeated the Bulldogs, 5–3, in the semifinals.

The Bulldogs claim 17 first-team All-Americans: Pat Boutette (1973), Ron Busniuk (1970), Keith Christiansen (1967), Chad Erickson (1990), Curt Giles (1978, 1979), Brett Hauer (1993), Bob Hill (1966), Murray Keogan (1970), Rick Kosti (1985), Tom Kurvers (1984), Walt Ledingham (1971, 1972), Junior Lessard (2004), Norm Maciver (1985, 1986), Chris Marinucci (1994), Mark Pavelich (1979), Derek Plante (1993) and Bill Watson (1984, 1985).

Thirty-four Bulldogs have gone on to play in the NHL, including Brett Hull, Curt Giles, Glenn Resch, Jim Johnson, Norm Maciver, Tom Kurvers and Shjon Podein. During the 1994–95 season, 11 Bulldog alumni were playing in the NHL.

University of Minnesota–Duluth Women's Hockey

Duluth's women's hockey team, coached by Shannon Miller, won the first three Division I women's hockey championships sponsored by the NCAA— in 2001, 2002 and 2003.

Minnesota State University–Mankato

The Mavericks played their first intercollegiate hockey game on January 16, 1970, where they lost to St. Cloud State, 8–2.

The Mavericks spent their first 26 seasons at the Division II or III level, appearing in the NCAA tournament 11 times. The Mavericks upgraded their program to Division I for the 1996–97 season. After three seasons as an independent, the Mavericks joined the WCHA for the 1999–2000.

St. Cloud State University

Hockey has been played at St. Cloud State since 1931, but the Huskies moved to the Division I level in 1987. In their first season at the Division I level, the Huskies, coached by Herb Brooks, went 25–10–1. In 1988 Craig Dahl became the Huskies coach. After two more seasons as an independent, the Huskies joined the WCHA in 1990. In 2001 the Huskies won the WCHA Final Five tournament. Prior to the 2005–06 season, Dahl resigned as the Huskies coach. Dahl coached the Huskies to a 338–309–52 record in 18 seasons.

Thirteen Huskies have gone on to play in the NHL. During the 2003–04 season, seven Huskies were in the NHL.

St. Thomas hockey team scrimmaging, 1924

The Huskies have had one first-team All-American player: Mark Hartigan (2002).

Bemidji State University

Bemidji State fielded its first hockey team in 1948. After four seasons, the school did not field a hockey team from 1951 to 1960.

The Beavers were coached by R. H. "Bob" Peters from 1966 until 2001. Peters coached the Beavers to a 702–293–49 record. Peters, who coached two seasons at the University of North Dakota before taking the Beavers job, was the first college hockey coach to win 700 games at one school.

Peters coached the Beavers to 13 national titles: the NAIA in 1968, 1969, 1970, 1971, 1973, 1979, 1980; NCAA Division II in 1984, 1993, 1994, 1995, 1997; and NCAA Division III in 1986.

In 1984 the Beavers capped a perfect season by winning the NCAA Division II national title. The Beavers were 31–0, just the sixth team in college hockey history to post an undefeated season. Their 31 victories are the most victories in an unbeaten season by a college hockey team. They were part of a 42-game winning streak—the longest in college hockey history.

Four Bemidji State alumni have gone on to the NHL, including Joel Otto, who was a member of the Calgary Flames Stanley Cup champion team in 1989.

Augsburg College

Augsburg College started its hockey program in 1926. Less than two years later, the Augsburg hockey team almost represented the United States at the 1928 Winter Olympics in Switzerland.

In January 1928, the Amateur Athletic Union's Ice Hockey Committee selected the Augsburg team, whose lineup featured five brothers, from a group of candidates to represent the United States in Switzerland. Among the teams Augsburg bested was Harvard, the University Club of Boston and Eveleth Junior College.

The only condition was the team had to raise $4,500—half of the cost of sending the team to Europe—in less than two weeks. The Minneapolis school, with an enrollment of 300, raised the amount and seemed to be poised to represent the United States. However, just days before the team was scheduled to leave for Switzerland, its endorsement by the United States Olympic Committee was overruled, and it was decided that the United States would not send a team to the games.

Major General Douglas D. MacArthur, the chairman of the United States Olympic Committee, made the announcement. MacArthur reportedly felt that the Augsburg team was "not representative of American hockey." Why the team was abruptly rejected is unclear. Speculation is that the committee felt that the five Hansen brothers, who were raised in Alberta before moving to Minneapolis, were not American enough. The committee was also pressured by a Boston amateur hockey group, which filed a protest saying that it should face Augsburg in a challenge match to determine the U.S. representative.

The Auggies recovered from the disappointment to win their second consecutive state title. The team, which consisted of Julius, Louis, Joe, Emil and Oscar Hansen and goaltender Joe Swanson, lost just once in two seasons.

Following their college careers, Oscar, Emil and another brother, Emory, went on to play professional hockey. Oscar Hansen went on to star for the Chicago Blackhawks.

Louis Hansen turned down professional hockey to earn a Ph.D. in chemisty. As a chemical engineer, he went on to hold several significant patents. Julius Hansen became a minister and Joe Hansen a teacher.

Oscar Hansen is a charter member of the Augsburg Athletic Hall of Fame. Louis Hansen was also inducted into the hall.

Hobey Baker Award

The Hobey Baker Award has been presented annually to the top player in NCAA Division I men's hockey since 1981. The award is named after Baker, who played hockey and football at Princeton in the early 20th century and is a member of the U.S. and Hockey Halls of Fame. A pilot during World War I, Baker died at age 26 in a training accident.

Since 1981, eight players from the University of Minnesota–Minneapolis or the University of Minnesota–Duluth have won the award: Neal Broten, Minnesota, 1981; Tom Kurvers, UMD, 1984; Bill Watson, UMD, 1985; Robb Stauber, Minnesota, 1988; Chris Marinucci, UMD, 1994; Brian Bonin, Minnesota, 1996; Jordan Leopold, Minnesota, 2002; Junior Lessard, UMD, 2004.

In 2005 Colorado College forward Marty Sertich, a junior from Roseville, Minnesota, won the Hobey Baker Award. Sertich was the WCHA Player of the Year and the league's scoring champion—with 17 goals and 25 assists in conference play. Sertich helped Colorado College reach the Frozen Four.

Minnesota Hosts the Frozen Four

The NCAA offered its first Division I hockey tournament in 1948. Since then, Minnesota has served as the host to Frozen Four tournament eight times.

The city of St. Paul has played host four times—1989, 1991, 1994 and 2002. In 1989 Harvard edged the Gophers, 4–3, in overtime for the championship. In 1991 Northern Michigan outlasted Boston University, 4–3, in three overtimes for the championship. In 1994 Lake Superior State defeated Boston University, 9–1, in the title game, and in 2002 the Gophers defeated Maine, 4–3, for the championship.

Duluth has hosted the tournament twice—1968 and 1981. Denver defeated North Dakota, 4–0, for the title in 1968. In 1981 Wisconsin, coached by Minnesota native Bob Johnson, defeated the Gophers, 6–3, in the championship game.

The University of Minnesota hosted twice—in 1958 and 1966. Denver defeated North Dakota, 6–2, in the 1958 championship game. In 1966 Michigan State defeated Clarkson, 6–1, for the championship.

High School
Sports

DID YOU KNOW ?

In 1999, the *Minneapolis Star Tribune* asked sportswriter Dave Mona to pick a five-player, all-time boys' state tournament basketball team. Mona's father, Luther, coached basketball at Minneapolis South High School from 1942 to 1975. Dave Mona has missed only two state tournaments since 1950. Along with cohost Sid Hartman (of a Sunday morning radio show on WCCO-AM), he picked this team: Jim McIntyre, Minneapolis Henry; Ron Johnson, New Prague; Mark Olberding, Melrose; Tom Nordland, Minneapolis Roosevelt; Khalid El-Amin, Minneapolis North.

MINNESOTA'S high schools fielded their first sports teams in the late 1800s. By the late 1890s school teams played baseball, basketball, football and hockey. In the 1900s track and field events joined the lineups.

In 1913 the first official state tournament took place when Carleton College in Northfield sponsored a state boys' basketball tournament. Three years later, an association called the State High School Athletic Association (SHSAA) formed. Its primary mission was to promote "pure" amateur sport in four sports—baseball, basketball, football and track and field—and to establish uniform eligibility rules for interscholastic activities.

During the 1920s state tournaments were added for golf, swimming and tennis. In 1929 the SHSAA changed its name to the Minnesota State High School League (MSHSL) and broadened its scope by including interscholastic activities, speech and debate. In 1974 the MSHSL allowed private high schools to join the association.

Girls in High School Sports

For the first 40 years of the 20th century, basketball was a popular sport for high school girls in the state. During the 1920s nearly 200 Minnesota high schools fielded girls' basketball teams.

As early as 1908, however, interscholastic athletics for girls was publicly criticized. The Amateur Athletic Union, the national body that governed amateur sports outside of high schools and colleges, declared it would not permit girls to play basketball in public places because such displays exploited women and led to undesirable traits. In the 1920s pressure against girls' sports mounted, when the women's division of the National Amateur Athletic Foundation (founded by Lou Henry Hoover, the wife of President Herbert Hoover) openly criticized what it viewed as commercialism in sport. This public stand caused even intramural basketball to decline in popularity.

After the mid-1920s, the number of girls' high school basketball teams in the state began to decline. One Minnesota town that managed to keep its girls' basketball team was Grand Meadow. The Grand Meadow team won all 94 games it played between 1929 and 1939.

In addition to basketball, girls in Minnesota had other "unofficial" athletic opportunities during the 1920s and 1930s. From 1924 to 1942, a girls' state swimming meet was regularly conducted, but during World War II interscholastic sports for girls disappeared entirely.

It was 1968 before the Minnesota State High School League's Representative Assembly asked the MSHSL's board of directors to draw up a bylaw for girls' interscholastic activities. On October 11, the MSHSL board voted to submit the proposed "Girls Athletic Bylaw" to the assembly for consideration. Two months later, on December 6, 1968, the assembly adopted the bylaw. The first "official" MSHSL sponsored event for girls was the 1972 state track and field meet.

In 1969 more than 400 state high schools had boys' athletic programs, while only 64 had girls' programs. By 1980 every high school in the state had a girls' sports program.

First State Tournaments and Meets

Boys

Baseball 1947; basketball 1913; cross country 1943; curling 1969 (last 1977); football 1972; golf 1928; gymnastics 1943 (last 1983); hockey 1945; skiing 1932; soccer 1974; swimming and diving 1924; tennis—individual 1929, team 1950; track and field 1921; wrestling 1938

Girls

Basketball 1974; cross country 1975; golf 1977; gymnastics 1975; hockey 1995; skiing 1976; soccer 1980; softball 1977; swimming and diving 1924, 1977; tennis 1974; track and field 1972; volleyball 1974

Most State Titles

The schools with the most state team championships in all sports (through the 2004–05 season) are:

94 Edina; **46** Stillwater; **43** Apple Valley; **37** Duluth Central; **36** Burnsville, Minnetonka, Rochester Lourdes; **34** Bloomington Jefferson; **33** Blake, Duluth East

Winning Streaks and Unbeaten Streaks

Probably the top dynasty in state high school athletics belonged to the Edina High School girls' tennis team. The Hornets won 15 consecutive state titles between 1978 and 1992. During that span, they won 205 consecutive matches—a streak ended by a 4–3 loss to Bloomington Jefferson on September 30, 1993. Other top streaks of games include:

86 Unbeaten streak by the South St. Paul girls' hockey team. The Packers' 63-game winning streak ended on December 2, 2003, after a 1–1 tie with Cloquet-Esko-Carlton; the Packers then extended their unbeaten streak to 86 consecutive games before a 3–1 loss to Eden Prairie in the first round of the 2004 Class AA state tournament.

81 Consecutive dual meets won by Apple Valley's wrestling team before a loss to Glenbard (Ill.) North in a tournament in Rochester, Minnesota, in January 2003.

79 Consecutive games won by the Eveleth boys' hockey team from 1948 to 1952. Hibbing ended the streak on February 9, 1952.

78 Consecutive games won by the Fosston girls' basketball team. The streak, which began in 1999, ended on March 9, 2002, with a 63–58 loss to Kittson Central.

69 Consecutive games won by the Edina boys' basketball team. The streak ended on February 16, 1968, with an 81–75 loss to Richfield, but the Hornets regrouped to win their third consecutive state championship—the first team to accomplish this feat.

66 Consecutive games won by Cretin–Derham Hall's baseball team. The streak ended in 1999, two games shy of the national high school record.

65 Consecutive games won by the Shattuck boys' basketball team. The streak ended on November 20, 1970, in a 50–48 loss to St. Paul Cretin.

60 Unbeaten streak for Minneapolis Washburn football. The Millers went 58–0–2 from 1966 to 1972, winning four "mythical" state titles and the first official state Class AA title (in 1972) in that span.

Nicknames

Nicknames are a big part of the tradition of high school athletics. Among the unusual nicknames are Aitkin Gobblers, Blooming Prairie Blossoms, Elgin-Millville Watchmen, Grand Meadow Superlarks, Hawley Nuggets, Jordan Hubmen, Lanesboro Burros, Little Falls Flyers, McGregor Mercuries, Proctor Rails, Sauk Centre Mainstreeters, Thief River Falls Prowlers, and the Two Harbors Agates.

Some memorable team nicknames at high schools that no longer exist include: Askov Danes, Derham Hall Dollies, Dilworth Locomotives, Freeborn Yeomen, Golden Valley Vikings, Granite Falls Kilowatts, Jasper Quartz-Siters, Minneapolis Vocational Volts, Minneapolis West Cowboys, Regina Raiders, St. Paul Mechanic Arts Trainers, St. Paul Washington Presidents, Trimont Orioles, Wykoff Wykats.

Basketball

Carleton College in Northfield hosted the first state basketball tournament in 1913. Originally, the tournament was an invitational with as many as 16 teams participating. In 1925 the tournament switched to an eight-team format, which remained unchanged until 1970.

During the 1950s and 1960s, the tournament was deemed the best-attended eight-team state tournament in the nation. In 1962 the tournament drew a record 87,951 for the six sessions. In 1971 the tournament was switched to two classes, and in 1997 it changed to a four-class format.

Through the years, the tournament has had seven homes—Carleton College, Kenwood Armory in Minneapolis, Minneapolis Auditorium, St. Paul Auditorium, Williams Arena, St. Paul Civic Center and Target Center.

Winningest Boys Basketball Coaches (through 2004–05)

Coach	School	Record
* Bob McDonald	Chisholm	827–345
* Bob Brink	Rocori	800–265
* Ziggy Kauls	Mounds View	622–279
* Lynn Peterson	Staples-Motley	599–179
John Nett	Winona Cotter	580–297
Jack Evens	Bloomington Jefferson	554–193
Hugo Goehle	Hills–Beaver Creek	554–223
Len Horyza	Cretin–Derham Hall	550–239
Darrell Kreun	Sibley East	533–185
Ron Ueland	Marshall County Central	532–322

*Active during the 2004–05 season

Most State Boys Basketball Tournament Appearances

28 Bemidji; **26** Austin; **22** Red Wing; **19** Minneapolis North; **18** Crosby-Ironton; **17** Mankato; **16** Chisholm; **14** Duluth Central, (Minneapolis) DeLaSalle; **13** Hopkins

Most one-class tournament appearances, 1913–70

	Number	School
Region 1	23	Austin
Region 2	17	Mankato
Region 3	8	New Ulm
Region 4	6	South St. Paul, St. Paul Mechanic Arts
Region 5	9	Buffalo

Edina vs. Duluth Central in the boys' state high school basketball tournament,
Williams Arena, 1968

Region 6	14	Moorhead
Region 7	11	Virginia
Region 8	26	Bemidji

Most consecutive appearances

Number	School	Year
8	Moorhead	1924–31
8	Tartan	1998–2005
7	Bemidji	1953–59
7	Minneapolis North	1980–86
6	Minneapolis Henry	1998–2003
6	New Ulm	1917–22
5	Crosby-Ironton	1944–48
5	Minneapolis DeLaSalle	1997–2001

DID YOU KNOW ?

On March 12, 1977, Winona Cotter defeated Pelican Rapids, 60–47, in the boys' state Class A basketball championship, making it the first private school to win a state basketball title. Two days earlier, in the first round of the tournament, Silver Bay defeated Minneapolis Marshall-U High School to end Marshall-U's 53-game winning streak. Marshall-U was in the middle of a six-year stretch that saw it compile a 139–9 record.

Top Boys and Girls High School Basketball Scorers (through 2004–05)

3,694 Katie Ohm, Elgin-Millville
3,300 Megan Taylor, Roseau
3,292 Joel McDonald, Chisholm
3,129 Janet Karvonen, New York Mills
3,037 Susan King, Holy Angels
3,036 Kierah Kimbrough, Badger-GMR
3,013 Jake Sullivan, Tartan

2,852   Norm Grow, Foley
2,829   Mitch Ohnstad, Faribault
2,811   Kelly Roysland, Fosston
2,804   Krissi Super, Badger-GMR
2,715   Kay Konerza, Lester Prairie
2,704   Kelly Skalicky, Albany
2,702   Shannon Schonrock, Blue Earth
2,693   Ashley Samuelson, Underwood
2,681   Grant Gunhus, Park Christian
2,655   Mary Jo Miller, Tracy-Milroy
2,524   Rhonda Birch, Wadena–Deer Creek

Glencoe vs. Redwood Falls in the Class A girls basketball tournament,
Met Sports Center, 1976

Girls' Basketball Standouts

Underwood's Ashley Samuelson, a 6-foot guard, is the only player in Minnesota girls' high school basketball history to have at least 2,600 points (2,693), 1,100 rebounds (1,166) and 600 steals (688). Samuelson holds the state record for steals.

Badger-Greenbush-Middle River's Kierah Kimbrough, a 6-foot-1 forward, set the single-season scoring record for girls' basketball by scoring 1,023 points during the 2004–05 season. Kimbrough, who averaged 34.1 points per game, finished her career with 3,036 points. Kimbrough is one of just seven players (boys or girls) to score more 3,000 points.

The winningest coach in state girls' basketball history is New London-Spicer's Mike Dreier. Dreier, who has coached 13 teams to the state tournament, has a 603–101 record. Rochester Lourdes coach Myron Glass, who has led 15 teams to the state tournament, has a 548–65 record. Lourdes won its eighth state title under Glass in 2005.

DID YOU KNOW **?**

On December 29, 1978, Minneapolis Edison's boys' basketball team defeated St. Paul Academy, 53–42, in the consolation round of the Centennial tournament. This ended a 71-game losing streak, which dated to the 1975–76 season. The Tommies had started the season with a 0–7 record.

National Interscholastic Tournament

In 1917 the University of Chicago began the National Interscholastic Tournament (NIT), the brainchild of legendary football coach Amos Alonzo Stagg. The tournament featured the top high school boys' basketball teams in the Midwest. The tournament was held until 1931.

The first team from Minnesota to compete was St. Paul Mechanic Arts, which went 1–1 at the 1917 tourney. In 1920 Minneapolis Central elected to bypass the Minnesota state tournament to play in the Chicago tournament (the two were being held at the same time). Minneapolis Central lost in the semifinals of the Chicago tournament.

Minnesota teams competing in tournament

1917 St. Paul Mechanic Arts; **1920** Minneapolis Central; **1921** Sandstone, Stillwater; **1922** Austin, Duluth Cathedral, Madison; **1923** Aurora; **1924** Two Harbors; **1925** St. Paul Mechanic Arts; **1926** Gaylord; **1927** Minneapolis South; **1928** Moorhead; **1929** Moorhead; **1930** Minneapolis South

Graded High School Tournament

From 1923 until 1927, this state basketball tournament, also known as the "Department" tournament, served teams not eligible or not members of the SHSAA. The tournament took place at Hamline in St. Paul. Beginning in 1928, the High School Department Athletic Association schools were allowed to compete in district tournaments with the bigger schools.

Champions

1923 East Chain; **1924** Stewart; **1925** Chisago City; **1926** Brewster; **1927** Henning

National Catholic Interscholastic Tournament

Loyola University in Chicago played host to the National Catholic Interscholastic Tournament from 1924 until 1941. One Minnesota team—Minneapolis's DeLaSalle High School—won the tournament in 1931, when the Islanders went 5–0. In the championship game, the Islanders defeated Jasper (Ind.) Academy, 23–21.

Minnesota teams competing in the tournament

1924 St. Thomas; **1925** St. Thomas; **1926** DeLaSalle, St. Thomas; **1927** DeLaSalle, Austin Columbus; **1928** St. Cloud Cathedral; **1929** St. Cloud Cathedral; **1930** DeLaSalle, St. John's Prep; **1931** DeLaSalle, Winona Cotter; **1932** DeLaSalle, Bird Island St. Mary's, Mankato Loyola, Cretin; **1933** DeLaSalle, St. Thomas, Cretin, Morris St. Mary; **1934** Cretin; **1935** DeLaSalle, Duluth Cathedral; **1936** DeLaSalle, Austin St. Augustine; **1937** DeLaSalle, Winona Cotter; **1938** St. Thomas, Austin St. Augustine; **1939** Austin St. Augustine, Cold Spring St. Boniface; **1940** Cretin; **1941** Cretin

Catholic School Tournaments

In 1974 the 47 nonpublic high schools in the state were invited to join the MSHSL. Prior to that time, private Catholic high schools had conducted their own state tournaments. Non-Catholic private schools also held a tournament.

State champions

Titles won	School	Years
9	DeLaSalle	1944, 1946, 1954, 1955, 1956, 1957, 1959, 1961, 1962
6	St. Thomas	1949, 1950, 1951, 1953, 1960, 1970
5	Austin St. Augustine—Austin Pacelli	1938, 1939, 1940, 1958, 1965
5	Cretin	1942, 1943, 1948, 1971, 1974
4	Rochester Lourdes	1966, 1967, 1968, 1973
2	Winona Cotter	1937, 1952
2	St. Cloud Cathedral	1947, 1969
2	Benilde	1963, 1964
1	Duluth Cathedral	1941
1	Mankato Loyola	1945
1	Fridley Grace	1972

NOTE: From 1971 to 1974, the Catholic and independent tournaments were combined.

March Weather Madness

1941

On March 15, 1941, a Saturday on which many high school district basketball championships were scheduled, 32 deaths were reported statewide from a blizzard. The hardest hit area was northwestern Minnesota, where winds of 75 mph were reported and the temperatures dropped 20 degrees in three hours. In the Red River Valley of Minnesota and North Dakota, 47 deaths were reported.

1951

Heading into the 1951 state tournament, the winter had already been the snowiest in Minneapolis in 35 years. On Saturday, March 10 (the weekend before the tournament), a storm hit Minnesota, leaving 7 inches of snow in Minneapolis and creating travel problems for fans and teams at regional tournaments.

The Canby team defeated Redwood Falls in St. Peter in the Region 3 championship game. The Canby team stayed overnight in St. Peter before setting out for home on Sunday morning.

By noon on Sunday, the team had made it to Tracy, about 45 miles from

Canby, where it was stranded because of impassable roads. The team was stuck in Tracy for 48 hours. On Tuesday, the team negotiated the final 45 miles in 4½ hours. The final portion of the trip involved the team having to get out and push or shovel most of the way home.

Most of Minnesota was paralyzed by winds and drifting snow. In parts of west-central Minnesota, around Wheaton, supplies were airlifted in by the Civil Air Patrol. At least six trains were stuck in snowdrifts—including the Minneapolis-bound Nightingale passenger train. With 350 passengers on board, it was stuck in a drift one mile west of Butterfield for 10 hours. Many local elections in the state that day were postponed because of blocked roads.

At 7:30 A.M. Wednesday, the Canby team left for Minneapolis, hoping to make a noon luncheon that honored the eight state tournament teams. An accident near Glencoe delayed the team and caused it to arrive in downtown Minneapolis at 2:30 P.M. When the team took the Williams Arena floor on Thursday against Hopkins, it was the first time in five days it had touched a basketball.

While Canby was encountering its travel difficulties, Williams Arena on the University of Minnesota campus also had weather-related issues. Just after noon on Monday—three days before the tournament started—a 120-foot section of retaining wall along the roof of the arena collapsed under the weight of the snow. The collapse, which injured two workers who were trying to clear snow off the roof, damaged the lobby on the south side of the arena. University officials nevertheless announced the tournament would start as scheduled.

Once the tournament began on Thursday, it was successful. Travel-weary Canby and tiny Gilbert reached the championship game. On Saturday, March 17, Gilbert defeated Canby for the title.

The next day—Palm Sunday—brought another snowstorm, which stranded many people in the Twin Cities for another day. The 9½ inches that fell in Minneapolis brought the season total to 81 inches—just four inches shy of the record 84.9 inches that fell in the winter of 1916–17. In the seven-day period, Minneapolis had received 21 inches of snow and in the first 18 days of March, 31 inches of snow had fallen in the city.

1965

On St. Patrick's Day, 1965, a blizzard with at least a foot of snow accompanied by strong winds created drifts 25 feet deep—and major statewide travel problems. On March 18, several high school regional basketball finals were postponed because of lingering poor road conditions. The storm was blamed for killing 90 percent of the state's ringneck pheasant population. The winter—called the worst in the state in 40 years—led to record flooding in the Minnesota River Valley in April.

1966

A late blizzard, powered by 60 mph winds, almost disrupted the 1966 state basketball tournament.The storm, which claimed four lives in Minnesota and two in South Dakota, was the worst snowstorm to hit during tournament week in the 54-year history of the tournament.

From the Black Hills to the Great Lakes, the storm dumped one to two feet of snow. The Twin Cities received 14 inches of snow—the third heaviest snowfall in a 24-hour period—the day before the tournament was scheduled to begin.

The weather affected travel for the eight teams. One team—Blooming Prairie—did not arrive in Minneapolis until the day of the tournament. The Blossoms arrived in Minneapolis around midday for their 7:30 P.M. game. A luncheon to welcome the tournament teams, which was scheduled for the day before the tournament, had to be canceled.

Curling

From 1969 until 1977, the Minnesota State High School League sponsored a statewide curling meet for boys. Hibbing won the first three meets and in 1973 and 1976. Mankato won in 1972. Other state curling champions were Virginia in 1974, International Falls in 1975 and Mankato East in 1977.

The MSHSL discontinued its sponsorship of curling, citing its policy that at least 5 percent of the league's membership (526 schools at the time) must compete in a sport for a state meet to be held. The final state curling meet was held February 25–26, 1977, at the Duluth Curling Club.

Football

The state's first high school football team was fielded in 1878 by Shattuck Academy in Faribault. The game resembled rugby at the time. In the 1880s Shattuck played college teams including the University of Minnesota and Carleton College. By 1889 Shattuck billed itself as football's "champions of the Northwest." In October 1894 Northfield and Faribault played the first football game between two Minnesota high schools.

By the early 20th century, teams argued over which was the state champion. In 1900 Minneapolis Central was called the champion of the "Northwest."

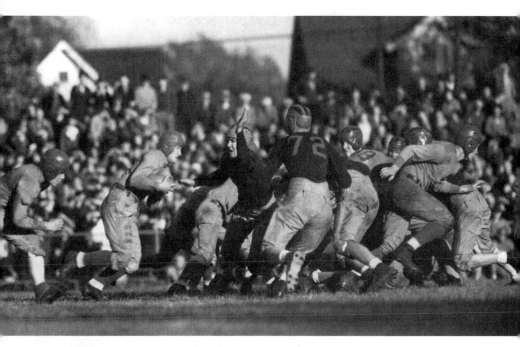

Minneapolis Central vs. Edison football game, 1936

Central, which opened the season with a 0–0 tie against the University of Minnesota, went 8–0–1 while outscoring opponents 291–5. Central defeated high schools in Madison, Wisconsin, and Elgin, Illinois, before completing its season with a 17–0 victory over St. Paul Central on Thanksgiving Day.

In 1907 Minneapolis North claimed the state title after going 7–0, while outscoring its opponents 237–0. Two of the victories came over colleges— St. John's and Hamline—and the Polars capped the season with a 36–0 victory over Chicago Oak Park High School before 5,000 in Minneapolis.

The next year, Faribault High School claimed the state championship with its 9–1 record. Faribault issued a challenge saying it would defend its claim against any team—anywhere—in the state.

According to the *Minneapolis Tribune*, from the day that Bernie Bierman became the football coach at the University of Minnesota in 1933, he hoped the Minnesota State High School League (MSHSL) would institute a play-off to determine a state high school champion. But Bierman, who had been a member of the Litchfield High School football team named the mythical state champion in 1911, never presented his idea to the MSHSL board of directors.

Wanting a more official determination of a state champion, University of Minnesota athletic director Ike Armstrong and Gophers football coach Wes Fesler presented a four-team playoff plan to the Minnesota State High School League's board of directors in 1951. The state of Texas already determined a state champion in football, and University of Oklahoma football coach Bud Wilkinson, a Minneapolis native and graduate of Shattuck and the University of Minnesota, spoke in favor of a playoff in Minnesota. It would be more than 20 years, however, before an official playoff was instituted.

In the interim, Ted Peterson of the *Minneapolis Tribune* began naming a "mythical" state champion in 1947. The newspaper continued the practice until 1971, when a state playoff plan was finally initiated.

State Champions (selected by the Minneapolis Tribune)

1947 Austin; **1948** Duluth Denfeld; **1949** South St. Paul; **1950** Austin; **1951** Austin; **1952** Bemidji; **1953** St. James; **1954** International Falls; **1955** Rochester; **1956** Minneapolis Roosevelt; **1957** Edina-Morningside; **1958** Robbinsdale; **1959** Minneapolis Washburn; **1960** Robbinsdale; **1961** Austin; **1962** Minneapolis Washburn; **1963** Richfield; **1964** Anoka; **1965** Edina-Morningside; **1966** Edina; **1967** Minneapolis Washburn; **1968** Albert Lea; **1969** Edina; **1970** Osseo; **1971** Moorhead

Winningest Coaches in Prep Football History (through 2004)

Coach	School	Record
George Larson	Cambridge	307–66–6
Mike Mahlen	Verndale	295–82–3
Ken Baumann	Mahnomen	287–65–2
George Thole	Stillwater	285–69–2
Ron Stolski	Brainerd	280–132–5
Grady Rostberg	Hutchinson	277–89–2
Jim Roforth	Osakis	267–111–3
George Smith	Mahtomedi	265–122–11
Neal Hofland	Chokio-Alberta	264–80–2
Les Dreschel	Red Lake Falls-Crookston	259–102–9
John Hansen	Osseo	259–105–13
Tom Mahoney	Fairmont	256–94–8

Most High-School Football Program Victories

544 Cambridge; **516** Mahnomen; **506** Fairmont; **469** Stillwater; **436** Redwood Valley; **435** Le Sueur-Henderson; **425** Le Center; **423** Owatonna; **420** Montevideo; **417** International Falls; **416** Detroit Lakes

Losing Streak Record

On September 12, 1986, Glenville-Emmons defeated Ellendale-Geneva, 14–8, to end a 70-game losing streak. The victory was Glenville-Emmons's first in eight years—following an 18–6 victory over Minnesota Lake on September 8, 1978. The losing streak was two games short of the national high school record held by Iberia, Missouri, set from 1965 to 1974.

Glenville-Emmons, which had recently been featured in a 12-page story in *Sports Illustrated,* had opened the 1986 season with losses to Cleveland and Waterville-Elysian. During the streak, Glenville-Emmons was shut out 38 times and outscored 1,803–259.

DID YOU KNOW ?

On November 17, 1972, Minneapolis Washburn defeated Richfield, 26–8, before 16,000 people at Metropolitan Stadium in the first Class AA state football title game. The victory was the 46th consecutive for the Millers and extended their unbeaten streak (which included two ties) to 60 games. When Washburn's Millers opened the 1973 season against Minneapolis Henry on August 31, 1973, Minneapolis Henry rallied for an 8–7 victory and ended the Millers' streak. The loss was the Millers's first since losing to Richfield during the 1966 season.

St. Paul and Minneapolis Conferences

The St. Paul City Conference is the state's second oldest conference in the state, predated only by Minneapolis's conference. St. Paul's conference was born on October 28, 1898, when Central and Mechanic Arts played the first football game between the two schools. Central won 25–0.

For many years, the biggest high school football game in the state was the annual Twin City Championship, which featured the St. Paul and Minneapolis City Conference champions. Played for years at the University of Minnesota's Memorial Stadium, the game attracted as many as 20,000 people. The series began in 1926. After a three-year hiatus, 1929–31, the game was played annually from 1932 to 1978. Discontinued in 1979, it was revived in 1990.

Through the 2004 season, Minneapolis schools lead the series, 40–24–1.

Girls in High School Football

According to the National Federation of State High School Associations, 1,473 girls in 31 states played high school football in 2005. Texas, with 503, and California, with 253, were the top two states for girls' participation.

In Minnesota Mary Nystrom was the place kicker for Robbinsdale Cooper High School in 1999. Nystrom succeeded her brother, Dan, as Cooper's kicker. Dan Nystrom went on to kick for the University of Minnesota.

In 2002 Minnesota teams had 14 girls playing football, and the next year, nine girls played statewide.

In 2004 only six girls played high school football in the Minneapolis–St. Paul Metropolitan Area. Among them was Koren Briggs, who played six years for Minneapolis Roosevelt High School.

All-State High School Football

The *Minneapolis Tribune* named its first all-state football team in 1940. Ted Peterson started picking the team in 1943. Only seniors were named, and no school could have more than one player. In 1956, for the first time, Minneapolis and St. Paul players made the roster. In 1977 the Associated Press picked the All-State team. From 1978 through 1995, the *Minneapolis Tribune* selected a team. Since 1996, the Associated Press has selected the all-state teams.

1940 E—Windmiller, Fergus Falls; Vogel, Austin; T—Musser, Fairmont; Hogan, Red Wing; G—Christianson, Marshall; Bukovich, Hibbing; C—Davidson, Mt. Iron; QB—Gambucci, Eveleth; HB—Luckemeyer, St. Cloud; Brown, Waseca; Mealey, Faribault; FB—Worth, Bemidji

1941 E—Bert Level, Dilworth; Lavton Ausen, Marshall; T—Pat Donohue, Faribault; Sid Nelson, Bemidji; G—Vincent Berra, Eveleth; F. Hendrickson, Redwood Falls; C—Ted Walters, Winona; QB—Wilfred Viitala, Mt. Iron; HB—Lloyd Loven, Ellendale; Russ Grotte, Fairmont; FB—Leo Trushenski, Foley

1942 E—Steve Nelson, Northfield; John Sundberg, Red Wing; T—Dewayne Hoberg, Bemidji; Dean Muetzel, Redwood Falls; G—Emil Steebe, Perham; G. Huntington, Waseca; C—Dick Lagergren, St. Cloud; QB—Bob Collison, Fairmont; HB—Dick Radatz, Winona; Wally Smith, Duluth Denfeld; FB—Alvin Lund, Moorhead

1943 LE—Rudy Branstrom, Duluth Denfeld; LT—Chuck Meiberg, Moorhead; LG—Gus Stromner, Cambridge; C—Francis Dwyer, Redwood Falls; RG—Danny Wagner, Morris; RT—Gordon Quist, St. Peter;

RE—Harold Sundberg, Red Wing; QB—James Graven, Hutchinson; HB—Frank Wright, Austin; Evvie Faunce, Fergus Falls; Willis Castle, Anoka; FB—Red Malcolm, Fairmont

1944 E—Richard Mundinger, Glenwood; T—Leo Meyer, Little Falls; G—George Dickinson, Bemidji; C—Vane Dummer, St. Peter; G—Howard Juliot, Lake City; E—Louis Brunsting, Rochester; Back—Donald Weber, Le Sueur; Bill Bye, Anoka; Frank Kuzma, Ely; Duane Euren, Moorhead

1945 LE—Guy Hollenbeck, Benson; LT—Milt Joecks, Hutchinson; LG—Godfrey Vacura, Jackson; C—Keith Stolen, Duluth Denfeld; RG—Herman Radig, Breckenridge; RT—Eldon Wolhart, St. Cloud Tech; RE—Irving Anderson, Clarkfield; Back—Bob Glover, Chatfield; Jim Malosky, Crosby-Ironton; Walt Hausken, Glenwood; Frank Kuzma, Ely

1946 E—Aldo DeMarkl, International Falls; T—Wayne Swanson, Brainerd; G—Sam Pitulla, Buhl; C—Bobby Hammel, Marshall; G—Jonathan Johnson, Willmar; T—Bill Nicolai, Granite Falls; E—Andrew Papke, Waseca; Back—Jack Sturdevant, Pipestone; Lawrence Tessier, Duluth Denfeld; Dick Brown, Austin; Buddy Brooks, Anoka

1947 LE—Clyde Slocum, Redwood Falls; LT—John Fauskee, Worthington; LG—Cliff Winter, St. Cloud Tech; C—Richard Oberstar, Chisholm; RG—Larry Devine, White Bear Lake; RT—George Fisch, Austin; RE—James Boo, Pine City; QB—Terry O'Hara, Glencoe; HB—Bennie Noland, Park Rapids; Bobby Thompson, Breckenridge; FB—Dave Koch, Wayzata

1948 E—Norm Kragseth, Duluth Central; T—Les Gieneart, Marshall; G—Roger Madson, Grand Rapids; C—Bob Gelle, Osakis; G—Ray Caspers, Melrose; T—Charles Kubes, Northfield; E—Bob McNamara, Hastings; Back—Charles Hren, Duluth Denfeld; Shorty Cochran, Rochester; Chuck Aakhus, Bemidji; Arnie Marudas, Milaca

1949 E—Richard Hugunin, Jackson; T—Gordon Ebel, Anoka; G—Dan Fritz, Luverne; C—Willis Wood, St. Cloud Tech; G—Robert Mancuso, Duluth Morgan Park; T—Glen Clafton, Grand Rapids; E—Herb Meier, Perham; Back—Marty Engh, Montevideo; Paul Giel, Winona; Don Nesheim, Spring Grove; Kermit Christianson, East Grand Forks

1950 E—Jerry Marsh, Austin; T—Bob Aufenthie, Redwood Falls; G—Jerry Leidl, Fergus Falls; C—Harold Pawlik, South St. Paul; G—Wally Eckstein, New Ulm; T—Dave Kragthorpe, Mound; E—Jim Soltau, Duluth Central; Back—Buzz Meighen, Preston; Dale Quist, Northfield; Geno Cappelletti, Keewatin; Jerry Helgeson, St. Cloud Tech

Alexandria vs. Glenwood high school football poster, 1936

1951 E—Don Anderson, Barnesville; T—John Komarek, New Prague; G—Gary Johnson, Litchfield; C—Maynard Meyer, Mountain Lake; G—Mike Falls, Bemidji; T—Jack Henderson, Mountain Iron; E—Dick Weber, Fairmont; Back—Dick LaPage, International Falls; Don Rasmussen, Austin; Dayle Rasmussen, Austin; Darrel Lassila, Esko; John Erickson, Thief River Falls

1952 E—Wayne Deden, Red Wing; T—Harold Drescher, Bemidji; G—Myron Loula, Montgomery; C—Scott Peterson, St. Cloud Tech; G—Vic Bittner, Stewartville; T—Chuck Machacek, Northfield; E—Omar Larson, Granite Falls; Back—Don Hedberg, Cambridge; Chuck Jasper, Duluth Morgan Park; Jim Joslin, Edina-Morningside; Larry Converse, Pipestone

1953 E—Bob Schmidt, Rochester; T—Frank Youso, International Falls; G—Dave Butler, Robbinsdale; C—Jerry Benda, Jackson; G—Bob Lieb, Kenyon; T—Bill Jukich, Duluth Morgan Park; E—Dick Cutler, Preston; Back—Dick Brown, Winona; Norman Anderson, St. James; Richard Borstad, Detroit Lakes, John Drazenovich, Nashwauk

1954 E—Nick Ellena, Duluth Morgan Park; T—Bronko Nagurski Jr., International Falls; G—Everett Gerths, Dodge Center; C—John Bush, Mankato; G—Bert Fristedt, Hopkins; T—Martin Amos, Willmar; E—Jim Reese, Marshall; Back—Sid Vraa, Thief River Falls; Robert Ilg, Montgomery; Willis Fjerstad, Red WIng; Jack Whiting, Bemidji

1955 E—Tom Moe, Edina-Morningside; T—Kirk MacKenzie, St. Peter; G—Norman Beckman, Worthington; C—Arnie Osmundson, Faribault; G—Don Hennessey, Hector; T—Bill Schilling, Walnut Grove; E—Gene Wiebusch, Lake City; Back—Roger Adair, Brainerd; Jim Sheldon, Spring Valley; Tom Robbins, Rochester; Jim Crotty, International Falls

1956 *Offense:* E—Jack Park, Aitkin; T—Dennis Albrecht, St. Paul Central; G—Gary Lytle, Richfield; C—Mike Suplick, Robbinsdale; G—Jim Porter, Minneapolis Washburn; T—John Willemssen, Worthington; E—Dick Aadelen, Red Wing; Back—Jack Halland, Fergus Falls; Dave Sieben, Melrose; L.C. Hester, Minneapolis Roosevelt; Gary Melchert, Morris

　　Defense: E—Gary Sprute, Farmington; T—Dick Maki, Proctor; C—Bill Nelson, Minneapolis Edison; T—Bob Johnson, Waseca; E—Dan Cunningham, Pipestone; LB—Chuck Wennerlund, Anoka; Chuck Benjamin, Hutchinson; Bob Hren, Duluth Central; HB—Nick Weller, White Bear Lake; Tom Kinnunen, Mountain Iron; S—T. Y. Moore, Rochester

1957 *Offense:* LE—Ken Hokeness, Northfield; LT—Tom Loechler, Robbinsdale; LG—Dennis Heeren, St. Paul Central; C—Tom Wagner, Buffalo; RG—T. Cooper, Rochester; RT—Tom Hecomovich, Coleraine; RE—Bob Stencel, Alden; Back—Roy Bostock, Edina-Morningside; Gary Schaar, Lamberton; Ron Meade, Canby; Jerry Ferguson, Minneapolis South

    Defense: LE—Dick Southard, Princeton; LT—Jerry Peterson, Austin; MG—Doug Backhaus, Alexandria; RT—Daryl Foster, Fosston; RE—Clarence Holman, Hutchinson; LB—Ken Wold, Crookston; Lloyd Nistler, Eden Valley; Arlo Brunsberg, Fertile; DB—Dick Bakke, St. James; Virg Riley, Melrose; S—Fred McSherry, Mounds View

1958 *Offense:* LE—Lawrence Johnson, Moorhead; LT—Tony Alleva, St. Paul Humboldt; LG—Dave Reinardy, Sauk Centre; C—Jerry Wherley, International Falls; RG—Clayton Schirmer, Minneapolis Washburn; RT—Cliff Nagengast, Osseo; RE—Jay Kessler, Redwood Falls; Back—Duane Tauer, Morgan; Jim Zak, Little Falls; Bill Brechler, Minneapolis South; Jerry Jones, St. Louis Park

    Defense: LE—Dennis Harvey, Willmar; LT—Jack Perkovich, South St. Paul; MG—Dick Grafe, Grand Meadow; RT—Terry Maus, Austin; Larry Maus, Austin; RE—Pete Bergman, Duluth Denfeld; LB—Julian Hook, Robbinsdale; Paul Benson, Granite Falls; Dick Riedberger, Hawley; DB—Bill Taylor, Crookston; Duane Blaska, Anoka; S—Harold Anderson, Cokato

1959 *Offense:* E—Tom Wilson, Mahtomedi; T—Mike Daley, Lewiston; G—Paul Moe, Albert Lea; C—Tom Gritton, Richfield; G—Howard McCarty, White Bear Lake; T—Gordy Kvern, Fergus Falls; E—Ronnie Braham; Back—Jerry Pelletier, Bloomington; Mike Doshan, Crosby-Ironton; Terry Hedstrom, Alexandria; John Collier, Minneapolis Washburn

    Defense: E—Clayton Reed, Austin; T—Lyle Gerdes, Worthington; MG—Lyle Stevens, Staples; T—Hank Moehrke, Cloquet; E—Dennis Anderson, International Falls; LB—Ronald Goetze, Waconia; Jack Puglisi, Duluth Denfeld; Jim Harder, Litchfield; DB—Dougal McLellan, St. Paul Harding; Doug Urness, Mahnomen; S—David Carey, Tracy

1960 *Offense:* E—Fred Warn, Minneapolis Roosevelt; T—Charles Stern, Austin; G—Doug Powers, Grand Rapids; C—Craig Olson, Bloomington; G—Rollie Olson, Crosby-Ironton; T—Duane Kropuensko, Luverne; E—Jim Tetzloff, Janesville; Back—John Hankinson, Edina; Mike Orman, Hastings; Steve Foster, Minneapolis Henry; Larry Peterson, Robbinsdale

Defense: E—Dick Fisher, Duluth East; T—Joe Hobson, LeCenter; MG—Jerry Cawley, Waseca; T—Fred Nord, Minneapolis Washburn; E—Dennis Dushaw, Sauk Rapids; LB—Lee Fawbush, Bemidji; Kraig Lofquist, Biwabik; Gene Rabel, Mahtomedi; DB—Jim Anderson, Montevideo; Dick Oliphant, Albert Lea; Jack Nielsen, Baudette; Pat O'Halloran, Olivia

1961 *Offense:* E—Bob Bruggers, Danube; T—Jim Osberg, Minneapolis Washburn; G—Wayne Lueders, Le Sueur; C—John Drury, Richfield; G—Jim Hennen, Ada; T—Jim Staebler, Morris; E—Jim Schwant, Sanborn; Back—Bob Grausnick, Winona; Tom Hardy, Austin; Tony Lynch, International Falls; Tom Drazenovich, Nashwauk

Defense: E—Jim Nesvold, Madison; T—Phil Fishbaugher, Harmony; MG—Roger Bonk, Appleton; T—Don Rosen, Rosemount; E—Allen Woitaszewski, Slayton; LB—Dale Brown, Brainerd; Doug Jones, Minneapolis Marshall; Brian Magnuson, Hopkins; DB—Earl Johnson, Willmar; Jim Schindler, Barnesville; Chuck Achterkirk, Mounds View

1962 *Offense:* E—Mike Rybak, Anoka; T—Roy Sutherland, Rochester; G— Jim Marxhausen, Minneapolis Washburn; C—Dennis Drummond, Perham; G—John Nefstead, Marshall; T—Bob Engebretson, Moorhead; E—Paul Sannes, Fertile; Back—Bob Haddorff, Mound; Mike Forrest, Cloquet; Paul Klungness, Thief River Falls; Hank Uberecken, St. Cloud Tech

Defense: E—Terry Hinz, Fairmont; T—Roger Nelson, Benson; MG—John Reiners, Minneapolis Edison; T—Pat Patten, Grand Rapids; E—Glen Stoltz, Owatonna; LB—Gary Reierson, Edina-Morningside; James Barle, Greenway; Chet Anderson, Duluth Central; DB—Tim Wheeler, Richfield; Joe Sauser, Lakeville; S—Dennis Aquiar, Bemidji

1963 *Offense:* E—John Tietz, Minneapolis Washburn; T—Dave Huber, Anoka; G—Randy Rajala, Bigfork; C—Nick Nahorniak, Mahtomedi; G—Ross Schmidt, Alden; T—Dave Griffin, Benson; E—Eddy Larson, Detroit Lakes; Back—Steve Lindell, Princeton; Don Parmeter, Littlefork; Harry Davis, Minneapolis Central; Ernie Maulsby, Edina-Morningside

Defense: E—Tom Langseth, Richfield; T—Ron Klick, Delano; MG— Bruce Walker, Hibbing; T—Leo Baxter, Walnut Grove; E—Rick Jahns, Albert Lea; LB—Pat Winkler, Bemidji; Dennis Hoglin, Orono; Mitch Rasmus, Moorhead; DB—Dave Nelson, Rochester; Gary Beher, St. Cloud Tech; Gary Sandbo, Tracy

1964 *Offense:* E—Jeff Hinz, Willmar; T—John Darkenwald, Edina-Morningside; G—Pete Rodman, Henning; C—Steve Lundeen, Minneapolis

Roosevelt; G—Ed Oliver, Cambridge; T—Eric Norri, Virginia; E—Tom Fink, Delano; Back—Marv Danielson, Anoka; Dennis Hale, Jackson; Scott Gernander, Duluth Denfeld; Bob Olson, St. Louis Park

Defense: E—Rich Field, Rochester; T—Tom Haugo, Litchfield; MG—Ron LeClaire, Melrose; T—Neil Ladsten, Littlefork-Big Falls; E—Noel Jenke, Owatonna; LB—Bob Fortier, Bemidji; Dick Fortier, Bemidji; Michael Swanke, Wheaton; Eldon Nelson, St. Cloud Tech; DB—Glen Nevlis, Minneapolis Central; Tom Williams, Fairmont; S—Doug Glynn, Grand Meadow

1965 *Offense:* E—Pat Kenney, Moorhead; T—Bob Bethke, Minneapolis Roosevelt; G—Mickey Stenson, Edina-Morningside; C—Tom White, Rochester; G—Doug Peterson, Madison; T—Charles Stuemke, White Bear Lake; E—Paul Kelly, Morris; QB—Doug Roalstad, Robbinsdale; HB—Paul Hatchett, Minneapolis Central; Glenn Leimbach, Jackson; FB—Jim Carter, South St. Paul

Defense: E—Terry Wirz, Milaca; T—Bryan Schultz, Blue Earth; G—Al Decker, Duluth Central; T—Larry Schwartz, Bemidji; E—Dave Brooker, North Branch; LB—James Pahula, Buhl; Ron Long, Pine River; John Branson, Delano; DB—Larry Kotek, Montgomery; Randy Stetler, Osseo; S—Hub Nelson, Golden Valley

1966 *Offense:* LE—Wayne Iverson, Robbinsdale; LT—Kim Brenckman, Blue Earth; LG—Greg Johnson, Crosby-Ironton; C—Darrell Gavie, Albert Lea; RG—Gerry Germundsen, Osseo; RT—Jan Nelson, Minneapolis Washburn; RE—Al Montgomery, St. Paul Washington; Back—Rick Heard, Austin; Bryce Kommerstad, Rochester; Jeff Wright, Edina; Cyd Maatala, Moorhead

Defense: LE—Gerald Brutlag, Henning; LT—Dave Colallio, Duluth Denfeld; MG—Jim Anderson, Belgrade; RT—Bob Eastlund, Cambridge; RE—Rich Varriano, Dilworth; LB—John Boyer, Bemidji; Ken Holker, Monticello; Greg Schneider, Chaska; DB—Kirk Pederson, Hastings; Jim Robinson, Minneapolis Central; S—Joe Nett, Albany

1967 *Offense:* D—Kevin Hamm, St. Cloud Tech; T—Bruce Dahl, Albert Lea; G—Craig Overhouse, Minneapolis Washburn; C—Ron King, Chatfield; G—Jerry Skogmo, Fergus Falls; T—Daryl Niemi, Cloquet; E—Mike Antilla, Esko; Back—Dan Hergott, Le Sueur; Bob Morgan, Robbinsdale; Tom Varichak, Chisholm; Doug Kingsriter, Richfield

Defense: E—Jack Babcock, Rochester Mayo; T—Richard Nielsen, St. Peter; MG—Pat McCarthy, Albany; T—Terry Reisinger, Mahtomedi; E—Larry Helgeson, Bemidji; LB—John Kukaska, Mounds View; Tom

Small, Worthington; Jim Kennedy, Grand Meadow; DB—Terry Domek, Fairmont; Bill Bordson, Duluth Denfeld; S—Al Brusven, Mahnomen

1968 *Offense:* E—Sheldon Joppru, Thief River Falls; T—Rolf Grudem, Jackson; G—Calvin Ludeman, Tracy; C—Clayton Scheuer, St. Cloud Tech; G—Tom Keckeisen, Hibbing; T—Joe Kotval, Pipestone; E—Matt Herkenhoff, Melrose; Back—Mike Cadwell, St. Louis Park; Jay Gustafson, Albert Lea; Jim Steinmueller, White Bear Lake; Dennis Kovash, Moorhead

Defense: E—Larry Wieker, Litchfield; T—Bruce Hanson, Minneapolis Roosevelt; MG—Steve Cook, Richfield; T—Steve McInerney, Two Harbors; E—Rick Poppitz, Chaska; LB—Tim Ball, Austin; Kevin Swanson, Fairmont; Marc Mayberg, Edina; DB—Chuck Ness, Duluth Central; Bob Bjorklund, Henning; S—Dan Quam, Kenyon

1969 *Offense:* QB—Dale May, Minneapolis Washburn; Back—Lindsay Hoyer, Edina; Bruce Reimer, Bloomington Kennedy; Terry Highum, Peterson; E—Scott Finley, Bloomington Lincoln; Keith Fahnhorst, St. Cloud Tech; T—Pat McNerney, Fairmont; Chet Stevenson, Princeton; G—David Lamb, Dilworth; Larry Wood, Austin; C—Dan Johnson, Anoka

Defense: MG—Greg Smith, Osseo; T—Scott Irwin, Duluth Central; Steve Haraldson, Bemidji; E—Terry Newman, Osseo; Mike Ramerth, Minneapolis Roosevelt; LB—Mark Schwarze, Hutchinson; Rick Vacura, Jackson; Mike Tintor, Hibbing; DB—Steve Holum, Moorhead; Marty Bonnell, Farmington; Tom Mandt, Adams

1970 *Offense:* QB—Craig Dahl, Albert Lea; Back—Dan Doshan, Armstrong; Walter Groce, Minneapolis Central; Tom Ruud, Bloomington Jefferson; C—John Chatley, Grand Rapids; G—Dan Fritsche, North St. Paul; Dave Mooers, Duluth Morgan Park; T—Tom Vaughan, Kellogg; Dennis Riesgraf, Belle Plaine; E—Bob Nelson, Stillwater; Mark Gibbons, Cambridge

Defense: MG—Greg Smith, Osseo; T—Dave Appleyard, Northfield; Bob Sims, Edina; E—Keith Rudeen, North St. Paul; John Frye, Richfield; LB—Don Joyce, Mahtomedi; George Rindelaub, Marshall; Scot MacDonald, Two Harbors; DB—Mike Pappas, Albert Lea; Brian Grover, St. Louis Park; Greg Wohnoutka, Olivia

1971 *Offense:* E—Steve Rukavina, White Bear Lake; Bob Verchota, Duluth East; T—Randy Hallstrom, Robbinsdale; Jim Johanson, Cloquet; G—Dave Clukey, Moorhead; Jeff Jacobson, Fergus Falls; C—Craig Everett, Pipestone; QB—Chuck McGrew, Edina; HB—Kevin Smith, Minneapolis North; Mike Jauss, Montevideo; FB—Brad Moen, Bloomington Lincoln

Defense: MG—Mike Smith, Minneapolis Central; T—Greg Shoff, Albert Lea; Jim Perkins, Red Wing; E—Wally Christopherson, Columbia Heights; Curt Olson, Bloomington Jefferson; LB—Gary Sargent, Bemidji; Dan Forsythe, North St. Paul; Bill Bunkers, Fulda; DB—Kurt Knoff, East Grand Forks; Paul Domholt, Minneapolis Washburn; Carl Hendrickson, Crosby-Ironton

1972 *Offense:* E—George Harris, Burnsville; Ken Spaeth, Mahnomen; T—Russ Anderson, Minneapolis Washburn; Joe Checco, Hibbing; G—Tom Young, Wadena; Kevin Gronlund, Cooper; C—Tim Kruger, Robbinsdale; QB—Loren Beste, Sauk Centre; RB—Jeff Huot, Moorhead; Dave Gervais, Hill-Murray; Ross Baglien, Minneapolis Washburn

Defense: E—Doug Ludeman, St. Cloud Tech; Mark Merrill, Kellogg; T—Jim Perkins, Red Wing; Terry Matula, Hastings; LB—Rick Budde, Richfield; Howie Gackstetter, Simley; Bruce Brenckman, Blue Earth;

Burnsville vs. Sauk Centre in the Class A state championship title game, 1972

DB—Dave Otness, Edina East; Todd Treichel, Cambridge; D. Van Der Heyden, Rochester John Marshall; Kent Smith, Thief River Falls

1973 *Offense:* E—Stan Drew, Bemidji; Steve Martin, Willmar; T—Steve Haney, Coon Rapids; Brian Mann, Luverne; G—Brian Mauer, St. Paul Harding; Mickey Reed, Rochester Lourdes; C—Steve Brandes, Minneapolis Edison; QB—Rick Chounard, Anoka; RB—Jeff Hawkins, Elk River; Kelly Fitzgerald, Preston; Ross Baglien, Minneapolis Washburn

Defense: E—Randy Christey, Owatonna; Steve Glocke, Burnsville; T—Tony Dorn, Thief River Falls; Steve Lindquist, Brooklyn Center; MG—Bill Barnett, Stillwater; LB—Andy Hvidston, Moorhead; J. D. Walker, Richfield; Stan Sytsma, Hutchinson; DB—Gary Frericks, St. Cloud Apollo; Rick Faust, Hopkins Lindbergh; Scott Bargfrede, Jackson

---

DID YOU KNOW ?

The Minnesota State High School League first instituted overtimes as a way to end ties games in football for the 1973 season.

1974 *Offense:* QB—Bob Beliveau, Alexandria; RB—Kent Kitzmann, Rochester John Marshall; Paul Larson, Coon Rapids; FB—Peter Assad, St. Thomas; C—Jeff Carter, Grand Rapids; G—Gery Wagner, Hastings; Bob Gastecki, Little Falls; T—Steve Tobin, Moorhead; Greg Cardelli, Minneapolis Southwest, E—Phil Verchota, Duluth East; WR—Scott Quittem, Simley; K—Scott Pederson, St. Louis Park

Defense: E—Phil Olson, Edina East; Ken Chenel, Centennial; T—Rick LaVoy, Mahnomen; Vince Whittley, Henning; LB—John Ruud, Bloomington Jefferson; Doug Nelson, Richfield; Scott Farnes, Albert Lea; Bruce Watson, White Bear Lake Mariner; DB—Harold Stevens, New Prague; Tom Klitzke, Cambridge; Jim Marcella, Virginia; P—Dave Petzke, Faribault

1975 *Offense:* E—Tim Laudner, Park Center; Dave Rockers, Austin Pacelli; T—Dave Dirkes, Albany; Mark Gramstad, Worthington; G—Russ Shroyer, White Bear Lake Mariner; Jay Klein, Hibbing; C—Brad Struck, Alexandria; QB—Mark Hustad, Battle Lake; RB—Glenn Lewis, Edina West; Brian Kaping, Hutchinson; Jeff Thompson, Bloomington Jefferson; K—Soren Gam, Stillwater

Defense: E—Kevin Berg, St. Thomas; Ken Holland, Emmons; T—Calvin Anderson, Minneapolis Central; Judd Sather, Anoka; LB—Jim Kelly, Red Wing; Ric Lager, St. Peter; Mark Mauer, St. Paul Harding; Steve Dronen, Richfield; DB—Mike Shaft, Faribault; Duane Southerland, Park Rapids; Randy Sonnenfeld, Robbinsdale

1976 *Offense:* QB—Greg Pylatiuk, Columbia Heights; HB—Tony Veith, Brainerd; Ron Straka, St. Peter; FB—Mike Schrader, Burnsville; C—Barry Berger, Worthington; G—Gret Milberger, Cloquet; Mark Eidem, Anoka; T—Mike Orgas, Park Center; Tim Femrite, Minneapolis Edison; TE—Steve Ferry, Cooper; WR—Al Markfort, St. Paul Harding; K—John Woodmansee, Shattuck

Marshall high school fans cheering for their team, about 1955

Defense: T—Jim Schleper, St. Cloud Cathedral; Gregg Gonsior, Fridley Grace; E—Wally Arnold, Rochester Lourdes; Perry Lundberg, Fridley; LB—Don Lucia, Grand Rapids; Dave Vanzo, Wayzata; Bob Slater, St. Thomas; Jim Fahnhorst, St. Cloud Tech; DB—Phil Frye, Rochester John Marshall; Pete Rockers, Austin Pacelli; Rodney Lewis, Minneapolis Central; P—Brian Bunkers, Fulda

1977 *Offense:* QB—Joe Lahti, Columbia Heights; HB—Gregg Thompson, Stillwater; Mike Sandor, Hibbing; FB—Chuck Lowell, White Bear Lake; C—Howard Holman, Columbia Heights; G—Scott Wierschem, Willmar; John Dingle, Rochester Mayo; T—Tom Halek, Fridley Grace; Jeff Kwapick, Centennial; E—Jay Barnett, White Bear Lake Mariner; Tony Freeman, Cooper; K—Tim Rohde, Waseca

Defense: NG—Don Borgenheimer, Hibbing; DL—Paul Franzmeier, Richfield; Mike Mazur, Mahtomedi; Kevin Kellin, Grand Rapids; Tim Biegert, Osseo; LB—Joe Wabner, Waseca; Randy Schmidt, Holdingford; Joe Slater, St. Thomas Academy; DB—Wayne Schlucter, St. Cloud Tech; Howard Nevanen, International Falls; Dave Hart, Minneapolis Washburn; P—Tim Sturdevant, Moorhead

1978 *Offense:* QB—Dennis Schleper, St. Cloud Cathedral; RB—Rick Bell, Cold Spring Rocori; Rob McGarry, Stillwater; Sean Maher, St. Thomas Academy; SE—Bruce Harman, Cooper; TE—Mark Gaworksi, Fairmont; T—Barry Young, Apple Valley; Don Williams, Minneapolis Washburn; G—Bill Dahlquist, Cambridge; Mark Downing, Minneapolis Roosevelt; C—Chris Bennett, Stillwater; K—Mike Gaffaney, Villard

Defense: E—John Olsonoski, Edina West; Brad Peterson, Brainerd; T—Steve Meyer, Pipestone; Todd Spratte, Rochester John Marshall; G—Pat Faber, Minneapolis Edison; LB—Paul Najarian, Minneapolis Central; Dick Maas, St. Louis Park; Mike Laliberte, Hibbing; John Houle, St. Paul Harding; DB—Bruce Larson, Fridley; Mark Selisker, Crosby-Ironton; P—Paul Blanchard, Wayzata

1979 *Offense:* QB—Scott Housh, Edina West; RB—Pat Juhl, Stillwater; Justin Taylor, Apple Valley; John Sachen, Red Wing; SE—Dale Olson, Eagle Bend; TE—Steve Veldmah, South St. Paul; T—Bob Anderson, Fridley Grace; Tim LaVoy, Mahnomen; G—Jeff Moritko, Minneapolis Edison, Kevin Thies, Gaylord; C—John Cierzan, Rochester Lourdes; K—Jim Gallery, Morton

Defense: E—John Alt, Columbia Heights; Mark Vonderhaar, Hibbing; T—Mike Stratton, Stillwater; Jesse Quam, Minneapolis Roosevelt; G—Ken Graeber, Armstrong; LB—Steve Garske, Richfield; Dave

Nickles, Apple Valley; Tyler Treichel, Cambridge; DB—Jeff Weyer, Redwood Falls; Ron Sannes, Fertile-Beltrami; Dave Strobel, Hill-Murray; P—John Scheuer, St. Paul Humboldt

1980 *Offense:* QB—Neil Stock, New Ulm; RB—Matt Hoffman, Pine Island; Clark Johnson, Alexander Ramsey; Gary Paulson, White Bear Lake; SE—Trent Johnson, Bloomington Lincoln; TE—Dave Bidinger, Morton; T—Eric Brust, Montevideo; Fred Hunt, Ortonville; G—Todd Kuss, Columbia Heights; Tom Ramboldt, Goodhue; C—Bert Duffy, Benilde–St. Margaret's; K—Craig Lewis, Simley

  Defense: E—Todd Chapman, Edina East; Greg Irons, Duluth East; T—Jon Lilleberg, Atwater; Korey Niesen, Park Center; LB—Joe Christopherson, Austin Pacelli; Pete Najarian, Minneapolis Central; Jon Dunbar, Cambridge; Jack Schlichting, Brooklyn Center; DB—Steve Johnson, Crookston; Dan Leighton, St. Thomas Academy; Barry Wohler, Bird Island-Lake Lillian; P—Adam Kelly, Minnetonka

1981 *Offense:* QB—Brett Sadek, Rosemount; RB—Chul Schwanke, Hutchinson; Brian Reis, Holdingford; Eric Borg, St. Anthony; E—Gary Schleper, Shakopee; Gary Anderson, Clarkfield; T—Kevin Blackmer, Minneapolis Central; Mike Praus, Wayzata; G—Mike Piel, North Branch; Robert Hepka, Argyle; C—Rich Hornung, Hill-Murray; K—Gary Potter, Hutchinson

  Defense: E—Ivan Zuber, Richfield; Steve Jordan, Minneapolis Washburn; T—Rick Spaeth, Mahnomen; Lawrence Hart, Park of Cottage Grove; G—Steve Emerson, Moorhead; LB—Jeff Gigstad, Alexandria; Jim Dick, Totino Grace; John Frawley, Red Wing; Dave Pederson, Duluth Morgan Park; DB—Todd DeBates, Stewartville; Brad Lembke, Burnsville; P—Dave Steveken, St. Thomas

1982 *Offense:* QB—Brett Sadek, Rosemount; Back—Willie Jacox, Bloomington Kennedy; Scott Roach, Mounds View; Back—Von Sheppard, St. Paul Central; SE—Mike Nelson, Starbuck; TE—Dave Lueth, Fairmont; T—Ray Hitchcock, St. Paul Johnson; Kevin Mell, Chaska; G—Greg Czech, St. Cloud Tech; Kevin Kampa, Becker; C—Bob Wagner, Faribault Shattuck

  Defense: E—Tom Copa, Coon Rapids; Rod Lossow, Minneapolis South; T—Darren Johnson, Osseo; Mike Seasly, Edina; G—Mark Fisher, Albany; LB—Brian Bonner, Minneapolis Washburn; Blaine Kolstad, St. James; Dana Muehlhauser, Sandstone-Finlayson; DB—Dan Lewis, St. Clair; Chad Van Hulzen, Fridley; Tony Zajac, White Bear Lake Mariner

Specialists: K—Mark Holsten, Stillwater; P—Dan Sorenson, Orono; Returner—Tim Veith, Brainerd

1983 *Offense:* QB—Mike McDevitt, Park Center; RB—Kermit Klesaas, Brooklyn Center; Dan Paulson, White Bear Lake; Dave Umland, Osseo; Receivers: John Mackedanz, Albany; Paul Weinberg, St. Paul Cretin; Line—Mike Berg, St. Charles; Mike Favor, Minneapolis North; Mark Mendel, Wayzata; John Williams, Bloomington Jefferson; Troy Wolkow, Lakeville

   Defense: Line—Jake Ford, Chisago Lakes; Greg Goenner, St. Cloud Tech; Mike Jindra, Montgomery-Lonsdale; Doug Phillips, Minneapolis Washburn; John Siekmeier, Mahtomedi; LB—Tom Mazur, Cloquet; Jon Scott, Coon Rapids; DB—Chris Garrett, St. Paul Central; Robbie Peterson, Barnum; Tom Serie, Minneapolis Edison; Greg Von Der Lippe, Blaine

   Specialists: K—Keith Kimberly, Apple Valley; P—David Balke, Waldorf-Pemberton

1984 *Offense:* TE—Tom Redalen, Chatfield; Line—J. J. Lennon, St. Thomas Academy; Landan Hegert, Bloomington Kennedy; Joel Maack, Breckenridge; Mark Schwegmann, Sauk Centre; C—Bill Anderson, Columbia Heights; WR—Kyle Loven, Swanville; QB—Steve Walsh, St. Paul Cretin; Andy Rostberg, Hutchinson; RB—Bob Kelly, Coon Rapids; Steve Shiner, Lakeville; Slot back—Cary Miller, Minneota

   Defense: DE—Jon Melander, Fridley; Brent Otto, Minneapolis Henry; Line—Dennis Ryan, Hill-Murray; Mike Kelley, Silver Bay; Tim England, St. Cloud Cathedral; LB—Snuffy Byers, Minneapolis Roosevelt; Mike Turgeon, Warren; Bryan Suess, Kasson-Mantorville; DB—Paul Friesen, Rosemount; Rick Rodgers, St. Cloud Tech; Dave Peterson, Worthington

   Specialists: P—Wade Begstad, Raymond; K—Pat Beaty, Bloomington Jefferson; Return—Steve Ehlert, Stewart

1985 *Offense:* TE—Kerry Miller, Rochester Mayo; Line—Kelly Day, Apple Valley, John Selvestra, Rosemount; Mark Braun, St. Charles; Derek Johnson, Bloomington Jefferson; C—Chris Mussman, Owatonna; WR—Todd Fultz, Forest Lake; QB—Tod Hartje, Anoka; RB—Ron Goetz, Waconia; Darrell Thompson, Rochester John Marshall; Pat Tingelhoff, St. Thomas Academy

   Defense: DE—Tom Donovan, Marshall; Bart Ludlow, Staples; Line—Bob Coughlin, Osseo; Dick Pundsack, Albany; Paul Bronson, Granite Falls; LB—George Pelawa, Bemidji; Jason Brouwer, Chandler-Lake

Wilson; DB—Gene Ollrich, Hutchinson, Brian Hennen, Burnsville; Tim Radosevich, Duluth Central; Harry Jackson, Minneapolis Roosevelt

Specialists: P—Cory Solberg, Spring Lake Park; K—Kevin Boe, Fergus Falls; Return—Mike Guckeen, Park Center

1986 *Offense:* TE—Barry Beck, Appleton; Line—Gary Isakson, Apple Valley; Troy Smutka, Hutchinson; Devin DeVore, Bloomington Jefferson; Dan Schmidt, Stewartville; C—Dick LaBorde, Wayzata; WR—Greg Dietel, Houston; QB—Trent Anderson, Alexandria; RB—Chris SanAgustin, Apple Valley; Kurt Gunning, Stillwater; Steve Severson, Wabasha-Kellogg

Defense: DE—Rob Phenix, Rosemount; Dan Donner, Echo-Wood Lake–Belview; DL—Jamie O'Brien, Rosemount; Jeff Julkowski, Forest Lake; Preston Stoltman, Argyle; LB—Mike Schwartz, Irondale; Scott Shiner, Lakeville; Rick Meyer, Granite Falls; DB—Gary Trettel, Mounds View; Kevin Lovegreen, St. Thomas Academy; Mike Doll, Bloomington Kennedy

Specialists: P—Pete Raether, Edina; K—Dean Kaufman, Sauk Centre; Return—Chad Mortenson, Osseo

1987 *Offense:* TE—Dave Anderson, Granite Falls; OL—Al Venske, Stillwater; Jeff Cech, Redwood Falls–Morton; Tom Markgraf, Osseo; Ted Harrison, Cooper; C—Paul Bartlett, Richfield; WR—Dan Carlson, Willmar; QB—Chris Meidt, Minneota; RB—Rod Smith, Roseville; Rick Meyer, Granite Falls; Mark Hansen, Owatonna; Jeremy Wicht, Cambridge

Defense: DE—John Bruley, Forest Lake; Adam Johnston, Minneapolis Edison; DL—Jeff Nelson, Stillwater; Joe Dimmen, Farmington; Adan Alonzo, Glyndon-Felton; LB—Monte Johnson, Osseo; Joel Staats, Winona; Shawn Stewart, Hallock; DB—Irving Hill, Burnsville; Sean Lumpkin, Benilde–St. Margaret's; Lance Sage, Warroad

Specialists: P—Pete Raether, Edina; K—Steve Tupy, New Prague; Return—Tom Menage, Luverne

1988 *Offense:* TE—Daren Danielson, Stillwater; OL—Brent Jensen, Richfield; Chuck Scripture, New Prague; Chris McElroy, Park Center; Tim Shaikoski, Fairmont; Dennis Scheel, Cambridge; C—Rod Carey, Wayzata; WR—Chris Essier, Sauk Centre; Eric Hennen, Minneota; QB—Justin Tomberlin, Greenway; RB—John Buzick, Blaine; John McCoy, St. Paul Como Park; David Christians, Herman-Norcross; Doug Doering, Willmar; Corey Fritz, Morristown

Defense: DE—Brad Ranum, Lakeville; Tony Poncelet, Goodhue; DL—Mitch Moorehead, Blaine; Jim Remme, Luverne; Scott Sether, Winona;

Lance Larson, Moorhead; LB—Paul Meyer, Minneapolis Henry; Matt Ellefson, Osseo; Jesse Harman, Mora; Jon Urban, Zumbrota-Mazeppa; DB—Jeff Rosga, Cretin–Derham Hall; Lance Wolkow, Lakeville; Mike Thomas, Apple Valley; Kyle Atherton, Waterville-Elysian

Specialists: Return—Arden Beachy, Staples-Motley; P—Matt Brzica, St. Thomas Academy; K—Chris Carlson, Park Center

1989 *Offense:* QB—Chris Weinke, Cretin–Derham Hall; RB—Parnell Charles, St. Agnes; Dennis Heinen, Osseo; Brad Loeffler, St. Clair; Chuck Rios, Roseville; Dan Seymour, New Prague; WR—T.R. McDonald, Totino-Grace; TE—Chad Pundsack, Albany; Mark Montgomery, St. Thomas Academy; OL—Rob Herrmann, Osseo; Scott Hosier, Burnsville; Jeff McCullough, Chaska; Pat O'Brien, International Falls; Erik Russek, Delano; Jason Slavik, Stillwater; Dave Vertin, Wayzata

Defense: DL—Brian Kohorst, St. Cloud Cathedral; Andy Kratochvil, New Prague; Todd Ratzlaff, Rosemount; Todd Schmidt, Staples-Motley; Ako Stafford, St. Thomas Academy; LB—Tim DeVlaeminck, Minneota; Joe Dziedzic, Minneapolis Edison; Brian Hamlin, Moorhead; Mike Mooney, Blaine; Todd Wolkow, Lakeville; DB—Eric Edmond, Burnsville; Robby Ott, Deer River; Troy Sladek, Battle Lake

Specialists: Return—John O'Neill, St. Bernard's; K—Omar Salas, Fridley; P—Terry Rasmussen, Farmington

1990 *Offense:* QB—Bryce Darnell, Brooklyn Center; Chris Walsh, Cretin–Derham Hall; RB—Chad Bohonek, Albert Lea; Mike Rudnick, Anoka; Marvin Sims, Apple Valley; WR—Jeremy Loretz, Anoka; Martez Williams, Minneapolis Henry; TE—Craig Wachholz, Mayer Lutheran; OL—Charlie Brown, Rochester Lourdes; Tait Christensen, Litchfield; Dan Jost, St. Cloud Apollo; Andy Kubena, Hibbing; Billy Pierce, Minneapolis Roosevelt; Marc Wiese, Owatonna; Erik Wilkinson, Wayzata

Defense: DL—Keith Bartholomaus, Brainerd; Amos Casey, Richfield; Shawn Ehrich, Blue Earth; Matt Reem, Concordia Academy; Dan White, Monticello; Mike Williams, Cretin–Derham Hall; LB—Bill Hjortaas, Richfield; Matt Jones, Elk River; Steve Sampson, Burnsville; Steve Walters, Stillwater; DB—Raylen Hicks, Minneapolis Edison; Mike Jaunich, Delano; Pete Roback, Anoka; Craig Sauer, Sartell

Specialists: K—Mike Chalberg, Forest Lake; Return—Jerry Reitan, Blaine; P—Todd Bouman, Russell-Tyler-Ruthton

1991 *Offense:* QB—Chris Walsh, Cretin–Derham Hall; RB—Shane Gunderson, Faribault; Jason Miller, Mahnomen; John Toth, Forest Lake; C—Bill Teas, Osseo; OG—Mike Doughty, Lakeville; Josh Fulwider, Spring

Lake Park; OT—Kurt King, Brainerd; Victor Robinson, Deer River; TE—Mark Tangen, Concordia Academy; WR—Skipp Schaefbauer, Elk River; Troy Stein, Rocori; Carl McCullough, Cretin–Derham Hall

Defense: DE—Kevin Hammond, Burnsville; Graham Gnos, Bloomington Jefferson; DT—Pat Larson, Stillwater; Mike McCullough, Chaska; LB—Curt Behrns, Kasson-Mantorville; Walter Binger, Cambridge; Jamal Clark, Hopkins; John DesRoches, Anoka; DB—Raylen Hicks, Minneapolis Edison; Kevin Pearson, Fergus Falls; Steve Rosga, Cretin–Derham Hall; Chad Weeks, Blaine; Jason Ziebarth, Cambridge

Specialists: K/P—Steve Opstad, Park Center; Return—Chris Veith, Brainerd

1992 *Offense:* QB—Jon Miller, Cambridge; Cory Sauter, Hutchinson; RB—Carl McCullough, Cretin–Derham Hall; Tony Paul, Warren; Tommy Reynolds, St. Paul Johnson; WR—Marcus Harris, Brooklyn Center; Andy Bogenholm, White Bear Lake; Skipp Schaefbauer, Elk River; TE—Paul Kratochvil, New Prague; OT—Luke Glime, Bemidji; Kyle Seifer, Fairmont; OG—Mike Doughty, Lakeville; Chad Larson, International Falls; C—Jon Jellum, Lakeville

Defense: DE—Donovan Dawson, Holdingford; Nate Rasmussen, Lakeville; DL—Jason DeVries, Forest Lake; Mike Greengard, Tartan; Luke Herkenhoff, Albany; LB—Happy Chakolis, Minneapolis North; John Hillman, Blaine; Jim Louis, Faribault; DB—Jason Birr, Albany; Chad Gomarko, BOLD; Rob Haedt, Austin; Adam Platte, Lakeville; Chad Strand, Blaine

Specialists: K—Nate Rasmussen, Lakeville; Return—Jason Suttle, Burnsville

1993 *Offense:* QB—J. J. Korman, Faribault Bethlehem Academy; Chad Rogness, Stillwater; RB—Jason Hall, Cambridge; Mike Mannausau, International Falls; Tommy Reynolds, St. Paul Johnson; WR—Kevin Conn, Apple Valley; Dave Watson, Bloomington Jefferson; TE—Troy Duerr, Buffalo; OT—Matt Birk, Cretin–Derham Hall; Keith Schulte, Wayzata; OG—David Everson, Mora; Graham Lomen, Apple Valley; C—Brian Woessner, Cretin–Derham Hall

Defense: DE—Chad Carlson, Apple Valley; Derrick Dierkhising, Albany; Bill Petrangelo, Chisholm; Jason Ziegler, Detroit Lakes; DL—Alex Sentyrz, Anoka; Ben Taylor, Lanesboro; LB—Gary Davis, Brainerd; Jeff Hoefs, St. Cloud Cathedral; Josh Mix, Bloomington Kennedy; Chris Vokal, Mankato East; DB—Chris Rainey, Minneapolis North; Jason Redfield, Moorhead; Tim Rosga, Cretin–Derham Hall

Specialists: Return—Ray Wilhelm, Stillwater; K—Tim Rosga, Cretin–Derham Hall; P—Brent Solheim, Rochester John Marshall

1994 *Offense:* QB—Kirk Midthun, Triton; Tom Soltys, Grand Rapids; C—Matt Blodgett, Orono; OL—Chad Johnson, International Falls; Craig Ploetz, North Branch; Dave Butler, Anoka; Casey Jensen, Eagan; Receivers—Tim Busch, Triton; Alex Hass, St. Peter; Mike McKinney, Apple Valley; RB—Matt Brechler, Rochester John Marshall; Brad Grossman, Park of Cottage Grove; Leroy McFadden, Eden Prairie; Tom Stark, Sartell

Defense: DL—Seth Becker, Madelia-Truman; Mike Cernoch, Burnsville; Rob Hansen, Wayzata; Pat Hau, Edina; LB—T. J. DeBates, Stewartville; Jay Hanson, Sauk Rapids; R. J. Nodland, Alexandria; Brandon Novak, Becker; DB—Brant Grimes, Bloomington Jefferson; Chris Rainey, Minneapolis North; Tim Rosga, Cretin–Derham Hall; Eric Vollbrecht, St. Michael–Albertville

Specialists: K—Louie Sylvester, South St. Paul; P—Tom O'Brien, Chaska; Return—Aaron Runk, Stillwater

1995 *Offense:* QB—Kirk Midthun, Triton; Andy Persby, Hill-Murray; Receivers: Tony Paquette, Hill-Murray; Conrad Emmerich, Foley; Ross Sannes, Breckenridge; Nino Zezza, Mahtomedi; OL—Justin Asher, Wayzata; Ben Beaudet, Stillwater; Dave Butler, Anoka; Ben Hamilton, Wayzata; Eric Larson, Cambridge; Ben Meyer, Pine Island; RB—Blaise Larson, Red Lake Falls; Aaron Run, Stillwater; Darren Smith, Woodbury; Josh Wilske, Lakeville

Defense: DB—Shawn Pogreba, St. Paul Johnson; Nate Schwieger, Spring Lake Park; Trenton Hyland, Kingsland; Steve Nolander, Albert Lea; DL—Adam Bunge, Totino-Grace; Javiar Collins, St. Thomas Academy; Nate Dwyer, Stillwater; Scott Mattis, Anoka; Beau Price, Rochester Mayo; John Schlecht, White Bear Lake; LB—Aaron Crowser, Alexandria; Josh Keyes, Detroit Lakes; Thad Olson, Burnsville; Brandon Novak, Becker; Willi Pung, Braham

Specialists: K—Todd Werner, Burnsville; Return—Brad Grossman, Park of Cottage Grove; P—Jeremy Belisle, Big Lake

1996 *Offense:* QB—Ryan Keating, Minnetonka; RB—Brian Day, Brainerd; Fred Harris, Mahtomedi; Aaron Krych, Holdingford; WR—Adam Runk, Stillwater; Jeremy Forsell, St. Cloud Apollo; TE—Rob LaRue, Minnetonka; OL—Derek Burns, Eden Prairie; Jeremy Dox, Cretin–Derham Hall; Eric Fredrickson, Northfield; Trevor Rolfes, Lakeville; Dan Schellhammer, Chatfield; Nate Scheuer, Blaine; Doug Schultz, Alexandria

Spectators at a Minneapolis Central–St. Paul Central High School basketball game, about 1985

Defense: DL—Nate Dwyer, Stillwater; Jared Enger, Cretin–Derham Hall; Scott Semst, Rochester John Marshall; LB—Wes Ahschlager, Russell-Tyler-Ruthton; Jared Bucksa, Totino-Grace; Travis O'Neel, Eden Prairie; DB—Shane Hall, Burnsville; Ryan Iverson, Eden Prairie; Mark Mokoff, Northfield; Scott Swanson, West Central

Specialists: K—Peter Nielson, Princeton; P—Jim Kopriva, Edina; KR—Jarrett Ealey, Minneapolis Roosevelt; Josh Savageau, Blaine; PR—Ryan Nodland, Alexandria; Jack Hannahan, Cretin–Derham Hall

Player of the year: Brian Day, Brainerd

1997 *Offense:* QB—Ryan Keating, Minnetonka; RB—Marvin Spencer, Blaine; Scott Schmitz, St. Cloud Tech; Thomas Tapeh, St. Paul Johnson; WR—Ryan Klocksien, Minnetonka; Ben Johnson, DeLaSalle; TE—Nick Hansgen, St. Cloud Apollo; OL—Chad Setterstrom, Northfield; Joe Palke, Mounds View; Mark Haffeman, Spring Lake Park; Matt Weineke, Adrian; Andy Nelson, St. Cloud Tech

Defense: DL—Dave Sykora, Bloomington Jefferson; Justin Viger, Blaine; Leif Murphy, Spring Lake Park; Ben Werner, Glencoe–Silver Lake; LB—Chris Stiernagle, Eden Prairie; Pete Zoller, Stillwater; Mike

Walrath, Sartell; DB—Ryan Iverson, Eden Prairie; Joel Kunza, Blaine; Nathan Loughran, Minneapolis Washburn; Jack Hannahan, Cretin–Derham Hall

Specialists: K—Eric Kalin, Eden Prairie; P—Barry Pederson, Cook County; Return—Terry Motz, Pelican Rapids; Joe Fritze, Eagan; Yarzue Slowon, Armstrong

Player of the year: Ryan Iverson, Eden Prairie

1998 *Offense:* QB—Ross Denne, Albany; RB—Thomas Tapeh, St. Paul Johnson; Louis Ayeni, Woodbury; Curt Jepsen, Rochester Mayo; WR—Jeff Hesse, Maple Grove; Ben Johnson, DeLaSalle; TE—Brent Swaggert, Buffalo; OL—Casey Knutson, Shakopee; Paul Howard, North Branch; Jed Ryan, Byron; Mark Haffeman, Spring Lake Park; Brad Schroeder, Rochester John Marshall

Defense: DL—Regis Eller, Breck; Robert Fedick, Blaine; Josh Muro, Maple Grove; Jason Cook, Spring Lake Park; LB—Phil Archer, Cretin–Derham Hall; Jareck Horton, Apple Valley; Eric Stenzel, Mankato West; Adam Hermann, Champlin Park; DB—Nate Howard, St. Thomas Academy; Barry Quickstad, Waseca; Jon David, Foley; Zach Zimmer, Milaca

Specialists: K—Adam Benike, Rochester John Marshall; P—Matt Konz, Adrian; Return—Reondo Davis, Blaine; Drew Carlson, Belle Plaine

Player of the year: Thomas Tapeh, St. Paul Johnson

1999 *Offense:* WR—Paul Martin, Elk River; Larry Fitzgerald, Holy Angels; TE—Mike Leach, Mounds View; OL—Mark McElroy, Cretin–Derham Hall; Rian Melander, Cretin–Derham Hall; Rob Satrom, Lakeville; Jeff Painter, St. Cloud Tech; Barry Smith, Champlin Park; QB—Joe Mauer, Cretin–Derham Hall; RB—Trevor Frischmon, Blaine; Preston Treichel, Cambridge-Isanti; Chris Boyer, Mankato West

Defense: DL—Derreck Robinson, DeLaSalle; Josh Jaskulke, Granada-Huntley-East Chain; Josh Zeithamer, Alexandria; Jason Frank, Lakeville; LB—Eric Stenzel, Mankato West; Charlie Cosgrove, Minneapolis Washburn; Winston Bell, Cretin–Derham Hall; Rashon Powers-Neal, Cretin–Derham Hall; DB—Dominique Sims, DeLaSalle; Darren Tietz, Westbrook-Walnut Grove; Adam Larson, Eastview

Specialists: K—Rob Reiling, Cretin–Derham Hall; Jared Swanson, Minnewaska; P—Scott Dirkes, Albany; Return—Walter Bowser, Cretin Derham-Hall; Justin Arneson, Fergus Falls

Player of the year: Dominique Sims, DeLaSalle

2000 *Offense:* WR—Larry Fitzgerald Jr., Holy Angels; Lee Clintsman, Hill-Murray; TE—Matt LeVoir, Eden Prairie; OL—Trevor McCulloch,

Brainerd; Andy Tidwell-Neal, Wayzata; Justin Shopbell, Woodbury; Taylor Murray, Cambridge-Isanti; Pat Bechdol, Orono; QB—Joe Mauer, Cretin–Derham Hall; RB—Riza Mahmoud, Champlin Park; Marion Barber III, Wayzata; Rashon Powers-Neal, Cretin–Derham Hall

Defense: DL—Rob Kraemer, Forest Lake; Sam Berg, Blaine; Jason Peterson, Eden Prairie; Matt Smude, Totino-Grace; LB—Digger Anderson, Coon Rapids; Jake Meixl, Mankato Loyola; Lawrence Pinson, Eagan; Matt Gwash, Cook County; DB—DeGeorge Tebbs, Minneapolis North; Terrell Fletcher, St. Louis Park; Marcus LeVesseur, Bloomington Kennedy; Sam Brown, Bloomington Jefferson

Specialists: K—Chris Brisson, White Bear Lake; P—Jacob Johnson, Maple Grove; Return—Dan Bowling, Hopkins

Player of the Year: Joe Mauer, Cretin–Derham Hall

2001 *Offense:* QB—Brian Kaufman, Hill-Murray; RB—Tyler Evans, McLeod West; Gino Guyer, Greenway; David Blom, Atwater-Cosmos-Grove City; OL—Joe Ainslie, Hopkins; Chris Adams, Atwater-Cosmos-Grove City; Mark Setterstrom, Northfield; Gabe Sweeney, Greenway; Ryan Harris, Cretin–Derham Hall; TE—Marcus Freeman, Cretin–Derham Hall; WR—Dominique Byrd, Breck; Justin Surrency, Concordia Academy

Defense: DL—Matt Hoffman, Champlin Park; Brent Hovis, Rochester John Marshall; Maurice Buchanan, Hopkins; Mark Fischbach, Cretin–Derham Hall; LB—Jake Meixl, Mankato Loyola; Brandon Archer, Cretin–Derham Hall; Jake Nordin, Atwater-Cosmos-Grove City; Jamie Steffensmeier, Mankato East; DB—Fletcher Terrell, St. Louis Park; DeGeorge Tebbs, Minneapolis North; Anthony Longe, St. Agnes; Tony Bizal, Blaine

Specialists: K—Stefan Turkula, Eden Prairie; P—Nick Nalezny, Edina; Return—Denis Jacobson, Duluth Denfeld

Player of the year: Tyler Evans, McLeod West

2002 *Offense:* QB—Craig Dahl, Mankato East; RB—John Majeski, Hastings; Randy Spring, Plainview-Elgin-Millville; Phil Porta, Cambridge-Isanti; OL—Ryan Harris, Cretin–Derham Hall; Barrett Anderson, Rochester Mayo; Marcus Coleman, Wayzata; Mitch Erickson, Hutchinson; Lydon Murtha, Hutchinson; TE—John Carlson, Litchfield; WR—Kyle Gearman, Alexandria; Rashad Turner, St. Paul Highland Park

Defense: DL—Tony Brinkhaus, Bloomington Jefferson; Trevor Laws, Apple Valley; Steve LeVoir, Eden Prairie; Richard Majerus, Rochester Mayo; LB—Tom Busch, Park of Cottage Grove; Jared Massey, Centennial; Brad McCamy, Mahtomedi; John Shevlin, Eastview; DB—

Dan Aagard, Edina; Mike Kootsikas, Rosemount; Chuck Miesbauer, Cretin–Derham Hall; Greg Winegarden, Eden Prairie

Specialists: K—Dan Ellering, St. Paul Johnson; P—Dan Ness, Rochester John Marshall; Return—Nathan Swift, Hutchinson

Player of the year: John Majeski, Hastings

2003 *Offense:* QB—Liam O'Hagan, Breck; RB—Nathan Swift, Hutchinson; Craig Luberts, Pierz; Brylee Callender, Lakeville; OL—Joe Vanstrom, Blaine; Lydon Murtha, Hutchinson; Jon Brost, Maple Grove; Jeff Dirkes, Albany; Aaron Weets, Rochester Mayo; TE—Matt Storlie, Byron; WR—Brandon Robinson, Breck; Vinny Flury, Lakeville

Defense: DL—Everette Pedescleaux, Armstrong; Troy Martin, Minneapolis North; Willie Van De Steeg, Glencoe–Silver Lake; Dustin Martin, Moorhead; LB—Michael Maresh, Champlin Park; Derek Potter, Becker; Nolan Oliver, Moorhead; Pat Sommerstad, Eastview; DB—Mike Odom, Mounds View; Garrett Adamson, Hill-Murray; Eric Scahumburg, Mahnomen; Pete Ruhl, Lakeville

Specialists: P—Brian Cristan, Mahtomedi; K—Britt Baumann, North Branch; Return—Dylan McAlpine, Elk River

Player of the year: Nathan Swift, Hutchinson

2004 *Offense:* QB—Nick Mertens, East Grand Forks; RB—Jay Thomas, Tartan; Kyle Minett, Russell-Tyler-Ruthton; Isaac Odim, Rochester Century; WR—Bryan Busack, Redwood Valley; Eric Decker, Rocori; TE—Chris Joppru, Minnetonka; OL—Paul Backowski, Foley; Rafael Eubanks, Cretin–Derham Hall; Pete Hiltner, Brainerd; Ryan Ruckdashel, Eastview; Lucas Meyer, Goodhue

Defense: DL—Walker Ashley, Eden Prairie; Jeff Bohlman, Sartell–St. Stephen; Matt Stommes, Eden Valley-Watkins; Hank Goff, Minnetonka; LB—James Laurinaitis, Wayzata; Derek Potter, Becker; Zach Larsen, Northfield; Ramon Humber, Champlin Park; DB—Tim Anderson, AlBrook; Mark Snow, St. Paul Highland Park; Ted Toune, Park Center; Ben Kuznia, BOLD

Specialists: P—Devin Swanberg, Chisago Lakes; K—Sam Buckman, Minnetonka; Return—Troy Harlander, Chaska

Player of the year: Nick Mertens, East Grand Forks

Hockey

High school hockey in Minnesota dates to the turn of the century. Throughout the 1920s and 1930s hockey was played at about two dozen high schools in the state. In 1942 several northern Minnesota high school hockey teams

High school skaters celebrating a goal at the boys' state hockey tournament, 1969

gathered in Roseau for a tournament. Two years later, Gene Aldrich, the athletic director for the St. Paul public schools from 1936 to 1959, thought the time had come for a "state" tournament. With the financial backing of several St. Paul businessmen—most prominently Elmer Englebert—and the approval of the MSHSL board of directors, Aldrich began planning the first tournament and organized the 26 high schools playing hockey into regions.

In February 1945 eight regional representatives—teams from Eveleth, Granite Falls, Rochester, Staples, St. Cloud Tech, St. Paul Washington, Thief River Falls and White Bear Lake—gathered at the St. Paul Auditorium for the first state-sponsored high school hockey tournament in the nation. Fred Hutchinson noted in the *St. Paul Pioneer Press* several days before the tournament that "with comparatively few of the state's league members playing hockey, some of the qualifiers lacked competition."

The day before the tournament, the *Minneapolis Tribune* named Eveleth, which was averaging 12 goals per game, the tournament favorite. The *Tribune* also pointed out that Thief River Falls brought an unbeaten record (12–0–1) into the tournament. Legendary St. Paul sportswriter Don Riley wrote in the

February 13 edition of the *St. Paul Pioneer Press,* "The stage has been set and sports history will be made this afternoon when the curtain goes up."

In the opening afternoon game, Thief River Falls defeated White Bear Lake, 3–2. In the first game of the night session, Eveleth showed why it was the favorite, with a 16–0 victory over Granite Falls. The next day's semifinals produced two mismatches as Thief River Falls skated past St. Cloud Tech, 12–0, and Eveleth defeated Washington, 10–0.

On Saturday, February 15, Eveleth scored twice in the third period to rally for a 4–3 victory over Thief River Falls in the first state championship.

Riley recapped the championship game in the February 16 *Pioneer Press:* "Eveleth's power-packed team today reigned as the first king of Minnesota's high school hockey domain after coming from behind to defeat a great Thief River Falls sextet for the championship before more than 5,000 screaming fans in the Auditorium Saturday night."

The inaugural tournament, underwritten by the backers for $4,500, was deemed a financial success after drawing 8,434 spectators and netting a profit of $135.06. The MSHSL assumed control of the tournament the next year.

For the next 23 years, the St. Paul Auditorium was home to the tournament before it was moved in 1969 to the new Met Center in Bloomington. In the last year in St. Paul, the tournament attracted 45,369 fans; in its first year at the larger Met Center, the tournament attracted 79,868.

In 1985, at the St. Paul Civic Center, the tournament attracted 103,096—a record for the one-class tournament. The final one-class tournament—held in 1991—drew 99,507.

In 1992 the tournament format changed. Following the recommendation of the state high school hockey coaches association, the MSHSL decided on a two-year experiment of conducting the tournament in two "tiers." The coaches suggested the tiers be based on performance and ability—unlike the enrollment standard used in every other MSHSL activity. At the end of the regular season, coaches in each section ranked their section's teams based on performance. The top eight in each section were placed in Tier I while the remaining teams were placed in Tier II. After the two-year trial, the MSHSL decided instead to classify the 146 hockey teams in the state by enrollment. Since 1994, Class A and Class AA tournaments have been held.

Longest Hockey Game

The longest game in the history of the Boys State Hockey Tournament was the Class AA semifinal between Apple Valley and Duluth East in 1996. Apple Valley eventually won 5–4 at 2:12 minutes in the fifth overtime on a goal by Aaron Dwyer. The game, which ended at 1:39 A.M., took 93 minutes, 12 seconds to decide. Apple Valley goalie Karl Goehring made a tournament-record 65 saves.

Prior to that marathon, the longest game in tournament history was a first-round matchup between Minneapolis South and Thief River Falls in 1955. Playing the first game of the Thursday night session, South won the game, 3–2, in 11 overtimes. But the overtime periods were just five minutes, so the game took just 87 minutes, 50 seconds to decide.

After nine overtime periods, the teams were given a break so that the session's second quarterfinal game could start. At 11:33 P.M., St. Paul Johnson and Roseau began their game. After the first period of that game, during the intermission, Minneapolis South and Thief River Falls played their 10th overtime. After Johnson and Roseau played their second period, South and Thief River Falls began their 11th overtime. Less than two minutes (1:50) into the overtime, Jim Westby scored for South, ending the marathon. The game, which concluded at 12:23 A.M., took nearly five hours (4:53) to complete.

Johnson went on to beat Roseau, 1–0, and then defeated South later that night, 3–1. In the championship game, Johnson defeated Minneapolis Southwest, 3–1, the first time the state championship game had featured two schools from the Metropolitan area.

Girls' Hockey

In the late 1980s and early 1990s girls' interest in hockey grew steadily. By 1992 there were 39 girls' and women's teams registered with the Minnesota Amateur Hockey Association. In the fall of 1993, eight high schools in the state fielded girls' hockey teams. Those teams concluded the 1993–94 season in February 1994 with an invitational tournament. Blaine-Coon Rapids defeated Anoka-Champlin Park, 3–0, in the tournament final.

Several weeks after that tournament, the MSHSL representative assembly voted to sanction girls' hockey as a varsity sport, making Minnesota the first state to support girls' hockey. (In 10 states, girls were allowed to play on boys' teams.)

The state's first "official" girls' hockey season began in November 1994 with 24 girls varsity teams in the state. The season kicked off on November 19, when South St. Paul defeated Holy Angels, 8–0.

The season culminated with four six-team sectional tournaments to determine the four teams that would compete in the first state girls' hockey tournament in U.S. history. Apple Valley, Henry Sibley, South St. Paul and

Stillwater won section titles to qualify for the tournament, to be held at Aldrich Arena in Maplewood.

Around 1 P.M. on February 24, 1995, with ESPN, CBS and other national media outlets broadcasting, the historic first puck was dropped for the semifinal between Apple Valley and Stillwater. Apple Valley won, 6–4, while South St. Paul defeated Henry Sibley, 4–0, in the other semifinal. The next day, a crowd of 3,255 watched Apple Valley defeat South St. Paul, 2–0, for the first state girls' hockey title.

Within eight years, 120 girls teams competed in the state.

Girls' Swimming

On March 14, 1924, the *Virginia Daily Enterprise* previewed the big high school sporting event slated for the next day in nearby Biwabik. The newspaper reported, "Miss Healy has developed another crack squad this season which has set its heart on being recognized as the initial title holders of the Minnesota girls swimming championships." Athletes from 13 schools were expected for the first annual meet of its kind, and each race was to "constitute a state record which future fair sex performers may aim at." The preliminaries of the meet were scheduled for 2 P.M., with the finals slated for 8 P.M.

Virginia, led by individual champions Leona Irvin (100 yard breaststroke) and Evelyn Peterson (diving) won the inaugural meet with 42 points.

On Monday, March 17, in the *Daily Enterprise,* Don MacIver recapped the event: "Girls high school athletics, and especially interscholastic swimming, assumed its rightful place Saturday when the first annual state high school swimming meet for girls was successfully staged in the Biwabik school natatorium with 83 youthful mermaids representing nine high schools participating." The newspaper reported that 1,000 enthusiastic fans watched the events.

The 1924 meet ended with these team standings: Virginia 42, Gilbert 22, Eveleth 20, Duluth Central 16, Biwabik 13, Nashwauk 5, Chisholm 1, Mountain Iron and Aurora 0. Event winners were: Gertrude Henderson, Biwabik (plunge); Mae Matt, Gilbert (25 yard freestyle, 50 yard freestyle); Caroline Schrodes, Eveleth (50 yard backstroke, 100 yard backstroke), Leone Irwin, Virginia (100 yard breaststroke); Evelyn Peterson, Virginia (dives); Effie Johnston, Nashwauk (50 yard breaststroke); Virginia (relay).

Over the next 17 years, the Virginia team, under the guidance of Coach Jean Healy, won the event 14 times.

One of the highlights of the meet occurred in 1932 when Chisholm's

Running the high hurdles at the Minneapolis school track meet, 1925

Anna Govednik set state records in the 50 yard breaststroke and the 100 yard breaststroke. Three weeks after the state meet, Govednik, under the auspices of the AAU, set a world record of 1:18.9 in the 100 yard breaststroke.

In late February 1942 the swimmers gathered for the 19th annual meet. A headline in the February 20, 1942, *Virginia Daily Enterprise* previewed the meet: "Nashwauk threatens long rule of Virginia mermaids." The newspaper reported, "Close to 80 high school girl swimmers, including some of the state's best, will compete in the 19th renewal of the Minnesota swimming meet, which opens at the Roosevelt pool here at 7:30 o'clock tonight." The newspaper's headline was prophetic—Nashwauk won the event with 57 points, 14 more than second-place Virginia. Chisholm finished third with 23 points, followed by Ely (21), Coleraine (12), Eveleth (8) and Aurora (4). The recap in the newspaper's Monday edition said, "The finals drew a good crowd of 500 to 600 persons, including a wildly cheering throng of Nashwauk boosters."

This 1942 swim was the last state meet held for girls—in any sport—until 1972.

Track and Field

In 1907 Dr. Henry Williams, the University of Minnesota football coach, and Dr. L. J. Cooke, the university's basketball coach and athletic director, decided that the university should stage a high school track and field meet. The first gathering, held on June 8, 1907, was won by Shattuck Academy of Faribault with 32 points.

This meet, which attracted high schools and academies from all over the Midwest, was held annually until 1920 (except for 1917).

On March 25, 1921, the State High School Athletic Association (now the MSHSL) decided to conduct an annual track and field meet for high school athletes only, to be held at the University of Minnesota's Northrop Field. On May 21, 1921, in the first "state" meet, Minneapolis West won the Class A meet (for Twin Cities schools) with 48 points. Winona won the Class B meet with 21 points.

The first "modern" state meet for girls was the 1972 state track and field meet. International Falls and White Bear Lake tied for the team title with 20 points. Virginia was third with 16, followed by Moorhead and Owatonna tied for fourth with 12 and Mound in sixth with 11. Sue Alstrom, of International Falls, won two events—shot put and discus.

The meet, held on May 27, 1972, at St. Cloud Apollo High School, attracted 458 girls from 108 schools.

Wrestling

Winningest Wrestling Coaches (through 2004–05)

Coach	School	Record
Scot Davis	Owatonna	710–104–4
Bill Sutter	Goodhue	670–132–8
Virg Vagle	Paynesville	661–148–6
Gary Hindt	Wabasso	501–150–6
Greg Greeno	St. Michael–Albertville	473–79–2
Ron Malcolm	Anoka, Worthington	464–119–5
Lyle Freudenberg	Foley	452–92–3
Ken Droegemueller	Osseo, Worthington	440–145–4
Bill Demarary	Apple Valley, Richfield	407–70–4
Don Dravis	Staples	401–51–4

Source: *The Guillotine*

Winningest Wrestlers (through 2004–05)

Wrestler	School	Record
Nate Matousek	Glencoe–Silver Lake	243–13
Mitch Kuhlman	Medford	233–11
Adam Aho	Frazee	225–36
Eric Sanders	Wabasha-Kellogg	223–27
Marcus LeVesseur	Bloomington Kennedy, Mpls. Roosevelt	218–12
Matt Nagel	Frazee	217–18
Jesse Jensen	Brooklyn Center	214–27
Charlie Falck	Apple Valley	213–11
Luke Becker	Cambridge-Isanti	210–18
Matt Kraft	Heron Lake-Okabena-Lakefield-Jackson	209–24

Source: *The Guillotine*

All-time State Wrestling Champs (by school, through 2004–05)

50 Blue Earth Area, Robbinsdale; **42** Apple Valley; **41** Anoka; **25** Albert Lea; **24** Faribault, Mound Westonka; **23** Bloomington Kennedy, Osseo, Wayzata; **22** Simley

Most Individual State Championships

Five championships

Wrestler	School	Years
Matt Nagel	Frazee	1997–2001
Eric Sanders	Wabasha-Kellogg	1999–2003

Four championships

Wrestler	School	Years
Jim Van Gordon	Minneapolis Marshall	1937–40
Steve Carr	Battle Lake	1976–78,
	Moorhead	1979
John Miller	Renville-Sacred Heart	1982–85
Ty Friederichs	Osseo	1992–95
Chad Erikson	Apple Valley	1994–97
Marcus LeVesseur	Minneapolis Roosevelt	1998–2000,
	Bloomington Kennedy	2001
Ty Eustice	Blue Earth Area	1997, 1999–2001
Jeff Pfaffinger	Blue Earth Area	1999–2002
Charlie Falck	Apple Valley	2001–04
Gabriel Mooney	Badger-Greenbush-Middle River	2001–04

Bronko Nagurski presents Nagurski cup to Barnum High School wrestling team, 1934

Scot Davis

On January 29, 2005, Owatonna wrestling coach Scot Davis earned the 700th victory of his coaching career in Owatonna's 52–3 victory over New Richland-Hartland-Ellendale-Geneva. Owatonna, which set a state record with 60 dual victories in 2004–05, went on to win the Class 3A state title in 2005. In 28 seasons as a high school wrestling coach, Davis has a 710–107–4 record. Davis has also coached at Bird Island-Lake Lillian, Hutchinson and Belcourt (N.D.).

Boys' State Champions

Baseball

One-class tournament

1947 St. Cloud Tech; **1948** Chisholm; **1949** Minneapolis Edison; **1950** Duluth Denfeld; **1951** Redwood Falls; **1952** Halstad; **1953** St. Paul Washington; **1954** Austin; **1955** Minneapolis Washburn; **1956** St. Paul Washington; **1957** Little Falls; **1958** St. Paul Johnson; **1959** Minneapolis Washburn; **1960**

Le Sueur High School baseball team, 1928

Minneapolis Washburn; **1961** North St. Paul; **1962** Richfield; **1963** Minneapolis Washburn; **1964** Austin; **1965** Richfield; **1966** Bloomington Kennedy; **1967** Hastings; **1968** Edina; **1969** Minneapolis Washburn; **1970** Albany; **1971** Richfield; **1972** Richfield; **1973** Bemidji; **1974** Owatonna; **1975** Bloomington Kennedy

Two-class tournament

1976 Hill-Murray (AA), Babbitt (A); **1977** St. Peter (AA), St. Cloud Cathedral (A); **1978** Grand Rapids (AA), Plainview (A); **1979** Little Falls (AA), St. James (A); **1980** Coon Rapids (AA), St. Cloud Cathedral (A); **1981** Cretin (AA), Sleepy Eye (A); **1982** Cretin (AA), Sauk Centre (A); **1983** Edina (AA), Staples (A); **1984** Grand Rapids (AA), Windom (A); **1985** St. Cloud Apollo (AA), Windom (A); **1986** Cretin (AA), Greenway (A); **1987** Willmar (AA), Greenway (A); **1988** Owatonna (AA), St. Cloud Cathedral (A); **1989** Cretin–Derham Hall (AA), Mankato Loyola (A); **1990** Cretin–Derham Hall (AA), Waseca (A); **1991** Stillwater (AA), Greenway (A); **1992** Cretin–Derham Hall (AA), Rocori (A); **1994** Henry Sibley (AA), Sibley East (A); **1995** Brainerd (AA), Crookston (A); **1996** Cretin–Derham Hall (AA), Rochester Lourdes (A); **1997** Cretin–Derham Hall (AA), Cherry (A); **1998** Cretin-Derham-Hall (AA), Sibley East (A); **1999** Hastings (AA), Montgomery-Lonsdale (A)

Three-class tournament

2000 Brainerd (3A), St. Michael–Albertville (2A), Sleepy Eye (A); **2001** Cretin–Derham Hall (3A), St. Cloud Cathedral (2A), St. Agnes (A); **2002** New Ulm (3A), Rochester Lourdes (2A), Sleepy Eye St. Mary's (A); **2003** Rochester Century (3A), St. Cloud Cathedral (2A), Howard Lake-Waverly-Winsted (A); **2004** Eden Prairie (3A), Jackson County Central (2A), Sleepy Eye St. Mary's (A); **2005** Lakeville (3A), Paynesville (2A), New Ulm Cathedral (A)

Basketball

One-class tournament

1913 Fosston; **1914** Stillwater; **1915** Red Wing; **1916** Virginia; **1917** Rochester; **1918** Waseca; **1919** Albert Lea; **1920** Red Wing; **1921** Minneapolis Central; **1922** Red Wing; **1923** Aurora; **1924** Two Harbors; **1925** St. Paul Mechanic Arts; **1926** Gaylord; **1927** Minneapolis South; **1928** Moorhead; **1929** Moorhead; **1930** St. Paul Mechanic Arts; **1931** Glencoe; **1932** Thief River Falls; **1933** Red Wing; **1934** Chisholm; **1935** Austin; **1936** Bemidji; **1937** Minneapolis Edison; **1938** Thief River Falls; **1939** Mountain Lake; **1940** Breckenridge; **1941** Buhl; **1942** Buhl; **1943** St. Paul Washington; **1944** Minneapolis Henry; **1945** Minneapolis Henry; **1946** Austin; **1947** Duluth Denfeld; **1948** Bemidji; **1949** St. Paul Humboldt; **1950** Duluth Central; **1951** Gilbert; **1952** Hopkins; **1953** Hopkins; **1954** Brainerd; **1955** Minneapolis Washburn; **1956** Minneapolis Roosevelt; **1957** Minneapolis Roosevelt; **1958** Austin; **1959** Wayzata; **1960** Edgerton; **1961** Duluth Central; **1962** St. Louis Park; **1963** Marshall; **1964** Luverne; **1965** Minnetonka; **1966** Edina; **1967** Edina; **1968** Edina; **1969** Rochester John Marshall; **1970** Sherburn

Two-class tournament with AA/A playoff

1971 Duluth Central (AA), Melrose (A), Duluth Central (playoff); **1972** Mounds View (AA), St. James (A), St. James (playoff); **1973** Anoka (AA), Chisholm (A), Anoka (playoff); **1974** Bemidji (AA), Melrose (A), Melrose (playoff); **1975** Little Falls (AA), Chisholm (A), Little Falls (playoff)

Two-class tournament

1976 Bloomington Jefferson (AA), Minneapolis Marshall-University (A); **1977** Prior Lake (AA), Winona Cotter (A); **1978** Prior Lake (AA), Lake City (A); **1979** Duluth Central (AA), Lake City (A); **1980** Minneapolis North (AA), Bird Island-Lake Lillian (A); **1981** Anoka (AA), Bird Island-Lake Lillian (A); **1982** Bloomington Jefferson (AA), Winona Cotter (A); **1983** Woodbury (AA), Barnum (A); **1984** White Bear Lake (AA), Pelican Rapids (A); **1985** White Bear Lake (AA), DeLaSalle (A); **1986** Bloomington Jefferson (AA),

Le Sueur (A); **1987** Bloomington Jefferson (AA), Norman County West (A); **1988** Rocori (AA), DeLaSalle (A); **1989** Owatonna (AA), Rushford (A); **1990** Owatonna (AA), Lake City (A); **1991** Cretin–Derham Hall (AA), Chisholm (A); **1992** Anoka (AA), Austin Pacelli (A); **1993** Cretin–Derham Hall (AA), Maple River (A); **1994** Minneapolis Washburn (AA), St. Agnes (A)

Sweet 16 format

1995 Minneapolis North; **1996** Minneapolis North

Four-class tournament

1997 Minneapolis North (4A), Simley (3A), Caledonia (2A), Hancock (A); **1998** Minnetonka (4A), St. Thomas Academy (3A), DeLaSalle (2A), Norman County East (A); **1999** Mounds View (4A), St. Paul Highland Park (3A), DeLaSalle (2A), Southwest Minnesota Christian (A); **2000** Tartan (4A), Minneapolis Henry (3A), Litchfield (2A), Southwest Minnesota Christian (A); **2001** Osseo (4A), Minneapolis Henry (3A), Kenyon-Wanamingo (2A), Southwest Minnesota Christian (A); **2002** Hopkins (4A), Minneapolis Henry (3A), Litchfield (2A), Southwest Minnesota Christian (A); **2003** Minneapois North (4A), Minneapolis Henry (3A), Litchfield (2A), Mankato Loyola (A); **2004** Chaska (4A), Mankato West (3A), Braham (2A), Russell-Tyler-Ruthton (A); **2005** Hopkins (4A), Shakopee (3A), Braham (2A), Russell-Tyler-Ruthton (A); **2006** Hopkins (4A), DeLaSalle (3A), Braham (2A), Rushford-Peterson (A)

Cross Country

One-class meet

1943 Duluth Central; **1944** Minneapolis Roosevelt; **1945** Duluth Central; **1946** Minneapolis Southwest; **1947** Minneapolis Southwest; **1948** Minneapolis Southwest; **1949** Duluth Central; **1950** Minneapolis Southwest; **1951** Duluth Central; **1952** Minneapolis Southwest; **1953** Minneapolis Southwest; **1954** Minneapolis Southwest; **1955** St. Louis Park; **1956** Duluth Central; **1957** Duluth Central; **1958** Minneapolis Roosevelt; **1959** Minneapolis Southwest; **1960** Hibbing; **1961** St. Louis Park; **1962** Minneapolis Southwest; **1963** Minneapolis Southwest; **1964** Minneapolis Southwest; **1965** Minneapolis Southwest; **1966** White Bear Lake; **1967** Austin; **1968** Alexander Ramsey; **1969** Minneapolis Southwest; **1970** Minneapolis Southwest; **1971** Minneapolis Southwest; **1972** Minneapolis Southwest; **1973** Minneapolis Southwest; **1974** Armstrong

Two-class meet

1975 Cretin (AA), Glenwood (A); **1976** Burnsville (AA), Blue Earth (A); **1977** Burnsville (AA), Blue Earth (A); **1978** Burnsville (AA), Rochester Lourdes

(A); **1979** Burnsville (AA), Rochester Lourdes (A); **1980** Minneapolis Southwest (AA), Rochester Lourdes (A); **1981** Lakeville (AA), Rochester Lourdes (A); **1982** Winona (AA), Staples (A); **1983** Alexander Ramsey/Frank B. Kellogg (AA), Staples (A); **1984** Esko-Cloquet (AA), Montgomery-Lonsdale (A); **1985** Esko-Cloquet (AA), Elgin-Millville (A); **1986** Burnsville (AA), Elgin-Millville (A); **1987** Winona (AA), Montevideo-Maynard (A); **1988** Minneapolis South (AA), Mesabi East (A); **1989** Minneapolis South (AA), Fairmont (A); **1990** Minneapolis South (AA), St. Paul Academy (A); **1991** Minneapolis South (AA), St. Paul Academy (A); **1992** Wayzata (AA), St. Paul Academy (A); **1993** Wayzata (AA), St. Paul Academy (A); **1994** Lakeville (AA), Sartell (A); **1995** Stillwater (AA), Canby-Minneota-Lincoln HI (A); **1996** Stillwater (AA), Staples-Motley (A); **1997** Stillwater (AA), Staples-Motley (A); **1998** Hopkins (AA), Staples-Motley (A); **1999** Hopkins (AA), Staples-Motley (A); **2000** Wayzata (AA), Paynesville (A); **2001** Hopkins (AA), Staples-Motley (A); **2002** Hopkins (AA), Staples-Motley (A); **2003** Marshall (AA), Staples-Motley (A); **2004** Marshall (AA), Eveleth-Gilbert (A); **2005** Willmar (AA), St. Cloud Cathedral (A)

Curling

1969 Hibbing; **1970** Hibbing; **1971** Hibbing; **1972** Mankato; **1973** Hibbing; **1974** Virginia; **1975** International Falls; **1976** Hibbing; **1977** Mankato East

Football

Five-class playoffs

1972 Minneapolis Washburn (2A), Burnsville (A), Mountain Iron (B), Gaylord (C), Rothsay (9-man); **1973** Rochester John Marshall (2A), Eveleth (A), New Prague (B), Gaylord (C), Lake Benton (9-man); **1974** Rochester John Marshall (2A), Alexandria (A), New Prague (B), Battle Lake (C), Lake Benton (9-man); **1975** Stillwater (2A), St. Thomas Academy (A), Gaylord (B), Esko (C), Ruthton (9-man); **1976** White Bear Lake (2A), St. Peter (A), Caledonia (B), New Richland-Hartland (C), Deer Creek (9-man); **1977** Minneapolis Washburn (2A), Fridley Grace (A), Granite Falls (B), Battle Lake (C), Deer Creek (9-man); **1978** Edina West (2A), Fridley Grace (A), New Richland-Hartland (B), Alden-Conger (C), Hoffman (9-man); **1979** Columbia Heights (2A), Rochester Lourdes (A), Gaylord (B), Bird Island-Lake Lillian (C), Russell (9-man); **1980** Burnsville (2A), Crookston (A), Mahnomen (B), Bird Island-Lake Lillian (C), Hoffman-Kensington (9-man); **1981** Rosemount (2A), St. Peter (A), Holdingford (B), Medford (C), Argyle (9-man); **1982** Stillwater (2A), Brooklyn Center (A), Le Center (B), Truman (C), Westbrook (9-man); **1983** Coon Rapids (2A), Hutchinson (A), Jordan (B), Southland (C), Silver

Lake (9-man); **1984** Stillwater (2A), Hutchinson (A), Granite Falls (B), Harmony (C), Norman County West (9-man);**1985** Burnsville (2A), New Prague (A), Jackson (B), Glyndon-Felton (C), Westbrook (9-man); **1986** Apple Valley (2A), Cambridge (A), Watertown-Mayer (B), Minneota (C), Argyle (9-man); **1987** Moorhead (2A), Cambridge (A), Granite Falls (B), Minneota (C), Silver Lake (9-man); **1988** Blaine (2A), Lakeville (A), Breckenridge (B), Minneota (C), Hallock (9-man); **1989** Burnsville (2A), Albany (A), Gibbon-Fairfax-Winthrop (B), Waterville-Elysian (C), St. Clair (9-man); **1990** Anoka (2A), Fridley (A), BOLD (B), Mahnomen (C), Chokio-Alberta (9-man); **1991** Burnsville (2A), Spring Lake Park (A), BOLD (B), Mahnomen (C), Chokio-Alberta (9-man); **1992** Lakeville (2A), Detroit Lakes (A), St. Cloud Cathedral (B), Mahnomen (C), Stephen (9-man); **1993** Apple Valley (2A), Detroit Lakes (A), St. Cloud Cathedral (B), Mahnomen (C), Chokio-Alberta (9-man); **1994** Anoka (2A), Sartell (A), Triton (B), Chatfield (C), Kittson Central (9-man); **1995** Stillwater (2A), Detroit Lakes (A), Kingsland (B), Chatfield (C), Cromwell (9-man); **1996** Eden Prairie (2A), Mora (A), Breck (B), Chatfield (C), Cromwell (9-man)

Six-class playoffs

1997 Eden Prairie (5A), Northfield (4A), Albany (3A), Pelican Rapids (2A), Cook County (A), Verndale (9-man); **1998** Woodbury (5A), Hutchinson (4A), Foley (3A), Mahnomen (2A), Cook County (A), Cromwell (9-man); **1999** Cretin–Derham Hall (5A), Mankato West (4A), DeLaSalle (3A), Waterville-Elysian-Morristown (2A), Cook County (A), Stephen-Argyle (9-man); **2000** Eden Prairie (5A), Cambridge-Isanti (4A), Glencoe–Silver Lake (3A), Triton (2A), Sleepy Eye (A), Westbrook-Walnut Grove (9-man); **2001** Hastings (5A), Detroit Lakes (4A), Jackson County Central (3A), Atwater-Cosmos-Grove City (2A), McLeod West (A), Hillcrest Lutheran (9-man); **2002** Eden Prairie (5A), Mankato West (4A), Plainview-Elgin-Millville (3A), Kingsland (2A), Rushford-Peterson (A), Verndale (9-man); **2003** Lakeville (5A), Totino-Grace (4A), Glencoe–Silver Lake (3A), Breck (2A), Goodhue (A), Stephen-Argyle (9-man); **2004** Minnetonka (5A), Totino-Grace (4A), East Grand Forks (3A), Pierz (2A), Rushford-Peterson (A), Stephen-Argyle (9-man); **2005** Wayzata (5A), Mahtomedi (4A), Becker (3A), Eden Valley-Watkins (2A), Springfield (A), Stephen-Argyle (9-man)

Golf

One-class meet

1943 Minneapolis University; **1944** Hopkins; **1945** Minneapolis Edison; **1946** Duluth Central; **1947** Duluth Central; **1948** Duluth Central; **1949**

Faribault; **1950** Anoka; **1951** Anoka; **1952** Albert Lea; **1953** St. Paul Central; **1954** Edina, St. Paul Central; **1955** St. Paul Central; **1956** Bemidji; **1957** No team title awarded; **1958** Minneapolis Roosevelt; **1959** Redwood Falls; **1960** Duluth East, Minneapolis Roosevelt; **1961** St. Paul Central; **1962** Red Wing; **1963** Minneapolis Roosevelt; **1964** North Branch; **1965** North Branch; **1966** North Branch; **1967** Austin; **1968** Duluth East; **1969** Virginia; **1970** Edina; **1971** White Bear Lake; **1972** Northfield; **1973** Edina West; **1974** Austin; **1975** Bemidji

Two-class meet

1976 Bloomington Lincoln, Virginia (AA), Albany (A); **1977** Edina West (AA), Waconia (A); **1978** Edina West (AA), Waconia (A); **1979** Austin (AA), Waconia (A); **1980** Austin (AA), Waconia (A); **1981** Austin (AA), Redwood Falls (A); **1982** Albert Lea (AA), Blake (A); **1983** Mahtomedi (AA), Sauk Centre (A); **1984** Winona (AA), Blake (A); **1985** Mankato West (AA), Fosston (A); **1986** Hastings (AA), Sauk Centre (A); **1987** Edina (AA), Sauk Centre (A); **1988** Bemidji (AA), Sauk Centre (A); **1989** Bemidji (AA), Le Sueur (A); **1990** Bemdiji (AA), Staples-Motley (A); **1991** Bemidji (AA), Mahtomedi (A); **1992** Apple Valley (AA), Fosston (A); **1993** Apple Valley (AA), Blue Earth Area (A); **1994** Wayzata (AA), Holy Angels (A); **1995** Grand Rapids (AA), Blue Earth Area, Rochester Lourdes (A); **1996** Mankato West (AA), Crosby-Ironton (A); **1997** Bemidji (AA), Blake (A); **1998** Wayzata (AA), Holy Angels (A); **1999** Eden Prairie (AA), Holy Angels (A); **2000** White Bear Lake (AA), Rochester Lourdes (A); **2001** Rochester Century (AA), Rochester Lourdes (A); **2002** Hibbing-Chisholm (AA), Rochester Lourdes (A); **2003** Benilde–St. Margaret's (AA), Rochester Lourdes (A); **2004** White Bear Lake (AA), Duluth Marshall (A); **2005** Eagan (AA), Rochester Lourdes (A)

Gymnastics

NOTE: From 1943 to 1952, state championships were awarded in each class. From 1953 to 1963, the championship was based on the highest total score in all three classes; in 1964 and 1965, on the highest total score in two classes; between 1966 and 1983, on the highest score in Class A.

1943 Minneapolis Roosevelt (Class C), Minneapolis North (B), Minneapolis Roosevelt (A); **1944** Minneapolis North (Class C), Minneapolis North (B), Minneapolis Roosevelt (A); **1945** Minneapolis North (Class C), Minneapolis North (B), Minneapolis Roosevelt (A); **1946** Minneapolis North (Class C), Minneapolis Roosevelt (B), Minneapolis Roosevelt (A); **1947** Minneapolis North (Class C), Minneapolis North (B), Minneapolis Roosevelt (A); **1948** Minneapolis North (Class C), Minneapolis Roosevelt (B), Minneapolis North (A); **1949** Minneapolis North (Class C), Minneapolis Roosevelt (B), Minneapolis

Roosevelt (A); **1950** Minneapolis Roosevelt (Class C), Minneapolis Roosevelt (B), Minneapolis Roosevelt (A); **1951** Minneapolis Roosevelt (Class C), Minneapolis North (B), Minneapolis Roosevelt (A); **1952** Minneapolis Roosevelt (Class C), Minneapolis North (B), Minneapolis North, St. Paul Johnson (A); **1953** Minneapolis North; **1954** Minneapolis North; **1955** Minneapolis North; **1956** Minneapolis North; **1957** Minneapolis North; **1958** Minneapolis Roosevelt; **1959** Minneapolis North; **1960** Minneapolis North; **1961** Minneapolis North; **1962** Minneapolis North; **1963** Alexander Ramsey; **1964** Alexander Ramsey; **1965** Minneapolis Marshall; **1966** Albert Lea; **1967** Minneapolis Marshall; **1968** Anoka; **1969** Anoka; **1970** Cooper; **1971** Cooper; **1972** Armstrong; **1973** Armstrong; **1974** Armstrong; **1975** Armstrong; **1976** Armstrong (winter), Armstrong (fall); **1977** Robbinsdale; **1978** Park Center; **1979** Robbinsdale; **1980** Park Center; **1981** Armstrong, Cooper; **1982** Edina; **1983** Bloomington Jefferson

---

DID YOU KNOW ?

The 1947 boys' hockey tournament was the first broadcast on radio. The tournament was televised for the first time in 1961.

Hockey
One-class tournament

1945 Eveleth; **1946** Roseau; **1947** St. Paul Johnson; **1948** Eveleth; **1949** Eveleth; **1950** Eveleth; **1951** Eveleth; **1952** Hibbing; **1953** St. Paul Johnson; **1954** Thief River Falls; **1955** St. Paul Johnson; **1956** Thief River Falls; **1957** International Falls; **1958** Roseau; **1959** Roseau; **1960** Duluth East; **1961** Roseau; **1962** International Falls; **1963** St. Paul Johnson; **1964** International Falls; **1965** International Falls; **1966** International Falls; **1967** Greenway; **1968** Greenway; **1969** Edina; **1970** Minneapolis Southwest; **1971** Edina; **1972** International Falls; **1973** Hibbing; **1974** Edina East; **1975** Grand Rapids; **1976** Grand Rapids; **1977** Rochester John Marshall; **1978** Edina East; **1979** Edina East; **1980** Grand Rapids; **1981** Bloomington Jefferson; **1982** Edina; **1983** Hill-Murray; **1984** Edina; **1985** Burnsville; **1986** Burnsville; **1987** Bloomington Kennedy; **1988** Edina; **1989** Bloomington Jefferson; **1990** Roseau; **1991** Hill-Murray

Two-tier format

1992 Bloomington Jefferson (Tier I), Greenway (II); **1993** Bloomington Jefferson (I), Eveleth-Gilbert (II)

Two-class format

1994 Bloomington Jefferson (AA), Warroad (A); **1995** Duluth East (AA), International Falls (A); **1996** Apple Valley (AA), Warroad (A); **1997** Edina (AA), Red Wing (A); **1998** Duluth East (AA), Eveleth-Gilbert (A); **1999** Roseau (AA), Benilde–St. Margaret's (A); **2000** Blaine (AA), Breck (A); **2001** Elk River (AA), Benilde–St. Margaret's (A); **2002** Holy Angels (AA), Totino-Grace (A); **2003** Anoka (AA), Warroad (A); **2004** Centennial (AA), Breck (A); **2005** Holy Angels (AA), Warroad (A); **2006** Cretin–Derham Hall (AA), St. Thomas Academy (A)

Skiing

NOTE: From 1934 to 1977 an overall team champion was calculated with a point system involving the scores achieved by schools' results in three events—cross country, slalom and jumping. In each event, the school with the two best scores was declared the champion.

Overall team champions

1934 Duluth Central; **1935** Duluth Central; **1936** Duluth Central; **1937** Greenway; **1938** Greenway; **1939** Duluth Central; **1940** Duluth Central; **1941** Duluth Central; **1942** Minneapolis North; **1943** Duluth Central; **1944** Duluth Central; **1945** Duluth Central; **1946** Duluth Central; **1947** Duluth Central; **1948** Duluth Central; **1949** Duluth Central; **1950** Duluth Central; **1951** Cloquet; **1952** Cloquet, Duluth Central; **1953** Duluth East; **1954** Duluth Central; **1955** Duluth East; **1956** Duluth East; **1957** Duluth Denfeld; **1958** Cloquet, Duluth Central; **1959** Duluth Central; **1960** Minneapolis North; **1961** Ely; **1962** Duluth Central, Ely; **1963** Cloquet; **1964** Duluth East; **1965** Cloquet; **1966** Cloquet; **1967** Cloquet; **1968** Cloquet; **1969** Cloquet; **1970** Cloquet; **1971** Cloquet; **1972** Bloomington Lincoln; **1973** Cloquet; **1974** Cloquet; **1975** Cloquet; **1976** Cloquet (won tie-breaker); **1977** Stillwater

Cross Country (before 1995)/Nordic

1935 Duluth Central; **1936** Duluth Central; **1937** Duluth Central; **1938** Greenway; **1939** No cross country held; **1940** Duluth Central; **1941** Duluth Central; **1942** Duluth Central; **1943** Duluth Central; **1944** Duluth Central; **1945** Duluth Central; **1946** Duluth Central; **1947** Duluth Central; **1948** Cloquet; **1949** Duluth Central; **1950** Duluth Central; **1951** Cloquet; **1952** Cloquet; **1953** Duluth Central; **1954** Duluth Central; **1955** Minneapolis Edison; **1956** Cloquet; **1957** Duluth Denfeld; **1958** Duluth Central; **1959**

Cloquet; **1960** Cloquet; **1961** Duluth Central; **1962** Duluth Central; **1963** Cloquet; **1964** Minneapolis North; **1965** Minneapolis North; **1966** Cloquet; **1967** Hopkins; **1968** Hopkins; **1969** Hopkins; **1970** Hopkins; **1971** Hopkins Eisenhower; **1972** Hopkins Eisenhower; **1973** Hopkins Eisenhower; **1974** Hopkins Eisenhower; **1975** Bloomington Lincoln; **1976** Hopkins Eisenhower; **1977** Stillwater; **1978** Stillwater; **1979** Stillwater; **1980** Armstrong; **1981** Edina West; **1982** Grand Rapids; **1983** Eden Prairie; **1984** Eden Prairie; **1985** Bloomington Jefferson; **1986** Bloomington Jefferson; **1987** Stillwater; **1988** Edina; **1989** Hastings; **1990** Stillwater; **1991** St. Paul Central; **1992** St. Paul Central; **1993** St. Paul Central; **1994** Winona; **1995** Hopkins; **1996** Stillwater; **1997** Hopkins; **1998** Duluth East; **1999** Duluth East; **2000** Duluth East; **2001** Duluth East; **2002** Hopkins; **2003** St. Louis Park; **2004** Duluth East; **2005** Forest Lake; **2006** Forest Lake

Ski jumping

1934 Duluth Central; **1935** Duluth Central; **1936** No senior high winner; **1937** Greenway; **1938** Duluth Central; **1939** Duluth Central; **1940** Duluth Central; **1941** Duluth Central; **1942** Greenway; **1943** Minneapolis Roosevelt; **1944** St. Paul Harding; **1945** Duluth Central; **1946** Duluth Central; **1947** Duluth Denfeld; **1948** Duluth Central; **1949** Duluth Central; **1950** Duluth Central; **1951** Duluth Denfeld; **1952** Duluth Central; **1953** Duluth Denfeld; **1954** Duluth Central; **1955** Duluth East; **1956** Duluth East; **1957** Duluth East; **1958** Duluth Central; **1959** Duluth Central; **1960** Minneapolis North; **1961** Ely; **1962** Duluth Central; **1963** Robbinsdale; **1964** Ely; **1965** Cloquet; **1966** Cloquet; **1967** Cloquet; **1968** Duluth Central; **1969** Robbinsdale; **1970** Robbinsdale; **1971** Robbinsdale; **1972** Cloquet; **1973** Cloquet; **1974** Duluth Central; **1975** Cloquet; **1976** Ely; **1977** Ely; **1978** Cloquet

Slalom (before 1997)/Alpine

1939 Duluth Central; **1940** Minneapolis North; **1941** Minneapolis Henry; **1942** Minneapolis North; **1943** Duluth Central; **1944** Duluth Central; **1945** Cloquet; **1946** Duluth Central; **1947** Duluth Central; **1948** Cloquet; **1949** Duluth Central; **1950** Cloquet; **1951** Cloquet; **1952** Cloquet; **1953** Duluth East; **1954** Duluth East; **1955** St. Louis Park; **1956** Duluth East; **1957** Cloquet; **1958** Grand Marais; **1959** Grand Marais; **1960** Duluth East; **1961** Duluth East; **1962** Grand Marais; **1963** Grand Marais; **1964** Grand Marais; **1965** Grand Marais; **1966** Grand Marais; **1967** Edina; **1968** Cloquet; **1969** Grand Marais; **1970** Grand Marais; **1971** Bloomington Lincoln; **1972** Bloomington Lincoln; **1973** Minneapolis Roosevelt; **1974** Minneapolis Roosevelt; **1975** St. Cloud Cathedral; **1976** Minneapolis Washburn; **1977** Bloomington Lincoln; **1978** Blake; **1979** Edina West; **1980** Edina West; **1981** Stillwater; **1982** Edina;

1983 Bloomington Jefferson; 1984 Bloomington Jefferson; 1985 Duluth East; 1986 Bloomington Jefferson; 1987 Bloomington Jefferson; 1988 Hastings; 1989 Woodbury; 1990 Duluth East; 1991 Duluth East; 1992 Bloomington Jefferson; 1993 St. Thomas Academy; 1994 Duluth East; 1995 Duluth East; 1996 Minnetonka; 1997 St. Thomas Academy; 1998 Minnetonka; 1999 Edina; 2000 Minnetonka; 2001 St. Thomas Academy; 2002 Edina; 2003 St. Thomas Academy; 2004 Benilde–St. Margaret's; 2005 Eden Prairie; 2006 Blake

Soccer

One-class tournament

1974 Bloomington Lincoln; 1975 Richfield; 1976 Bloomington Lincoln; 1977 Mounds View; 1978 Cooper; 1979 Robbinsdale; 1980 Burnsville; 1981 Bloomington Kennedy; 1982 Burnsville; 1983 Hopkins; 1984 Apple Valley; 1985 Wayzata; 1986 St. Paul Academy; 1987 St. Paul Academy; 1988 Apple Valley; 1989 Apple Valley; 1990 Burnsville; 1991 St. Paul Academy; 1992 Apple Valley; 1993 Burnsville; 1994 St. Paul Academy; 1995 Stillwater; 1996 Stillwater

Two-class tournament

1997 Apple Valley (AA), Benilde–St. Margaret's (A); 1998 Apple Valley (AA), Rochester Lourdes (A); 1999 Edina (AA), Rochester Lourdes (A); 2000 Edina (AA), Benilde–St. Margaret's (A); 2001 Edina (AA), Southwest Minnesota Christian (A); 2002 Eden Prairie (AA), Totino-Grace (A); 2003 Armstrong (AA), Benilde–St. Margaret's (A); 2004 Bloomington Jefferson (AA), Totino-Grace (A); 2005 Wayzata (AA), Breck (A)

Swimming and Diving

One-class meet

1924 Minneapolis Central; 1925 Virginia; 1926 Virginia; 1927 Hibbing; 1928 Chisholm; 1929 Chisholm; 1930 Chisholm; 1931 Chisholm; 1932 Virginia; 1933 Chisholm; 1934 Hibbing; 1935 Hibbing; 1936 Hibbing; 1937 Virginia; 1938 Hibbing; 1939 Hibbing, Virginia; 1940 Virginia; 1941 Virginia; 1942 Hibbing; 1943 Hibbing; 1944 Hibbing; 1945 Austin; 1946 Austin; 1947 Hibbing; 1948 Hibbing; 1949 Ely; 1950 Hibbing; 1951 Hibbing; 1952 Hibbing; 1953 Rochester; 1954 Rochester; 1955 Rochester; 1956 Rochester; 1957 Rochester; 1958 Rochester; 1959 Rochester; 1960 Biwabik; 1961 Biwabik; 1962 Rochester; 1963 Rochester; 1964 Rochester; 1965 Edina; 1966 Hopkins; 1967 Edina; 1968 Edina; 1969 Hopkins; 1970 Hopkins; 1971 Golden Valley; 1972 Golden Valley; 1973 Irondale; 1974 Hopkins Eisenhower; 1975 Hopkins Eisenhower; 1976 Hopkins Eisenhower; 1977 Hopkins Eisenhower;

1978 Minnetonka; **1979** DeLaSalle; **1980** Bloomington Jefferson; **1981** Mounds View; **1982** Lakeville; **1983** Mounds View; **1984** Edina; **1985** Burnsville; **1986** Edina; **1987** Edina; **1988** Minnetonka; **1989** Apple Valley; **1990** Minnetonka; **1991** Minnetonka; **1992** Minnetonka; **1993** Minnetonka; **1994** Bloomington Jefferson; **1995** St. Thomas Academy; **1996** Minnetonka; **1997** Minnetonka

Two-class meet

1998 Hutchinson (AA), Red Wing (A); **1999** Alexandria (AA), St. Thomas Academy (A); **2000** Alexandria (AA), St. Thomas Academy (A); **2001** Apple Valley (AA), St. Thomas Academy (A); **2002** Eden Prairie (AA), St. Thomas Academy (A); **2003** Eden Prairie (AA), St. Thomas Academy (A); **2004** Edina (AA), Sauk Rapids-Rice (A); **2005** Eden Prairie (AA), St. Thomas Academy (A); **2006** Lakeville North (AA), St. Thomas Academy (A)

Tennis

One-class meet

1950 Rochester; **1951** Rochester; **1952** Minneapolis Southwest; **1953** Rochester; **1954** St. James; **1955** Rochester; **1956** Rochester; **1957** Minneapolis Central; **1958** Minneapolis Marshall; **1959** Edina; **1960** Stillwater; **1961** Greenway; **1962** Rochester; **1963** Rochester; **1964** Rochester; **1965** Rochester; **1966** Edina, North St. Paul; **1967** Edina; **1968** Edina; **1969** Austin; **1970** Cooper; **1971** Edina; **1972** Edina; **1973** Edina East; **1974** Minnetonka; **1975** Edina East; **1976** St. Cloud Tech; **1977** Blue Earth; **1978** Edina East; [*] **1983** St. Cloud Tech; **1984** Blake; **1985** St. Cloud Tech; **1986** Minnehaha Academy

Two-class meet

1979 Edina East (AA), Blake; **1980** Edina West (AA), Blue Earth (A); **1981** Edina East (AA), Blake (A); **1982** Austin (AA), Blake (A); [*] **1987** Edina (AA), Blake (A); **1988** Edina (AA), Blue Earth-Frost-Winnebago (A); **1989** Edina (AA), Litchfield (A); **1990** Mounds View (AA), Staples-Motley (A); **1991** Blake (AA), Staples-Motley (A); **1992** Edina (AA), Blake (A); **1993** Wayzata (AA), St. Paul Academy (A); **1994** Bloomington Jefferson (AA), Blake (A); **1995** Edina (AA), Breck (A); **1996** Bloomington Jefferson (AA), Blake (A); **1997** Stillwater (AA), Breck (A); **1998** Edina (AA), Breck (A); **1999** Wayzata (AA), Winona Cotter (A); **2000** Edina (AA), Blake (A); **2001** Minneapolis South (AA), Breck (A); **2002** Edina (AA), Blake (A); **2003** Edina (AA), Blake (A); **2004** Mounds View (AA), St. Paul Academy (A); **2005** Mounds View (AA), Mounds Park Academy (A)

*One-class meets were held 1983–86; two-class meets were held 1979–82.

Track and Field

Two-class meet

1923 Minneapolis Central (A), Duluth Central (B); **1924** Minneapolis Central (A), Faribault (B); **1925** Minneapolis Central (A), Eveleth (B); **1926** Minneapolis West (A), Mankato (B); **1927** Minneapolis Central (A), Eveleth (B); **1928** Minneapolis Central (A), Sleepy Eye (B)

One-class meet

1929 Moorhead; **1930** Duluth Central; **1931** Minneapolis West; **1932** Montevideo; **1933** Minneapolis Edison; **1934** Minneapolis West; **1935** Duluth Central; **1936** Duluth Central; **1937** Minneapolis West; **1938** Minneapolis West; **1939** Minneapolis West; **1940** Minneapolis Washburn; **1941** Minneapolis Washburn; **1942** Minneapolis Washburn; **1943** Minneapolis North; **1944** Minneapolis Central; **1945** Minneapolis South; **1946** Minneapolis Southwest; **1947** Minneapolis Washburn; **1948** Minneapolis North; **1949** Duluth Denfeld; **1950** Owatonna; **1951** Mankato; **1952** Minneapolis Central; **1953** Minneapolis Central; **1954** St. Paul Central; **1955** Minneapolis Southwest; **1956** Minneapolis Southwest; **1957** Minneapolis Washburn; **1958** St. Louis Park; **1959** Minneapolis Central; **1960** Minneapolis Central; **1961** Hibbing; **1962** St. Louis Park; **1963** St. Louis Park; **1964** Minneapolis Central; **1965** St. Louis Park; **1966** St. Louis Park; **1967** Moorhead; **1968** Moorhead; **1969** Edina; **1970** Edina; **1971** White Bear Lake; **1972** Moorhead

Three-class meet

1973 Moorhead (AA), Glenwood (A), Elbow Lake, Kiester (B); **1974** Edina East (AA), Crookston (A), Gaylord (B); **1975** White Bear Lake Mariner (AA), Glencoe (A), Barnesville (B)

Two-class meet

1976 Minnetonka (AA), Glencoe (A); **1977** Wayzata (AA), Silver Bay (A); **1978** Burnsville (AA), Slayton (A); **1979** St. Paul Central (AA), Staples (A); **1980** Minneapolis Central, Wayzata (AA), Breckenridge (A); **1981** Owatonna (AA), Redwood Falls (A); **1982** Minneapolis Central (AA), Breckenridge (A); **1983** Northfield (AA), Austin Pacelli (A); **1984** Wayzata (AA), Austin Pacelli (A); **1985** Armstrong (AA), Brooklyn Center, Redwood Falls (A); **1986** Apple Valley (AA), Byron (A); **1987** Moorhead (AA), Elgin-Millville (A); **1988** White Bear Lake (AA), Rushford-Peterson-Houston (A); **1989** St. Paul Central (AA), Staples-Motley (A); **1990** Minneapolis Henry (AA), Lake Crystal-Wellcome Memorial (A); **1991** Apple Valley (AA), Glyndon-Felton-Dilworth (A); **1992** Apple Valley (AA), Atwater-Grove City-Cosmos,

Rocori (A); **1993** Moorhead (AA), St. Paul Academy (A); **1994** Minneapolis Washburn (AA), Mahtomedi (A); **1995** Wayzata (AA), Minnesota Valley Lutheran (A); **1996** Stillwater (AA), Park Rapids (A); **1997** Stillwater (AA), Stewartville (A); **1998** Stillwater (AA), Morris (A); **1999** Mounds View (AA), St. Michael–Albertville (A); **2000** Mounds View (AA), Plainview (A); **2001** Mounds View (AA), Chisholm (A); **2002** Armstrong (AA), Plainview (A); **2003** Mankato East (AA), Plainview (A); **2004** Mankato West (AA), Staples-Motley (A); **2005** Roseville (AA), Hermantown (A)

Wrestling

One-class meet

1938 Minneapolis Marshall; **1939** Minneapolis Marshall; **1940** Minneapolis Marshall, Robbinsdale; **1941** Minneapolis Vocational, Robbinsdale, Wayzata; **1942** Robbinsdale; **1943** Robbinsdale; **1944** Robbinsdale; **1945** Robbinsdale; **1946** Robbinsdale; **1947** Mound; **1948** Austin; **1949** Anoka; **1950** Anoka; **1951** Faribault, Wayzata; **1952** Wayzata; **1953** Blue Earth, Wayzata; **1954** Owatonna; **1955** Anoka; **1956** Blue Earth; **1957** Blue Earth; **1958** Blue Earth; **1959** Anoka; **1960** Alexander Ramsey; **1961** Robbinsdale; **1962** Owatonna; **1963** Hopkins; **1964** Mankato; **1965** Cooper; **1966** Albert Lea; **1967** Fridley, Hopkins; **1968** Hopkins; **1969** Cooper; **1970** Caledonia; **1971** Albert Lea; **1972** St. James; **1973** Fridley; **1974** Minnetonka; **1975** Fridley

Two-class meet

1976 Albert Lea (AA), Canby (A); **1977** Anoka (AA), Canby (A); **1978** Anoka (AA), Staples (A); **1979** Fridley (AA), Canby (A); **1980** Bloomington Kennedy (AA), Goodhue, Staples (A); **1981** Albert Lea (AA), Staples (A); **1982** Brainerd (AA), Staples (A); **1983** Apple Valley (AA), Staples (A); **1984** Bloomington Kennedy (AA), Staples (A); **1985** Apple Valley (AA), Staples (A); **1986** Apple Valley (AA), Canby (A); **1987** Simley (AA), Paynesville (A); **1988** Simley (AA), Canby (A); **1989** Simley (AA), St. James, Foley (A); **1990** Anoka (AA), Paynesville (A); **1991** Apple Valley (AA), Paynesville (A); **1992** Simley (AA), Frazee (A); **1993** Forest Lake (AA), Foley (A); **1994** Apple Valley (AA), Canby, Foley (A); **1995** Apple Valley (AA), Canby (A)

Three-class meet

1996 Hastings (AA), St. Michael–Albertville (A), Wheaton-Herman-Norcoss (B); **1997** Apple Valley (3A), St. Michael–Albertville (2A), Hayfield (A); **1998** Owatonna (3A), Dassel-Cokato (2A), St. James (A); **1999** Apple Valley (3A), Jackson County Central (2A), Frazee (A); **2000** Apple Valley (3A), Jackson County Central (2A), Paynesville (A); **2001** Apple Valley (3A), Blue Earth

St. Paul Central Class AA girls state basketball champions,1979

Area (2A), Goodhue (A); **2002** Apple Valley (3A), Blue Earth Area (2A), Medford, Frazee (A); **2003** Apple Valley (3A), Litchfield (2A), BOLD (A); **2004** Apple Valley (3A), St. Michael–Albertville (2A), Pierz (A); **2005** Owatonna (3A), St. Michael–Albertville (2A), Pierz (A); **2006** Apple Valley (3A), St. Michael–Albertville (2A), Canby (A)

Girls' State Champions

Basketball

One-class tournament

1974 (fall) Glencoe; **1975** (winter) Holy Angels

Two-class tournament

1976 St. Paul Central (AA), Redwood Falls (A); **1977** Burnsville (AA), New York Mills (A); **1978** Bloomington Jefferson (AA), New York Mills (A); **1979** St. Paul Central (AA), New York Mills (A); **1980** Little Falls (AA), Albany (A);

1981 Coon Rapids (AA), Heron Lake-Okabena (A); **1982** St. Cloud Apollo (AA), Moose Lake (A); **1983** Albany (AA), Henderson (A); **1984** Little Falls (AA), Chisholm (A); **1985** Little Falls (AA), Staples (A); **1986** St. Louis Park (AA), Midwest Minnesota (A); **1987** Mankato East (AA), Rochester Lourdes (A); **1988** Edina (AA), Tracy-Milroy (A); **1989** Osseo (AA), Storden-Jeffers (A); **1990** St. Louis Park (AA), Rochester Lourdes (A); **1991** Burnsville (AA), Rochester Lourdes (A); **1992** Burnsville (AA), Tracy (A); **1993** Bloomington Jefferson (AA), Rochester Lourdes (A); **1994** Bloomington Jefferson (AA), Blake (A); **1995** Rochester Mayo (AA), Rochester Lourdes (A); **1996** Hastings (AA), Tracy-Milroy (A)

Four-class tournament

1997 Rochester Mayo (4A), Alexandria (3A), New London-Spicer (2A), Hancock (A); **1998** Bloomington Jefferson (4A), Minneapolis North (3A), Blake (2A), Christ's Household of Faith (A); **1999** Cretin–Derham Hall (4A), Minneapolis North (3A), Blake (2A), Brandon-Evansville (A); **2000** Osseo (4A), New Prague (3A), Rochester Lourdes (2A), Fosston (A); **2001** Lakeville (4A), Marshall (3A), St. Michael–Albertville (2A), Fosston (A); **2002** Lakeville (4A), Marshall (3A), New London-Spicer (2A), Kittson Central (A); **2003** Woodbury (4A), Minneapolis North (3A), Rochester Lourdes (2A), Fosston (A); **2004** Hopkins (4A), Minneapolis North (3A), Breck (2A), Wabasso (A); **2005** Bloomington Kennedy (4A), Minneapolis North (3A), Rochester Lourdes (2A), Elgin-Millville (A); **2006** Hopkins (4A), Benilde–St. Margaret's (3A), Cannon Falls (2A), Fulda (A)

Cross country

One-class meet

1975 Regina; **1976** Armstrong; **1977** White Bear Lake Mariner

Two-class meet

1978 Armstrong (AA), Hinckley (A); **1979** Owatonna (AA), Montgomery-Lonsdale (A); **1980** Eden Prairie (AA), Esko (A); **1981** Minnetonka (AA), Rochester Lourdes (A); **1982** Minnetonka (AA), Redwood Falls (A); **1983** Hopkins (AA), Redwood Falls-Morton (A); **1984** Faribault (AA), Hermantown (A); **1985** Alexandria (AA), Hermantown (A); **1986** Winona (AA), St. Cloud Cathedral (A); **1987** Alexandria (AA), Windom-Storden-Jeffers (A); **1988** Fairmont (AA), Windom-Storden-Jeffers (A); **1989** Winona (AA), Hawley-Ulen-Hitterdal (A); **1990** Rochester John Marshall (AA), Plainview (A); **1991** Minnetonka (AA), Hawley-Ulen-Hitterdal (A); **1992** Duluth East (AA), International Falls (A); **1993** Duluth East (AA), Canby-Minneota (A);

Apple Valley's girls celebrate a goal in the nation's first girls' state hockey tournament, 1995

1994 Duluth East (AA), Rochester Lourdes (A); **1995** Duluth East (AA), Sartell (A); **1996** Duluth East (AA), Wadena-Deer Creek (A); **1997** Duluth East (AA), Lake City (A); **1998** Duluth East (AA), Wadena-Deer Creek (A); **1999** Bloomington Jefferson (AA), Deer River-Northland (A); **2000** Grand Rapids (AA), New London-Spicer (A); **2001** Hopkins (AA), New London-Spicer (A); **2002** Hopkins (AA), New London-Spicer (A); **2003** Lakeville (AA), Staples-Motley (A); **2004** Minnetonka (AA), Glencoe–Silver Lake (A); **2005** Lakeville North (AA), Adrian (A)

Golf

One-class meet
1977 Alexandria; **1978** Alexandria

Two-class meet
1979 Chaska (AA), Albany (A); **1980** Hopkins Eisenhower (AA), Albany (A); **1981** Hopkins Eisenhower-Lindbergh (AA), Wadena (A); **1982** Milaca (AA), Le Sueur (A); **1983** Edina (AA), Le Sueur (A); **1984** Edina (AA), Caledonia (A); **1985** Willmar (AA), Long Prairie (A); **1986** Stillwater (AA), Long Prairie (A); **1987** Stillwater (AA), Long Prairie (A); **1988** Edina (AA), Caledonia/Spring

Grove (A); **1989** Princeton (AA), Cottonwood (A); **1990** Burnsville (AA), Caledonia/Spring Grove (A); **1991** Richfield (AA), Cottonwood/Echo-Wood Lake (A); **1992** Alexandria (AA), Fosston (A); **1993** Edina (AA), Fosston (A); **1994** Edina (AA), Fosston (A); **1995** Edina (AA), Caledonia/Spring Grove (A); **1996** Grand Rapids (AA), Caledonia/Spring Grove, Orono (A); **1997** Edina (AA), Belle Plaine (A); **1998** Little Falls (AA), Staples-Motley (A); **1999** Brainerd (AA), Staples-Motley/Pillager (A); **2000** Burnsville (AA), Roseau (A); **2001** Red Wing (AA), Roseau (A); **2002** Red Wing (AA), Pequot Lakes (A); **2003** Red Wing (AA), Caledonia/Spring Grove (A); **2004** Bemidji (AA), Pequot Lakes (A); **2005** Elk River (AA), Caledonia/Spring Grove (A)

Gymnastics
One-class meet

1975 Burnsville, Richfield; **1976** Robbinsdale; **1977** Burnsville; **1978** Burnsville

---

DID YOU KNOW ❓

The first boys' state gymnastics meet was held in 1943. The MSHSL sponsored a state boys' gymnastics meet for the next 40 years.

The final state meet was held at Bloomington Jefferson High School in November 1983. The host Jaguars won the meet. Only 17 high schools participated in the state sponsored boys' gymnastics that final year.

Two-class meet

1979 Edina West (AA), Jackson (A); **1980** Edina East (AA), Jackson (A); **1981** Edina West (AA), Blake (A); **1982** Burnsville (AA), Mahtomedi (A); **1983** Armstrong (AA), Blake (A); **1984** New Prague (AA), Jackson (A); **1985** Edina (AA), Mahtomedi (A); **1986** Lakeville (AA), Jackson (A); **1987** Eden Prairie (AA), Mahtomedi (A); **1988** Eden Prairie (AA), Mahtomedi (A); **1989** Apple Valley (AA), Mahtomedi (A); **1990** Hopkins (AA), Mahtomedi (A); **1991** Eden Prairie (AA), Mahtomedi (A); **1992** Eden Prairie (AA), Mahtomedi (A); **1993** Lakeville (AA), Mahtomedi (A); **1994** Mounds View (AA), Melrose (A);

1995 Lakeville (AA), Melrose (A); **1996** Lakeville (AA), Mahtomedi (A); **1997** Lakeville (AA), Sauk Rapids (A); **1998** Lakeville (AA), Waseca (A); **1999** Lakeville (AA), Big Lake (A); **2000** Lakeville (AA), Big Lake (A); **2001** Apple Valley (AA), New Prague (A); **2002** Lakeville (AA), Mankato East (A); **2003** Lakeville (AA), New Prague (A); **2004** Park of Cottage Grove (AA), Perham (A); **2005** Eden Prairie (AA), Perham (A); **2006** Roseville (AA), Perham (A)

Hockey

One-class tournament

1995 Apple Valley; **1996** Roseville; **1997** Hibbing; **1998** Apple Valley; **1999** Roseville; **2000** Park Center; **2001** Bloomington Jefferson

Two-class tournament

2002 South St. Paul (AA); Benilde–St. Margaret's (A); **2003** South St. Paul (AA), Blake (A); **2004** Elk River (AA), Benilde–St. Margaret's (A); **2005** South St. Paul (AA), Holy Angels (A); **2006** Eden Prairie (AA), South St. Paul (A)

Skiing

Overall team champions
(based on results of cross country and slalom)

1976 Bloomington Lincoln; **1977** Cloquet

Cross country (before 1995)/ Nordic

1976 Cloquet; **1977** Cloquet; **1978** Cloquet; **1979** Blaine; **1980** Wayzata; **1981** Aurora-Hoyt Lakes; **1982** Stillwater; **1983** Stillwater; **1984** Stillwater; **1985** Stillwater; **1986** Stillwater; **1987** Stillwater; **1988** Winona/Winona Cotter; **1989** Brainerd; **1990** Mesabi East; **1991** St. Paul Central; **1992** Hastings; **1993** Hopkins; **1994** Elk River; **1995** Roseville; **1996** Duluth East; **1997** Stillwater; **1998** Duluth East; **1999** Duluth East; **2000** Roseville; **2001** Hopkins; **2002** Hopkins; **2003** Hopkins; **2004** Grand Rapids; **2005** Grand Rapids; **2006** Grand Rapids

Slalom (before 1997)/Alpine

1976 Stillwater; **1977** Cloquet; **1978** Blake; **1979** Stillwater; **1980** Stillwater; **1981** Blake; **1982** Stillwater; **1983** Duluth East; **1984** Stillwater; **1985** Stillwater; **1986** Stillwater; **1987** Minnetonka; **1988** Stillwater; **1989** Stillwater; **1990** Stillwater; **1991** Edina; **1992** Blake; **1993** Minnetonka; **1994** Duluth East; **1995** Duluth East; **1996** Orono; **1997** Edina; **1998** Edina; **1999** Edina; **2000** Benilde–St. Margaret's; **2001** Edina; **2002** Edina; **2003** Duluth East; **2004** Edina; **2005** Edina; **2006** Duluth East

Soccer

One-class tournament

1980 Bloomington Jefferson; **1981** Minneapolis Washburn; **1982** Bloomington Jefferson; **1983** Irondale; **1984** Bloomington Jefferson; **1985** Coon Rapids; **1986** Edina; **1987** Coon Rapids; **1988** Roseville; **1989** Anoka; **1990** Park of Cottage Grove; **1991** Wayzata; **1992** Burnsville; **1993** Burnsville; **1994** Stillwater; **1995** Apple Valley; **1996** Wayzata

Two-class tournament

1997 Henry Sibley (AA), Mahtomedi (A); **1998** Stillwater (AA), Minnehaha Academy (A); **1999** Woodbury (AA), Mahtomedi (A); **2000** Wayzata (AA), Blake (A); **2001** Minnetonka (AA), Totino-Grace (A); **2002** Wayzata (AA), Totino-Grace (A); **2003** Woodbury (AA), Holy Angels (A); **2004** Woodbury (AA), Mahtomedi (A); **2005** Eden Prairie (AA), Mahtomedi (A)

Softball

One-class tournament

1977 Coon Rapids; **1978** Cambridge

Two-class tournament

1979 Rosemount (AA), Wadena (A); **1980** Austin (AA), Jordan (A); **1981** Austin (AA), Moose Lake–Barnum (A); **1982** Henry Sibley (AA), Moose Lake (A); **1983** Hill-Murray (AA), La Crescent (A); **1984** North St. Paul (AA), Sleepy Eye St. Mary's (A); **1985** Cooper (AA), St. Bernard's (A); **1986** Mankato East (AA), St. Bernard's (A); **1987** Austin (AA), Glencoe (A); **1988** Mankato East (AA), Southland (A); **1989** Mankato East (AA), St. Bernard's (A); **1990** Mankato West (AA), St. Bernard's (A); **1991** Mankato East (AA), Hermantown (A); **1992** Richfield (AA), Maple River (A); **1993** Park of Cottage Grove (AA), New Ulm Cathedral (A); **1994** St. Cloud Tech (AA), New Ulm Cathedral (A); **1995** Stillwater (AA), New Ulm Cathedral (A); **1996** Stillwater (AA), Maple River (A); **1997** Hopkins (AA), Mound Westonka (A); **1998** Stillwater (AA), Esko (A); **1999** Minnetonka (AA), Wabasso (A)

Three-class tournament

2000 Minnetonka (3A), Holy Angels (2A), St. Bernard's (A); **2001** Armstrong (3A), Maple River (2A), Mankato Loyola (A); **2002** Eden Prairie (3A), Hermantown (2A), St. Bernard's (A); **2003** Eastview (3A), Winona Cotter (2A), New Ulm Cathedral (A); **2004** Burnsville (3A), Jackson County Central (2A), St. Bernard's (A); **2005** Burnsville (3A), Jackson County Central (2A), New Ulm Cathedral (A)

Swimming

One-class meet

1924 Virginia; **1925** Virginia; **1926** Virginia; **1927** Eveleth; **1928** Biwabik; **1929** Biwabik; **1930** Virginia; **1931** Virginia; **1932** Virginia; **1933** Virginia; **1934** Virginia; **1935** Virginia; **1936** Virginia; **1937** Virginia; **1938** Virginia; **1939** Virginia; **1940** Virginia; **1941** Virginia; **1942** Nashwauk; **1975** Minnetonka; **1976** Minnetonka; **1977** Irondale; **1978** Hopkins Lindbergh; **1979** Hopkins Lindbergh; **1980** Richfield; **1981** Burnsville; **1982** Burnsville; **1983** Burnsville; **1984** Edina; **1985** Burnsville; **1986** Edina; **1987** Edina; **1988** Edina; **1989** Hastings; **1990** Apple Valley; **1991** Woodbury; **1992** Edina; **1993** Woodbury; **1994** Apple Valley; **1995** Hastings; **1996** Eden Prairie

Two-class meet

1997 Eden Prairie (AA), Hutchinson (A); **1998** Eden Prairie (AA), Northfield (A); **1999** Eden Prairie, Edina (AA), Rosemount (A); **2000** Edina (AA), Red Wing (A); **2001** Edina (AA), Red Wing (A); **2002** Burnsville (AA), Red Wing (A); **2003** Edina (AA), Hutchinson (A); **2004** Edina (AA), Hutchinson (A); **2005** Stillwater (AA), Visitation (A)

Tennis

One-class meet

1974 Minnetonka; **1975** Minnetonka; **1976** St. Paul Academy; **1977** St. Paul Academy

Two-class meet

1978 Edina East (AA), Rochester Lourdes (A); **1979** Edina East (AA), St. Paul Academy; **1980** Edina East (AA), St. Paul Academy (A); **1981** Edina (AA), St. Paul Academy (A); **1982** Edina (AA), St. Paul Academy (A); **1983** Edina (AA), St. Paul Academy (A); **1984** Edina (AA), Blake (A); **1985** Edina (AA), Blue Earth (A); **1986** Edina (AA), St. Paul Academy (A); **1987** Edina (AA), Blake (A); **1988** Edina (AA), St. Paul Academy (A); **1989** Edina (AA), Virginia (A); **1990** Edina (AA), Blake (A); **1991** Edina (AA), Blake (A); **1992** Edina (AA), Blake (A); **1993** Bloomington Jefferson (AA), Blake (A); **1994** Hopkins (AA), Orono (A); **1995** Bloomington Jefferson (AA), Orono (A); **1996** Bloomington Jefferson (AA), Breck (A); **1997** Edina (AA), Rochester Lourdes (A); **1998** Edina (AA), Rochester Lourdes (A); **1999** Edina (AA), Rochester Lourdes (A); **2000** Edina (AA), Rochester Lourdes (A); **2001** Edina (AA), Rochester Lourdes (A); **2002** Edina (AA), Rochester Lourdes (A); **2003** Edina (AA), Rochester Lourdes (A); **2004** Edina (AA), Rochester Lourdes (A)

Track and Field

One-class meet

1972 White Bear Lake, International Falls; **1973** Moorhead; **1974** Moorhead; **1975** Moorhead

Two-class meet

1976 Owatonna (AA), Buffalo Lake (A); **1977** St. Paul Central (AA), Austin Pacelli (A); **1978** St. Paul Central (AA), Buffalo Lake (A); **1979** South St. Paul (AA), Plainview (A); **1980** St. Cloud Apollo (AA), Mt. St. Benedict (A); **1981** Anoka (AA), Mt. St. Benedict, Rochester Lourdes (A); **1982** Anoka (AA), Rochester Lourdes (A); **1983** Minnetonka (AA), Greenway (A); **1984** Rosemount (AA), Blooming Prairie (A); **1985** Minnetonka (AA), Blue Earth (A); **1986** Minnetonka (AA), Belgrade/Brooten (A); **1987** Rocori (AA), Windom (A); **1988** Park of Cottage Grove (AA), Windom (A); **1989** Minnetonka (AA), Byron, Hawley/Ulen-Hitterdal (A); **1990** Roseville (AA), Byron (A); **1991** Roseville (AA), Byron (A); **1992** Minnetonka (AA), Plainview (A); **1993** Apple Valley (AA), Plainview (A); **1994** Apple Valley, St. Paul Central (AA), Sartell (A); **1995** Apple Valley (AA), Esko (A); **1996** Coon Rapids (AA), Breck (A); **1997** Apple Valley (AA), Breck (A); **1998** St. Louis Park (AA), St. Michael–Albertville (A); **1999** Moorhead (AA), Roseau (A); **2000** Anoka (AA), Holdingford (A); **2001** Moorhead (AA), Blake (A); **2002** Lakeville (AA), Holdingford (A); **2003** Lakeville (AA), Mayer Lutheran (A); **2004** Apple Valley (AA), Cedar Mountain (A); **2005** Lakeville (AA), Lac qui Parle Valley/Dawson-Boyd (A)

Volleyball

One-class meet

1974 Osseo

Two-class meet

1975 Hibbing (AA), Moose Lake (A); **1976** Minnetonka (AA), Hermantown (A); **1977** St. Paul Highland Park (AA), Sartell (A); **1978** Coon Rapids (AA), Gaylord (A); **1979** St. Paul Johnson (AA), Gaylord (A); **1980** Armstrong (AA), Moose Lake (A); **1981** Armstrong (AA), Moose Lake (A); **1982** Armstrong (AA), Mayer Lutheran (A); **1983** Armstrong (AA), St. Michael–Albertville (A); **1984** Armstrong (AA), Concordia Academy (A); **1985** Apple Valley (AA), Greenway (A); **1986** Columbia Heights (AA), Clarissa (A); **1987** Columbia Heights (AA), Concordia Academy (A); **1988** Moorhead (AA), Win-E-Mac (A); **1989** Columbia Heights (AA), Cook (A); **1990** Columbia Heights (AA), Tracy-Milroy (A); **1991** Chaska (AA), Tracy-Milroy (A); **1992** Apple Valley

Girls volleyball game between Pipestone and Windom high school teams, 1978

(AA), Tracy-Milroy (A); **1993** Chaska (AA), United South Central (A); **1994** Chaska (AA), Tracy-Milroy (A); **1995** Alexandria (AA), Tracy-Milroy (A); **1996** Chaska (AA), Tracy-Milroy (A); **1997** Eagan (AA), Stewartville (A); **1998** Alexandria (AA), Jackson County Central (A)

Three-class meet

1999 Alexandria (3A), Jackson County Central (2A), Central Minnesota Christian (A); **2000** Armstrong (3A), Stewartville (2A), Central Minnesota Christian (A); **2001** Eagan (3A), Tracy-Milroy-Balaton (2A), Fosston (A); **2002** Armstrong (3A), Renville County West (2A), Fosston (A); **2003** Eagan (3A), Jackson County Central (2A), Faribault Bethlehem Academy (A); **2004** Marshall (3A), Tracy-Milroy-Balaton (2A), Fosston (A); **2005** Chaska (3A), Lake of the Woods (2A), Faribault Bethlehem Academy (A)

Bowling, Golf, Lacrosse, Soccer, Tennis, and Volleyball

7

AMERICAN BOWLING CONGRESS

ABC

ST. PAUL   1951

Bowling

EUROPEANS brought bowling—played in England as early as the fourteenth century—to the United States in the early 19th century. The American Bowling Congress formed in New York City in 1895, an event that spurred standardization of the sport and national competitions.

According to Minneapolis sports writer George Barton, the first bowling alley in Minneapolis was probably located in Harmonia Hall, on Nicollet Avenue between Washington and Third Street, in the early 1890s. Another alley was probably installed in a downtown Minneapolis hotel in 1901. The State Bowling Association was formed in 1903, and the first state tournament was held that same year. A team from Minneapolis entered the American Bowling Congress tournament in Indianapolis in 1903.

In 1925 the *Minneapolis Tribune* organized the Northwest Singles Classic, which became a very popular bowling event for the next 50 years. Since the founding of the American Bowling Congress tournament in 1901, St. Paul has hosted three times—1941, 1951 and 1965.

Minnesota State Bowling Association Hall of Fame

A Norm Abrams, St. Paul; Joel Albrecht, New Ulm; G. "Hots" Anderson, Duluth; **B** Bill Baden, Minneapolis; Bud Bahr, Rochester; Clarence Bell, Winona; Maynard Bergs, Hutchinson; Elmer Beyer, St. Paul; Roger Blad, Burnsville; John Blum, Austin; Vince Bovitz, St. Paul; Arden Bullert, Glencoe; **C** Jim Collier, Minneapolis; LeRoy Cook, Minneapolis; Art Cumming, Minneapolis; **D** Paul Doherty, St. Paul; John Dorek, Edina; Bill Drouches, Minneapolis; Jerry Dutler, Mankato; **E** John Eiss, Brooklyn Park; Virgil Enger, Bloomington; A. S. Ernst, St. Paul; Jerry Ernster, St. Paul; **F** Sonny Feind, Rochester; Richard Finke, Minneapolis; Bruce Forsland, Minnetonka; **G** Arnold Gautschi, St. Paul; Paul Goeb, Duluth; **H** Hal Halverson, Minneapolis; Dale Hanson, St. Paul; Robert Hanson, Minneapolis; William Harich, Minneapolis; Bill Hengen, Minneapolis; John Henry, Minneapolis; **J** Albert Joyner, Osseo; **K** Roland Keena, Princeton; Robert Kosidowski, Winona; **L** Chuck Leone, Rochester; Jim Lindquist, Minneapolis; Alan Loth, Arden Hills; **M** Jim Madden, Minneapolis; Ed Mady, St. Paul; Edward Maehren, St. Paul; Leo Mann, St. Paul; Norm Marietta, Minneapolis; Richard Mattson, Buffalo; Leroy Meyer, Alexandria; Jack Miller, St. Paul; Fran Morrisette, St. Paul; **N** Arnie Ness, Barnesville; **P** Joe Page, Winona; Fran Penfield, Cannon Falls;

George Peterson, Crystal; Clark Poelzer, Arden Hills; Vic Poganski, St. Paul; **R** Ossie Ragogna, St. Paul; **S** Dennis Savoy, Duluth; Bob Schabert, St. Paul; Dennis Schacht, St. Paul; Terry Schacht, Oakdale; **T** Jerry Tessman, St. Paul; Syl Thiel, Lake City; Ray Throne, Winona; Rod Toft, St. Paul; Tom Trainer, Plymouth; **W** Jack Wallisch, St. Paul; Einar Wick, Minneapolis; Clarence Wittman, St. Paul; **Y** Jess Young, Minneapolis

---

DID YOU KNOW **?**

On December 9, 2004, a New Prague man became the first Minnesotan to roll a 900 series (three consecutive perfect 300 games). Darin Pomije, a bowling alley owner, accomplished the feat during league play to become just the seventh American to roll a 900 since 1997. Pomije, age 30, had rolled eleven 300 games prior to his 900.

Golf

Minnesota has a long and rich golf tradition. The state is home to the nation's second-oldest continuously played golf course and the oldest course west of New Jersey, St. Paul's Town and Country Club. The Town and Country Club opened in June 1893, a year before golf's national governing body, the United States Golf Association (USGA), was formed.

Minnesota is the only state to have hosted all 13 USGA championships, as well as the Walker and Curtis Cup matches and the USGA state championships.

Minnesota Golfing Legends

Les Bolstad, the long-time coach at the University of Minnesota and mentor to Patty Berg, was the youngest golfer ever to win the U.S. Amateur Public Links championship. He won in Buffalo, New York, in 1926 at the age of 18.

Harrison "Jimmy" Johnston and **John Harris** are the only two Minnesotans to win the U.S. Amateur. Johnston, a St. Paul investment broker, won the 1929 U.S. Amateur at Pebble Beach, California. Harris, a former University of Minnesota golfer and hockey player, won the 1993 U.S. Amateur in Houston, Texas.

Tom Lehman, an Alexandria native, is a former University of Minnesota All-American. In 1996 Lehman won the British Open and was named the PGA Tour's Player of the Year.

Patty Berg, a founding member of the Ladies Professional Golf Association, won 28 amateur titles in a seven-year span before turning pro in 1940. The Minneapolis native won three professional tournaments in 1941 before a knee injury suffered in a car accident sidelined her for 18 months. In 1943

Les Bolstad, a Gopher golfer in the 1920s and coach, 1947–76

Berg enlisted in the Marines and was eventually commissioned a lieutenant. While in the service, she won two tournaments in 1943 and another tournament in 1945. She won three more titles in 1946 before winning the first U.S. Women's Open in September 1946. The six-day tournament offered the largest purse ever for a women's tournament—$19,700. Berg earned $5,600 for her title. Between 1948 and 1962, Berg won 44 more titles. She was named the Associated Press Female Athlete of the Year three times—in 1938, 1943 and 1956.

DID YOU KNOW ?

According to the Minnesota Golf Association in 2005, Minnesota is the nation's top golf state, based on per capita participation. Minnesota has more than 450 golf courses.

Solomon Hughes

Hughes learned to play golf after he began caddying at age 12 in Gadsden, Alabama. By the 1930s, Hughes was playing in events sponsored by the United Golf Association, a national association for African American golfers. In 1935, at age 26, Hughes won the National Negro Open. During the 1940s, Hughes won the Joe Louis Open in Detroit, the Midwest Open in Toledo and the Des Moines Open.

In 1944 Hughes moved his family to Minneapolis. After joining an association of African American golfers called the Twin Cities Golf Club, Hughes started giving golf lessons.

In 1948 Hughes and Ted Rhodes filed an entry fee to play in the St. Paul Open, a PGA tournament played annually at Keller Golf Course. The PGA refused to let Hughes and Rhodes into the tournament because they were not members of the PGA. At the time, African Americans were prohibited from joining the PGA.

In 1951, with the support of one of the tournament's sponsors—the St. Paul Jaycees—Hughes again sent in an entry form to the tournament and was again turned down.

One year later, after boxing legend Joe Louis had generated considerable publicity about the PGA's exclusion of African Americans, the PGA altered its policies for a few tournaments. In 1952 Hughes and Rhodes were allowed to play in the St. Paul Open. (In 1959 Charles Sifford became the first African American to receive a PGA card.) Hughes died in 1987 at age 78.

Memorable Moments in Minnesota Golf History

Bobby Jones winning the 1930 U.S. Open at Interlachen to earn his third major title of the year.

Sam Snead shooting a Western Open–record, 20-under par, 268 to win the 1949 Western Open at Keller Golf Course in St. Paul.

Solomon Hughes in 1948, the year he tried to enter the St. Paul Open tournament

Rob Rosburg winning the 1959 PGA Championship at Minneapolis Golf Club.

Jack Nicklaus, age 19, winning the 1959 Trans-Mississippi Tournament at Woodhill Country Club in Wayzata.

Tony Jacklin winning the 1970 U.S. Open at Hazeltine National in Chaska and **Payne Stewart** edging **Scott Simpson** in an 18-hole playoff to win the 1991 U.S. Open at Hazeltine in Chaska.

Hollis Stacy defeating **Nancy Lopez** by two strokes to win the 1977 U.S. Women's Open at Hazeltine.

Rich Beem outlasting **Tiger Woods** by one stroke before a crowd of 40,000 to win the PGA Championship at Hazeltine in 2002.

DID YOU KNOW ?

Prescott Sheldon Bush, the father of President George H. W. Bush and president of the USGA, presented the winner's medal to Patty Berg at the 1935 U.S. Women's Amateur tournament at Interlachen Country Club. Prescott Bush later became a U.S. Senator from Connecticut.

Keller Golf Course

In 1932, the year it hosted the PGA Championship for the first time, St. Paul's Keller was called the finest public course in the world. Through the years, it has hosted 31 PGA tour events. It hosted an LPGA event—the Patty Berg Classic—from 1973 to 1980. For more than 30 years, beginning in 1930, the course hosted the St. Paul Open (renamed the Minnesota Classic in 1966).

USGA Events

The United States Golf Association (USGA), formed in 1894, sponsors 13 championships, and Minnesota is the only state to have played host to each.

Event	Year	Course
USGA Open	1916	Minikahda
	1930	Interlachen

	1970	Hazeltine
	1991	Hazeltine
USGA Senior Open	1983	Hazeltine
USGA Amateur	1927	Minikahda
	1950	Minneapolis Golf Club
USGA Senior Amateur	1956	Somerset
	1986	Interlachen
USGA Mid-Amateur	1994	Hazeltine
USGA Junior Amateur	1958	University of Minnesota
	1984	Wayzata Country Club
USGA Public Links	1931	Keller
	1947	Meadowbrook
	1964	Francis Gross
	1976	Bunker Hills
	1992	Edinburgh USA
	2004	Rush Creek
USGA Women's Open	1956	Northland
	1966	Hazeltine
USGA Women's Amateur	1935	Interlachen
	1951	Town and Country Club
	1988	Minikahda
USGA Senior Women's Amateur	1995	Somerset
USGA Women's Mid-Amateur	1993	Rochester Golf and Country Club
USGA Junior Girls	1988	Golden Valley
USGA Women's Public Links	1979	Braemer

Cups

The **Walker Cup** is a biennial international golf competition started in 1922 to foster interest in golf on both sides of the Atlantic Ocean. It has been held in Minnesota twice—in 1957 at Minikahda and in 1993 at Edina's Interlachen. In 1957 the United States won, 8–3. In 1993 the U.S. won, 19–5.

The **Curtis Cup** is a biennial amateur women's golf competition between the United States and Great Britain. The event has been held in Minnesota once—in 1998 at Minneapolis's Minikahda. The United States defeated Great Britain/Ireland, 10–8.

The **Solheim Cup** is a biennial, trans-Atlantic team match-play competition between U.S.-born players from the LPGA Tour against European-born players from the Ladies European Tour. The event has been held in Minnesota once—at Interlachen in 2002. The U.S. won 15½ to 12½.

Senior Tour

The PGA Senior tour has made a stop in Minnesota since 1993. Now named the 3M Championship, the tournament has been won by Chi Chi Rodriguez (1993), Dave Stockton (1994), Raymond Floyd (1995), Vicente Fernandez (1996), Hale Irwin (1997, 1999 and 2002), Leonard Thompson (1998), Ed Dougherty (2000), Bruce Lietzke (2001), Wayne Levi (2003) and Tom Kite (2004).

DID YOU KNOW ?

In 2003, Hilary Homeyer Lunke, of Edina, became the 14th player in LPGA history to make the U.S. Women's Open her first LPGA tour victory. Lunke defeated Angela Stanford and Kelly Robbins in an 18-hole playoff to win the tournament in Portland, Oregon. Her winner's check of $560,000 was the largest ever for an LPGA event. The 2004 and 2005 U.S. Women's Open winners also earned $560,000.

Women's Golf

The Women's Golf Association was formed in 1915, when representatives from six courses joined to encourage women in the state to take up the sport. The first women's match-play championship was held at Town and Country Club in September 1915. Eleanor Lightner of Town and Country won the tournament, which featured 62 golfers.

One of the state's top female golfers is Bev Gammon Vanstrum. Between 1953 and 1968, Vanstrum won the Minnesota Women's Golf Association's match-play title seven times, the medal-play title six times and four women's state amateurs. In 1957 Vanstrum became the first to win all three in the same season.

Women's Professional Golf

The first Ladies Professional Golf Association (LPGA) event held in Minnesota was the American Women's Open, played at Brookview in 1958 and

Golfer Patty Berg, winner of 28 amateur championships in the 1930s

1959 and at Hiawatha in 1960 and 1961. Patty Berg won the tournament in 1958—her first professional tournament appearance in Minnesota—and 1960. Bev Hanson won in 1959 and Judy Kimball in 1961.

The Patty Berg Classic was called the St. Paul Ladies Open in 1973 and 1974 before being renamed in 1975. The winners were: Sandra Palmer (1973), JoAnne Carner (1974), JoAnn Washam (1975), Kathy Whitworth (1976), Bonnie Lauer (1977), Shelley Hamlin (1978), Beth Daniel (1979 and 1980).

The LPGA returned to Minnesota in 1990 with the Northgate Classic. The tournament was renamed the Minnesota LPGA Classic in 1993 and held several other names and sponsors in its times in Minnesota. The tournament moved from Edinburgh USA in Brooklyn Park to Rush Creek Golf Course in Maple Grove in 1997.

The winners were Beth Daniel (1990), Cindy Rarick (1991), Kris Tschetter (1992), Hiromi Kobayashi (1993 and 1998), Liselotte Neumann (1994 and 1996), Julie Larsen (1995), and Danielle Ammaccapane (1997).

University of Minnesota Golf

Two golfers in the University of Minnesota men's program have won NCAA individual titles. **Louis Lick**, a 20-year-old medical student, won the title in 1944. In the final round, Lick defeated the University of Michigan's John Jenswold, one up. Jenswold, who was from Duluth, had won the Western Conference (Big 10) title earlier in the year.

James McLean won in 1998. McLean, a native of Australia, shot a 72-hole total 271 to tie the tournament record held by Justin Leonard, Phil Mickelson and John Inman. Going into the 2005–06 season, McLean had four of the five lowest rounds by a Gopher (since 1979). During his university career, McLean shot rounds of 63, 64 and two 65s.

Les Bolstad and Conference Titles

Les Bolstad served as the Gophers men's golf coach from 1946 to 1976. He coached teams to two Big Ten titles—in 1963 and 1972, and the Gophers finished in second place at the conference tournament in 1961 and 1970.

Prior to becoming the Gophers' coach, Bolstad helped the team win the first Big Ten title. In 1927 Bolstad was the medalist at the conference meet. Two years later, he again was the medalist at the conference meet, held at University Golf Course, when the Gophers won the title. The Gophers won their second conference title in 1938.

In addition to Bolstad's two conference titles, six other Gophers have won conference titles: James Teale (1943), Bill Brask (1968), Dave Haberle (1971), Jim Bergeson (1972), John Harris (1974) and Matt Anderson (2003).

Tom Lehman

Tom Lehman, born in Austin, Minnesota, was a three-time All-American for the Gophers—in 1979, 1980, and 1981. He is the only golfer in school history to achieve this success.

In Big Ten meets, Lehman finished third in 1979, tied for 17th in 1980 and tied for second in 1981. At the NCAA meet, Lehman finished 36th in 1979 and 20th in 1980. He missed the cut at the NCAA meet in 1981.

As a professional golfer, Lehman has won five PGA tour events. As of April 1, 2005, Lehman's career winnings on the PGA tour were $16.68 million.

Gophers Women's Golf

The University of Minnesota fielded its first women's golf team in 1976. The team has won two Big Ten Conference titles.

In 1978 the Gophers tied for first at the rain-shortened conference meet, shooting an 18-hole 331. In 1989 the Gophers won the conference tournament and then finished 12th at the NCAA meet, their only NCAA appearance.

The Gophers have finished second at the Big Ten meet in 1984, 1986, 1988 and 1992.

The only Gopher to win a Big Ten individual title is Kate Hughes, who won back-to-back titles in 1988 and 1989.

Surviving the Cut

In April 2002 the University of Minnesota announced that its men's and women's golf programs, as well as the men's gymnastics program, would be eliminated at the end of the school year because of budget problems.

Three weeks after the announcement, the Gophers won their first Big Ten Conference title in 30 years. A month later, the Gophers rallied to win the NCAA team title—the first "Northern" school to win the title since Ohio State in 1979.

But the Gophers had almost been sent home early from the NCAA meet in Columbus, Ohio. Weather hampered the first two days of the tournament. With more rain predicted for the third round, NCAA officials discussed trimming the field of 30 teams in half for the final two rounds before electing to let the entire field complete the tournament. Had the NCAA trimmed the field, the Gophers would not have won the title. They were tied for 16th place—one stroke out of 15th place—after two rounds.

In the third round, played in high winds and rain, the Gophers shot a 1-under par 283 to move into fourth place—three strokes out of first—heading into the final round.

On the final day, the Gophers shot a 6-under par 278 to finish with a 72-hole total of 1,134—four strokes better than first-ranked Georgia Tech.

The Gophers were the only team to shoot below par on the final two days of the tournament. Their previous best finish at the NCAA meet was a second-place finish in 1944, and they had had not ranked higher than No. 18 all season.

Justin Smith, who shot a final round 69, was the Gophers' top finisher. Smith finished in a tie for fourth—5-under 279. Matt Anderson, who shot a career-best 66 in the final round, finished in a tie for eighth with a 281. Smith and Anderson each earned All-American status.

A "Save Gophers Sports" fund-raising campaign raised enough money to save the golf and men's gymnastics programs. The Gophers repeated as Big Ten champions in 2003.

DID YOU KNOW ?

Bois de Sioux Golf Course is the only public golf course in the nation to have nine holes in one state and nine holes in another. The front nine is in Wahpeton, North Dakota, and the back nine in Breckenridge, Minnesota.

Amateur Golf

Top Minnesota amateur golfers have had ample opportunities to compete with top amateurs from around the country. From the 1940s through the 1980s—nearly 40 years running—three major competitions lasting three consecutive weeks were held in Minnesota's "Resort Country": the Birchmont Invitational in Bemidji, Resorters in Alexandria and Pine-to-Palm in Detroit Lakes.

Joe Coria

Between 1934 and 1952, Joe Coria won the Minnesota State Open a record seven times and finished second four other times. Coria finished in the tournament's top ten 19 consecutive times. In all, Coria made 38 appearances in the event, also a record.

Coria won 11 golfing titles in Minnesota—seven state opens, two Public Links championships (1933 and 1934) and two state PGA titles (1943 and

1944). During one round in the 1940s, he shot a course-record 57 at Phalen Golf Course, a record that still stands.

In 1941 he led the St. Paul Open at Keller Golf Course in St. Paul through 63 holes, before losing to Horton Smith by four strokes. Finishing in a tie for second place with Coria was the legendary Ben Hogan.

Title Holders

Joe Coria is tied for second among Minnesota golfers with 11 "major" state titles. First-place George Shortridge won 15 state championships—the state open twice and 13 state PGA titles. Harry Legg won 11 state titles—the state amateur 10 times and the state open once. H. R. "Jimmy" Johnston and Les Bolstad each won nine state titles. Johnston won the state amateur seven times and the state open twice, while Bolstad won the state open four times, the state PGA and state Public Links twice and the state amateur once.

[1] MGA Men's Amateur Champions

1901 Theodore Thurston; **1902** Harold Bend; **1903** Michael Doran Jr.; **1904** Harold Bend; **1905** Harry Legg; **1906** Clive Jaffray; **1907** Lynn Johnson; **1908** Harry Legg; **1909** Harry Legg; **1910** Harry Legg; **1911** Harry Legg; **1912** Harry Legg; **1913** Harry Legg; **1914** Richard Patrick; **1915** Dudley Mudge Jr.; **1916** Dudley Mudge; **1917** Harry Legg; **1918** Robert Hopwood; **1919** Harry Legg; **1920** Harry Legg; **1921** H. R. Johnston; **1922** H. R. Johnston; **1923** H. R. Johnston; **1924** H. R. Johnston; **1925** H. R. Johnston; **1926** H. R. Johnston; **1927** H. R. Johnston; **1928** Rudy Juran; **1929** Frank Brokl Jr.; **1930** Charles Sawyer; **1931** Les Bolstad; **1932** Charles Sawyer; **1933** Carson Herron; **1934** Bobby Campbell; **1935** Albert Clasen; **1936** Richard Sawyer; **1937** Bobby Campbell; **1938** Kenneth Young; **1939** George Wright Jr.; **1940** Thomas Hamper Jr.; **1941** Neil Croonquist; **1942–44** No tournament; **1945** Albert Clasen; **1946** Charles Sawyer; **1947** Lawrence Karkhoff; **1948** Charles Sawyer; **1949** Lawrence Karkhoff; **1950** Adrian Simonsen; **1951** Adrian Simonsen; **1952** William Zieske; **1953** Henry Ernst; **1954** Spero Daltas; **1955** Thomas Hadley; **1956** William Waryan; **1957** Clayton Johnson; **1958** Robert Henrikson; **1959** Ted Vickerman; **1960** Neil Croonquist; **1961** Gene Hansen; **1962** Gene Hansen; **1963** Rolf Deming; **1964** Bob Barbarossa; **1965** James Archer; **1966** Norbert Anderson; **1967** Robert Magie III; **1968** Gary Burton; **1969** Gary Burton; **1970** Mike Fermoyle; **1971** Dave Haberle; **1972** Rick Ehrmanntraut; **1973** Mike Fermoyle; **1974** John Harris; **1975** Steve Johnson; **1976** Bill Israelson; **1977** Bill Israelson; **1978** Bill Israelson; **1979** John

McMorrow; **1980** Mike Fermoyle; **1981** Tom Lehman; **1982** Chris Perry; **1983** Chris Perry; **1984** Dave Tentis; **1985** Dave Nordeen; **1986** Dave Nordeen; **1987** John Harris; **1988** Jon Christian; **1989** John Harris; **1990** Dan Croonquist; **1991** James Scheller; **1992** Tim Herron; **1993** Mike Sauer; **1994** Aaron Barber; **1995** Mike Christensen; **1996** Joe Stansberry; **1997** David Christensen; **1998** James McLean; **1999** Adam Dooley; **2000** John Harris;

H. R. ("Jimmy") Johnston, 1908, winner of the National Amateur Golf Championship in 1929

2001 Ben Meyers; **2002** Bowen Osborn; **2003** Kane Hanson; **2004** Eric Deutsch; **2005** Joe Stansberry

NOTE: Match play from 1901 to 1966 (except for stroke play in 1945). Stroke play with 72 holes started in 1967; stroke play with 54 holes began in 1971.

Women's Amateur Champions

1954 Beverly Gammon; **1955** Beverly Gammon; **1956** Gloria Brandsness; **1957** Beverly Gammon Vanstrum; **1958** Carole Pushing; **1959** Nancy Brown; **1960** Carole Pushing; **1961** Betty Swanson; **1962** Beverly Gammon Vanstrum; **1963** Betty Swanson; **1964** Darlene Anderson; **1965** Betty Swanson; **1966** Joan Garvin; **1967** Kris Gilbertson; **1968** Lynn Zmistowski; **1969** Joan Garvin; **1970** Lynn Zmistowski; **1971** Joan Garvin; **1972** Joan Garvin; **1973** Joan Nesset; **1974** Joan Garvin; **1975** Julie Gumlia; **1976** Anne Zahn; **1977** Joan Garvin; **1978** Jody Rosenthal; **1979** Kelly Varty; **1980** Betsy Seitz; **1981** Anne Zahn; **1982** Lisa Kluver; **1983** Nancy Harris; **1984** Nancy Harris; **1985** Nancy Harris; **1986** Dawn Ginnaty; **1987** Julie Hennessy; **1988** Nancy Harris; **1989** Nancy Harris; **1990** Jodi Krafka; **1991** Kelly Varty Burley; **1992** Kelly Varty Burley; **1993** Kelly Varty Burley; **1994** Nancy Harris Blanchard; **1995** Kris Lindstrom; **1996** Alissa Herron; **1997** Alissa Herron; **1998** Alissa Herron; **1999** Claudia Pilot; **2000** Claudia Pilot; **2001** Megan George; **2002** Karla Schuldt; **2003** Katie Nicoll; **2004** Laura Olin; **2005** Chrissie McArdle

NOTE: From 1954 to 1971, the tournament was known as the Minnesota Women's Amateur Championship. It was abandoned after the 1971 season, when the Minnesota Women's Golf Association's 54-hole Stroke Play Championship became known as the Minnesota Women's State Amateur Championship.

Lacrosse

Minnesota's latest professional franchise debuted on January 1, 2005, when the Minnesota Swarm of the National Lacrosse League played their season-opener. The Swarm arrived in Minnesota when Minnesota Sports and Entertainment, the parent company of the Minnesota Wild of the NHL, purchased the rights to the dormant Montreal Express for $1 million.

Swarm officials were confident that the Twin Cities would support the team. The Minnesota Lacrosse Association has more than 5,000 members. The team, which plays its home games in the Xcel Energy Center in St. Paul, sold more than 4,000 season tickets.

Of the 23 players on the roster, 22 of them were Canadian. Teams in the league play a 16-match schedule.

The 12-team league started as a four-team league in 1987.

Minnesota Swarm lacrosse action with defenseman Brock Boyle

Soccer—Minnesota Thunder

After a six-year break, professional "outdoor" soccer returned to Minnesota in 1994 when the United States Independent Soccer League fielded a team known as the Minnesota Thunder. Buzz Lagos co-founded the Thunder with Tom Engstrom in 1990. Lagos had previously coached the St. Paul Academy boys soccer team to a 256–55–35 record and four state championships. On August 1, 2005, Lagos announced that he would retire as Thunder coach at the end of the 2005 season.

The Thunder's record number of goals in a season is 21, scored by Johnny Menyongar in 2000. Menyongar, a member of the Liberian national team, led the A-League in scoring (17 goals) during the regular season and then added four goals in the playoffs.

The Thunder's all-time leading scorer is Amos McGee. McGee had 64 goals and 39 assists.

The Thunder reached the A-League Championship game six times: 1994, 1995, 1998, 1999, 2000 and 2003. The Thunder won the championship game in 1999.

In 2005 the Thunder moved from the A-League to the USL First Division. Following the 2005 season, Buzz Lagos retired as coach. McGee was named to replace him.

Minnesota Thunder Year-by-Year
Outdoor

Season	Coach	Record
1994	Buzz Lagos	18–0
1995	Lagos	19–1
1996	Lagos	10–8
1997	Lagos	13–15
1998	Lagos	19–9
1999	Lagos	22–6

Amos Magee, a leading Minnesota Thunder scorer and head coach

2000	Lagos	20–4–4
2001	Lagos	9–15–2
2002	Lagos	14–9–5
2003	Lagos	17–9–2
2004	Lagos	13–9–6
2005	Lagos	7–11–10

DID YOU KNOW ?

Strikers coach Alan Merrick played for the Minnesota Kicks from 1976 to 1979 and again in 1981. Merrick, a defender, scored six goals in 115 games.

Goalkeeper Tino Lettieri, who played for the Kicks and the Strikers, was inducted into the Canada Soccer Hall of Fame in 2001. Lettieiri played for the Canadian Olympic team in 1984.

Gregg Thompson, a football standout at Stillwater High School, played for the Strikers, too. Thompson was the Minnesota High School Athlete of the Year in 1978 before playing college soccer at Indiana University. He earned All-American honors by helping the Hoosiers win the NCAA title in 1982. In the championship game, Thompson, a defender, scored both goals in the Hoosiers' 2–1 victory over Duke in eight overtimes. At the time it was the longest game in NCAA soccer history.

Minnesota Strikers

Minnesota was without professional soccer in 1982 and 1983, but in 1984 the world's game returned to Minnesota when the Robbie family relocated the Fort Lauderdale Strikers, owned by Elizabeth Robbie, the wife of Minneapolis lawyer Joe Robbie, to Minnesota. Joe Robbie owned the Miami Dolphins of the National Football League.The Strikers went 14–10 in their first season in Minnesota but missed the playoffs.

Following the 1984 season, the NASL and Major Indoor Soccer League (MISL) merged. The Strikers and three other teams joined the MISL, which had been created in 1978 as the first indoor professional soccer league.

The Strikers began their inaugural MISL season on November 3, 1984, with a 10–2 loss in San Diego. They made their home debut six days later with a 6–3 victory over Tacoma before 7,754 at Met Center. The Strikers finished their first season with a 24–24 record and reached the semifinals of the MISL playoffs before being eliminated by three-time defending league champion San Diego.

The largest crowd to see a soccer match in Minnesota numbered 52,621, fans gathered at the Metrodome on May 28, 1984, who watched the Strikers defeat Tampa Bay, 1–0. Following the game, the Beach Boys put on a concert.

In the 1985–86 playoffs, the Strikers reached the finals, where they lost to San Diego again. The Strikers, who were trying to become the first Minnesota team to win a pro title since the Minneapolis Lakers won the NBA title in 1954, had led the best-of-seven series, 3–1, but the Sockers won the final three games for their fifth consecutive MISL title.

The Strikers would last two more seasons before folding on June 22, 1988, citing financial losses. Four other MISL teams folded following the 1987–88 season, but the league lasted four more seasons.

Minnesota Strikers Year-by-Year

Outdoor (1984)

Coach: David Chadwick; **Record:** 14–10 (3rd, West); **Playoffs:** None; **Home attendance:** 14,263 average (2nd in league); **Scoring leader:** Alan Willey, 15 goals, 4 assists: **NASL All-Star:** Ray Hudson

Indoor year-by-year

Season	Coach	Record
1984–85	Alan Merrick	24–24 (4th, East)
1985–86	Merrick	26–22 (2nd, East)
1986–87	Merrick	26–26 (4th, East)
1987–88	Merrick	31–25 (1st, East)

Playoffs

1984–85   7–5; vs. Wichita (W 2–1, L 8–3, W 3–2 OT); vs. Las Vegas (W 6–5, L 6–4, W 3–2, W 4–1); vs. San Diego (L 8–1, L 6–5 OT, W 8–5, W 4–3 shootout, L 8–0)

1985–86   9–6; vs. Dallas (W 5–3, W 7–2, L 4–1, W 7–4); vs. Cleveland (L 5–2, W 6–2, W 5–4 OT, W 7–3); vs. San Diego (L 7–2, W 6–1, W 7–2, W 4–3, L 7–4, L 6–3, L 5–3)

1986–87   2–3; vs. Cleveland (W 5–4 OT, L 7–6, L 6–5 OT, W 5–4, L 7–3)

1987–88   4–5; vs. Baltimore (W 5–3, W 4–2, L 5–1, W 9–4); vs. Cleveland (L 7–3, W 7–0, L 5–4, L 5–2, L 7–2)

NOTE: Total playoff record: 22–19. Reached semifinals in 1985 and 1988; finals in 1986.

Strikers Players Records

Goals: 58 by Hector Marinaro, 1987–88
Assists: 42, by David Byrne, 1987–88

Minnesota Kicks

The first professional soccer game in state history occurred on May 9, 1976, when the Minnesota Kicks played host to San Jose in their North American Soccer League (NASL) home opener. The start of the game was delayed 15 minutes because of the large crowd outside Metropolitan Stadium waiting to buy tickets, and more than 2,000 fans were simply let in free.

The Kicks, who had relocated to Minnesota after two seasons as the Denver Dynamo, went on to defeat San Jose, 4–1. Two weeks earlier, the teams had opened the season in San Jose. The Kicks won that game, 4–2.

One month after their home opener, the Kicks played host to the New York Cosmos. An NASL record crowd of 46,164 turned out to watch the Cosmos and the legendary Pele defeat the Kicks, 2–1. The Kicks closed out their first season by winning 9 of the final 10 games and winning their division with a 15–9 record.

Crowds continued to show up as the Kicks opened the playoffs with a 3–0 victory over Seattle before an NASL playoff record crowd of 41,505 at Metropolitan Stadium. Four days later, the Kicks defeated San Jose, 3–1, before another record crowd of 49,571 at the Met, earning a spot in the NASL championship game. On August 28, 1976, Toronto defeated the Kicks, 3–0, before 25,765 in the championship game in Seattle.

The Kicks enjoyed tremendous success in their first four seasons in Minnesota, winning a division title in each season.

In August 1981 the Kicks closed out their sixth season in Minnesota with a 2–1 victory over Dallas before 18,635 at Metropolitan Stadium. Earlier that month the largest home crowd of the season, 28,604, watched the Kicks defeat the Cosmos, 2–1, in overtime.

The Kicks, who had finished second in their division with a 19–13 record, opened the playoffs with a 3–1 victory in Tulsa—the first road playoff victory in franchise history. On August 26, the Kicks defeated Tulsa again, 1–0, in a shootout before 10,722 at Met Stadium. After a 3–0 loss in Fort Lauderdale, Florida, on September 2, the Kicks' season came to an end four days later with another 3–0 loss to Fort Lauderdale before 10,000 at Memorial Stadium on the University of Minnesota campus.

New York Cosmos player Pele tangles with Minnesota Kicks player Alan Merrick at
Met Stadium, 1976

Less than two months later, the NASL folded the Kicks franchise. The
team had withheld players' checks and was in a dispute over a future lease
with the Metrodome. Team owner Ralph Sweet, who had purchased the
team the previous November, had warned he would move the team because
of financial losses.

In six "outdoors" seasons, the Kicks averaged 24,381 fans per home game.
The Minnesota Kicks also competed in the NASL Indoor League in the winters of 1979–80 and 1980–81, going 8–4 and 12–6.

Three of the top five all-time points leaders in NASL history played for
the Kicks. Alan Willey ranks third with 129 goals and 48 assists (306 points);
Ron Futcher is fourth with 119 goals and 58 assists (296 points) and Patrick

"Ace" Ntsoelengue is fifth with 87 goals and 82 assists (256 points). Giorgio Chinaglia is the all-time points leader with 193 goals and 81 assists (467 points). Karl-Heinz Granitza is second with 128 goals and 101 assists (357 points).

Willey is the second-leading goal scorer in NASL history, with 129 goals in nine seasons. Futcher is fourth with 119 goals in nine seasons. Ntsoelengue is eighth with 87 goals in 11 seasons, while Ricardo Alonso is 16th with 67 goals in six seasons.

Minnesota Kicks Year-by-Year
Outdoor year-by-year

Season	Coach	Record
1976	Freddie Goodwin	15–9 (1st, West Division)
1977	Goodwin	16–10 (1st, West)
1978	Goodwin	17–13 (1st, Central)
1979	Roy McCrohan	21–9 (1st, Central)
1980	Goodwin	16–16 (2nd, Central)
1981	Goodwin/G. Barnett	19–13 (2nd, Central)

Playoffs

1976   2–1; beat Seattle (3–0), beat San Jose (3–1), lost to Toronto (3–0)
1977   0–1; lost to Seattle (2–1, OT)
1978   2–1; beat Tulsa (3–1), beat Cosmos (9–2), lost to Cosmos (4–0), lost to Cosmos (1–0) in mini-game tie-breaker
1979   0–2; lost to Tulsa (2–1, OT), lost to Tulsa (2–1, OT)
1980   0–2; lost to Dallas (1–0), lost to Dallas (2–0)
1981   2–2; beat Tulsa (3–1, 1–0), lost to Fort Lauderdale (3–1, 3–0)

Home attendance

1976   23,117 average (2nd in league)
1977   32,771 (2nd)
1978   30,860 (2nd)
1979   24,580 (3rd)
1980   18,279 (7th)
1981   16,605 (7th)

Scoring leaders

1976   Alan Willey, 16 goals
1977   Willey, 14 goals
1978   Willey, 21 goals (team record); Willey also scored seven goals in four playoff games
1979   Willey, 21 goals (team record)

1980   Rod Futcher and Patrick "Ace" Ntsoelengue, 13 goals each. (Ntsoelengue had a team-record 17 assists)

1981   Futcher, 14 goals; Ntsoelengue, 12 goals

NASL All-Stars

Alan West (1977) and Ace Ntsoelengue (1979)

Indoor year-by-year

Season	Coach	Record
1979–80	Freddie Goodwin	8–4 (2nd, West)
1980–81	Goodwin	12–6 (2nd, Central)

Playoffs

1979–80   2–1; beat Tulsa (3–2), beat Memphis (6–3), lost to Memphis (4–3, OT), lost to Memphis (1–0) in mini-game tie-breaker

1980–81   0–2; lost to Atlanta (10–8), lost to Atlanta (5–4, OT)

Women's Soccer

Briana Scurry has been successful at every level of soccer she has played. In 1989 the Dayton, Minnesota, native helped Anoka to the girls' state soccer title and received All-American honors as a goalkeeper.

At the University of Massachusetts, she helped lead her team to the NCAA women's soccer Final Four in 1993. In her college career, Scurry posted a 48–13–4 record with 37 shutouts.

Since graduating, Scurry has been a member of three U.S. women's Olympic soccer teams. The U.S. won a gold in 1996, a silver in 2000 and the gold in 2004. From 2001 to 2003 Scurry also played in the Women's United Soccer Association, an eight-team professional league.

Tennis

Minnesotans first played tennis in the 1880s. Late in that decade tennis could be seen at four sites in St. Paul: the Hamline Turf Club, White Bear Yacht Club, Town and Country Club and Ashland Courts. In Minneapolis, the sport was being played at the Minikahda Club and the Hotel Lafayette–St. Louis. In 1886 the Burton family of Deephaven started the Northwest Lawn Tennis Tournament. The tournament continued until 1941. Ward C. Burton ran most of the early tournaments at the grass courts on his family estate.

John W. Adams Jr. of Deephaven was another leading tennis figure in the area for nearly 60 years. Adams won the St. Paul singles championship in 1905 at age 16. Four years later, playing for the University of Minnesota, he won both Western Conference (Big Ten) singles and doubles titles. He repeated as champion of both in 1911. Adams, who went on to serve as the president of the Northwest Lawn Tennis Association, won the state championship several times.

The first Minnesota tennis player to be nationally ranked was George Belden, who was ranked No. 10 in 1898. Belden, who played in the singles final of the grass court championships nine consecutive years (1888–97), served as president of the Minnesota Tennis Association.

In 1913 national rankings were started for women. Gwendolyn Rees was the first Minnesota woman to be ranked. She tabbed at No. 10 that year.

Almost 60 years later—in 1972—high school senior Peggy Brenden was the plaintiff in a groundbreaking federal lawsuit, *Brenden v. Independent School District 742*. This was one of the first cases nationwide to address the issue of equal rights for girls in high school sports. Brenden earned the right to play on her high school tennis team at St. Cloud Tech, an opportunity that had previously been available only to boys. The decision not only made her one of the first, if not the first, girl in Minnesota to play high school tennis, but it also stimulated the growth and development of girls' and women's sports across the country.

Jeanne Arth

Jeanne Arth was the first Minnesotan to play Centre Court at Wimbledon. She dominated the United States Tennis Association's Northern Section for nearly 20 years.

Growing up, Arth practiced at the St. Paul Tennis Club. She excelled in national junior competition before entering the College of St. Catherine in St. Paul. From 1954 to 1956, she was a three-time singles finalist at the National College Girls tournament in St. Louis.

Arth, who began her career as a teacher and counselor, in 1957 teamed with Californian Darlene Head to win the U.S. doubles title in 1958. The unseeded duo upset the top-seeded team of Althea Gibson and Maria Bueno. Arth and Head won the U.S. doubles title again in 1959.

In 1959 Arth and Head, who was from Montebello, California, defeated Beverly Baker Fleitz from Long Beach and Christine Truman from Great Britain, 2–6, 6–2, 6–3, to win the Wimbledon doubles title. Later that year, Arth was a member of the U.S. team, which won the Wightman Cup.

Arth retired from tennis at the peak of her game in her mid-30s. She is a member of at least four halls of fame—Minnesota Tennis, Minnesota Sports,

Delta Lawn Tennis Club, St. Paul, 1880s

International Tennis and St. Paul Central High School. She told the *Minne-apolis Tribune* in 1986 that the doubles championship in 1958 was the high-light of her career.

Norm McDonald

Norm McDonald, a sporting goods salesman, brought the 1964 Davis Cup match to the Twin Cities. A member of the Minnesota Tennis Hall of Fame, McDonald won more than 200 local championships during his playing career.

McDonald was honored as the Urban Tennis Man of the year by the board of the Urban Tennis Association in 1989.

David Wheaton

Minnesotan David Wheaton became a Wimbledon champion in 2004. Wheaton, of Tonka Bay, teamed with T. J. Middleton to win the men's 35-and-older doubles championship. Wheaton played on the professional tennis tour for 13 years and had reached Wimbledon's singles semifinals, as an unseeded player, in 1991. He peaked in the world's rankings that year at No. 12.

During 1991, Wheaton also saw his biggest payday as a professional, when he won the Grand Slam Cup Championship and earned $2 million for the

David Wheaton reached the semifinals of Wimbledon in 1991 and teamed with T. J. Middleton to win the Wimbledon 35-over doubles championship in 2004.

title. Prior to that victory, in his first six years on the tour, Wheaton had won one tournament and earned $960,000.

Davis Cup

In August 1964, international tennis came to Minnesota when the final of the Davis Cup American Zone was held at the Nicollet Tennis Center in South Minneapolis. Australia defeated Chile, 5–0, in the match that was held over three days. A capacity crowd of 600 attended the event each day (top ticket price was $3). Australia, whose team included Fred Stolle, Roy Emerson and John Newcombe, went on to defeat the United States for the Davis Cup championship.

In 1992 the Davis Cup competition returned to Minneapolis, when the United States defeated Sweden, 4–1, in a World Group semifinal at Target Center. The match featured five of the top 10 men's tennis players—Sweden's Stefan Edberg (who was No. 1 in the world at the time), and John McEnroe, Jim Courier, Andre Agassi and Pete Sampras for the United States.

Pan-Am Trials

In 1967 the Pan-American tennis trials were held in Minnesota. Tennis legend Arthur Ashe was one of those who competed in the three-day event at Minikahda Country Club.

Pro Women's Tour

In January 1977 the women's professional tour made a stop at Met Center for the $100,000 Virginia Slims of Minnesota Tournament. Martina Navratilova won the seven-day competition, which featured 32 players. The event drew 20,000 fans—4,000 for the Navratilova/Sue Barker final. In August 1977, it was announced that the tournament, which had lost money, would not return to Minnesota the following January.

The Twin Cities market got a second chance, when the U.S. Women's Indoor tournament was revived after a one-year hiatus (after it had failed in Atlanta). Held in Bloomington in October 1978, the tournament was won by Chris Evert. In 1979 the tournament returned to Bloomington and was won by Evonne Goolagong.

Team Tennis

Tennis star Billie Jean King conceived the idea of team tennis, which debuted as the 16-team World Team Tennis league. A Minnesota team, the Buckskins, played its first match on May 7, 1974, losing to the Houston E-Z Riders, 30–28, before 2,317 at Met Center. Ann Hayden-Jones, who won the Wimbledon singles title in 1969, was a member of the Buckskins.

The Buckskins concluded their 44-match season on August 17 with a 26–17 victory over the Hawaii Leis before 1,294 at Met Center. The Buckskins, who had compiled a 27–17 record in the regular season, reached the second round of the playoffs—edging Houston, 48–47, before losing to the Denver Racquets.

The Buckskins were a one-season wonder in Minnesota. Despite drawing 9,300 for a match against King and her Philadelphia Freedom team, the franchise folded after one season in Bloomington.

In 1993 Minnesota had another one-year fling with World Team Tennis. The Minnesota Penguins—one of five new World Team Tennis teams—played their first match on July 9, 1993. The Penguins lost to Newport Beach, 28–24, before an estimated crowd of 1,000 at the Flagship Athletic Club in Eden Prairie. The Penguins, whose roster included Edina native Ginger Helgeson, averaged 1,468 for their seven home matches. The team finished last in the 14-team league in attendance. Following the season, the team, which was run by the Minneapolis office of the International Management Group, announced it would move to Charlotte, North Carolina.

Clay Courts in Minneapolis

For many years Minneapolis featured 10 clay courts near Lyndale Avenue South and Wayzata Boulevard. Built in 1932 the courts, which were the scene of many state opens, were the only "public" clay courts in the city. Tennis legend Bill Tilden played an exhibition there, as did Wimbledon champion Alice Marble. The courts were torn down in 1988 to make way for a new ice arena.

DID YOU KNOW ?

In April 1948 nearly 2,700 fans gathered at the Minneapolis Auditorium to watch Jack Kramer and Bobby Riggs continue their tennis challenge series. The *Minneapolis Sunday Tribune* said it was the "first showing of big time professional tennis in the Twin Cities since Don Budge, Bill Tilden and Co. appeared here several years ago."

The 6-foot-2 Kramer defeated the 5-foot-6 Riggs, 6–3, 6–2. It was Kramer's 48th victory over Riggs in 66 matches in the series, which had started the previous December. In his career, Kramer won 13 U.S. singles and doubles titles and was elected to the International Tennis Hall of Fame in 1968. Riggs, who had won at Wimbledon in 1939, was elected to the International Tennis Hall of Fame in 1967.

USTA Northern Section Hall of Fame

The United States Tennis Association (USTA) Northern Section was founded on January 9, 1961, as the Northwestern Tennis Association to serve Minnesota, North Dakota, South Dakota and the northwestern section of Wisconsin.

In 1979 *Tennis Midwest Magazine* inaugurated a Minnesota Tennis Hall of Fame. In the 1990s, the name changed to the USTA/Northern Section Hall of Fame.

Minnesotans in the Hall of Fame

J. J. Armstrong (1979); Jeanne Arth (1979); Howe Atwater (1898); George Belden (2002); Charlie Boone (2001); Peggy Brenden (2003); Chuck Britzius (1993); Ward C. Burton (1979); Marjorie Champlin (2005); Steven Champlin (2005); Muriel Magnusson Cooper (1979); Marguerite Davis (1987); Jack Dow (1983); Ernie Greene (1997); Marvin Hanenberger (1985); David Healey (1993); Janet Marie Hoffman (1997); Percy Hughes (2003); Trafford Jayne (2002); Cammy Johnson (2001); Les Johnson (1997); Bill Kuross (1979); Pat Lamb (1991); Bob Larson (1993); Norm MacDonald (1979); Sandy Martin (2003); John Matlon (2003); John Mattke (1999); Janet Marie McCutcheon (1997); David Nash (1991); Jerry Noyce (1983); Bucky Olson (1985); Wendell Ottum (1981); Wes Painter (1999); Jerry Pope (1999); Harvey Ratner (1985); Lachlan Reed (1987); Gwendolyn Rees (2002); Jack Roach (1983); Robert Rockwell (1981); Rosemary Rockwell (1981); Bill Schommer (1999); Justin Smith (1983); Betty Swanson (2001); Al Teeter (1987); Frank Voigt (1979); Ed Von Sien (1989); Joan Warner (1981); Fred Wells (2003); David Wheaton (2005); Marnie Wheaton (1993); Dr. Bill Widen (1987); Steve Wilkinson (1983); Marvin Wolfenson (1985); Gregg Wong (2003); David Yorks (2003)

College Tennis

University of Minnesota

The Gophers men's tennis program has won or shared 15 Big Ten Conference titles. Eight of the titles came in a 12-season span (1984–95). The Gophers won four consecutive titles from 1992 to 1995. They have appeared in the NCAA tournament 12 times—including nine consecutive times from 1996 to 2004.

The Gophers have had six individual Big Ten champions at No. 1 singles: J. J. Armstrong (1911, 1912), Charles Britzius (1933), Bill Schommer (1935), Jim Ebbit (1972) and Fredrik Pahlett (1983).

The Gophers women's tennis program fielded its first team in the 1974–75 season. The Big Ten offered its first women's tennis championship in 1982. The Gophers have not won a conference title but have made five appearances in the NCAA tournament.

Two Minnesotans have been part of a team that won an NCAA doubles tennis championship. In 1903 Minnesotan Edwin Clapp and his Yale team-mate Fredrick Colston won. Ten years later, Minnesotan J. J. Armstrong and Harvard teammate Watson Washburn also won.

Gustavus Adolphus

Gustavus Adolphus men's tennis coach Steve Wilkinson is the winningest NCAA Division III tennis coach. He is just one of four college coaches to have won 800 matches.

Going into the 2004–05 season—his 35th at Gustavus—Wilkinson's teams had compiled an 806–242 record. In 34 seasons, Wilkinson's teams won 31 MIAC titles. In that time, Gustavus won 301 of 302 conference dual matches. The Gusties won NCAA Division III championships in 1980 and 1982.

The Gustavus women's program has been successful as well. In 2004–05 Jon Carlson was entering his 16th season as the Gusties coach. In his first 15 seasons, the Gusties won 14 MIAC titles and compiled a 151–1 record in conference duals. Overall, the Gusties were 314–104 in that time. The Gusties won the NCAA Division III championship in 1990.

Volleyball

Minnesota has seen two attempts at establishing women's professional vol-leyball. In 1987 the Major League Volleyball league was formed with six teams—Chicago, Dallas, Los Angeles, New York, San Jose, and Minnesota.

The Minnesota Monarchs were successful on the court. In 1989 they were unbeaten in 13 matches, but the league folded in March of that year. In 1990 the Monarchs played a schedule as an independent team.

In 2002 the four-team United States Professional Volleyball League fielded a team named The Chill based in Rochester, Minnesota. The league's other franchises were Chicago, Grand Rapids (Michigan) and St. Louis.

The Chill was also successful on the court, winning the league champion-ship. The Chill defeated the Chicago Thunder in the championship series. Former University of Minnesota volleyball players Nicole Branagh and Lind-sey Berg and Lakeville native Elisabeth "Wiz" Bachman played for the Chill. Branagh was named the MVP of the league championships series. The league canceled its 2003 season due to lack of funds.

Wrestling and Boxing

Wrestling

OR NEARLY 40 years, one man—Verne Gagne—defined wrestling in Minnesota. Gagne's professional wrestling career spanned the years 1949 to 1985. In his final professional match, he teamed with his son Greg to defeat Nick Bockwinkle and Saito before 16,901 fans at the St. Paul Civic Center.

Gagne's promotional group, the American Wrestling Association, dominated professional wrestling in the Midwest for decades. The American Wrestling Association's weekly televised wrestling cards had stellar ratings. The popular Wally Karbo, who began working for Minneapolis promoter Tony Stecher in 1935, served as a foil for the bad guys on the show. Karbo remained in the business until his death in 1993 at age 77.

Before Gagne made his name, the biggest name in wrestling was also the biggest name in football, Bronko Nagurski. Arguably the greatest player in the history of University of Minnesota football, Nagurski played eight seasons with the Chicago Bears of the NFL before retiring after the 1937 season. During that time, Nagurski was named All-NFL five times. Nagurski returned to play one more season with the Bears in 1943.

Following his retirement from football—which landed him in both the College and Pro Football halls of fame—Nagurski forged a 15-year career in professional wrestling. Nagurski eventually found a talented tag-team partner—Gagne. Before Nagurski retired to International Falls, he won the world heavyweight wrestling title three times—first in 1937, again in 1939 and finally in 1941.

Other Champions and Notables

Walter Miller of St. Paul won three world titles—welterweight, middleweight and light heavyweight. His first was in 1914 and his final in 1924.

Ted Thye of Northfield won the world light heavyweight title in 1910.

Norwegian-born **Henry Ordemann** of Minneapolis was one of America's top heavyweights for nearly 10 years. He won the American heavyweight title in 1910 and held it until losing it in 1914.

Stan "Krusher" Kowalski (nee Bert Smith) wrestled and played fooball at the University of Minnesota before serving in the navy during World War II. He wrestled more than 6,600 matches in a professional career that

307

Professional wrestlers, about 1940

extended from 1951 to 1976. Kowalski and his tag-team partner, Tiny Mills, were dubbed "Murder Inc." During his 25-year professional career, Kowalski won 19 titles.

Italian-born **Leo Nomellini** earned All-American honors as a football player for the University of Minnesota before embarking on a 14-year career in professional football. During the off season, Nomellini, who was inducted into both the College Football and Pro Football Halls of Fame, moonlighted as a wrestler. He teamed with Gagne to win a world tag-team title in 1956.

Ric Flair, who made his professional wrestling debut in 1972, won eight National Wrestling Alliance (forerunner of World Championship Wrestling) heavyweight titles. In the 1990s, Flair won the WCW world title nine times. He retired from pro wrestling at age 55.

Jesse Ventura

Jesse "The Body" Ventura (formerly James Janos) competed in football and swimming at Minneapolis Roosevelt High School before serving in the navy.

He made his professional wrestling debut in 1975 and joined Verne Gagne's AWA in 1978. Ventura teamed with Adrian Adonis to win the AWA tag-team title in 1980. He retired from wrestling in 1983, became a commentator for Vince McMahon's World Wrestling Federation, and during the mid-1980s appeared in several movies. In the late 1980s, he served as a commentator for Ted Turner's WCW.

In 1991 Ventura turned his attention to politics. He was mayor of Brooklyn Center from 1991 to 1995. Then, on November 3, 1998, Ventura was elected the 38th governor of Minnesota. During his tenure, Ventura served as a referee for a wrestling "pay-per-view" match at the Target Center between Stone Cold Steve Austin, Hunter Hearst Helmsley (Triple H) and Mankind. The event—the World Wrestling Federation's "SummerSlam"–drew 19,404. Ventura said he would donate the $100,000 fee he received for working the event to charity. There were published reports that estimated Ventura would make an additional $1 million or more in undisclosed payments related to the event.

In early 2001 Ventura served as a commentator on XFL football broadcasts on NBC. The league, which last just one season, was a joint venture of the World Wrestling Federation and NBC. In 2004 Ventura was inducted into World Wrestling Entertainment's Hall of Fame.

University of Minnesota Wrestling

The University of Minnesota fielded its first Gophers team in 1910 and had its first NCAA individual champion in 1937, John Whitaker. Two more Gophers—Dale Hanson in 1939 and Leonard "Butch" Levy in 1941—earned NCAA individual titles.

Verne Gagne arrived on campus in the fall of 1943. He won his first Big Ten heavyweight title in 1944 before having his college career interrupted by military service. He returned to the university in 1946 to win Big Ten titles in 1947, 1948 and 1949 and NCAA titles in 1948 and 1949. Gagne is the school's lone four-time Big 10 champion.

The Gophers wrestling program has won two NCAA titles and eight Big Ten conference titles. The Gophers have been the NCAA runner-up three times. The Gophers have finished in the top eight at the NCAA meet every year since 1997. From 1997 until 2003, the Gophers finished no lower than third at the national meet. The Gophers finished eighth in 2004 and fifth in 2005.

The Gophers have finished either first or second at the last nine Big Ten conference meets.

NCAA Titles

The Gophers won back-to-back NCAA championships in 2001 and 2002. The Gophers went 38–1 in dual meets (19–1 in 2000–01 and 19–0 in 2001–02) during those two seasons. The Gophers' only dual-meet loss in that time was a 25–12 loss to Oklahoma State on January 7, 2001.

At the 2001 NCAA meet, the Gophers finished first with 138½ points. All 10 Gopher wrestlers earned All-American honors. At the 2002 meet, the Gophers won with 126½ points. Seven Gophers earned All-American honors in 2002.

The Gophers were the NCAA runner-up in 1998, 1999 and 2003.

Gopher Coaching Records

Coach	Seasons	Record
Wally Johnson	34	392–209–11
J Robinson*	19	278–101–3
Dave Bartelma	13	82–32–5

*J Robinson is the winningest active Big Ten wrestling coach.

Gopher Individual Leaders

Career victories

159 Ed Giese; **142** Billy Pierce; **135** Leroy Vega; **133** Tim Hartung; **132** Jason Davids; **130** Jared Lawrence; **127** Tim Harris, Jacob Volkmann; **126** Luke Becker; **121** Willy Short

Career pins

51 Pierce; **48** Hartung; **47** Marty Morgan; **40** Chad Erikson; **38** Davids; **34** Volkmann; **33** Lawrence; **32** Michael Foy, Mike McArthur; **29** Jim Martinez, Luke Becker

Consecutive victories

58 Hartung (1998–99); **39** Morgan (1990–91); **36** Short (1993–94); **32** Ryan Lewis (2001–02), Morgan (1989–90)

Gopher Olympians

The Gopher wrestling program has produced 10 Olympians: Verne Gagne (1948), Alan Rice (1956), Dan Chandler (1976, 1980 and 1984), Evan Johnson (1976), Jim Martinez (1984), Michael Foy (1988 and 1992), Gordan Morgan

(1996), Dave Zuniga (1996), Brandon Paulson (1996) and Garrett Lowney (2000).

Martinez won a bronze medal and Paulson won a silver medal in Greco-Roman wrestling. Lowney, an Appleton, Wisconsin, native, won a bronze in Greco-Roman.

Transplanted Minnesotan Dennis Koslowski, a South Dakota native who wrestled at the University of Minnesota–Morris, won silver medals in Greco-Roman wrestling at the 1988 and 1992 Olympics. Another Minnesota wrestler to compete at the Olympics was Brad Rheingans, who finished fourth in Greco-Roman at the 1976 Olympics.

Augsburg College

Augsburg College in Minneapolis fielded its first wrestling team in 1949. Since then the Auggies have dominated small-college wrestling.

The Auggies have won nine national championships and finished runner-up on eight other occasions. Through the 2004–05 season, the Auggies have compiled a 551–123 record (an .818 winning percentage) in dual meets.

The Auggies' ninth national title came in 2005, when they won the NCAA Division III meet with 162 points. The meet was held at St. Olaf College in Northfield—the first time the meet had been held in Minnesota. For the second year in a row, the Auggies tied an NCAA Division III record with four individual champions. That has been accomplished five other times—Carroll in 1975, Montclair State in 1976, Augsburg in 2000, and both Augsburg and Wartburg in 2004.

The four individual champions in 2005 increased Augsburg's total to 33 individual national champions. Augsburg also had 10 wrestlers earn All-American honors, tying the mark set by Wartburg in 2003.

The Auggies' 2005 champions were Marcus LeVesseur (157 pounds), Mark Matzek (133 pounds), Joe Moon (174 pounds) and Matt Shankey (125 pounds). All four wrestlers defended titles they had won in 2004.

LeVesseur's victory in the championship match improved his career record to 124–0, the second-longest winning streak in college wrestling (all divisions) history. (Iowa State's Cael Sanderson won 159 consecutive matches from 1999 to 2002.) With his third title, LeVesseur became one of seven in NCAA history to win three titles in any weight class and the first since 1999.

The Auggies have also won national titles in 1991, 1993, 1995, 1997, 1998, 2000, 2001 and 2002.

Women's Wrestling

In 1995 the University of Minnesota–Morris was the first college in the nation to offer women's wrestling as a varsity intercollegiate sport. The program was a club team during the 1994–95 season but became a varsity sport in the 1995–96 season.

In 1997 the Cougars, coached by Doug Reese (who also coached the Minnesota–Morris men's squad), won the team championship in USA Wrestling's first-ever U.S. Women's University National Wrestling Championships. The freestyle tournament, which was held in Morris, featured female wrestlers between the ages of 17 and 24. The Cougars had four individual champions— Lisa Berbue, Jen Teske, Kristy Jeffry and Wendy Murphy. Jeffry was named the outstanding wrestler of the meet.

In nine seasons, 10 women wrestlers from Morris represented the United States in the world championships. Reese coached the United States women's team to a silver medal at the 1998 Pan American Games (held in Winnipeg, Manitoba).

In 2003 three former Minnesota–Morris wrestlers won a gold medal at the Pan American Games: Tina George, Sarah McMann and Sally Roberts. All three went on to win a gold medal at the 2003 World Championships.

In 2004 the school announced that it would cut both men's and women's wrestling because of state budget cuts. This move left eight U.S. colleges (and three Canadian colleges) offering women's wrestling as a varsity sport.

Boxing

Minnesota played an early role in the development of boxing in the United States. The state's first professional fight was held in Winona in 1871. Bare-knuckle fighter Dan Carr knocked out Jim Taylor in the 18th round.

In the 1880s some of the greatest fighters in the country—including legendary heavyweight champion John L. Sullivan—fought in Minnesota. On November 26, 1883, Sullivan knocked out Morris Hefey in the third round in St. Paul.

In February 1891 one of the longest matches in boxing history took place in Minneapolis when Danny Needham of St. Paul knocked out Tommy Ryan of Syracuse, New York, in the 76th round. The fight, held at the Twin City Athletic Club in downtown Minneapolis, lasted more than five hours.

Three months after that marathon match, two Minnesota promoters announced they would stage a world middleweight championship bout in St. Paul in July 1891. This match between Australians Bob Fitzsimmons and

Jim Hall earned so much pre-fight publicity nationally that it aroused reform-
ers, who wanted the state to outlaw boxing. The state had passed a statute
in 1890 that banned prize fighting in the state, but it had been ignored. Governor William R. Merriam, who initially said he wouldn't intervene, reluc-
tantly agreed to stop the fight after a group of citizens threatened him with
impeachment. In the next session, the state legislature passed a law making
prizefighting a felony. Boxing remained illegal in the state for the next 23
years.

George Barton, a Minneapolis sportswriter for 50 years, recalled in his
1958 autobiography that, "passage of the anti-prizefighting bill was followed
by nearly a quarter century of 'sneak' fights." Fights were conducted in tiny
gyms in Minneapolis and St. Paul, in barns, and in wooded areas along the
Mississippi and St. Croix rivers. The fights were promoted only by word-of-
mouth so they wouldn't draw undue attention.

In 1915 boxing became legal in Minnesota again, and the state quickly
produced two world champions—bantamweight Johnny Ertle (in 1915) and
middleweight Mike O'Dowd (in 1917)–and contenders including Mike and
Tommy Gibbons and Del Flanagan.

In one of the most famous matches in boxing history, Tommy Gibbons
fought defending champion Jack Dempsey for the heavyweight title in Shelby,
Montana, in 1923. The town of Shelby, which had promoted the fight, went
bankrupt when the fight proved to be a financial disaster. Dempsey won the
15-round fight. For Gibbons it was one of just four losses in 62 career fights.
Gibbons had a career record of 57 wins, 4 losses and one draw.

Dempsey, who first won the title in 1919, retained the title after he defeated
St. Paul's Billy Miske in Benton Harbor, Michigan, in 1920.

On March 27, 1925, American light heavyweight champion Gene Tunney
defeated world middleweight champion Harry Greb at the St. Paul Auditorium. George Barton refereed the 10-round fight. Three months later, on June
25, 1925, Tunney knocked out Tommy Gibbons of St. Paul in the 12th round
of a scheduled 15-round fight. It was Gibbons's final professional fight and
the only time in his 14-year career that he was knocked out. Gibbons, who
had a 57–4–1 record (with 43 no-decisions), became the Ramsey County
sheriff after retiring from boxing. Tunney was the world heavyweight champion from 1926 to 1928.

Through the years, Minnesota has produced other standout boxers like
Duane Bobick and Scott LeDoux. Bobick, from Bowlus, Minnesota, won the
U.S. Golden Gloves heavyweight title in 1972 before competing in the 1972
Olympics. LeDoux was a professional boxer for 13 years. In April 1976, a
crowd of 13,789—a record for a fight held in the state—gathered at the Met

Fighters Jack Dempsey (left) and Billy Miske with referee George Barton, 1918

Center in Bloomington to watch Bobick defeat LeDoux. Three years later, a Met Center crowd of 7,500 watched LeDoux lose to Ken Norton. In 1980 a fight between LeDoux and World Boxing Council heavyweight champion Larry Holmes drew 8,000 to the Met Center. Holmes retained his title.

In the last 20 years, several other Minnesotans have had noteworthy careers. In August 1986, St. Paul boxer Rocky Sekorski defeated former heavyweight champion Leon Spinks in a bout held in Detroit Lakes. The next month, Brian Brunette lost to Patrizio Oliva of Italy for the World Boxing Association junior welterweight title.

In 1994 Mike Evgen of St. Paul lost to Rafeal Ruelas of Las Vegas in a fight for the International Boxing Federation lightweight championship. In 1998

Will Grigsby, who trained in St. Paul, won the International Boxing Federation flyweight title. Two years later, Grigsby won the World Boxing Organization's junior flyweight crown.

Women Boxers

According to USA Boxing, women's participation in boxing has grown steadily since it first sanctioned women's bouts in 1993. The organization held its first women's national championship in 1997. Of the 2,401 women registered with

Brainerd-born Susan "KO" Carlson fought Minnesota's first professional women's boxing match in 1978 at the Minneapolis Auditorium.

USA Boxing in 2004, 63 were from Minnesota. Many of them train at Uppercut in Minneapolis, which was established in 1996 by Lisa Bauch.

Duane Bobick

In 1972 Bobick, a native of Bowlus, Minnesota, won the Upper Midwest Golden Gloves and U.S. Golden Gloves heavyweight championship. Bobick defeated future heavyweight champion Larry Holmes at the U.S. Olympic boxing trials to make the Olympic team. Later that year, he fought Cuban Teofilo Stevenson for the gold medal at the Olympics. Bobick had defeated Stevenson in 1971, but Stevenson defeated Bobick for the first of the three gold medals. That loss ended a 62-match winning streak for Bobick.

Following the Olympics, Bobick turned professional and won his first 38 fights. Thirty-two of those victories were by knockout. His winning streak came to end when he was knocked out by Ken Norton on May 11, 1977. Bobick, who was 26, was ranked No. 5 in the world heavyweight rankings. Bobick's professional career lasted two more years. He retired in 1979, with a 48–4 professional record.

Johnny Ertle

Austrian-born Ertle began his professional boxing career in 1913 at the age of 16. On September 10, 1915, he fought bantamweight Kid Williams in St. Paul. Ertle was awarded a victory by the referee and laid claim to the title, but, according to Minnesota boxing historian George Blair, the claim was never fully recognized.

Four years later, Ertle fought bantamweight champion Pete Herman in Minneapolis. Herman won the bout with a fifth-round knockout. In a 10-year career, Ertle compiled a 20–11 record with three draws. He won 14 fights by knockout and had 45 no-decisions.

The Flanagans

Brothers Del and Glen Flanagan are two of the best fighters Minnesota has ever produced. Glen Flanagan, a featherweight, made his professional debut in 1946 at age 20. In a career that spanned 141 fights (115–19–7 record), he was ranked as high as No. 3 in *Ring Magazine*'s ratings.

Del Flanagan, a welterweight, was ranked as high as No. 2 by *Ring Magazine* in a career that featured 129 fights (104–22–2 with one no-contest). Flanagan won his first 52 fights as a professional. In 1957 he defeated Virgil

Atkins, the reigning world welterweight champion, in a 10-round fight at the St. Paul Auditorium, but the fight was considered a "nontitle" fight. In his career, he defeated eight former or future world champions.

Scott LeDoux

In a 13-year professional career, LeDoux, a heavyweight, fought Muhammed Ali, Ken Norton, George Foreman and Larry Holmes. LeDoux, who had his first pro fight in 1974, had a 38–12–2 professional record.

DID YOU KNOW ?

Only two Minnesotans have been inducted into the International Boxing Hall of Fame in Canastota, New York: brothers Mike Gibbons, 1992, and Tommy Gibbons, 1993.

Billy Miske

St. Paul-born Miske turned professional in 1913 at the age of 19. After Minnesota re-legalized boxing in 1915—it had been made illegal in 1892—Miske fought St. Paul's Tommy Gibbons in the first legitimate bout.

In 1918 Miske fought legendary Jack Dempsey twice. On May 3, Dempsey and Miske fought a 10-round fight—refereed by *Minneapolis Tribune* sports editor George Barton—that was ruled a no-decision. On November 28, they had a rematch in Philadelphia, and their six-round bout was also ruled a no-decision.

About seven months after that fight, on July 4, 1919, Dempsey became the world heavyweight champion when he defeated Jess Willard with a third-round knockout in Toledo, Ohio. Dempsey would remain the champion until 1926.

On September 6, 1920, Dempsey defended his title with a bout against Miske in Benton Harbor, Michigan. Dempsey knocked out Miske in the third round. It was the only time in 112 career fights that Miske was knocked out.

Miske's final professional fight was on November 7, 1923. Miske defeated Bill Brennan in a four-round bout in Omaha, Nebraska.

Miske's career record was 43–2–1 (with 34 knockouts) and 56 no-decisions. Miske, known as the "St. Paul Thunderbolt," died on January 1, 1924, at the age of 29.

Mike O'Dowd

O'Dowd, born in St. Paul, was Minnesota's first "recognized" world champion. Turning professional in 1913 at age 18, O'Dowd went on to defeat Al McCoy in Brooklyn, New York, on November 14, 1917, to claim the world middleweight championship. Known as the "Harp," O'Dowd held the title for 2½ years until he was defeated by Johnny Wilson in Boston on May 6, 1920. Wilson won a 12-round referee's decision.

O'Dowd was a prolific fighter—fighting 17 times in 1915 and 23 times in 1920. In 121 career fights, O'Dowd had a 56–8–3 record with 54 no-decisions and 41 knockouts. O'Dowd himself was knocked out just once in his career—by Jock Malone in his final fight on March 16, 1923. After his fighting career, O'Dowd owned a nightclub in St. Paul. He died in 1957 at age 62.

Golden Gloves

In 1923 *Chicago Tribune* sports editor Arch Ward convinced his newspaper to sponsor a citywide amateur boxing tournament. Each weight-class winner was given a miniature golden glove, which became the name of the tournament.

In 1927 the *New York Daily News* sponsored a boxing tournament similar to Ward's that served as a championship for East Coast boxers. The next year, the winners from the New York and Chicago tournaments fought for a national championship.

During the 1930s newspapers around the country sponsored regional Golden Gloves tournaments. Charles O. Johnson, the sports editor of the *Minneapolis Star,* encouraged his newspaper to sponsor the Upper Midwest Golden Gloves tournament.

Phyllis Wheatley Boxers

During the Depression of the 1930s, citizens on Minneapolis's north side often gathered at the Phyllis Wheatley House, an independent social service agency. One of the agency's programs, designed to keep young men occupied, was boxing.

Golden Gloves outdoor boxing event in St. Paul, 1984

The Phyllis Wheatley boxing program flourished in the 1940s and 1950s, winning nine team titles at the Upper Midwest Golden Gloves. Community leader Harry Davis started out as a boxing coach at the center in 1943 and led the boxing program for the next 23 years, until it was discontinued in 1966. Davis was involved in Golden Gloves boxing in the Upper Midwest for nearly 50 years, and he managed the 1984 U.S. Olympic boxing team.

Golden Gloves Champions

In April 2005, James Taylor of Minneapolis won the championship of the 201-pound class and became the fifth fighter to win six Upper Midwest Golden Gloves titles. Other boxers to win at least six titles were Gilbert Mitchell (6), Dan Schommer (6), Mike Evgen (6) and South Dakotan John Richman (7). Also at the 2005 meet, Champlin's Joey Abell won his fifth Upper Midwest Golden Glove title. He won four consecutive titles, 1998–2001. Abell also played football at South Dakota State from 2002 to 2004.

The first Upper Midwest Golden Gloves boxer to win a national title was Minneapolis's Jack Graves, who won the 118-pound title in 1942. Since then seven others have taken national titles.

Roland Miller of Minneapolis is the only Upper Midwest boxer to win two national titles. Miller won the 112-pound title in 1965 and 1967.

Among the other national champions from the Upper Midwest was Jimmy Jackson of the Phyllis Wheatly program. Jackson won the 112-pound title in 1957 before competing in the U.S. Olympic boxing trials in 1960. The other national champions were Don Sargeant of Minneapolis (147 pounds in 1959), Pat O'Connor of Minneapolis (112 pounds in 1967), Duane Bobick of Minneapolis (heavyweight in 1972), Virgil Hill of Minneapolis (165 pounds in 1984) and Dave Sherbrooke of Minneapolis (heavyweight in 1987).

University of Minnesota Athletics

Gymnastics

YMNASTICS is one of the oldest sports on the University of Minnesota campus. The Gophers fielded their first team in 1903.

Ralph Piper coached the Gophers for 36 seasons (1930–56, 1958–62, 1964–65 and 1967–68). Fred Roethlisberger coached for 33 seasons (1972–2004).

Although the Gophers have yet to win an NCAA Championship, they finished in the top five on seven occasions: second (1941, 1949 and 1990), third (1989), fourth (1991 and 1992) and fifth (1993). They have won 20 Big Ten conference team championships and finished runner-up at the conference meet 16 times. Seventeen Gophers gymnasts have won a total of 28 conference all-around championships.

University of Minnesota Champions

NCAA All-around Titles

Newt Loken	1941
John Roethlisberger	1991, 1992, 1993

Individual event NCAA champions

Vault	Jim Peterson 1948
Parallel bars	Bob Hanning 1940, Roethlisberger 1991
Horizontal bar	Loken 1941
Flying rings	Delver Daly 1941, Ken Bartlett 1953
Pommel horse	Roethlisberger 1993, Clay Strother 2001, 2002
Floor exercise	Strother 2001, 2002

Gymnasts with three or more individual titles

Earnest Carlson	1916, 1921, 1922
James Peterson	1947, 1948, 1949
Tim LaFleur	1976, 1977, 1978
John Roethlisberger	1990, 1991, 1992, 1993

John Roethlisberger

John Roethlisberger, son of the long-time Gophers gymnastics coach, competed in three Olympics—in 1992, 1996 and 2000—and five World Championships. Born in Wisconsin, Roethlisberger was a four-time U.S. All-Around champion. His seventh-place finish in the all-around at the 1996 Olympics was the highest individual finish by an American in a nonboycotted Olympics since 1932.

Gophers Women's Gymnastics

The Roethlisberger name also dominates University of Minnesota women's gymnastics. Marie Roethlisberger, older sister of John Roethlisberger, was an alternate on the 1984 Olympic team. An elbow injury prevented her from competing at the Olympics. During her college career, she won seven Big Ten conference championships and won the uneven bars title at the 1990 NCAA championships. She earned All-American honors in four events.

Roethlisberger was 1987 and 1989 Big Ten All-Around champion. She was the Big Ten women's gymnast of the year three times: 1987, 1988 and 1989. She later graduated from the University of Minnesota Medical School.

Robin Huebner is another standout for the Gophers. She won four Big Ten conference championships in 1988, 1989, 1991 and 1998. Huebner was a three-time AIAW All-American and a six-time Big Ten champion.

Swimming and Diving

The University of Minnesota organized a men's swimming team in 1905. The first intercollegiate Gophers team competed in the 1919–20 season. They have claimed 17 event titles at the NCAA championships. The most successful swimmer in the program's history is six-time NCAA champion Steve Jackman.

University of Minnesota Champions

Individual NCAA Champions

Athlete	Year	Event
John Faricy	1925	200 backstroke
Jim Hill	1926	150 backstroke
Lowell Marsh	1931	150 backstroke
Steve Jackman	1961, 1962	100 freestyle
	1962, 1963	50 freestyle
Virgil Luken	1962	200 backstroke
Walt Richardson	1963, 1964	100 butterfly
Craig Lincoln (diving)	1972	3-meter diving
P. J. Bogart (diving)	1993	platform
	1995, 1996	1-meter

NCAA Relay Titles

Year	Event	Winners
1927	300 medley	Jim Hill, Charles Purdy, Sam Hill
1962	400 freestyle	John Bergman, Ralf Allen, Danny Crocker, Steve Jackman
1963	400 medley	Alfred Erickson, Virgil Luken, Walt Richardson, Steve Jackman

Gopher P. J. Bogart, three-time NCAA diving champ

Coaches

Niels Thorpe, 1920–57 (37 seasons)   Big Ten conference titles, 1922, 1926
Dennis Dale*, 1985–present   Big Ten conference titles, 1996, 2001, 2002, 2003, 2005

*Under Dale, who previously coached the Burnsville High School boys and girls swimming teams to four state titles, the Gophers have finished no lower than second at the Big Ten meet since 1989.

NCAA Meets

Third place   1943, 1962
Fourth place   1963
Fifth place   1964

The Gophers finished in the top ten in five consecutive years (2000–04) and finished 11th in 2005.

Gopher Women's Swimming

The University of Minnesota fielded its first women's swimming and diving team in 1970. The Gophers have won two Big Ten conference team championships—in 1999 and 2000—and had 59 individual champions.

Women's National and All-American Swimming and Diving Champions

Year	Winner	Event
1981	Chris Curry	3-meter diving, Association of Intercollegiate Athletics for Women (AIAW)
1997	Gretchen Hegener	100 breaststroke champion, NCAA championships
1974	Terry Ganley*	backstroke, AIAW

*University of Minnesota's first female All-American

University of Minnesota Aquatic Center

Built where Memorial Stadium once stood, the Aquatic Center opened in 1990. The facility has hosted these national events: 1990 Olympic Festival; 1991 United States Open; 1991 U.S. Diving Championships; 1993 and 1998 NCAA women's championships; 2005 NCAA men's championships.

Track and Field

Steve Plasencia

University of Minnesota men's cross country coach and assistant men's track and field coach Steve Plasencia is one of the top distance runners in state history. At the university, Plasencia, who attended Robbinsdale Cooper High

School, was a two-time All-American in outdoor track and field and a three-time All-American in cross country. He set three university records in track and field and three in cross country.

Plasencia qualified for the U.S. Olympic team in 1988 and 1992. In 1988 he did not qualify for the finals in the 10,000 meters. At the 1992 games in Barcelona, he did not place in the 10,000.

In 1996 he just missed qualifying for a third Olympics when he finished fourth at the U.S. Olympic Marathon Trials. He also just missed qualifying by finishing fifth in the 5,000 at the U.S. Track and Field Championships.

Plasencia competed in four World Championships. He was the U.S. champion in the 10,000 in 1990. In 1996 he was elected to the Minnesota Track and Field Hall of Fame. That same year, he was named coach at the

Track meet at Memorial Stadium, about 1940

University of Minnesota, only the third men's cross country coach at the university since 1938.

Track and Field Championships

The University of Minnesota won the NCAA Division I outdoor track and field championship in 1948. The Gophers, coached by Jim Kelly and led by Fortune Gordien, finished with 46 points in the meet, which was held in Minneapolis.

Another Twin Cities school, the University of St. Thomas, has won eight NCAA Division III national championships in cross country and in track and field: men's cross country, 1984 and 1986; women's cross country, 1981, 1982, 1984, 1986 and 1987; and men's indoor track, 1985.

Gophers Hall of Fame

1996 Colin Anderson, Ron Backes, Garry Bjoklund, Ron Daws, Buddy Edelen, Roy Griak, Fortune Gordien, Janice Klecker, Van Nelson, Steve Plasencia

1997 Karl Anderson, Jane Oas Benson, Cathie Twomey Bellamy, Al Halley, Jim Kelly, Bob Kempainen, Mark Lutz,

1998 Bill Andberg, Orv Bies, Tom Lieb, Ted Nelson, Mark Nenow, Mike Slack

1999 Jim Deane, Jan Ettle, Bob Fitch, Bob Hoisington, Rick Kleyman, Bruce Mortenson, Leslie Seymour

2000 Dave Griffith, Jody Eder-Zdechlik, Tim Heikkila, Steve Hoag, Jack Moran, Alex Ratelle, Byrl Thompson

2001 Dick Beardsley, Jack DeField, Steve Holman, Pat Lanin, Ray Tharp, Don Timm

2002 Lynne Anderson, Bev Docherty, Dave Odegaard, Jan Arenz Pearson, Kent Stahly, Fred Watson, R. Eugene "Lefty" Wright

2003 Ed Hendrickson, Loyd LaMois, Bill Miles, Paul Noreen, Kathleen Borgwarth Reynolds

2004 none

Volleyball

The University of Minnesota fielded its first volleyball team in 1972. The Gophers made their first appearance in the NCAA championships in 1989. Since then they have made nine other appearances.

Cassie Busse, All-American Gopher volleyball player

In 2003 the Gophers advanced to the NCAA Final Four for the first time. In 2004 the Gophers again advanced to the Final Four and reached the championship match. Stanford defeated the Gophers for the title.

Mike Hebert has coached the Gophers to a 231–81 record in nine seasons. Hebert, who has also coached at Pittsburgh, New Mexico and Illinois, is the fifth-winningest active volleyball coach, with 802 victories.

Gopher Volleyball Honors

All-Americans	**1981** Jill Halsted; **1996** Katrien DeDecker; **2003** Cassie Busse and Paula Gentil
Big Ten Conference Player of the Year	**1983** Martie Larsen; **2000** Nicole Branagh; **2003** Busse
Big Ten Conference championship	**2002**
School record	**1996** Katrien DeDecker, for 738 kills

Racing

Marathons, Horses, and Autos

Marathons

HE FINAL event of the first modern Olympic games, held in Athens in 1896, was the marathon. After the games, athletes from Boston returned home excited about the race they had witnessed. This led to the establishment of the Boston Marathon, which has been run every year since 1897.

In Minnesota, the Minnesota Distance Running Association created in 1963 the first marathon in the Twin Cities—the Land of Lakes Marathon. Five participants—all male—ran the 26.2-mile course through Minneapolis. The winner, Ron Daws, would go on to represent the United States in the 1968 Olympics in Mexico City. Daws, who had competed in track and cross country at the University of Minnesota, finished 22nd at the Olympics.

The Land of Lakes Marathon was renamed the City of Lakes Marathon in 1976. In 1981 St. Paul held its own marathon—the St. Paul Marathon. The next year, the races were combined to form the Twin Cities Marathon. The first "combined" Twin Cities Marathon attracted 4,563 entrants, at the time an American record for a "first-time" race.

Between 1982 and 2003, over 100,000 runners completed the Twin Cities Marathon. The 2004 race, held on October 3, attracted 10,000 entrants; 7,408 (4,536 men and 2,872 women) finished the race.

The course record for the Twin Cities Marathon is held by Phil Coppes, who ran a 2:10.05 in 1985. The women's record is held by Zinaida Semenova of Russia, who ran a 2:26.51 in 2001.

Several other major marathons are held in Minnesota. In 1977 a group of runners planned a scenic road race from Two Harbors to Duluth. This race, known as Grandma's Marathon, received its name from its first major sponsor—a Duluth-based group of restaurants called Grandma's. The first race attracted 150 participants. This race, held annually in June, attracted more than 9,000 entrants in 2004.

The top finish time by a Minnesotan is claimed by Dick Beardsley, who completed the course in 2:09.37 in 1981. Minnesotan Garry Bjorklund has two of the race's top 10 times—2:10.20 (second) in 1980 and 2:11.31 (seventh) in 1981.

Dick Beardsley

On April 18, 1982, Dick Beardsley of Rush City and world-record holder Alberto Salazar ran what is considered the most exciting Boston Marathon ever. The two runners ran neck-and-neck until a motorcycle cop accidentally cut into Beardsley's path 100 yards from the finish line. Salazar was able to win the race by two seconds—2:08.51 to 2:08.53. Their times were the two fastest ever run by Americans.

An injury prevented Beardsley from qualifying for the 1984 Olympic team, and he failed to qualify for the 1988 Olympic team.

Beardsley won Grandma's Marathon twice, and he still holds the course record—set in 1981. As of 2002, his time was still the fourth-fastest marathon time by an American. Salazar's time stood for 12 years before it was broken by another Minnesotan—Bob Kempainen.

Bob Kempainen

Kempainen made his marathon debut at age 25 in 1991 in the Twin Cities Marathon. He finished second. Two years later, in just his fourth marathon, Kempainen finished second at the New York City Marathon. His time of 2:11:03 was the fastest of the year by an American.

On April 18, 1994, he finished seventh at the Boston Marathon with a time of 2:08.47, breaking the U.S. record set by Salazar. It was just his fifth marathon.

As a 29-year-old medical student, he finished 31st at the 1996 Olympics.

Inline Roller Skating

In 1980 two Minnesota hockey-playing brothers—Scott and Brennan Olson—discovered an inline skate while browsing at a sporting goods store. They refined the design into one on which hockey players could train during the off-season when there was no outdoor ice. The first "rollerblade" was made in the basement of their parents' Minneapolis home.

On September 14, 1996, more than 1,200 skaters took part in the first North Shore Inline Marathon. The marathon, the largest in the United States, follows the course of Grandma's Marathon from Two Harbors to Duluth. More than 3,000 participants skated in the 2004 inline marathon.

Horse Racing

Horse racing has had mixed success in Minnesota in recent decades. In 1982 Minnesotans voted to allow pari-mutuel betting in the state by a 64–36 percent margin. Less than three years later, Minnesota's first and only pari-mutuel racetrack opened. On June 26, 1985, a crowd of 15,079 joined Governor Rudy Perpich on the first day of racing at Canterbury Park near Shakopee. The crowd wagered $867,627 on the inaugural nine-race card.

Faiz, a seven-year-old bred in England, won the first race at Canterbury Downs (now Canterbury Park). Owned and trained by Martin Kenney of Washington, Faiz defeated Forty Eight Facets in the one-mile race. It was the seventh career victory for Faiz.

The next year, Canterbury enjoyed its peak year, when some $135 million was wagered at the track. But just one year later, attendance began to decline, a drop that continued until 1992. Canterbury Park closed in December 1992, when average daily attendance dropped under 2,900. The track remained idle in 1993 and 1994 before re-opening in 1995 under new ownership. By 1997, the track was profitable, and it has continued to prosper financially.

Through the 2005 season, the top jockey in track history is Scott Stevens, with 651 victories and more than $5.3 million in earnings.

Wally's Choice

On November 21, 2004, Wally's Choice, a horse co-owned by the Curtis Sampson family and Wally (the Beerman) and Joyce McNeil, won the $150,000 Oklahoma Derby. This made him the first Minnesota-bred horse in 13 years to win a graded-stakes race. Before the victory of Wally's Choice, which had gone off at 33–1 odds, the most recent Minnesota-bred horse to win a stakes race was Blair's Cove, which won the 1991 Stars & Stripes at Arlington Park in Illinois.

Mike Smith

Mike Smith rode at Canterbury Park for three years, and in 1985 he earned the riding title with 72 winners. Smith, who is in the Canterbury Park Hall of Fame, won his 1000th race in 1988.

In 2005, in his 12th Kentucky Derby appearance, Mike Smith rode Giacomo to victory. It was Smith's first victory at the Kentucky Derby. Giacomo went off at 50-to-1.

Dan Patch

On September 8, 1906, for the second time in five days, a large crowd gathered at the State Fairgrounds to watch one of the top athletes in state history attempt to set a world record. The crowd, estimated at 25,000, witnessed Dan Patch, the top harness racing horse in the country, beat the world record for the mile. Dan Patch ran a 1:55, breaking his own world record of 1:55¼ set the previous year.

Five days earlier, the opening day of the State Fair, Dan Patch had fallen short in his bid to break the mile record of 1:55. That day, a crowd estimated by one newspaper at more than 90,000 people, watched him do a mile in 1:56½. That was a state record, but the time fell short of the world record, which was not bettered for more than 50 years.

Dan Patch, purchased by Minneapolis businessman Marion W. Savage in 1901, started racing in 1900 at the late age of four. Between 1900 and July 22, 1902, the horse was unbeaten. After being bought by Savage, the horse stopped racing against other pacers.

Racing at Donnybrooke Speedway, Brainerd, about 1970

During his career, Dan Patch set 10 world records and earned a reported $2 million for Savage. After the horse was retired in 1910, tourists from all over the United States traveled to the Savage farm to see him.

On July 11, 1916, Dan Patch died at age 20. Savage, who was recovering from minor surgery in a Minneapolis hospital at the time, was reportedly so shocked and grief-stricken by the news that he passed away the next day—32 hours after his horse—from heart failure. Savage had insured the horse's life for $120,000, while he had no life insurance for himself.

DID YOU KNOW ?

Greg LeMond, born in California in 1961, won the grueling Tour de France bicycle race three times. After his first win in 1986, LeMond moved to Minnesota. LeMond told the New York Times that Minnesota's "winter climate provides excellent conditioning."

LeMond was seriously injured in a hunting accident in 1986 and missed the Tour de France in 1987 and 1988 while recovering from the injuries. In 1989, he returned to win the Tour de France a second time. He won his third title the next year.

LeMond, who retired from racing in late 1994, lives in a suburb of Minneapolis.

Auto Racing

In the 1960s, George Montgomery, a commercial pilot living in Edina, caught the racing bug after attending a race in Wisconsin. He bought a car, raced competitively and determined to build a road-racing track.

In 1968 Montgomery's vision became reality when Donnybrooke Speedway, near Brainerd, opened. Despite staging Trans-American and Canadian-American races, the track struggled financially. Following the 1972 season, it closed and went through bankruptcy. It remained idle through the 1973 season, except for private events.

In late 1973 Jerry Hansen—the winningest amateur driver in Sports Car Club of America (SCCA) history with 27 national titles—convinced a friend, Dick Roe, to join him in an effort to revive the race track, renamed the Brainerd International Raceway. In 1974 the Land O'Lakes Region of the SCCA supported the efforts of Hansen and Roe by helping purchase new equipment. One spectator event was held in 1974—the amateur Uncola Nationals, which attracted 17,000 fans.

In 1975 at the Pepsi Trans-Am, the first professional race at the Brainerd International Raceway since it had closed in 1972, actor Paul Newman set a lap record.

In 1982 the track acquired some grandstands from Metropolitan Stadium, which had closed the year before, in order to prepare for the Quaker State North Star Nationals. Among the highlights for the more than 50,000 fans that attended the event was seeing Newman win his first pro race. Willy T. Ribbs won the race the next three years.

Through the years, other events have been added at Brainerd—drag racing, the Camel GT series, the Can-Am series, and the Superbike World Championship.

Warren Johnson

Johnson, a native of Virginia, Minnesota, is one of the top drag racers in the history of the National Hot Rod Association (NHRA). He won his first race in 1963 at Minnesota Dragway in Coon Rapids, a track used from 1958 to 1977. Johnson made his first NHRA Pro Stock appearance in 1971. Johnson was ranked No. 7 among NHRA's all-time Top 50 drivers.

In April 2005 Johnson became the oldest driver to win a race in the history of professional drag racing. He was 61 years, 9 months when he won the Pro Stock event at the O'Reilly Spring Nationals. The victory was the 93rd of his pro career and guaranteed him his 24th consecutive season with at least one final-round appearance.

State Fair Racing

Auto racing was a regular feature of the Minnesota State Fair for nearly 100 years. From 1907 until 2002, racing took place at every fair, sometimes every day, but from 1985 to 2002, it was limited to the fair's final day, Labor Day.

Over the years, the Labor Day race became one of the American Speed Association's biggest events. In October 2002, however, the Minnesota State Fair board voted unanimously to make the changes that ended the annual Labor Day race. The board approved a $5.5 million grandstand renovation but did not invest an additional $4.5 million to update the track, last paved in 1964. Gary St. Amant won the final race in 2002.

Fishing, Hunting, and Other Outdoor Sports

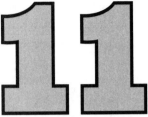

Young man with large northern pike, about 1940

INNESOTA has been a frontrunner in conservation practices and protection of its natural resources. In 1906 a group of 36 hunters formed what is probably the first wildlife conservation group in the state. On the upper arm of North Heron Lake in northern Jackson County, they signed a gentleman's agreement to oversee their own duck hunting on the lake. In 1911 the state appointed Carlos Avery as its first head of the Game and Fish Department and William Cox as its first forester.

The state opened its first pheasant-hunting season in October 1924. According to the *Minneapolis Tribune*, "For a three-day period, from Wednesday morning until Friday night, hunters were allowed to shoot ringneck pheasants in parts of Hennepin County and Carver County, adjoining the Minnetonka game refuge." Game and fish commissioner J. F. Gould signed an order that month allowing hunting in Independence, Medina and Plymouth townships, west of Medicine Lake, in an area covering approximately 10,000 acres.

The state issued its first fishing licenses in 1927 at a cost of 50 cents for individuals and $1 for families. Four years later, the state established the Minnesota Department of Conservation.

In 1951 Minnesota Bureau of Game supervisor Dick Dorer began the state's "Save the Wetlands" program. In 1971 the Department of Conservation became the Department of Natural Resources. Because of several severe winters and the over-harvest of does, deer season was closed. The state held its first bear and moose seasons that year.

The state began a nongame wildlife program in 1980, and in 1991 the Minnesota Wetlands Conservation Act passed. In 1998 the state legislature passed and voters approved an amendment to the state constitution that protected the privilege to hunt and fish.

Fishing

Minnesota has 3,000 official public accesses to lakes and rivers. About 1,500 are managed by the Minnesota Department of Natural Resources (DNR). According to the DNR, Minnesota has 11,482 lakes of 10 acres or more. Of those, 5,483 are considered fishing lakes. Minnesota ranks fourth in the nation in number of anglers—2.2 million.

The popularity of fishing contests has forced the state to enforce fishing tournament regulations. A 2000 law limits the number of tournaments and requires permits for open-water tournaments with more than 30 participants. In 2004 almost 60,000 anglers competed in the 82 ice-fishing contests that required permits. One tournament, the Brainerd Jaycees $150,000 Ice Fishing Extravaganza, held on Gull Lake, is billed as the largest ice fishing contest in the world. In 2005 it drew about 9,000 anglers in a snowstorm. At least three other contests—in Alexandria, Forest Lake and Park Rapids—offer more than $100,000 in prizes.

Many fishing contests are also held during the summer and fall. One of the biggest tournaments is the Muskie Classic on Lake Vermilion in September. The state also hosts about 20 major bass and walleye tournaments.

Top 10 Ice-fishing Contests (2004)

Brainerd Jaycees $150,000 Ice-Fishing Extravaganza (12,000 anglers)
American Legion Fishing Derby in Park Rapids (4,862)
Perch Extravaganza on Lake Mille Lacs (3,500)
Alexandria Ice Fishing Challenge (3,351)
Lincoln Area Business Association Fishing Derby (3,000)
International Eelpout Festival on Leech Lake (2,207)
Golden Rainbow Ice Fishing Tournament on Forest Lake (2,100)
Rainy Lake Sportfishing Club Family Fishing Derby (1,500)
Wolf Lake VFW Fishing Derby (1,500)
Warroad Chamber of Commerce Fishing Derby (1,300)

State Record Fish (DNR, 2005)

Bass (largemouth)	8 pounds–15 ounces, Auburn Lake (Carver County)
Bass (rock)	2–0, Osakis Lake (Todd) and Lake Winnibigoshish (Cass)
Bass (smallmouth)	8–0, West Battle Lake (Otter Tail)
Bass (white)	4–2.4, Mississippi River Pool 5 (Wabasha)
Bluegill	2–13, Alice Lake (Hubbard)
Bowfin	10–15, Mary Lake (Douglas) and French Lake (Rice)
Buffalo (bigmouth)	41–11, Mississippi River (Goodhue)
Buffalo (black)	20–0, Minnesota River (Nicollet)
Buffalo (smallmouth)	20–0, Big Sandy (Aitkin)
Bullhead (black)	3–13, Reno Lake (Pope)
Bullhead (brown)	7–1, Shallow Lake (Itasca)
Bullhead (yellow)	3–10, Osakis Lake (Todd)
Burbot	19–3, Lake of the Woods (Lake of the Woods)
Carp	55–5, Clearwater Lake (Wright)

Carpsucker (river)	3–15, Mississippi River (Ramsey)
Catfish (channel)	38–0, Mississippi River (Hennepin)
Catfish (flathead)	70–0, St. Croix River (Washington)
Crappie (black)	5–0, Vermillion River (Dakota)
Crappie (white)	3–15, Lake Constance (Wright)
Drum (freshwater)	35–3, Mississippi River (Winona)
Eel (American)	6–9, St. Croix River (Washington)
Gar (longnose)	16–12, St. Croix River (Washington)
Gar (shortnose)	4–10, Mississippi River (Hennepin)
Goldeye	2–13, Root River (Houston)
Hogsucker (northern)	1–15, Sunrise River (Chisago)
Mooneye	1–15, Minnesota River (Redwood)
Muskellunge	54–0, Lake Winnibigoshish (Itasca)
Muskellunge (tiger)	34–12, Lake Elmo (Washington)
Perch (yellow)	3–4, Lake Pantaganette (Hubbard)
Pike (northern)	45–12, Basswood Lake (Lake)
Pumpkinseed	1–6, Leech Lake (Cass)
Quillback	6–14, Mississippi River (Ramsey)
Redhorse (golden)	3–14, Bigfork River (Koochiching)
Redhorse (greater)	12–11.5, Sauk River (Stearns)
Redhorse (river)	12–10, Kettle River (Pine)
Redhorse (shorthead)	7–15, Rum River (Anoka)
Redhorse (silver)	9–15, Bigfork River (Koochiching)
Salmon (atlantic)	12–13, Baptism River (Lake)
Salmon (chinook)	33–4, Poplar River (Cook) and Lake Superior (St. Louis)
Salmon (coho)	10–7, Lake Superior (Lake)
Salmon (kokanee)	2–15, Caribou Lake (Itasca)
Salmon (pink)	4–8, Cascade River (Cook)
Sauger	6–3, Mississippi River (Goodhue)
Splake	13–6, Larson Lake (Itasca)
Sturgeon (lake)	94–4, Kettle River (Pine)
Sturgeon (shovelnose)	5–5, Mississippi River (Goodhue)
Sucker (blue)	14–3, Mississippi River (Wabasha)
Sucker (longnose)	3–10.6, Brule River (Cook)
Sucker (white)	9–1, Big Fish Lake (Stearns)
Sunfish (green)	1–4.8, Arbor Lakes (Hennepin)
Sunfish (hybrid)	1–12, Zumbro River (Olmsted)
Trout (brook)	6–5, Pigeon River (Cook)
Trout (brown)	16–12, Lake Superior (St. Louis)
Trout (lake)	43–8, Lake Superior (Cook)

Trout (rainbow, steelhead)	16–6, Devil Track River (Cook)
Trout (tiger)	2–9, Mill Creek (Olmsted)
Tullibee (cisco)	5–12, Little Long (St. Louis)
Walleye	17–8, Seagull River (Cook)
Walleye-Sauger hybrid	9–13, Mississippi River (Goodhue)
Whitefish (lake)	12–5, Leech Lake (Cass)
Whitefish (menominee)	2–8, Lake Superior (Cook)

DID YOU KNOW ❓

Minnesota businessman Irwin Jacobs is one of the most powerful men in fishing. He started the RCL Walleye Tour and is the chairman of the world's largest recreational boat company, Genmar. He leads FLW Outdoors, the company responsible for five professional fishing circuits.

Redhorse World Record

On May 20, 2005, according to the *Minneapolis Star Tribune*, 19-year-old Robin Schmidt, of Freeport, Minnesota, caught not only a state record but a world-record greater redhorse, when he pulled a 12-pound, 11½-ounce fish from just below the Sauk River dam in Melrose. The fish dwarfed the previous world record holder—an 8-pound, 12-ounce redhorse caught in Ontario.

Smelt Run

For many years the annual "smelt run" along Lake Superior was one of the state's great fishing events. Smelt, a small, silvery, salmonlike food fish, usually headed up streams and rivers to spawn along the North Shore in late April, when the temperature in streams remained at a minimum of 40 degrees overnight. Anglers traditionally waded in the water with nets and scooped out great quantities.

In the 1990s, smelt runs along the North Shore became much smaller than in previous decades. The 1996 run was one of the worst in years because of lingering ice and cold temperatures.

Babe Winkelman

Babe Winkelman, raised on a farm near Duelm in central Minnesota, is one of Minnesota's outdoors legends. His company—Babe Winkelman Productions—dates to the early 1970s. The company produces two network and cable programs, *Good Fishing* and *Outdoor Secrets*, on fishing and on hunting and conservation, viewed throughout North America. Winkelman is a member of three Halls of Fame: Fresh Water Fishing Hall of Fame (inducted 1988), Sports Legends Hall of Fame (1992) and Minnesota Fishing Hall of Fame (2001). He co-founded the Minnesota Bass Federation and the Masters Walleye Circuit (MWC).

Boat Registrations

Minnesota has the highest number of boat registrations per capita in the nation—about one boat for every six people. In 2004 boat registrations in the state numbered 854,000.

The number of boat registrations has increased five-fold since 1959, the first year of registration, when 158,000 boats were registered. There were 285,000 in 1970; 580,000 in 1980; 715,000 in 1980; and 812,000 in 2004.

Hunting

Minnesota claims 1,300 public wildlife management areas. These 1.1 million acres of habitat provide recreation for hunters. Among the hunting seasons are small-game, fur-bearing animals, deer, bear, moose, goose and pheasant. According to the Minnesota Department of Natural Resources, there are nearly 500,000 deer hunters in the state.

Jimmy Robinson

Robinson, born in Kent, Minnesota, in 1897, began writing for *Sports Afield* magazine in 1928. He went on to become the *Minneapolis Star*'s first "outdoors" writer. In addition to writing numerous books on hunting and trap shooting, Robinson ran the Sports Afield duck camp in Manitoba. Each spring he conducted a survey of breeding ducks and water conditions, and he was the creator of the annual waterfowl forecast for America's duck and goose hunters. Dennis Anderson, writing for the *Minneapolis Star Tribune*, has described Robinson as the "most notable Minnesota sportsman" of the 20th century. Robinson died in 1986 at age 88.

Bear Hunting

The DNR reports that about 20,000 black bears roam the forests of northern Minnesota. In 2004 about 3,300 were harvested. In 2003 a hunter in northern Minnesota shot a 462-pound black bear. Adult black bears typically stand two to three feet at the shoulders and weigh between 250 and 300 pounds.

DID YOU KNOW ?

In 2004, Minnesota held its first dove hunting season in 57 years. The first Minnesota hunting season for this most commonly hunted game bird in the United States was in 1897. Minnesota became the 40th state to have a dove-hunting season.

Trophy Whitetail and Big Deer

Minnesota ranks second among states with recorded trophy-class whitetail deer, according to the Boone and Crockett Club. The state's Boone and Crockett score of 608 puts it second for whitetail only to Iowa (with a score of 615).

The state's record for the largest "typical" whitetail has stood since 1918, when John Breen shot a large buck near Funkley (northeast of Bemidji). In 1960 the 10-point buck (a "typical" whitetail because of its symmetrical antlers) was scored under the Boone and Crockett Club system as 202–0/8—the first "typical" deer to score higher than 200. For six years, the deer was a world record, and it still ranks in the top 10 in the world.

Wild Turkey Hunting

About 30,000 wild turkeys live in Minnesota. During the spring of 2004, some 4,349 turkeys were shot. The number of wild turkeys in the state is increasing, and Minnesota's 2005 wild turkey season attracted 32,000 hunters.

Trapshooting

Two Minnesotans have won the Grand American Handicap trapshooting event. In 1922 J. S. Frink of Worthington broke 96 targets at a distance of 22 yards. Frink finished first out of 588 entrants. In 1974 John Steffen of Minneapolis broke 99 targets at 24½ yards. Steffen finished first out of 3,932 entrants.

Deer hunters, about 1940

Four Minnesotans have been inducted into the Trapshooting Hall of Fame in Vandalia, Ohio: Loral I. Delaney, Bob and Lou Ann Munson and Jimmy Robinson.

Northwest Sports Show

The Northwest Sports Show, held annually in Minneapolis, is the longest-running sports show in the United States. It was founded in 1933 by hockey legend Nick Kahler. For 72 years, the show at the Minneapolis Auditorium and Minneapolis Convention Center was locally owned.

Phil Perkins, who bought the show from Kahler, worked with the show for 43 years. In 2004 Dave Perkins of Edina, who had purchased the show from his father, Phil, sold it to the National Marine Manufacturers Association, a nonprofit trade group based in Chicago.

During the 1950s, the show was so popular that it took scheduling precedence over the auditorium's tenant—the Minneapolis Lakers basketball team.

Hunters and the Armistice Blizzard

On November 11, 1940, a sudden, ferocious blizzard caused 49 fatalities statewide. Twenty of the deaths were duck hunters, who were caught outside as the temperatures fell from the 60s to below zero in less than 24 hours. Gusts of 60 mph wind were accompanied by 16 inches of snow over a 24-hour period.

Curling

Curling dates to the seventeenth century in Scotland. North America's first curling club was formed in Montreal in 1807, and 25 years later, the first American curling club was founded in Detroit.

Since the mid-1800s, curling has thrived in upper midwestern states including Wisconsin, Minnesota and North Dakota. A curling club started in Milwaukee in 1845 is the oldest continuous operating club in the United States.

Minnesota's oldest existing curling club is the Duluth Curling Club, formed in 1891; Minneapolis and St. Paul both had clubs prior to 1900 as well. Minneapolis's Minnesota Curling Club folded around 1940. St. Paul's Nashua Curling Club and Capitol City Curling Club merged in 1912 to form the St. Paul Curling Club, which has remained in the same location at 470 Selby Avenue since that date.

The Duluth Curling Club, which has played host to two world championships and the U.S. Olympic trials, is the second-largest club in the United States. Only the St. Paul Curling Club has more members.

The Bemidji Curling Club was founded in 1935. Teams from the club have captured more than 50 state and national titles. Curling debuted as a medal sport in the 1998 Olympics and the Bemidji Curling Club was home to both the U.S. men's and women's curling teams, which competed in the 2006 Turin Olympics. The men's team, the Pete Fenson rink, won the bronze medal. Team member Scott Baird became the oldest American to medal at the Winter Olympics. The women's team, the Cassie Johnson rink, did not medal at Turin.

Stacy Liapis, born in Bemidji, is a two-time Olympian curler. Liapis, who has been curling since she was 12, competed in the 1998 Olympics in Nagano, Japan, and the 2002 Olympics in Salt Lake City.

Figure Skating

In April 1921 the United States Figure Skating Association (USFSA) formed in New York City. The Twin City Figure Skating Club was one of the seven charter members. In 1926 Minnesotan Chris Christenson represented the club and earned the Men's Senior National title. He was 50.

In 1929 the Twin City Figure Skating Club was re-organized and renamed the Figure Skating Club of Minneapolis. In 1935 Edeth and Arthur Preusch organized the St. Paul Figure Skating Club in their living room. The next year, they won the Mid-Western Ice Dance championship.

The Figure Skating Club of Minneapolis produced many national champions and Olympians—most notably Robin Lee, National Senior Men's champion from 1935 to 1939. Lee, who had won his first title at age 13 and competed at the 1936 Olympics, continued to train skaters at the club until his retirement in 1991.

Jill Trenary

Trenary began figure skating while living in Minnetonka. She moved to Colorado Springs at age 16 to train under Carlo Fassi, who had coached 1968 Olympic gold medalist Peggy Fleming. Trenary won three U.S. National Championships—in 1987, 1989 and 1990—and won the World Championship in 1990.

At the 1988 Olympics in Calgary, Trenary just missed a medal by finishing fourth. East Germany's Katarina Witt won the gold, Canada's Elizabeth

Manley the silver, and American Debi Thomas the bronze. Trenary competed as a professional figure skater in 1992–93 and again in 1996–97, before retiring from competition. In 1994 she married British ice dancing champion Christopher Dean.

Powderhorn Park

Powderhorn Park, located in south Minneapolis features more than 65 acres of land and 12 acres of water. For 20 years, from 1930 to 1950, Minneapolis was considered the hub of speed skating in the United States. The Powderhorn Speedskating Club was nationally known. In January 1934, a crowd of 30,000 turned out to watch the U.S. Outdoor Speedskating championships.

DID YOU KNOW ?

During the 2004–05 winter season, Tony Benshoof of White Bear Lake won a total of seven luge medals between the World Cup, Challenge Cup, and championship competitions. He was selected as USA Luge's male athlete of the year. At the 2006 Olympics in Turin, Italy, Benshoof finished fourth in the luge—missing a bronze medal by .153 second.

Ice Follies

Oscar Johnson, a St. Paul chemist, and Eddie Shipstad, a typewriter salesman, began their sporting careers as speed skaters. After watching figure skaters on Lake Como, Johnson and Shipstad decided to join the Hippodrome Figure Skating Club.

In the early 1920s they worked out a doubles routine and became the featured performers in shows put on by the club. They perfected a comedy act, which was presented for the first time in 1924 at the club's annual ice carnival. The act received great reviews. They began performing it between periods of hockey games in Minneapolis and St. Paul and soon took the act to Boston, New York and Pittsburgh. The duo was eventually joined by Eddie Shipstad's younger brother, Roy Shipstad.

In 1934 Lyle Wright, manager of the Minneapolis Auditorium, asked the trio to produce a show for the Figure Skating Club of Minneapolis. In April, the trio teamed with the St. Paul Children's Hospital to raise money for the hospital.

The trio got its big break in 1935, when it was booked to do a four-week show—with female skaters—in Chicago. The show was so successful that its run was extended to 16 weeks. While in Chicago, the trio came up with the idea of creating a show to take on the road.

Oscar Johnson and Eddie Shipstad, Ice Follies skaters, 1938

In October 1936 the Shipstad and Johnson Ice Follies was booked for the first time into the Minneapolis Auditorium. The next month, the show went on its first tour with 36 skaters.

The Ice Follies continued to perform in St. Paul until 1939, when the Shipstad family moved to Southern California. In 1947 the show's engagement at the Minneapolis Auditorium drew 140,000. The next year the show's stay in Minneapolis was extended by a week and drew a record crowd of 173,000.

Outdoor Adventurers

For most of the 20th century, Admiral Robert E. Peary was credited with being the first explorer to reach the North Pole in 1909. But in September 1988, the National Geographic Society, citing evidence in Peary's diary, recognized that he had missed the pole by 30–100 miles. Credit for being the first person to reach the North Pole now goes to Ralph Plaisted, of St. Paul. In 1967 his 10-man team heading to the pole fell short, but in March 1968 he set out again. Traveling for 43 days and 474 miles via snowmobiles, the 40-year-old Plaisted and his group reached the top of the world.

In 1990 a team led by Will Steger, of Ely, became the first to traverse Antarctica at its widest distance. Four years earlier, Steger and Paul Schurke, of Ely, had reached the North Pole.

In 1990 Ann Bancroft became the first woman to cross the Arctic to the North Pole. She was a member of the expedition led by Steger and Schurke.

Three years later, on January 14, 1993, Bancroft became the first woman to travel overland to both poles, when she reached the South Pole on skis. Bancroft and three other women covered 660 miles in 67 days. In 2001 Bancroft and Liv Arneson became the first women to ski across Antarctica.

Skiing

Minnesota boasts more than 2,100 miles of cross-country ski trails. One of the most scenic is the North Shore Ski Trail, which covers 196 kilometers (121 miles) and runs from Temperance River State Park to north of Cascade River State Park. Southern Minnesota has the popular 67.6-kilometer (41.6 mile) Root River State Trail.

The Twin Cities Metropolitan area has some 160 miles of trails. Among the highlights are trails at Lake Elmo Park Reserve, Ritter Farm Park Ski Trail in Lakeville, William O'Brien State Park in Marine-on-St. Croix and Fort Snelling State Park.

"America's Champion Boy Skier," Oliver Kahldahl of Glenwood, 1917

The North Star Ski Touring Club, formed in 1967, is the largest ski-touring club in the lower 48 states. Based in St. Paul, it has 1,000 members, sponsors outings all over North America, and provides lessons for beginning skiers.

National Ski Hall of Fame

Fifteen Minnesotans have been inducted into the U.S. National Ski Hall of Fame and Museum in Ispheming, Michigan: Harold Grinden, Duluth (1958); Lars Haugen, Minneapolis (1963); Asario Aution, Ely (1966); Grace Carter Lindley, Wayzata (1966); Julius Blegen, Minneapolis (1968); Ole Mangseth, Coleraine (1968); George Kotlarek, Duluth (1968); Col. George Emerson Leach, Minneapolis (1969); John E. P. Morgan, White Bear Lake (1972); Sverre Fredheim, St. Paul (1973); Carl Holmstrom, Duluth (1973); Sigurd Overby, St. Paul (1976); Cindy Nelson, Lutsen (1976); Eugene Wilson, Coleraine (1982); Jimmy Johnson, Minneapolis (1996).

Cindy Nelson

Nelson, whose family owned a ski resort on Minnesota's North Shore, was a member of the U.S. national team for 14 years. She started her career on the U.S. team as a 15-year-old. In 1976 the 17-year-old Nelson won a bronze medal in downhill skiing at the Innsbruck Olympics. Four years later, at the Olympics in Lake Placid, New York, she won the silver medal in combined downhill. Before her retirement from international skiing in 1985, she won seven World Cup races and was a seven-time winner at the U.S. National Championships.

Mora Vasaloppet

In 1922 a 90-kilometer cross-country ski race was held in Sweden. It was inspired by a run made by King Gustav Vasa in 1520. The Swedish Vasaloppet, now held annually on the first Sunday in March, is the oldest, longest and biggest cross-country ski race in the world.

Since 1981, a sister race has been held annually on the second Sunday of February in Mora, Minnesota. Second only to the American Birkebeiner (North America's largest cross-country race, held in Cable, Wisconsin), the Mora Vasaloppet is one of Minnesota's strongest winter traditions. The Mora event attracts about 1,500 participants who ski in three adult races ranging in length from 35 to 58 kilometers. The race begins with a traditional dynamite blast, and blueberry soup is served at aid stations.

A top competitor is Jan Guenther, owner of a ski shop in Long Lake. Guenther is a five-time Mora Vasaloppet champion.

Ski Resorts

Minnesota has 11 downhill skiing venues—Afton Alps (Hastings), Andes Tower Hills (Alexandria), Buck Hill (Burnsville), Giants Ridge (Biwabik), Hyland (Bloomington), Lutsen (Lutsen), Mount Kato (Mankato), Powder Ridge (Kimball), Spirit Mountain (Duluth), Welch Village (Welch) and Wild Mountain (Taylors Falls). Lutsen, which opened on the shore of Lake Superior in 1948, has a vertical rise of 1,088 feet and one slope two miles in length. Lutsen receives more than 100 inches of snow a winter. *Ski Magazine* has rated Giants Ridge, which opened in the mid-1950s, and Lutsen among the top 10 ski resorts in the northern United States.

DID YOU KNOW ?

The annual Beargrease race, first held in 1983, covers more than 400 miles on its round-trip course from Duluth to Grand Marais along the North Shore of Lake Superior. Teams of up to 14 dogs race in honor of John Beargrease, who delivered mail along the North Shore from 1887 to 1904. Beargrease, the son of an Ojibwe leader, made a biweekly run from Two Harbors to Grand Marais.

Snowmobiling

Attempts at developing mechanized vehicles that could travel over snow date to the first years of the 20th century. Using various track designs, combined with skis and some form of engine power, the vehicles were called snow sleds, motorized toboggans or sleighs. A Ford dealer coined the term "snowmobile" to describe the Model T Ford automobile that he had mounted on tracks and skis.

Snowmobiling as a recreational sport had its start in Roseau, Minnesota, in the mid-1950s. David Johnson, Alan Heteen and Edgar Heteen, partners in a farm-equipment business, developed the first modern vehicles for sale. Their company became Polaris Industries.

International 500 Snowmobile Race

From 1966 to 1982, the International 500, the longest snowmobile race in the world, kicked off the St. Paul Winter Carnival winter festivities. The race started west of Winnipeg, Manitoba, on the Assiniboine River, and finished at Lake Phalen in St. Paul. The race was grueling for drivers.

In 1969 only 19 of the 118 starters finished. In 1972 only 162 of the 301 drivers, who began the race in -37° weather, completed the first 176-mile leg to Crookston.

Water Skiing

In 1922 a Lake City teenager set out to answer the question, "If you could ski on snow, why not on water?" Eighteen-year-old Ralph Samuelson purchased 15-pound, 9-foot-long pine boards at a lumberyard. After boiling and curving the tips of the boards, he strapped them onto his feet and hitched himself to a 24-horsepower motorboat. Three days later, he was skiing the waters of Lake Pepin. Samuelson, who owned a turkey farm near Mazeppa, Minnesota, as an adult, went on to give shows and demonstrations nationally.

In 1967 the American Water Ski Association certified him as the inventor, but he never accepted a formal award. "I never thought it mattered," Samuelson said in the *Minneapolis Tribune*. "I knew I was the first one and that is all I cared about."

Venues, Commentators, Officials, and the Poll

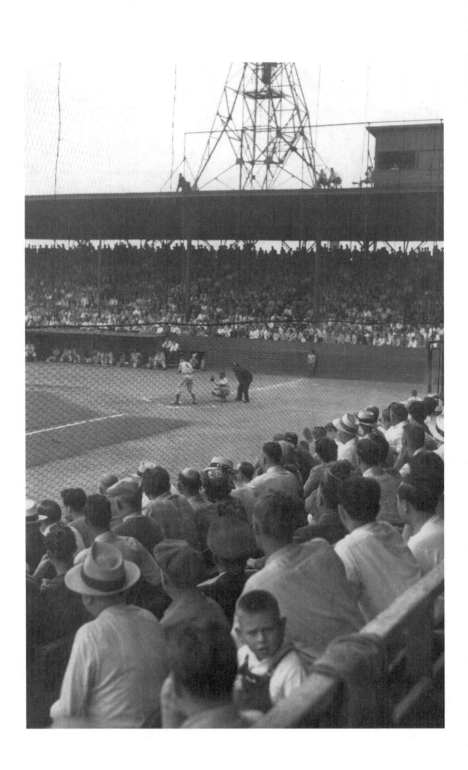

Major Sports Venues

WHILE Native Americans and early settlers enjoyed sporting contests on the open prairie or in vacant urban lots, Minnesotans developed the first venues exclusively for sports sometime in the mid-1880s. On June 23, 1884, professional baseball teams from Minneapolis and St. Paul played each other for the first time before a crowd of 4,000 at St. Paul's West 7th Street grounds.

Baseball historian Stew Thornley writes that the Minneapolis team had several homes during its first few seasons. The team initially played at a ballpark that could accommodate about 2,300 fans near 17th Street between Portland and Chicago avenues. After only a few years, the Millers moved to a small ballpark just off Lake Street and Minnehaha Avenue. In 1889 the team, then a member of the eight-team Western Association, moved into a new ballpark—**Athletic Park,** located behind the West Hotel at 6th Street and 1st Avenue North in downtown Minneapolis (the site of Butler Square).

DID YOU KNOW ?

From 1895 through 1909 the Minneapolis Millers played Sunday home games at Minnehaha Driving Park because regular home parks were in neighborhoods that frowned on playing baseball on the Sabbath.

Athletic Park was the home to the Minneapolis Millers for just seven years. The state's first "stadium controversy" arose in 1896, when the Millers were given a 30-day notice to vacate Athletic Park, to be converted to other commercial uses. The Millers played their final home game on May 23 and then embarked on a lengthy road trip, not knowing where they would play when they returned home.

Four sites were considered for the Millers before a site at 31st Street and Nicollet Avenue was chosen and a ballpark constructed—within three weeks.

Three Minneapolis newspapers ran a contest to name the new ballpark, which had cost $4,000 to build and could seat 4,000 fans. The name "Wright

Field" was chosen, but the Millers didn't like the name. For the next year, the park was simply called "the new ballpark."

The Millers played their first game in their new home on June 19, 1896. The ballpark, eventually named **Nicollet Park**, served as their home for the next 60 seasons.

Across the river the St. Paul Saints played their first game in **Lexington Park** at Lexington and University in 1897. The park would be the Saints' primary home for the next 60 seasons. From 1903 to 1909, the Saints also played home games at a downtown St. Paul ballpark bounded by Robert, Minnesota, 12th and 13th streets.

DID YOU KNOW ?

On December 12, 1948, Horace Stoneham, owner of the New York Giants baseball team, announced the Giants had purchased 20 acres in St. Louis Park with the intention of building a new stadium for their farm team— the Minneapolis Millers. Stoneham hoped the new facility would be ready in 1950, but it was never built.

Midway Stadium vs. Metropolitan (Met) Stadium

By the 1950s, business leaders in the Twin Cities had their eyes on major league baseball. On November 3, 1953, voters in St. Paul passed a city bond issue—by a margin of 48,883 to 17,082—that included $2 million to be used to build Midway Stadium. The city claimed that it would be the "beginning of an athletic plant, which could house the majors if the opportunity arose."

Ten months later—on August 13, 1954—a commission backed by the cities of Minneapolis, Bloomington, and Richfield picked the southeast corner of the intersection of Cedar Avenue and Highway 100 in Bloomington as the future site for a stadium. The commission paid $478,899 for the 164-acre site.

On June 20, 1955, about 500 people watched as ground was broken for the future Metropolitan Stadium. A bond drive, led by a group called the Minneapolis Minutemen, helped raise money for the project, which would eventually cost $10.3 million. When the stadium opened in 1956, it was

Metropolitan Sports Center (left) and Metropolitan Stadium, Bloomington, 1967

pronounced by baseball observers to be the last word in stadium construction. Its "cantilever" structure meant there were no obstructed-view seats.

On April 24, 1956, Metropolitan Stadium's first crowd of 18,366 fans watched the Minneapolis Millers lose to Wichita, 5–3.

Met Stadium was home to baseball for 25 years. After the Minnesota Twins played their final season at the stadium in 1981, Minnesota Twins owner Calvin Griffith praised the stadium's legacy. "It was a hell of a business venture," Griffith told the *Minnesota Daily.* "The people built it with private money. There was no bond issue, no government or city money."

Met Stadium hosted its final event on December 20, 1981, a football game with the Vikings playing the Kansas City Chiefs. Until the stadium was demolished several years later, on January 28, 1985, it sat empty. One real estate developer hoped to move the structure to either Clearwater or Monticello, but the plan fell through.

Bloomington's Mall of America sits on the site of the former Metropolitan Stadium. When the city council approved construction plans, its "condition of approval" included "remembering" Metropolitan Stadium in the mall. A replica brass plate, inscribed "Metropolitan Stadium Home Plate 1956–1981," marks the exact spot of the old one. It is embedded in a concrete floor near the Northwood Stage in the Park at Mall of America, 14 feet above what was once Met Stadium's infield.

The longest home run in Metropolitan Stadium history is also remembered in the mall. To mark the landing point of Harmon Killebrew's 522-foot home run on June 3, 1967, a seat is suspended over the Paul Bunyan chute ride, also in the amusement park. For Vikings fans, the Park at Mall of America's fountain stands near the 50-yard line on what was the east side of the football field.

DID YOU KNOW ?

The largest crowd in Metropolitan Stadium history was an estimated 65,000 for a concert by the Eagles on August 1, 1978. On August 21, 1965, about 30,000 fans—according to the *Minneapolis Tribune,* "mostly squirming, writhing, clapping teenagers"—gathered at Metropolitan Stadium for a one-hour, second-tour concert by the Beatles. It was one of the few on the tour that didn't sell out. The day before, more than 43,000 people had gathered at Metropolitan Stadium for the Vikings' 35–21 exhibition over the Philadelphia Eagles.

Metropolitan Sports Center (Met Center)

In February 1966 the NHL announced that an expansion team had been awarded to Minnesota. The league insisted that the team, to begin play in the 1967–68 season, have a new arena—not the existing Minneapolis Auditorium or St. Paul Auditorium.

Ten months later, ground was broken just north of Metropolitan Stadium in Bloomington for a 15,500-seat arena, to be called Metropolitan Sports Center, or Met Center.

On October 21, 1967, the Minnesota North Stars played their first game in the new arena, hosting the expansion California Seals.

The next day, the arena played host when professional basketball returned to Minnesota. The Minnesota Muskies of the American Basketball Association played the Kentucky Colonels. In 1969 Met Center hosted the state high school hockey tournament for the first time. Through the years, the arena was the home to team tennis, boxing matches, professional indoor soccer, and concerts.

In October 1992 Minnesota North Stars owner Norm Green began talking about the team's financial problems. Green suggested remodeling the arena and connecting it by skyway to its neighbor, the Mall of America. When his proposal was ignored, Green hinted the team might be forced to move unless it received an improved lease. Among the potential new homes for the North Stars were Minneapolis, St. Paul, and Anaheim, California.

On January 30, 1993, Green received bids from Target Center in downtown Minneapolis and the St. Paul Civic Center. Green did not like either bid, and on March 10, 1993, he announced he had reached an agreement to move the franchise to Dallas.

On April 13, 1993, the North Stars, who were battling for a playoff spot, skated their final home game. The Chicago Blackhawks held on, defeating the North Stars, 3–2, before a crowd of 15,445. The North Stars, who played their final two games on the road, missed the playoffs.

The next spring, the Metropolitan Sports Facilities Commission announced that the 27-year-old Met Center would be demolished. On December 13, 1994, the arena was imploded.

St. Paul Civic Center

In 1971 the state legislature authorized the city of St. Paul to construct a new arena. The city built a 16,000-seat facility at the corner of West 7th Street and Kellogg Boulevard using city funds. The St. Paul Civic Center, adjacent to the old St. Paul Auditorium, opened on January 1, 1973, with a crowd of 11,701 watching the Minnesota Fighting Saints and the Houston Aeros of the World Hockey Association skate to a 4–4 tie.

For the next 25 years, the arena—modestly called the greatest hockey arena in North America—played host to high school tournaments, professional hockey, professional wrestling and concerts. Renamed RiverCentre in 1996, the final sporting event at the arena was the 1998 boys' state high school basketball tournament. In the final game of the tournament, Minnetonka defeated Eagan, 65–57, in the state Class 4A championship game.

On March 31, 1998, the final concert was held at the arena, when Eric Clapton played to a crowd of 15,825. In April workers began removing seats, and the structure was soon demolished. Over the years, the city of St. Paul spent $170 million on the complex.

Hubert H. Humphrey Metrodome

Talk of replacing Metropolitan Stadium could be heard as early as 1969. In January 1969 the Minneapolis City Council requested that the Metropolitan Area Sports Commission study the area's long-range needs for major league sports venues. In October 1972 the Minneapolis Charter Commission refused to permit a referendum on whether the city should build a proposed $49 million downtown stadium with parking ramp.

In April 1975 Governor Wendell Anderson announced he was convinced that the Twins and Vikings would leave the state without passage of stadium legislation. After much debate in three legislative sessions, a no-site bill—the idea of Rep. Al Patton (DFL-Sartell)—passed in 1977. The bill created a seven-member commission to select a stadium site and design.

DID YOU KNOW ❓

The Metrodome is the only stadium in the world to play host to the World Series (in 1987 and 1991), baseball's All-Star game (1985), the Super Bowl (1992), and the NCAA Division I men's basketball Final Four (1992 and 2001).

The commission, whose members were appointed by Governor Rudy Perpich, received three financial parameters: It could spend $37.5 million if it chose to build a new football stadium in Bloomington and improve Metropolitan Stadium for baseball; it could spend $25 million if it chose to remodel Metropolitan Stadium as a multi-purpose stadium; or it could spend no more than $55 million if it decided to build a domed stadium anywhere else.

In 1979 the Commission weighed eight proposals for a stadium—two from Minneapolis, one from St. Paul, another from the "Midway" area between St. Paul and Minneapolis, and others from Bloomington, Brooklyn Center, Coon Rapids, and Eagan. The choice came down to Minneapolis and Bloomington. By a 4–3 vote, the commission selected downtown Minneapolis.

Construction of the Hubert H. Humphrey Metrodome began on December 20, 1979. With its roof inflated on October 2, 1981, the Metrodome was completed in April 1982, on time and under budget. The final price: $55 million.

After two exhibition games, the Twins played their first regular-season game in the Metrodome on April 6, 1982, when they lost to the Seattle Mariners, 11–7. Outside, it was 28°.

Target Center

Target Center, in downtown Minneapolis, has been the home of the Minnesota Timberwolves since 1990. The arena, which took 27 months to build, cost an estimated $104 million. Marv Wolfenson and Harvey Ratner, owners of the Timberwolves franchise, originally owned the arena as well. They sold it to the city of Minneapolis in March 1995.

The Timberwolves played their first game in Target Center on October 16, 1990. The Philadelphia 76ers defeated the Timberwolves, 102–96, in the preseason game before 18,296 fans.

Xcel Energy Center

Almost immediately after the Minnesota North Stars relocated to Dallas in 1993, Twin Citians began exploring ways to lure the National Hockey League back to Minnesota. In November 1996, after being spurned by two NHL franchises that had considered relocating to the Twin Cities, a Minnesota group formally applied for an NHL expansion franchise.

In April 1997 NHL officials toured the St. Paul Civic Center to assess its suitability for a future team. Finding the building inadequate, NHL commissioner Gary Bettman told St. Paul mayor Norm Coleman that the city would need a new arena before it could be awarded an expansion franchise.

The city of St. Paul, which had been considering a $51 million renovation of the arena, quickly developed a plan to build a new arena instead on the Civic Center site. Financing for the $130 million arena would be split evenly between the state of Minnesota and the city of St. Paul.

On June 25, 1997, St. Paul was awarded an expansion team, which would begin play in the 2000–01 season. On June 23, 1998, ground was broken for the new arena. It took 27 months to complete. On October 11, 2000, the Minnesota Wild played its first regular-season game in the 18,632-seat arena.

University of Minnesota Sports Venues

Northrop Field

Prior to 1899, the Gophers, who first fielded a football team in 1882, played games on several fields, including Athletic Park in downtown Minneapolis. In 1899 Northrop Field, named in honor of University of Minnesota president Cyrus Northrop, became the home to Gophers football.

The Gophers played their first game there on November 4, 1899, losing to Northwestern, 11–5. Their final game on the field was November 17, 1923, when 26,000 saw the Gophers defeat Iowa, 20–7. Probably the most famous game at Northrop Field was the first "Little Brown Jug" game between Michigan and Minnesota on October 31, 1903. The teams played to a 6–6 tie.

Memorial Stadium

On March 6, 1924, despite snow and a cold wind, about 500 people gathered to watch groundbreaking for a new University of Minnesota football stadium. The horseshoe-shaped stadium, at the corner of University Avenue SE and Oak Street SE, took just seven months to complete. With 56,000 seats, the facility cost $572,000. It opened on October 14, 1924, when the Gophers defeated North Dakota, 14–0.

Memorial Stadium was the home to Gophers football for the next 57 years. The Gophers' final game was played on November 21, 1981, when the team lost to Wisconsin, 26–21. In March 1982, the university's Board of Regents, after considering renovating the stadium, decided to move Gophers football games to the Metrodome. Memorial Stadium was demolished in 1989.

Williams Arena and Mariucci Arena

In 1927 the University of Minnesota started construction on what would become one of the most famous college basketball arenas in the country. On February 4, 1928, the arena, called simply the Fieldhouse, was christened. Dr. James Naismith, the "inventor" of basketball, was on hand to watch Ohio State defeat the Gophers, 42–40. The building, which cost $650,000, had an original capacity of 14,100.

In 1950 the building was remodeled and renamed in honor of Dr. Henry L. Williams, who coached the Gophers football team from 1900 to 1921. It was divided into a hockey arena at the west end and a basketball arena with a seating capacity of 18,025 on the east end. From 1950 to 1971, Williams Arena had the largest capacity of any collegiate basketball arena in the country.

In 1993 the arena was again renovated. The changes reduced the capacity of the arena to 14,625. In February 2003 the arena celebrated its 75th anniversary. With its trademark raised floor, Williams Arena is the fifth oldest NCAA Division I basketball arena in the country.

The Gophers hockey team played its first game in the remodeled arena on February 17, 1950. A crowd of 3,734 saw the Gophers defeat Michigan State, 12–1. The arena, called Mariucci Arena, was home to the Gophers

University of Minnesota Memorial Stadium (center), with Williams Arena (right), about 1955

hockey team until 1993. The largest crowd to see a hockey game there—9,490 fans—watched on January 18, 1958, when the Gophers played North Dakota. Crowd capacity for the arena in its final season was 7,594.

On October 15, 1993, the Gophers played their first game across the street from Williams Arena in the new John Mariucci Arena, named for the legendary Gopher hockey player and coach. The new arena cost a reported $20 million has a capacity of 10,000.

Amateur Sports Venues

The first **Minneapolis Auditorium** was built as part of the Northwestern National Life Insurance Company's headquarters at 11th Street and Nicollet Avenue. It opened in 1905.

The first **Minneapolis Armory** was completed in 1907 on a site near Lyndale Avenue and Kenwood Parkway. From 1923 to 1927 the Armory was home to the boys' state high school basketball tournament. Construction-settling problems forced its condemnation in 1929.

The second Minneapolis Armory opened in 1936, on a block bounded by 5th and 6th streets, 5th Avenue South, and Portland Avenue South in downtown Minneapolis. It was built on the site of the Judd House, once the "most showy" residence in the city, which had been razed in 1926.

According to Larry Millett in *Lost Twin Cities*, the **St. Paul Auditorium**, which opened in 1907, was one of the most "sophisticated, multipurpose auditoriums of its day." Built in downtown St. Paul for a cost of $460,000, it was razed in 1982.

National Sports Center

The National Sports Center in Blaine is one of the largest amateur sports complexes in the world. The complex, which opened in 1990, features 52 regulation-sized soccer fields, four sheets of Olympic-sized ice, a 13,000-capacity track-and-field/soccer stadium, track cycling velodrome, a 200-meter indoor track, and a dormitory. The latest addition to the complex is an 18-hole putting course that is the first phase of the National Youth Golf Center. The center will eventually have an 18-hole championship course and a three-hole learning center for youth golfers.

The Guinness Book of World Records verifies that the complex is the largest soccer complex in the world. In fall 2006, the addition of four more ice sheets will make it the world's largest indoor ice facility.

Sports Commentators

Newspapers first began adding sections devoted exclusively to sports in the early 1900s. Before that time, coverage of sporting events was spotty and hard to find.

One of the first "sporting" editors in Minneapolis was **Frank Force** of the *Minneapolis Tribune*. Force covered the legendary Gophers-Michigan football game in November 1903. The game, which ended in a 6–6 tie, is one of the most famous in Gophers history for several reasons. The game was the only nonvictory during a 56-game unbeaten streak for the Wolverines. The six points scored by the Gophers were the only points allowed by Michigan all season. Finally, the game was the first "Little Brown Jug" game.

Here is how Force described the game in the next day's *Minneapolis Sunday Tribune:*

> Minnesota, Minnesota, Minnesota. You have reason to feel proud today, for yesterday eleven of your sturdiest sons won honor for themselves and you . . . not a victory in the score, for this stands but a tie.

A tie it will be counted in the football records of the year. But in the minds of those who saw the contest, the Minnesota-Michigan game at Northrop Field, October 31, 1903, will be considered one of the greatest victories Minnesota ever won—Michigan the mighty has fallen.

Since that day over 100 years ago, Minnesotans have been fortunate to witness the exploits of many athletic greats—Bronko Nagurski, Bruce Smith, Paul Giel, George Mikan, Patty Berg, Harmon Killebrew, Fran Tarkenton, Dave Winfield, Paul Molitor, Kirby Puckett, and Kevin Garnett. Minnesotans have also been fortunate to have some extraordinary members of print and broadcast media chronicle the feats of these athletes. A handful of these observers stand out for their talent and longevity.

DID YOU KNOW ?

The year 1960 was the most important year in Minnesota sports history, says sports writer Sid Hartman. Consider the highlights: In January the Lakers survived a plane crash in northwest Iowa, and the NFL awarded an expansion team, to begin play in 1961, to a Minnesota group. In February the U.S. Olympic hockey team, with eight Minnesotans on the roster, won the gold medal. In March tiny Edgerton won the boys' state basketball tournament. On the same night, the Lakers played their final game. In April, the Lakers owner Bob Short announced he was moving the team to Los Angeles. In June, the Gophers baseball team, coached by Dick Siebert, won its second NCAA baseball title in five seasons. In October, Calvin Griffith announced he would move his baseball team to Minnesota. In November, the Gophers football team defeated top-ranked Iowa and went on to earn its first-ever berth in the Rose Bowl.

George Barton's newspaper career lasted 55 years, from 1902 to 1957. In addition to the newspaper work, Barton officiated boxing matches—more than 12,000 during his career. *Ring Magazine* rated him as one of the top five boxing officials of all time.

Bruce Bennett was born in Marquette, Michigan, without forearms and hands. He had a nearly 40-year career as a sports writer in Duluth, working at the *Duluth News-Tribune* from 1959 to 1997.

Herb Carneal was introduced to the Upper Midwest in 1961 as the CBS-TV voice of the Minnesota Vikings. The next spring, he became the radio voice for the Minnesota Twins. The 2006 season was Carneal's 43rd as a Twins announcer and 54th as a baseball announcer. In 1996 Carneal was honored by the National Baseball Hall of Fame for his contributions to baseball.

Ray Christensen broadcast University of Minnesota basketball and football games for more than 50 years. He graduated from the university in 1949 and began doing football play-by-play in 1951, first on university-owned KUOM, then on WLOL-AM, and in 1963 on WCCO. He added Gophers men's basketball duties at WLOL in 1956. On September 2, 2000, Christensen broadcast his 500th Gophers football game. He retired after the 2000–01 Gophers basketball season—his 45th season of basketball. In all, he called some 1,300 Gophers basketball games.

Dick Cullum started at the *Minneapolis Journal* in 1921. He retired as a full-time columnist for the *Minneapolis Tribune* in 1976 but continued to cover boxing and write a weekly column until 1982. His last column appeared on April 15, 1982, shortly before his death at age 87.

George Edmond worked at the *St. Paul Pioneer Press* and *Dispatch* from 1925 to 1970 (excluding three years of military service during World War II). Born in Minneapolis, he became the executive sports editor of the *St. Paul Pioneer Press* and *Dispatch* in 1934. In 1959 he became sports editor of the evening *Dispatch*, and he retired in 1970.

Halsey Hall had lengthy careers in newspaper and radio. His newspaper career, with his trademark "It's a Fact" column, extended from 1919 to 1961, while his radio career stretched from 1923 to 1972. As a personality on WCCO radio, he broadcast Gophers football and Twins baseball. He was the first to call the Gophers football team "Golden."

Sid Hartman was hired in November 1944 as an intern by *Minneapolis Times* sports editor Dick Cullum. It was the beginning of a long, influential newspaper career. When the *Times* folded in 1948, Hartman moved to the *Minneapolis Tribune*, his first byline running on May 18, 1948. In 1947 Hartman helped bring professional basketball to the area. In 1955 he began working for WCCO-radio. In September 2003 the Naismith Memorial Basketball Hall of Fame honored Hartman for his outstanding contributions to basketball. Hartman still works for the *Star Tribune* and WCCO.

Charles Johnson had a long newspaper career spanning 1916 to 1968. As executive sports editor of the both the *Minneapolis Star* and the *Minneapolis*

Announcers Herb Carneal (1), Merle Harmon (center), and Halsey Hall (r), about 1967

Tribune, Johnson was influential in helping lure major league baseball and pro football to the area.

Jim Klobuchar, who retired in 1995, had a 43-year career writing for the *Minneapolis Star Tribune.* He has also authored almost two dozen books, several about the Minnesota Vikings.

Ted Peterson covered college, high school, and amateur sports in the Upper Midwest for the Associated Press and the *Minneapolis Tribune* for 40 years before retiring in 1969. He was regular at the state basketball tournament and state amateur baseball tournament. For many years, Peterson picked all-state football teams and a "mythical" state champion in football.

Patrick Reusse, a native of Fulda, has been a sportswriter and columnist for nearly 40 years. After stops in Duluth and St. Cloud, Reusse worked in St. Paul before joining the *Minneapolis Star* and *Tribune.*

Don Riley's newspaper career lasted for more than 40 years. Riley, who covered the first high school hockey tournament in 1945, wrote a popular column called "The Eye Opener" in the *St. Paul Pioneer Press* from the late 1950s through the 1980s.

Jimmy Robinson was the first "outdoors" writer for the *Minneapolis Star.* He also wrote for *Sports Afield* magazine for more than 60 years (1926–88).

Al Shaver became the radio voice of the Minnesota North Stars in 1967 after broadcasting Canadian Football League games for a dozen years.

He remained in that position until the team moved to Dallas in 1993. In 1993 Shaver became a media honouree of the Hockey Hall of Fame in Toronto.

Ben Sternberg had a long career with the *Rochester Post-Bulletin* beginning in 1957 and continuing with a column for the paper into the 1990s. He was also a successful boxing promoter in Rochester and in the Twin Cities. He began promoting amateur boxing events in the 1930s, and one of his top boxers was Rochester's Pat O'Connor during the 1970s.

Charley Walters began writing for the St. Paul newspapers in 1982. The Minneapolis native had played seven years of professional baseball, appearing in six games with the 1969 Minnesota Twins, managed by Billy Martin, before embarking on a journalism career.

Other Announcers

Jim Kaat entered his fourth season with the New York Yankees "YES" network and 23rd season overall as a baseball television commentator in 2005. A Michigan native, Kaat began his broadcasting career while still an active major leaguer. During the strike of 1981, Kaat served as an analyst on minor league baseball games. After retiring from play in 1983, he was a baseball correspondent for ABC's *Good Morning America*. Since then, Kaat has worked for WPIX-TV, WTBS, CBS, ESPN, and NBC. During the 1988 season, Kaat also served as an analyst on 75 Twins broadcasts on WCCO-TV. When he retired as a major league pitcher, he had played more seasons (25) than any other player in modern major league history. (Nolan Ryan eventually surpassed Kaat when he retired after 27 seasons.) In 898 career appearances, Kaat won 283 games, struck out 2,461 hitters, and threw 31 shutouts. The left-hander also won 16 Gold Glove Awards. Kaat played with the Twins from 1961 to 1973.

Bert Blyleven, who made his major league debut with the Minnesota Twins in 1970 as a 19-year-old, began his 10th season as a Twins announcer in 2005. Blyleven has earned a following for "circling" fans with a telestrator during Twins broadcasts. (On September 26, 2002, the Twins gave a CD to the first 10,000 fans attending the game against the White Sox. The CD included a song called "Circle Me Bert," written by Jim Pellinger.) Blyleven spent 22 seasons—11 with the Twins—in the major leagues. Going into the 2005 season, Blyleven ranked fifth on major league baseball's all-time strikeout list (3,701), ninth in games started (685), and ninth in shutouts (60). He won 287 games (24th best all-time) in his career. Blyleven is only the second pitcher in major league history to win a game before his 20th birthday and after his 40th birthday.

Dick Nesbitt played in the NFL before going to work as a sportscaster for KSTP-TV. **Ray Scott** announced pro football on radio and television. **Rollie Johnson** anounced at WCCO radio. **Jules Perlt** served as the Gophers' public address announcer for more than 50 years.

Sports Officials

Jerry Seeman, a Minnesota native, began officiating Minnesota high school football in 1963 and joined the NFL in 1975. He spent 16 years as a game official and worked two Super Bowls before becoming the league's officiating director in 1991. During his 10-year tenure, Seeman modernized the training and grading system for officials and increased communication

Managers and umpires going over ground rules at Metropolitan Stadium, 1956

between the league and the teams. He was also instrumental in developing an instant replay system.

Bernie Kukar is an NFL official with a 21-year career (as of the 2004 season). Kukar first started officiating Minnesota high school and small college football in 1963. He worked his first Super Bowl in 1999.

DID YOU KNOW ?

Wheaties, the cereal known as the "Breakfast of Champions," is a Minnesota product promotion. Introduced to the public by Minneapolis's Washburn Crosby Company (predecessor to General Mills) in 1924, Wheaties began advertising on baseball broadcasts and sponsoring radio broadcasts of the Minneapolis Millers baseball games on WCCO in 1934. The sponsorship included a sign on the left-field wall of Nicollet Park that introduced the phrase, "Breakfast of Champions." The cereal eventually won testimonials from sports stars such as Babe Ruth, Jack Dempsey, and Johnny Weismuller. Baseball Hall of Famer Lou Gehrig was the first athlete to appear on a Wheaties box in 1934.

After the Minnesota Twins won the World Series in 1987, General Mills featured not a single player but the entire team on the front of a box. Some 500,000 packages were distributed in the Upper Midwest only.

Several hundred amateur and professional athletes have been recognized on the front of Wheaties boxes. Other teams with Minnesota connections include the U.S. Men's Olympic Hockey team in 1997 and the Women's Olympic Hockey team in 1998. Among the individuals are Dave Winfield, Kirby Puckett, Patty Berg, and Bronko Nagurski.

Ken Mauer Jr., who played baseball for the University of Minnesota, started refereeing high school "B" squad basketball as an 18-year-old in 1974. Within three years, Mauer was officiating small-college basketball games in the state. In 1986 Mauer was added to the NBA staff. At the age of 30, he was one of the two youngest officials in a pool of 32.

Joe Brinkman, a Little Falls native, began his 32nd season as a major league umpire in 2005. He began his umpiring career in the Class A Midwest League in 1968. He reached the major leagues in 1973. During his big-league career, he has worked three All-Star games and in the World Series three times. He has worked in the playoffs nine times. From 1981 to 1998, Brinkman owned and operated the Joe Brinkman Umpire School.

Tim Tschida, a St. Paul native, began his 19th season as a major league umpire in 2005. After attending Cretin–Derham Hall High School, he began his umpiring career in the Class A California League in 1981. During his big-league career, he has worked two All-Star games and two World Series. He has also worked in the playoffs nine times.

Jeffrey Nelson, a Bethel College graduate, became a major league umpire in 1999. Beginning his umpiring career in the Pioneer League in 1989, he has worked in the playoffs three times.

Jimmy Lee, an African American from St. Paul, was the state's most famous basketball referee and amateur baseball umpire. According to Patrick Reusse of the *Minneapolis Star Tribune,* Lee's competence and personality did more to improve race relations in outstate Minnesota than any other ambassador. Lee was inducted into the Minnesota Sports Federation's Softball Hall of Fame in 1982, and a St. Paul recreation center in the Rondo neighborhood carries his name.

Minnesota Poll on Sports

"It were not best that we should all think alike; it is a difference of opinion that makes horse races," wrote Mark Twain in 1894.

The *Minneapolis Tribune* (now the *Star Tribune*) began measuring public opinion in the state in 1944 with its Minnesota Poll. Over the last 60 years the poll, now run by Rob Daves, has dealt with a variety of sports issues and attitudes. While the most frequent concerns have been baseball and stadiums, the polls have looked at subjects ranging from bowling to the Olympics.

One of the first polls, taken in August 1945, asked Minnesotans outside of the metropolitan area what entertainment they sought when the ventured to the Twin Cities. Nearly one-fifth (17 percent) said the state fair, 12 percent said football, and 9 percent said the Ice Follies. More than one-third (36 percent) said they had attended a Gophers football game in the previous 10 years.

Three years later—in July 1948—Minnesotans named their favorite sports. Some 35 percent named fishing; 20 percent, watching or playing in ballgames; 11 percent, swimming; and 5 percent, golf. Fifty years later, a 1998

Opening Day crowd at Midway Stadium, St. Paul, 1957

Minnesota Poll asked similar questions. Some 47 percent said they had been warm-weather fishing in the previous 12 months, down from the 61 percent in a 1959 poll. Some 18 percent said they were hunters (another 8 percent were hunters but hadn't hunted in the previous 12 months), down from 20 percent in 1992 and 22 percent in 1965. Asked if they thought hunting was a natural activity for people, 64 percent said yes (down from 72 percent in 1992).

As early as 1953, Minnesotans were interested in the Twin Cities acquiring a major league baseball team. Nearly two-thirds polled said they would rather have a major league team than the towns' two existing minor league teams. Asked how much personal interest they had in baseball, those responding a "great deal" ranged from 21 percent in 1957 to 10 percent in 2000. The number peaked at 38 percent in September 1965, the month the Twins clinched their first American League pennant.

When Minnesotans were asked their opinion in 1954 about legalized betting on horse racing, 51 percent opposed betting while 39 percent supported it. By 1971, 60 percent favored pari-mutuel betting.

Minnesotans were sophisticated enough in 1953 to realize that "professional wrestling" was primarily a "show." Nearly two-thirds (65 percent) said it was mainly entertainment; more than two-thirds (69 percent) had seen a match, either in person or on TV.

In 1973 as the city of Minneapolis considered a domed stadium for the Minnesota Vikings, 44 percent in a Minnesota Poll said a stadium complex would benefit the city. In the same poll, 64 percent said Bloomington was the best home for the Vikings.

In 1977 the state legislature passed a stadium bill creating the Metropolitan Sports Facilities Commission and gave the commission a deadline of December 1, 1978, to announce whether a new stadium would be built or not. Five days before the deadline, a Minnesota poll said 42 percent opposed a new stadium, while 38 percent favored one, and 30 percent said they didn't care. Of those who favored it, 49 percent wanted a multipurpose stadium in downtown Minneapolis, while 29 percent wanted a new stadium for football and soccer in Bloomington with Metropolitan Stadium being remodeled. One-fifth (20 percent) wanted a new open-air stadium in Bloomington. On December 1, 1978, the Metropolitan Sports Facilities Commission chose downtown Minneapolis as the site for a new stadium.

In recent years, opposition to public funding for a new stadium has remained nearly constant—strongly opposed by 61 percent (October 1997), 68 percent (July 1999), 58 percent (December 2001), and 59 percent (March 2002). In May 2005, 67 percent statewide opposed using public money for stadiums. Of Hennepin County respondents, 58 percent opposed the plan.

Metropolitan Stadium, Bloomington, 1965

Bibliography

Barton, George. *My Lifetime in Sports.* Minneapolis: Olympic Press, 1957.

Bernstein, Ross. *55 Years—55 Heroes: A Celebration of Minnesota Sports.* Minneapolis: Nodin Press, 2002.

———. *Frozen Memories: Celebrating a Century of Minnesota Hockey.* Minneapolis: Nodin Press, 1999.

———. *The Hall: Celebrating the History and Heritage of the United States Hockey Hall of Fame,* 2000.

———. *Hardwood Heroes: Celebrating a Century of Minnesota Basketball.* Minneapolis: Nodin Press, 2001.

———. *Legends and Legacies: Celebrating a Century of Minnesota Coaches.* Minneapolis: Nodin Press, 2003.

Blashfield, Jean. *Awesome Almanac Minnesota.* Fontana, WI: B & B Publishing, 1993.

Brown, George, III. *100 Years of Minnesota Golf: Our Great Tradition.* Edina, MN: Minnesota Golf Inc., 2001.

Carlson, Kenneth. *College Football Scorebook* (2nd ed.). Lynnwood, WA: Rain Belt Publishing, 1984.

Charlton, Jim, ed. *Road Trips.* Cleveland, OH: Society for American Baseball Research, 2004.

Dent, Jim. *Monster of the Midway: Bronko Nagurski, the 1943 Chicago Bears and the Greatest Comeback Ever.* New York: Thomas Dunne Books, an imprint of St. Martin's Press, 2003.

Diamond, Dan, James Duplacey, Igor Kuperman and Eric Zweig, eds. *Total Hockey: The Official Encyclopedia of the National Hockey League.* Kingston, NY: Total Sports Publishing, 1998.

Fisher, Richard Charles, ed. *Who's Who in Minnesota Athletics.* Minneapolis: Who's Who in Minnesota Athletics Publishing, 1941.

Godin, Roger A. *Before the Stars: Early Major-League Hockey and the St. Paul Athletic Club Team.* St. Paul: Minnesota Historical Society Press, 2005.

Greiner, Tony, comp. *The Minnesota Book of Days: An Almanac of State History.* St. Paul: Minnesota Historical Society Press, 2001.

Grossmann, Mary Ann, and Tom Thomsen, eds. *The Minnesota Almanac* (3rd ed.). Taylors Falls, MN: John L. Brekke, 1987.

Grundman, Adolph. *Golden Age of Amateur Basketball: The AAU Tournament, 1921–68.* Lincoln: University of Nebraska Press, 2004.

Hosier, Tom, with Stew Thornley and George Rekala. *Mac Is Back: The Story Behind the Ending of College Football's Longest Losing Streak.* Minneapolis: Stanton Publishing Services, 1991.

Johnson, Lloyd and Miles Wolff. *The Encyclopedia of Minor League Baseball.* Durham, NC: Baseball America, Inc., 1997.

Jones, Thomas B. "Caucasians Only: Solomon Hughes, the PGA, and the 1948 St. Paul Open Golf Tournament," *Minnesota History* 58 (Winter 2003): 383–92.

Kelley, James. *Minnesota Golf: 90 Years of Tournament History.* Edina, MN: Minnesota Golf Association, Inc., 1991.

Kirchoff, Maggie, ed. *Let's Play Hockey Presents a Complete History of the Minnesota Boys and Girls High School Hockey Tournament, 1945–2000.* Minneapolis: D & M Publishing, Inc., 2000.

Koppett, Leonard. *24 Seconds to Shoot: An Informal History of the NBA.* New York: The MacMillan Co., 1970.

Lannin, Joanne. *A History of Basketball for Girls and Women: From Bloomers to the Big Leagues.* Minneapolis: Lerner Publishing Group, 2000.

Lazenby, Ronald. *The Lakers: A Basketball Journey.* Indianapolis, IN: The Master's Press, 1995.

Lovett, Charlie. *Olympic Marathon.* Westport, CT: Greenwood Publishing Group, Inc., 1997.

McClellan, Keith. *The Sunday Game: At the Dawn of Professional Football.* Akron, OH: The University of Akron Press, 1998.

McDermid, Chris, ed. *The Minnesota Almanac* (4th ed.) Taylors Falls, MN: John Brekke & Sons, Publisher, 1999.

Millett, Larry. *Lost Twin Cities.* St. Paul: Minnesota Historical Society Press, 1993.

Mona, Dave. *Twenty-Five Seasons: The First Quarter Century of the Minnesota Twins.* Minneapolis: Mona Publications, 1986.

Monroe, Cecil O. "The Rise of Baseball in Minnesota," *Minnesota History* 19 (June 1938): 162–81.

Neft, David S., Richard M. Cohan and Rick Korch. *The Football Encyclopedia: The Complete History of Professional Football from 1892 to the Present.* New York: St. Martin's Press, 1991.

The Ohio Sports Almanac. Wilmington, OH: Orange Frazer Press, Inc., 1992.

O'Neal, Bill. *The American Association: A Baseball History, 1902–1991.* Austin, TX: Eakin Press, 1991.

Palmer, Pete, and Gary Gillette. *The Baseball Encyclopedia.* New York: Barnes & Noble Publishing, 2004.

Papas Jr., Al. *Gopher Sketchbook.* Minneapolis: Nodin Press, 1990.

Phillips, Gary L. *Skate for Goal! Highlights from Minnesota's Hockey Tournament.* Afton, MN: Afton Press, 1982.

Rippel, Joel A. *75 Memorable Moments in Minnesota Sports.* St. Paul: Minnesota Historical Society Press, 2003.

Sloan, Dave, comp. *Complete Pro Football Draft Encyclopedia.* St. Louis, MO: Sporting News Books, 2004.

Soucheray, Joe. *Once There Was a Ballpark.* Edina, MN: Dorn Books, 1981.

Surgent, Scott Adam. *The Complete Historical and Statistical Reference to the World Hockey Association, 1972–79.* Tempe, AZ: Xaler Press, 1995.

Thornley, Stew. *Basketball's Original Dynasty: The History of the Lakers.* Minneapolis: Nodin Press, 1989.

———. *On to Nicollet: The Glory and Fame of the Minneapolis Lakers.* Minneapolis: Nodin Press, 1988.

Media Guides and Record Books

American Association Record Book
Bemidji State University Men's Hockey
Canterbury Park
Dallas Stars
Ladies Professional Golf Association
Minnesota Lynx
Minnesota State High School League Yearbook
Minnesota Timberwolves
Minnesota Twins
Minnesota Vikings
Minnesota State University–Mankato, Women's Basketball
NBA Official Guide
NBA Official Register
NHL Official record book
Northern League Media Guide
St. John's University football
University of Minnesota baseball, men's basketball, women's basketball, football, men's hockey, women's hockey and wrestling

Newspapers

Chicago Tribune
Minneapolis Star

Minneapolis Star Tribune
Minneapolis Times
Minneapolis Tribune
Minnesota Daily
St. Paul Pioneer Press
Virginia Daily Enterprise

Other Publications

Augsburg Alumni Magazine
Augsburg Yearbook
University of Minnesota Alumni Weekly

Web sites

Harvard-Yale "The Game"
Metropolitan Sports Facilities Commission
Minnesota Curling Association
Minnesota Intercollegiate Athletic Conference
North Central Conference
Northern Sun Intercollegiate Conference
Rec Sport Soccer Statistics Foundation
St. Paul City Athletic Conference
United States Hockey Hall of Fame
United States Olympic Committee
Women's National Basketball Association

The photo on p. 5 is courtesy the National Baseball Hall of Fame Library, Cooperstown, New York; 2, 4, 16, 167, 193, 197, 277, 325, and 329, University of Minnesota Athletics; 18 (Carlos Gonzalez), *Star Tribune/Minneapolis–St. Paul;* 26 and 41, Minnesota Twins; 55, St. Paul Saints; 124 and 148, Minnesota Timberwolves/NBAE/Getty Images; 176 (Minnesota Wild), 290 (Minnesota Swarm), and 291 (Minnesota Thunder), Bruce Kluckhohn; 119, St. John's University, Collegeville; 188, AP/Wide World; 190 and 191, Donald Clark Collection; 265 (Jean Pieri), *St. Paul Pioneer Press;* 279, Solomon Hughes Family; and 300, David Wheaton/*Springfield News Leader.*

All the other images are from the Minnesota Historical Society, including the following: p. ii–iii (Freeman), 28 (Dennis "Buzz" Magnuson), 29 (Spence Hollstadt), 82 (Hollstadt), 178, 181 (John Doman), 209 (Hollstadt), 228 (Neale Van Ness), 295 (Steve Schluter), 376, and 384—all from the St. Paul Dispatch–Pioneer Press collection; 107, 211 (Bruce Bisping), 242, 327, and 340—all from the Minneapolis Star Journal Tribune Collection; and 62 (A. P. Rhodes), 71 (John Runk), 115 (Monroe Killy), 151 (Peter Hohn), 238 (Charles Chamblis), 299 (Ingersoll), 319 (Chamblis), 336 (Countryman-Klang), and 347 (Runk).

Souvenir hunters dismantle the scoreboard at Metropolitan Stadium after the last game, 1981